Negotiation Games
Revised Edition

The concept of Negotiation is critical to coping with all manner of strategic problems that arise in the everyday dealings that people have with each other and with organizations. Game theory illustrates this to the full and shows how these problems can be solved.

This is a revised edition of a classic book and uses some wonderfully adroit case studies that remain relevant today. *Negotiation Games* covers such themes as:

- trade offs and the game of chicken
- the effects of power in the cease-fire game
- the use of threat power in sequential games
- fallback bargaining and rational negotiation

Written by one of the leading game theorists of the generation, this book will be greatly appreciated not only by academics and students involved in game theory, economics, business and international relations, but also by those involved in diplomacy and international business.

Routledge Advances in Game Theory
Edited by Christian Schmidt

Volume 1
Game Theory and Economic Analysis
A Quiet Revolution in Economics
Christian Schmidt

Volume 2
Negotiation Games
Applying Game Theory to Bargaining and Arbitration
Steven J. Brams

Negotiation Games
Revised Edition
Applying Game Theory to Bargaining
and Arbitration

Steven J. Brams

Routledge
Taylor & Francis Group

LONDON AND NEW YORK

First published 1990
by Routledge
29 West 35th Street, New York, NY 10001

Revised Edition first published 2003 by Routledge
11 New Fetter Lane, London EC4P 4EE

Simultaneously published in the USA and Canada
by Routledge
29 West 35th Street, New York, NY 10001

Routledge is an imprint of the Taylor & Francis Group

© 2003 Steven J. Brams

Printed and bound in Great Britain by
St Edmundsbury Press Ltd, Bury St Edmunds, Suffolk

British Library Cataloguing in Publication Data
A catalogue record for this book is available from the British Library

Library of Congress Cataloging in Publication Data
A catalog record for this book has been requested

ISBN 0–415–30894–1 (hbk)
ISBN 0–415–30895–X (pbk)

Contents

List of Figures   ix

List of Tables   xi

Preface to the Second Edition   xiii

Preface   xxi
  Modeling Negotiations   xxi
  Overview and Level   xxiii
  Acknowledgments   xxvi

1. Negotiations in the Bible   1
  1.1. Introduction   1
  1.2. Cain and Abel: Bargaining with God   3
  1.3. Rahab and the Spies: Making a Just Agreement   9
  1.4. Solomon's Arbitration: Discovering the Truth   17
  1.5. Conclusions   25
      Notes   26

2. Bargaining Procedures and the Problem of Honesty   29
  2.1. Introduction   29
  2.2. The Honesty Problem   34
  2.3. The Bonus Procedure   39
  2.4. The Bonus Appraisal Procedure   45
  2.5. The Penalty Procedure   48
  2.6. The Penalty Appraisal Procedure   51
  2.7. The Expansive Appraisal Procedure   53
  2.8. Camp David: The Logic of the Procedures Applied   57
  2.9. Conclusions   60
      Notes   62

3. Arbitration Procedures and the Problem of Convergence   64
  3.1. Introduction   64
  3.2. Different Arbitration Procedures   66

3.3.	Trade-Offs and Implicit Arbitration	68
3.4.	Final-Offer Arbitration (FOA)	71
3.5.	FOA in Practice: The Importance of Winning	75
3.6.	Bonus FOA	79
3.7.	Combined Arbitration	81
3.8.	Two-Stage and Multistage FOA	86
3.9.	Is Convergence in Stages Desirable?	91
3.10.	Kissinger's Shuttle Diplomacy: A Case of Multistage Negotiations	93
3.11.	Conclusions	96
	Notes	99

4.	Superpower Crisis Bargaining and the Theory of Moves	101
4.1.	Introduction	101
4.2.	Prisoners' Dilemma and Chicken	102
4.3.	The Cuban Missile Crisis as a Game of Chicken	104
4.4.	Deception and Power in the Cuban Missile Crisis	110
4.5.	A Sequential View of the Cuban Missile Crisis	113
4.6.	The 1973 Alert Decision	116
4.7.	Nonmyopic Equilibria and the Theory of Moves: A Digression	120
4.8.	Stability in the Cease-Fire Game	127
4.9.	Was There an Alternative to the Alert?	130
4.10.	The Possible Effects of Power in the Cease-Fire Game	132
4.11.	Conclusions	134
	Notes	136

5.	Threats and Reputation in Bargaining	138
5.1.	Introduction	138
5.2.	Repeated Play of a Sequential Game	141
5.3.	Threat Outcomes in Repeated Play of a Game	148
5.4.	The Sequential-Primary Game	154
5.5.	Conclusions	163
	Notes	165

6.	Threats in Two Domestic Crises	168
6.1.	Introduction	168
6.2.	The Use of Threat Power in Poland, 1980–81	169
6.3.	The White House Tapes Case: The Players and Their Preferences	175
6.4.	The White House Tapes Case: The Trap	181
6.5.	Conclusions	186
	Notes	187

7.   Bargaining in Legislatures   189
     7.1.   Introduction   189
     7.2.   Judgments about Vote Trading   191
     7.3.   Definitions and Assumptions about Vote Trading   192
     7.4.   Sincere and Insincere Voting   195
     7.5.   Initial Trades and the Paradox of Vote Trading   199
     7.6.   Subsequent Trades and the Instability
            of Vote Trading   202
     7.7.   The Consequences of Refusing to Trade   204
     7.8.   The Consequences of Forming Coalitions   206
     7.9.   Empirical Examples of the Paradox
            of Vote Trading   209
     7.10. Choosing a Governing Coalition in a Multiparty
            System: Coalition Voting   211
     7.11. Majority, Minimal Majority, and Governing
            Coalitions   215
     7.12. Measuring Bargaining Strength under
            Coalition Voting   217
     7.13. Possible Uses of Coalition Voting   221
     7.14. Conclusions   223
            Notes   225

8.   Bargaining Power   227
     8.1.   Introduction   227
     8.2.   Power in the U.S. Federal System   228
     8.3.   What Should a Power Index Measure?   231
     8.4.   The Power of Approval and Disapproval   236
     8.5.   Empirical Evidence of Presidential Power   242
     8.6.   The Paradox of the Chair's Position   244
     8.7.   The Chair's Counterstrategy of Deception   249
     8.8.   The Geneva Conference Game   252
     8.9.   Conclusions   258
            Notes   261

9.   Epilogue   263

Glossary   266
Bibliography   273
Index   287

Figures

1.1. Game Tree of Cain's Murder of Abel   8

1.2. Outcome Matrix of Rahab's Game   11

1.3. Rahab's Game Revised   13

1.4. Region in Which $E(K) > E(B)$ 17

1.5. Outcome Matrix of Solomon's Game   19

1.6. Game Tree of Solomon's Game   21

1.7. Payoff Matrix of Solomon's Game   22

2.1. Linear Symmetric Equilibrium Strategies of B and S
     under Chatterjee-Samuelson Procedure   35

2.2. Discrete Bargaining under the Bonus Procedure   43

2.3. Settlement Regions for Penalty Appraisal Procedure
     and Expansive Appraisal Procedure: B's View   57

3.1. Final Offers of A (a) and B (b) for Uniform Distribution 73

3.2. Gap with and without the Bonus under FOA   79

3.3. Use of Conventional Arbitration and FOA under
     Combined Arbitration   82

3.4. Final Offers of A (a) and B (b) for Triangular Distribution 83

4.1. Prisoners' Dilemma and Chicken   103

4.2. Cuban Missile Crisis as a Game of Chicken   105

4.3 Payoff Matrix of Alternative Representation of the
     Cuban Missile Crisis   107

4.4. Game Tree and Payoff Matrix of Sequential Choices
     in the Cuban Missile Crisis   114

4.5. Payoff Matrix of Cease-Fire Game   118

4.6. Game Tree of Moves, Starting with Row, from (3,3)
     in Chicken   123

x / Figures

4.7.   Revised Chicken, with Final Outcomes   126
4.8.   1973 Cease-Fire Game (with Alert) as Prisoners' Dilemma   128
4.9.   Cease-Fire Game, with United States as Honest Broker   131
5.1.   Moves in Chicken and Prisoners' Dilemma   142
5.2.   Ordinal 2 × 2 Outcome Matrix   143
5.3.   Game Illustrating a Deterrent Threat of Row   146
5.4.   Category 1 Games in Which Neither Player Has a
       Threat Strategy   149
5.5.   Category 2 Games in Which One Player Has a
       Threat Strategy   150
5.6.   Five Category 3 Games in Which Both Players Have
       a Threat Strategy and Power Is Ineffective   151
5.7.   Fifteen Category 3 Games in Which Both Players Have
       a Threat Strategy and Power Is Effective   153
5.8.   Game Tree in One Primary Election   156
5.9.   Payoff Matrix in One Primary Election (Player A Weak)   157
5.10. Payoff Matrix in One Primary Election (Player A Strong)   161
6.1.   Payoff Matrix of Polish Game, 1980–81   171
6.2.   Outcome Matrix of White House Tapes Game   179
6.3.   Payoff Matrix of White House Tapes Game   182
6.4.   Revised Payoff Matrix of White House Tapes Game   183
8.1.   Sophisticated Voting Outcome, Given X Chooses
       "Vote for x"   247
8.2.   Tacit Deception Outcome, Given X Chooses "Vote for y"   251

Tables

7.1.	Utility of Positions and Salience of Roll Calls for Two Members	192
7.2.	Positions and Utilities before Trading	196
7.3.	Positions and Utilities after Trading	197
7.4.	Positions and Utilities of Left-Out Member before and after Trading	199
7.5.	Positions of Members before Initial Trades on Six Roll Calls	201
7.6.	Positions of Members after Initial Trades on Six Roll Calls	202
7.7.	Preferences of Members for Trades	209
7.8.	Example of Coalition Voting	218
8.1.	Banzhaf and Johnston Power in Weighted Voting Body [3; 2,1,1]	234

Preface to the Second Edition

The 1990 edition of *Negotiation Games* was written partly in response to a dearth of literature on applications of game theory to bargaining and arbitration. Additionally, I sought to synthesize and interpret theoretical results in the negotiation literature that offered insights into why some negotiations succeeded and some failed.

Thus, for example, in chapter 2 I analyzed the problem of honesty in bargaining and showed that there was no free lunch: No bargaining procedure can induce the bargainers to be honest without extracting a price. Specifically, either a third party would have to add a bonus, or there would have to be a penalty – in the form of negotiations failing on occasion or not delivering their full potential – to induce two bargainers to be truthful. As a case in point, I argued that these features induced Menachem Begin and Anwar Sadat, under the prodding of Jimmy Carter, to reach an agreement after ten days of difficult negotiation at Camp David in 1978.

Likewise in chapter 3, I showed that the presence of an arbitrator, who can force a resolution if the two bargainers do not reach an agreement, does not promote their convergence under final-offer arbitration (FOA). The use of FOA in major-league baseball and public-employee disputes illustrates this proposition.

But there are arbitration procedures that induce convergence or partial convergence. For example, the multistage procedure analyzed in Brams, Kilgour, and Weber (1991) models, at least informally, Henry Kissinger's successful shuttle diplomacy in the Middle East in 1973–75.

In other chapters in *Negotiation Games*, I used different game-theoretic models to analyze bargaining processes and outcomes, from biblical times to the present. For each model, I gave real or hypothetical examples of situations, most involving political conflict, that the model illuminated.

These models, in my opinion, remain relevant today, even if there are more recent examples to illustrate them. Of course, new models of bargaining and arbitration have been developed in the past twelve years, but many seem quite far removed from any practical applications. These include those discussed in two edited collections (Young, 1991; Zeckhauser, Keeney, and Sebenius, 1996), which highlight the role of theory but give short shrift to empirical examples of negotiation. The edited collection of Bates *et al.* (1998) errs in the opposite direction, emphasizing cases at the expense of formal models.

Because of the continuing relevance of the models I analyzed in 1990, I have decided to leave this second edition of *Negotiation Games* intact (except for making small corrections). To provide a current perspective, I now briefly discuss new models and applications of game theory to negotiation that update the different chapters to 2002. While I focus on my own work, I cite the research of others wherein game theory sheds new light on negotiations, especially the strategic issues in a conflict.

Chapter 1. Negotiations in the Bible

Brams (2002) is a revised edition of Brams (1980), which was referenced in the 1990 edition. It includes a new chapter, "Beyond Biblical Games" in which, among other things, I revisit one Bible story (Abraham's attempted sacrifice of Isaac) to illustrate how a character (Abraham) might have acted differently from the way he did to achieve a preferred outcome. Although Abraham's negotiations with God probably would have been quite delicate if, counterfactually, he had not heeded God's command to sacrifice Isaac, the analysis suggests that Abraham probably would have succeeded not only in saving Isaac's life but also in defying God's command without suffering severe punishment or traumatizing his son.

Other literary works to which game theory has been applied – novels, short stories, plays, and epic poems – are reviewed in Brams (1994a). In several of these fictional accounts of conflict and intrigue, the characters bargain over their differences, sometimes successfully, but more often they are beset by betrayals, violence, and mayhem that sabotages any peaceful resolution of their conflicts.

Chapter 2. Bargaining Procedures and the Problem of Honesty

In Brams and Kilgour (1996) a rigorous development of the theoretical results in this chapter is given. The alternating-offers model of Rubinstein (1982), which was referenced in the 1990 edition and became probably the most influential bargaining model of the last generation, is now the subject of a large literature that is synthesized in Muthoo (1999).

If by "applications" one means to real-life cases, the title of Muthoo

(1999), *Bargaining with Applications*, is a misnomer. There are no such applications but, instead, extensions of Rubinstein's original model to a variety of different circumstances, such as the possibility of outside options.

Kennan and Wilson (1993) provide a good survey of bargaining models in which there is private information. In these models, a bargainer knows his or her own valuation of the goods but has only incomplete information about the valuation of the other bargainer (in most models there is only one other bargainer; for an exception, see Brams and Doherty (1993)).

Conflict resolution has been an impetus behind the development of many game-theoretic bargaining models; an excellent collection of these and related models that pinpoint barriers to conflict resolution can be found in Arrow *et al.* (1995). Game theory has also been used to show how negotiations can attenuate conflict, both in general situations (Brams, 1992) and in more specific contexts, such as arms control (Kilgour and Brams, 1992).

Chapter 3. Arbitration Procedures and Problems of Convergence

There have been refinements and further developments of arbitration models (Kilgour, 1994; Armstrong and Hurley, 2001). An innovative proposal by Zeng, Nakamura, and Ibaraki (1996), which allows bargainers to make double offers, induces them, as in combined arbitration, to converge, obviating the need for an arbitrated settlement. Models in which, after an alternating-offers bargaining stage, there is arbitration if the parties disagree, may lead to very different outcomes from those in which there is no arbitration at the end (Manzini and Mariotti, 2001). Put another way, the *possibility* of arbitration, whether or not it is used to reach an agreement, can significantly affect the nature of the bargaining that precedes it.

Chapter 4. Superpower Crisis Bargaining and the Theory of Moves

Chapter 5. Threats and Reputation in Bargaining

Chapter 6. Threats in Two Domestic Games

I group these three chapters together, because parts of the "theory of moves" (TOM) are used in all of them. In Brams (1994b), I developed a framework that subsumed these different parts and interrelated them.

To summarize, TOM, while based on the classical theory of games, proposes major changes in its rules to render it a dynamic theory. By postulating that players think ahead not just to the immediate consequences of making moves, but also to the consequences of countermoves to these moves, counter-countermoves, and so on, it extends the strategic analysis of conflicts into the more distant future. It also elucidates the role that different kinds of power – moving, order, and threat – may have on conflict outcomes, and it shows how misinformation, perhaps caused by misperceptions or deception, affects player choices. Both in Brams (1994b) and in about 20 subsequent articles by me and others, TOM has been applied to a series of cases drawn from politics, economics, sociology, and fiction.

TOM, in my view, offers not only a parsimonious explanation of their outcomes but also shows why they unfolded as they did. This view is not unanimous. While most reviews of Brams (1994b) have been positive and several highly laudatory, some have been critical of parts of the book.

But no review has painted a more bleak, dark, and sinister a picture than Randall Stone's (2001) article-length critique of TOM, which finds no redeeming value in the theory. Because I responded at length to this critique (Brams, 2001), wherein I cite the TOM literature since the appearance of *Theory of Moves*, I think no more needs to be said about this controversy – interested readers can judge for themselves the merits of the opposing arguments.

What I think is worth stressing is that TOM is history-dependent; the players do not start from a *tabula rasa*, as assumed when players independently select strategies in the normal or strategic form of a game. Instead, TOM postulates that players may move from state to state in a payoff matrix, according to specified rules of play.

These moves reflect the give-and-take of bargaining, including the offers and counteroffers that one often observes bargainers make in the course of negotiations. The path they choose is often the key to whether their negotiations are successful (e.g., lead to a nonmyopic equilibrium in TOM) or fail.

I refer the reader to the TOM literature, especially its diverse applications, to obtain a better understanding of whether TOM might be applicable to the kinds of negotiation in which he or she is interested. As just one example from the more recent literature, catch-22 situations, in which a kind of vicious cycling occurs, have been identified in medieval witch trials, international conflicts, and literary plots.

The modeling of these wrenching conflicts as games illustrates how moving power can break an impasse. But the exercise of such power can be extremely damaging to the player who does not have the wherewithal to hold out indefinitely in negotiations (Brams and Jones, 1999; Brams, 1999).

Chapter 7. Bargaining in Legislatures

Vote-trading, which is modeled in the first part of chapter 7, is not the only kind of bargaining that occurs in legislatures. In recent years, game-theoretic models have been used to explain, among other phenomena, why legislative coalitions in the US Congress tend to be bipartisan and of supermajority size (Krehbeil, 1998).

The frequent occurrence of minimal majorities, as well, on important bills is explained by another model of coalition formation (Brams, Jones, and Kilgour, 2002a); a related model gives conditions under which disconnected coalitions (e.g., comprising the left and right but not the center) form when voters have single-peaked preferences (Brams, Jones, and Kilgour, 2002b). These models are based on "fallback bargaining," whereby bargainers successively fall back to less acceptable outcomes in order to reach an agreement (Brams and Kilgour, 2001).

Bargaining is a central focus of Grossman and Helpman (2001), which shows how special interests can influence legislation through lobbying and campaign contributions. How presidential vetoes, or the threat of vetoes, affects a president's bargaining with Congress – especially when the government is divided (the party of the president differs from the majority party in at least one house of Congress) – is modeled and tested in Cameron (2000). Bargaining is, of course, commonplace in parliamentary systems, as the models and empirical analysis of Laver and Shepsle (1996) show.

Coalition voting (Brams and Fishburn, 1992), and a simple variant called yes-no voting (Brams and Fishburn, 1993), allow voters to indicate coalitional preferences. In the case of the former, a measure of bargaining strength was proposed in chapter 7. While coalition voting and yes-no voting give voters some leverage over the make-up of a coalition government, it is the parties that join the government that must bargain over ministries for their members.

A reform recently adopted in Northern Ireland eliminates this kind of bargaining by letting the parties choose ministries in a sequence specified by a divisor apportionment method (O'Leary, Grofman, and Elklit, 2001). This mechanism for allocating cabinet ministries is not without its problems, however, if parties can anticipate each others' choices in the sequence (Brams and Kaplan, 2002).

The properties of different apportionment methods and allocation procedures are the subject of a burgeoning literature (Young, 1994; Brams and Taylor, 1996, 1999; Balinski and Young, 2001; Moulin, 2003). The role of bargaining is reduced, but not necessarily eliminated, by the use of mechanisms founded on principles of fair division.

Chapter 8. Bargaining Power

Felsenthal and Machover (1998) provide a comprehensive analysis of the voting power indices, both in theory and practice. There is a continuing controversy over the use of these indices, however, as seen in "Symposium. Power Indices and the European Union" (1999) and in a power analysis of the US Supreme Court (Edelman and Chen, 2001).

Conditions under which power relationships can be represented as weighted voting games have been investigated theoretically and empirically (Taylor and Zwicker, 2000). That large size may be a liability in minimal winning coalitions (Brams and Fishburn, 1995; Fishburn and Brams, 1996), and that the possession of moving power may work to a player's disadvantage (Brams, 1994b), are good examples of subtleties in the study of power that game theory helps to make perspicuous.

Conclusion

Negotiations are critical to coping with all manner of strategic problems that arise in dealings people have with each other and with organizations. Not only does game theory offer important insights into why this is the case, but it also shows how some of these problems can be ameliorated if not solved.

References

Armstrong, Michael J., and W. J. Hurley (2002). "Arbitration Using the Closest Offer Principle of Arbitrator Behavior," *Mathematical Social Sciences* 43, no. 1 (January): 19–26.

Arrow, Kenneth, Robert H. Mnookin, Lee Ross, Amos Tversky, and Robert Wilson (eds.) (1995). *Barriers to Conflict Resolution*. New York: W.W. Norton.

Balinski, Michel L., and H. Peyton Young (2001). *Fair Representation: Meeting the Ideal of One Man, One Vote*, 2nd ed. New Haven, CT: Yale University Press.

Bates, Robert H., Avner Greif, Margaret Levi, Jean-Laurent Rosenthal, and Barry R. Weingast (eds.) (1998). *Analytic Narratives*. Princeton, NJ: Princeton University Press.

Brams, Steven J. (1992). "A Generic Negotiation Game," *Journal of Theoretical Politics* 4, no. 1 (January): 53–66.

———. (1994a). "Game Theory and Literature." *Games and Economic Behavior* 6, no. 1 (January): 32–54.

———. (1994b). *Theory of Moves*. New York: Cambridge University Press.

———. (1999). "To Mobilize or Not to Mobilize: Cathch-22s in International Crises," *International Studies Quarterly* 43, no. 4 (December): 621–640.

———. (2001). "Response to Randall Stone: Heresy or Scientific Progress?" *Journal of Conflict Resolution* 45, no. 2 (April): 245–256.

——. (2002). *Biblical Games: Game Theory and the Hebrew Bible,* rev. ed. Cambridge, MA: MIT Press.

Brams, Steven J., and Ann E. Doherty (1993). "Intransigence in Negotiations: The Dynamics of Disagreement," *Journal of Conflict Resolution* 37, no. 4 (December): 692–708.

Brams, Steven J., and Peter C. Fishburn (1992). "Coalition Voting." In Paul E. Johnson (ed.), *Mathematical and Computer Modelling (Formal Theories of Politics II: Mathematical Modelling in Political Science)* 16, no. 8/9 (August/September): 15–26.

——. (1993). "Yes-No Voting," *Social Choice and Welfare* 10: 35–50.

——. (1995). "When Is Size a Liability? Bargaining Power in Minimal Winning Coalitions," *Journal of Theoretical Politics,* 7, no. 3 (July): 301–316.

Brams, Steven J., and Christopher B. Jones (1999). "Catch-22s and King-of-the-Mountain Games: Cycling, Frustration, and Power," *Rationality and Society* 11, no. 2 (May): 139–167.

Brams, Steven J., Michael A. Jones, and D. Marc Kilgour (2002a). "Forming Stable Coalitions: The Process Matters." Preprint, Department of Politics, New York University.

——. (2002b). "Single-Peakedness and Disconnected Coalitions," *Journal of Theoretical Politics* 14, no. 3 (July): 359–383.

Brams, Steven J., and Todd R. Kaplan (2002). "Dividing the Indivisible: Procedures for Allocating Cabinet Ministries to Political Parties in a Parliamentary System." Preprint, Department of Politics, New York University.

Brams, Steven J., and D. Marc Kilgour (1996). "Bargaining Procedures That Induce Honesty," *Group Decision and Negotiation* 5: 239–262.

Brams, Steven J., D. Marc Kilgour, and Shlomo Weber (1991). "Sequential Arbitration Procedures: Dynamic Versus Static Models of ADR." In Stuart S. Nagel and Miriam K. Mills (eds.), *Systematic Analysis in Dispute Resolution.* New York: Quorum, pp. 199–220.

Brams, Steven J., and Alan D. Taylor (1996). *Fair Division: From Cake-Cutting to Dispute Resolution.* Cambridge, UK: Cambridge University Press.

——. (1999). *The Win-Win Solution: Guaranteeing Fair Shares to Everybody.* New York: W.W. Norton.

Cameron, Charles M. (2000). *Veto Bargaining: Presidents and the Politics of Negative Power.* New York: Cambridge University Press.

Edelman, Paul, and Jim Chen (2001). "The Most Dangerous Justice Rides Again: Revisiting the Power Pageant of the Justices," *Minnesota Law Review* 86: 131–226.

Felsenthal, Dan S., and Moshé Machover (1998). *The Measurement of Voting Power: Theory and Practice, Problems and Paradoxes.* Cheltenham, UK: Edward Elgar.

Fishburn, Peter C., and Steven J. Brams (1996). "Minimal Winning Coalitions in Weighted-Majority Voting Games." *Social Choice and Welfare* 13: 397–417.

Grossman, Gene M., and Elhanan Helpman (2001). *Special Interest Politics.* Cambridge, MA: MIT Press.

Kennan, John, and Robert Wilson (1993). "Bargaining with Private Information," *Journal of Economic Literature* 31, no. 1 (March): 45–104.

Kilgour, D. Marc (1994). "Game-Theoretic Properties of Final-Offer Arbitration." *Group Decision and Negotiation* 3: 285–301.

Kilgour, D. Marc, and Steven J. Brams (1992). "Putting the Other Side 'On Notice' Can Induce Compliance in Arms Control," *Journal of Conflict Resolution* 36, no. 3 (September): 395–414.

Krehbiel, Keith (1998). *Pivotal Politics: A Theory of U.S. Lawmaking.* Chicago: University of Chicago Press.

Laver, Michael, and Kenneth A. Shepsle (1996). *Making and Breaking Governments: Cabinets and Legislatures in Parliamentary Democracies.* Cambridge, UK: Cambridge University Press.

Manzini, Paola, and Marco Mariotti (2001). "Perfect Equilibria in a Model of Bargaining with Arbitration," *Games and Economic Behavior* 37, no. 1 (October): 170–195.

Moulin, Hervé (2003). *Fair Division and Collective Welfare.* Cambridge, MA: MIT Press.

Muthoo, Abhinay (1999). *Bargaining Theory with Applications.* Cambridge, UK: Cambridge University Press.

O'Leary, Brendan, Bernard Grofman, and Jorgen Elklit (2001). "The Use of Divisor Mechanisms to Allocate and Sequence Ministerial Portfolio Allocations: Theory and Evidence from Northern Ireland." Preprint, Department of Political Science, University of Pennsylvania.

Stone, Randall W. (2001). "The Use and Abuse of Game Theory in International Relations: The Theory of Moves." *Journal of Conflict Resolution* 45, no. 2 (April): 216–244.

"Symposium. Power Indices and the European Union" (1999). *Journal of Theoretical Politics* 11, no. 3 (July): 291–366.

Taylor, Alan D., and William S. Zwicker (2000). *Simple Games: Desirability Relations, Trading, Pseudoweightings.* Princeton, NJ: Princeton University Press.

Young, H. Peyton (ed.) (1991). *Negotiation Analysis.* Ann Arbor, MI: University of Michigan Press.

Young, H. Peyton (1994). *Equity in Theory and Practice.* Princeton, NJ: Princeton University Press.

Zeckhauser, Richard J., Ralph L. Keeney, and James K. Senenius (eds.) (1996). *Wise Choices: Decisions, Games, and Negotiations.* Boston: Harvard Business School Press.

Zeng, Dao-Zhi, Shinya Nakamura, and Toshihide Ibaraki (1996), "Double-Offer Arbitration," *Mathematical Social Sciences* 31, no. 3 (June): 147–170.

Preface

Modeling Negotiations

Everybody engages in negotiations. It is therefore not surprising that negotiation processes and outcomes are studied in political science, economics, psychology, and sociology. In addition, courses on negotiation are now commonplace in business schools and law schools, principally because negotiation skills are highly prized in both business and law.

If negotiations are ubiquitous, their analytic study is not. Under the rubric of "alternative dispute resolution" (ADR), for example, negotiation is seen as a purely pragmatic means for reconciling differences and reaching settlements to avoid costly litigation. To coax agreement out of negotiators, claim advocates of ADR, requires good will, forthright exchanges, and persistence on the part of the negotiators.

I do not dispute this claim, but I would argue, as few ADR advocates would, that rigorous theory is also essential to their enterprise. The primary reason is that many conflicts *do* have a rational basis: they cannot be understood as simply the hapless product of misperceptions or poor communication that some enlightened effort can overcome.

Thus, for example, because it is almost always rational for the parties in a dispute to exaggerate their positions, the attempt to find common ground may fail. Despite the parties' best intentions to hammer out an agreement, they soon come to realize that by being completely honest and straightforward, they may end up giving away too much. Consequently, posturing, emotional outbursts, and even outright deception are often the best prescription for doing well in negotiations.

Not only do first-hand observations support this melancholy conclusion, but it also has a strong theoretical basis. By conceding more when negotiations run amok, one may well end up being the sucker; all the good will in the world cannot eradicate this problem. On the other hand, the usual nostrums and quick fixes for avoiding humiliation—

for example, that exhort one boldly to seize the initiative and concede nothing—may create a tide of bitterness and resentment that deepens and prolongs a conflict.

But the situation is not totally bleak, which is precisely where the role of theory comes into play. For one thing, a theory based on the parties' own calculations of gain and loss helps one to understand how rationality—not the usual culprit, some ill-conceived notion of "irrationality"—interferes with bargaining and may derail a settlement. For another, it may provide a key to unlocking how rationality itself may be put to the service of devising better approaches, and even implementing practicable procedures, that help parties build up trust and reach agreements.

The purpose of this book is to explore the rational foundations of conflicts that negotiations may help to resolve. By *negotiations* I mean *exchanges between parties designed to reconcile their differences and produce a settlement*. These exchanges may take different forms, from coolly discussing the terms of a contract to blatantly threatening an adversary with some untoward action—and taking that action if the threat is ignored. Thus, negotiations include exchanges of deeds as well as words, because the former as much as the latter may signal the possible terms of a settlement.

The process of negotiation, as I shall use the term, subsumes both bargaining and arbitration. Arbitration involves a third party that can dictate a settlement if the bargainers cannot reach an agreement on their own. However, this third party may not have complete freedom to impose its own will but may be restricted, as under final-offer arbitration, to selecting one or the other of the two parties' so-called final offers.

Most of this book is about bargaining, wherein the parties are on their own, so to speak. To be sure, they may receive help from mediators or others with an interest in a settlement, but the settlement cannot be imposed; it must be agreed to by the parties themselves. Accordingly, I focus on what actions the parties might take, cognizant of the interests of others, that might smooth over differences and lead to a settlement.

The intersecting yet conflicting interests of the different parties are what make the problem of reaching an agreement a "game"—that is, the outcome depends on the choices of *all* the players. Insofar as no players have reason to abrogate an agreement, the game is said to be "noncooperative": the agreement, because it is in the mutual interest of the parties, is self-enforcing, obviating the need for an outside party to make it stick. Most of the models I shall develop are founded on *noncooperative games*, which do not assume that a binding agreement can be imposed and instead focus on the choice of strategies. *Cooperative games*, which presume such an agreement can be made, concern how the surplus generated by the agreement might be reasonably divided among the players.

The models in the first six chapters, with the exception of one game in Chapter 5, are based on two-person game theory. Many, but by no means all, conflicts can indeed be reduced to two-person games without distorting them unduly. In the last two chapters, I develop models of negotiations involving more than two parties within legislatures, among the different branches of government, and in international relations.

By "models" I mean simplified representations of a situation that, nevertheless, abstract the essential features that one wishes to study. Because game theory provides a powerful set of tools for analyzing interdependent decision situations, it is obviously relevant to negotiations, wherein the players' choices are interactive, each impinging on everybody else's.

I emphasize tools (in the plural) rather than a single methodology because game theory, as a mathematical theory, is perhaps most notable for its richness and diversity. Thus, for example, there are several different representations of a game, which I consider a virtue for modeling purposes because one can select that which is most appropriate for capturing what one wants to model. On the other hand, the lack of a single unified mathematical theory, coupled with a plethora of solution concepts, has provoked some serious disagreements about which are the most fruitful approaches, and what are the most significant problems, in the field.

Overview and Level

I personally find this intellectual ferment stimulating, but in this book I eschew more arcane mathematical issues in favor of constructing models that illuminate problems connected with negotiations. In Chapter 1, I gently ease into the theory—introducing only elementary game-theoretic concepts—by analyzing three biblical stories in which negotiations played a central role. I raise the level of theoretical discourse considerably in Chapter 2, wherein I discuss five different bargaining procedures that can induce two players to be honest, some of which involve an outside party that pays bonuses or offers appraisals. Although this discussion is quite abstract, I suggest in the end that the procedures help to explain how Jimmy Carter was able to persuade both Anwar Sadat and Menachem Begin to make major concessions at Camp David in 1978.

In Chapter 3, I analyze both extant and proposed arbitration procedures, giving special attention to the degree to which they promote the convergence of two parties and thereby diminish the need for an arbitrator. Henry Kissinger's shuttle diplomacy in the Middle East over the 1973–75 period is interpreted in terms of a sequential arbitration procedure that induces the disputants to move toward the position of the arbitrator—or, in the personification of Kissinger, the mediator and bargainer as well.

I introduce the "theory of moves" in Chapter 4, explicating this theory mainly through the moves and countermoves made in two superpower bargaining crises (the Cuban missile crisis of 1962 and the Yom Kippur War of 1973). In Chapter 5, I extend the theory of moves to repeated games in order to analyze different kinds of threats and their effects over time. The costs and benefits of reputation in a sequential-primary game with 21 players are also examined.

The threat analysis is applied to the Polish crisis of 1980–81 in Chapter 6. Also in this chapter, I reconstruct a game that explains why Richard Nixon's threat to abide by a "definitive" decision of the Supreme Court backfired in the Watergate crisis, inducing the Court to rule unanimously against him and ultimately forcing his resignation.

Models of n-person games (i.e., games with more than two players) are developed in the last two chapters. In Chapter 7, I show how vote-trading in legislatures can cause everybody to be worse off, despite the fact that individual legislators always benefit from their own trades. In addition, I describe a new voting system, called "coalition voting," that is intended to induce political parties to form coalitions in multiparty systems based on proportional representation. I analyze the bargains that parties might strike before an election, and illustrate a measure of bargaining strength, in a cooperative game under this system. This measure takes account of the competing claims of parties for, say, ministerial posts in a new government and, in so doing, addresses the problem of a fair division of the spoils.

A more general measure of bargaining power is developed in Chapter 8 and applied to the U.S. federal system, comprising the president, senators, and representatives. I briefly compare the results of the theoretical calculations with empirical data on presidential vetoes and the record of Congress in overriding them. Finally, the limitations of this measure are discussed in the context of how the players' knowledge of each others' preferences may hurt the ostensibly most powerful player (measured in terms of its resources) under "sophisticated voting." The applicability of this analysis to nonvoting games is illustrated by modeling the 1954 Geneva conference over the future status of Vietnam as a three-person game, wherein deception was apparently involved.

The case studies and examples I use to illustrate the game-theoretic models are almost all "political," including arguably the Bible stories. In part they reflect my background and interests as a political scientist; examples from business, law, or other fields could also be used. These cases are not presented as anecdotes, described in a paragraph or two, but are developed in sometimes copious detail. My purpose is to show how, by interweaving a game-theoretic model with empirical information, one can achieve a depth of understanding of the strategic choices of the players, and the resulting outcomes of negotiations, that a more superficial recounting does not offer.

Emphatically, the raison d'être of developing game-theoretic models of negotiations is not to dress up a situation in fancy mathematical garb that looks flashy but is really meant only for display. Rather, it is to elucidate why players act the way they do in conflicts in which their choices affect those of others and how, through negotiations, they may break an impasse.

Both the theory and applications in this book suggest that virtually all negotiations can be conceptualized as games. The intellectual challenge is to construct game-theoretic models that illuminate the nonobvious strategic choices players make and, just as important, reveal how alternative procedures might foster more frequent and enduring agreements.

Let me offer some advice on reading this book. Game theorists will notice immediately that I have left out portions of the standard theory (e.g., I never define a "characteristic function," though such functions are implicit in calculations in Chapters 7 and 8.) The reason is that, by expunging mathematical details that underlie the more formal results, I hope to make the models as accessible as possible to social scientists and practitioners. In my opinion, these details are not essential if one can provide a systematic development of underlying ideas, and set up and illustrate game-theoretic calculations, that convey an understanding of the overarching argument.

Everybody should be able to follow my exegesis of the Bible stories and the reconstructions of most of the real-life cases without much difficulty. On the other hand, the reasoning in the more theoretical sections often relies on a relatively nontechnical but sustained and subtle deductive argument, which may be arduous to follow every step of the way.

If this is the case, go on—and come back to the less yielding parts later. Knowing where the reasoning leads can often help in filling in the gaps later. Also, use the glossary if you forget definitions, and study the figures carefully, including the "keys" and "notes" that are intended to clarify matters.

Game theory provides a way of looking at both the cases and the glue that holds them together. If you think the glue does not bind things well, it can be undone. But then try, using the methodology, to reglue things as you see them, which may require extending the theory.

In this way you can make the theory serve your own ends. Indeed, it can be an exhilarating experience to construct your own model that forges links in a tight logical chain—and may even suggest some practical procedures for conflict resolution never thought of, much less applied, heretofore.

From our happiness in families to our satisfaction in careers to our collective well-being on earth, much hinges on negotiation. A fundamental understanding of this colossal subject, I maintain, cannot be built either on well-meaning platitudes about being generous and open-minded or on hard-boiled tactical advice about being aggressive or deceptive. The intellectual tools are there to improve the study and practice of negotiation, but they first need to be understood in order to be put to good use.

Acknowledgments

It is a pleasure to thank my coauthors of articles and papers on which much of this book is based: Paul J. Affuso, Peter C. Fishburn, Marek P. Hessel, D. Marc Kilgour, Samuel Merrill, III, Douglas Muzzio, William H. Riker, Shlomo Weber, Donald Wittman, and Frank C. Zagare. They are, of course, not responsible for the way I have assembled material, especially the parts I have added to and subtracted from our joint work to try to make the book more coherent. I am grateful for the financial support I have received over the years from the National Science Foundation, the Guggenheim Foundation, the Alfred P. Sloan Foundation, and the U.S. Institute of Peace for reseach on various topics in this book. Finally, I thank Samuel Merrill, III, several anonymous reviewers, and my wife, Eva, for meticulously reading the entire manuscript and making numerous valuable suggestions.

Chapter 1
Negotiations in the Bible

1.1. Introduction

It may seem odd indeed to go back to the Bible for examples of negotiations. But, on reflection, there is no good reason why the beginning of Western recorded history should not contain instances of bargaining and arbitration. In fact, one can argue that the cast of characters in most of the great biblical narratives—God included—generally thought carefully about the goals and consequences of their actions. They often were skillful in negotiating agreements that were in their mutual interest.

To be sure, the Bible is a sacred document to millions of people; it expresses supernatural elements of faith that do not admit of any natural explanations. At the same time, however, some of the great narratives in the Bible do appear to be plausible reconstructions of real events.

I have chosen for analysis three stories in the Hebrew Bible, or Old Testament: (1) Cain's murder of Abel and his bargaining with God not to be killed for his crime; (2) Rahab's negotiation with Israelite spies in Jericho, whom she harbored in return for being saved when Jericho was destroyed; and (3) Solomon's arbitration of a dispute between two women, both of whom claimed maternity of a baby. That I analyze negotiations in these stories in secular terms is not meant to diminish the religious significance or sacred value that they may have.

Some elementary game theory will be introduced both to aid the strategic exegesis of the stories and to illustrate the application of game theory to the analysis of negotiations. Although the popular notion of a game focuses on entertainment, in game theory players are not assumed to act frivolously. Quite the contrary: they are assumed to think carefully about their choices and the possible choices of other players. The outcome of a game—whether comic or tragic, mundane or momentous, fair or unfair—depends on individual choices. Yet because these choices may have ramifications not only for the individuals involved but also for an entire people, they are unmistakably political.

1

Game theory is a tool ideally suited for penetrating the complex decision-making situations often described in the Bible. Because its appplication requires the careful unraveling of a tangle of character motivations and their effects, it imposes a discipline on the study of these situations that is usually lacking in more traditional literary-historical-theological analyses of the Bible.

The game theory in this chapter is supplemented by verbal explications that use ideas from game theory but not its formal apparatus. Indeed, in some instances a rote application of game-theoretic tools would be forced or silly; at those times I resort to a more informal analysis.

The three cases of biblical negotiation analyzed here are but a sampling of the biblical stories in which bargaining or arbitration figure prominently. Other cases that might have been included are

- Abraham's bargaining with God to save the sinful cities of Sodom and Gomorrah if as few as fifty innocent inhabitants could be found, with haggling eventually bringing the number down to ten;

- the bargaining between the twins, Jacob and Esau, over the sale of Esau's birthright (Esau was born first);

- the intercession of the twins' mother, Rebekah, in the negotiations about who would receive the blessing of their father, Isaac;

- Laban's disputed agreements with Jacob about the tasks that Jacob would have to perform in order to be able to marry Laban's daughter, Rachel, who was beautiful and whom Jacob preferred to Laban's older daughter, Leah;

- Joseph's mercurial dealings with his brothers and his father, Jacob, which included both betrayal and reconciliation within the family;

- Moses's bargaining with God first about assuming leadership of the Israelites, later about whether God would spare the Israelites after their idolatry at Mount Sinai, and finally about obtaining relief from the burdens of leadership;

- Jonah's defiance and later acceptance of God's command to warn Nineveh of its imminent doom, and then his angry confrontation with God after the city was spared;

- Esther's delicate negotiations with King Ahasuerus, linking Haman's conspiracy against the Jews to his seeming designs on her, in order to discredit Haman and then bring about his demise; and

- Satan and God's bargaining about how Job would be tested.

I have used game theory in a previous work to analyze some of these conflicts—as well as the three analyzed in this chapter—though not with a specific focus on the negotiations between the disputing parties (Brams 1980).

Elementary game-theoretic concepts and analysis will be introduced in this chapter. In order to avoid introducing too much material too soon, however, I reserve for later chapters a discussion of more sophisticated concepts and more complex forms of analysis.

1.2. Cain and Abel: Bargaining with God

After being expelled from the garden of Eden, Adam and Eve became parents first to Cain and then to Abel. Cain was a tiller of the soil and Abel a shepherd. The conditions for conflict immediately became apparent[1]:

> In the course of time, Cain brought an offering to the LORD from the fruit of the soil; and Abel, for his part, brought the choicest of the firstlings of his flock. The LORD paid heed to Abel and his offering, but to Cain and his offering He paid no heed. Cain was much distressed and his face fell. (Gen. 4:3–5)

Unlike the impersonal prohibition on eating from the forbidden fruit in the garden of Eden, God appears to meddle directly in the affairs of the brothers by playing favorites, naturally antagonizing the one not favored.

True, Cain's offering was apparently inferior to Abel's, because it was simply from the "fruit of the soil" (Gen. 4:3) but not, like Abel's, the "choicest" (Gen. 4:4). Yet, if God was disappointed by its meagerness, He did not say so but instead ignored Cain's offering. By contrast, God had not been silent about His distress with Adam and Eve's transgressions.

It seems that God's primary motive was less to chastise Cain than to stir up jealousy between the brothers—and then await the fireworks. If this was His goal, He was not to be disappointed.

As support for this position, consider God's incredible question after refusing Cain's offering and observing his anger:

> Why are you distressed,
> And why is your face fallen? (Gen. 4:6)

Without awaiting an answer, which I presume God knew and did not want to respond to, God offered a poetic message of hope and fear:

> Surely, if you do right,
> There is uplift.
> But if you do not do right
> Sin couches at the door;
> Its urge is toward you,
> Yet you can be its master. (Gen. 4:7)

Having issued this warning, God immediately observed the divine consequences of His provocation of Cain:

> Cain said to his brother Abel [Ancient versions: "Come, let us go into the field"] . . . and when they were in the field, Cain set upon his brother Abel and killed him. (Gen. 4:8)

Next comes another incredible question from God, reminiscent of the rhetorical question He asked Adam ("Where are you?" [Gen. 3:9]) after Adam and Eve ate the forbidden fruit and tried to hide from God: "Where is your brother Abel?" (Gen. 4:9). Cain's memorable response is less than forthcoming: "I do not know. Am I my brother's keeper?" (Gen. 4:9).

This laconic answer in the form of a question, which I assume was uttered with some acerbity (the tone of Cain's voice is obviously not known), gives us as much insight into Cain's strategic calculations as it does into his shaky morality. First, there seems little doubt that his murder of Abel was premeditated, for he set upon Abel "in the field" (Gen. 4:8), to which, it seems, they journeyed together.[2] Second, warned by God of the presence of sin at his door, Cain cannot plead ignorance of the fact that his murder might have adverse consequences, even if their exact nature could not be foretold.

Seething with anger and jealousy over the favoritism shown Abel, and unable to strike out against God directly (even if he had wanted to), Cain did the next best thing—he murdered God's apparent favorite. Under the circumstances, this response to God's taunting from a terribly aggrieved man seems not at all irrational.

What is harder to understand is Cain's reply about being his brother's keeper. In my opinion, it can be read as a cleverly constructed challenge to God's own morality in meddling in the affairs of the brothers.[3] Not that Cain necessarily knew that God had fomented trouble to test Cain's susceptibility to sin—and make punishment of his crime a precedent for others. Whoever was to blame, however, Cain felt deeply wronged and was driven to take revenge.

But how does one justify fratricide, and what can one do after the act to mitigate one's punishment for the crime? Cain had at least three courses of action open to him:

1. Admit the murder.
2. Deny the murder.
3. Defend his morality.

Admittedly, the third course of action would seem hard to execute shamelessly, except when it is recalled that the conditions that led to the crime do not leave God with virtuous intent intact.

Whether one perfidy excuses another, the salient fact is that Cain did not think his act unjustified. Even if he did not question the purity of God's motives, he could still perhaps defend himself by pleading no responsibility for his brother's welfare.

Cain's defense is actually more subtle than simply a plea of inculpability. He first says he does not know where his brother is. Could not this imply that God does or should know, and that He bears some responsibility for Abel, too? The notion that Abel is not Cain's sole responsibility is then reinforced by Cain's famous question.

This, in my opinion, is a brilliant defense, because it eloquently contrasts God's responsibility and his own, implicitly suggesting that there may be questionable morality on both sides. God, in His response to Cain's (unadmitted) crime and rhetorical defense, begins with His own rhetorical question, which He quickly follows with a stiff sentence for a tiller of the soil:

> What have you done? Hark, your brother's blood cries out to me from the ground! Therefore, you shall be more cursed than the ground, which opened its mouth to receive your brother's blood from your hand. If you till the soil, it shall no longer yield its strength to you. You shall become a ceaseless wanderer on earth. (Gen. 4:10–12)

Acting as his own defense attorney, Cain responded to God's sentence with a plea for mercy:

> My punishment is too great to bear! Since You have banished me this day from the soil, and I must avoid Your presence and become a restless wanderer on earth—anyone who meets me may kill me! (Gen. 4:13-14).

Note that the crux of Cain's plaintive remonstration is that he might be killed, not that the sentence itself is unjust or inappropriate. Reminded of this consequence of His sentence, God finds it unpalatable and answers Cain by saying:

"I promise, if anyone kills Cain, sevenfold vengeance shall be taken on him." And the LORD put a mark on Cain, lest anyone who met him should kill him. (Gen. 4:15)

The reason, I believe, that God finds Cain's death unpalatable is because only "a ceaseless wanderer on earth" (Gen. 4:12) can spread far and wide the message of God's retribution for fratricide. If Cain were quickly dispatched, God's great power—and even greater mercy in sparing the murderer's life—would of course not get communicated to the world.

I postulate that God considered two strategies in response to Cain's murder of Abel:

1. Kill Cain.
2. Punish Cain.

If Cain had either admitted his crime or denied it, I believe God would probably have chosen to kill Cain. Murder, especially of one's brother, is too serious a crime to ignore or cover up. Moreover, the execution of the murderer would set an impressive precedent.

If there were extenuating circumstances, on the other hand, punishment short of death could be considered. But there was no serpent, as in the Adam and Eve story, that could be implicated and used as exculpation for Cain's sin. The only possible extenuating circumstance was God's complicity—or at least His failure to accept any responsibility for stirring up trouble in the first place, or for not coming to Abel's aid just before his murder.

This failure is exactly what Cain plays upon in his reply to God. It is as if Cain said, "He's your responsibility, too; why did you not protect him from my rage, which after all you incited?" If God is not disturbed by this implied question, why would He say that Abel's blood "cries out *to Me* from the ground" (Gen. 4:10; my italics)—not to Cain, not to the world, but to God Himself. God is responsible, too.

God can hardly condemn a man to death when He is also culpable. Whether this implies God felt "guilty," however, is more difficult to say. Guilt seems a peculiarly human trait, and I know of no open admission of this attribute by God anywhere in the Bible. But even if one rules out remorse on God's part in this story, He had good reason only to banish Cain from the ground where his brother's blood was shed and spare his life.

In fact, as I have already indicated, Cain is able to extract still more from God: a mark that signals to anyone meeting him that he should not be killed. Two explanations for this concession from God suggest themselves. First, because God is personally troubled (and perhaps guilt-ridden) by Abel's murder, He is attentive to Cain's plea of mercy. Second, because of God's desire—evident in many other biblical stories (Brams 1980)—to promulgate to the world both His power and His mercy, it is sensible, on purely strategic grounds, to commute Cain's sentence. I believe there is more support for the second explanation, based on its consistency with the other stories.

My exegesis of the Cain and Abel story in rational-choice terms is summarized as a game played between Cain and God in Figure 1.1. This representation is called a *game in extensive form,* or *game tree,* and describes the sequence of moves in the story (read from top to bottom): God first chooses between creating jealousy between the brothers or not; if He does, Cain next chooses between murdering or not murdering Abel. If Cain commits the murder, God interrogates him, after which Cain has the choice of admitting the crime, denying it, or defending his morality; finally, God can either kill Cain or punish him in some other way.

For God, I give a three-tier ranking of outcomes (good, medium, or bad), and for Cain I give a two-tier ranking (medium or bad), at each level of the tree. Starting at the bottom level, I rate all outcomes as "medium" or "bad" for God, except that of punishing Cain after he mounts a defense of his morality that indirectly implicates God. Whether or not this defense creates guilt or shame in God, as an astute ruler, I believe, He would prefer to act mercifully (if given good reasons) than to act

- too harshly by killing Cain—"medium" outcomes in Figure 1.1; or
- too benevolently by sparing him (without good reasons)—"bad" outcomes in Figure 1.1.

In fact, these "medium" and "bad" outcomes for God at the bottom of the tree could be reversed without changing the results of the subsequent analysis. At the top of the tree, I consider God's failure to create jealousy between the brothers to be "bad" not only because He probably felt genuinely slighted by Cain's offering but also because there was a better alternative: He could, by provoking Cain, use any misbehavior on Cain's part to send a message about the retribution that recalcitrants would suffer for defying Him.

Instead of killing Cain, letting him live as a marked man provides God with not only a message but also a messenger who can tell the world that although God punished him, He mercifully spared his life. This will be "good" for God's image—and salve His possibly disquieting feelings about the episode. For Cain, this is a better outcome ("medium") than any

Figure 1.1. Game tree of Cain's murder of Abel

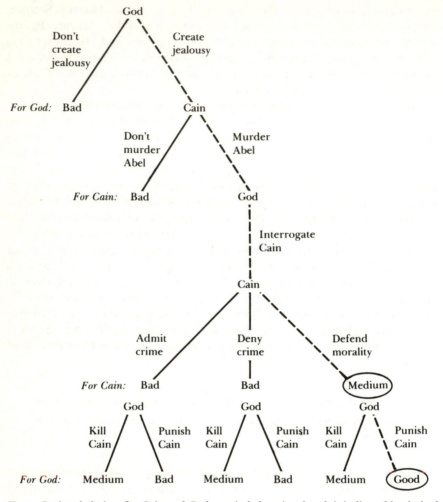

Key: Rational choices for Cain and God are circled; rational path is indicated by dashed line.

other (the remainder are "bad"), including suppressing his murderous instinct—if this is even possible—and not murdering Abel.

The determination of rational choices from the game tree is based on a backward reasoning process, which I shall formalize in later chapters. More informally, to begin the process one asks what the last-moving player (God) would choose if play got to His choice point (or *move*) at the bottom of the tree. Clearly, He would prefer to kill Cain if either he admits or denies his crime; but if Cain defends his morality, God would prefer to punish him less severely.[4] Hence, God's best choice depends on Cain's prior choice.

Because I assume this to be a *game of complete information*, each player knows the preferences of the other as well as the sequence of play. Proceeding up the tree, Cain, therefore, can anticipate God's subsequent choices, depending on what he (Cain) does at the next-to-last stage. Assuming that God will punish him, giving him a "medium" outcome, if he defends his morality, Cain will choose this course of action over the "bad" alternatives at this stage. It is a *rational choice* because it leads to a preferred outcome.

In turn, Cain will murder Abel rather than feeling self-pity in not avenging his humiliation, for the latter "bad" outcome is inferior to the former "medium" outcome resulting from Abel's murder, Cain's defense, and God's punishment. At the top of the tree, it is clearly rational for God, anticipating future rational choices, to incite jealousy between the brothers—with ultimate favorable consequences for the image He wants to create—rather than to do nothing.

Having reconstructed rational choices via this backward reasoning, the players now can reverse this process and look ahead to the consequences of their choices, starting at the top of the tree. The dashed line through the tree indicates the path that rational players would follow, beginning with God's choice of creating jealousy at the top and ending with His punishment of Cain at the bottom. Note that God's interrogation of Cain after the murder of Abel is not shown as a choice but an occurrence, which sets up possible future choices for Cain. While the choice of noninterrogation by God is in principle possible, it would end the game at an evidently inferior outcome for God and, consequently, would not be made.

Both the origin and resolution of the family conflict between Cain and Abel are obviously affected by the heavy hand of God. Indeed, I do not consider Abel even to be a player, capable of making choices, in my game-theoretic treatment of his murder and its aftermath. In the next story, God's hand is less heavy; the focus of negotiation shifts to the rationality of subscribing to an agreement with another party.

1.3. Rahab and the Spies: Making a Just Agreement

After the death of Moses, Joshua became leader of the Israelites and prepared for the occupation of Canaan by sending out two spies to reconnoiter the country:

They came to the house of a harlot named Rahab and lodged there. The king of Jericho was told, "Some men have come here tonight,

> Israelites, to spy out the country." The king of Jericho thereupon sent
> orders to Rahab: "Produce the men who came to you and entered your
> house, for they have come to spy out the whole country." (Josh. 2:1–3)

Rahab admitted to seeing the two men but said they had already left. She
claimed not to know where they had gone but urged that they be pursued.

The pursuit was fruitless, because Rahab had in fact hidden the men
on her roof among stalks of flax. The reason she gave to the spies for
deceiving her king was based on the fearsome reputation of the Israelites
and their God:

> I know that the LORD has given the country to you, because dread of
> you has fallen upon us, and all the inhabitants of the land are quaking
> before you. For we have heard how the LORD dried up the waters of
> the Sea of Reeds [Red Sea] for you when you left Egypt, and what you
> did to Sihon and Og, the two Amorite kings across the Jordan, whom
> you doomed. When we heard about it, we lost heart, and no man had
> any more spirit left because of you; for the LORD your God is the only
> God in heaven above and on earth below. (Josh. 2:9–11)

As a prostitute (and business woman), Rahab was certainly knowledgeable about the exchange of favors. Not intending to let her hiding of the
spies go unrewarded, she put the following proposition to them:

> Now, since I have shown loyalty to you, swear to me by the LORD that
> you in turn will show loyalty to my family. Provide me with a reliable
> sign that you will spare the lives of my father and mother, my brothers
> and sisters, and all who belong to them, and save us from death. (Josh.
> 2:12–13)

Recognizing a good deal when they saw one, the spies willingly accepted
the proposition, but with the proviso that Rahab continue to support
them:

> Our persons are pledged for yours, even to death! If you will not disclose
> this mission of ours, we will show you true loyalty when the LORD gives
> us the land. (Josh. 2:14)

Abetting the escape of the spies from her roof, Rahab offered them some
sage advice:

> Make for the hills, so that the pursuers may not come upon you. Stay
> there in hiding three days, until the pursuers return; then go your way.
> (Josh. 2:16)

Figure 1.2.   Outcome matrix of Rahab's game

Spies

		Save Rahab	Don't save Rahab
Rahab	Hide spies	Barter made, everybody lives	Rahab killed, spies live
	Don't hide spies	Spies killed, Rahab lives	Barter not made, everybody killed

The spies, in turn, after reminding Rahab that their deal was binding only if she did exactly what they said, told her:

> When we invade the country, you tie this length of crimson cord to the window through which you let us down. Bring your father, your mother, your brothers, and all your family together in your house. (Josh. 2:18)

Rahab followed their instructions to the letter, as the spies followed Rahab's advice. After hiding for three days in the hills, the spies escaped detection and returned safely to Joshua, reporting to him what had transpired and what they had observed.

With not inconsequential assistance from God, Jericho was captured after the sound of rams' horns and the shouts of the Israelite army brought its walls crashing down. "Man and woman, young and old, ox and sheep and ass" (Josh. 6:22) were exterminated with the sword. Before the city was destroyed by fire, the two spies led Rahab and her familty to safety, "for she had hidden the messengers that Joshua sent to spy out Jericho" (Josh. 6:25).

There seems nothing very complex about the game played between Rahab and the spies: Rahab could either hide or not hide the spies; they could either save or not save Rahab after Jericho was taken (assuming that it was). These are the *strategies,* or courses of action, that each player may follow. A *player* is simply an actor or set of actors that can make strategy choices in a *game,* which is an interdependent situation—the outcomes depend on the choices of *all* players—which can be represented in different forms (the extensive form, or game tree, was illustrated in Section 1.2).

The consequences of these strategy choices are shown in the *outcome matrix* of Figure 1.2, whose entries—at the intersections of the different strategies of the players—are described verbally. However, this representation does not reflect the fact that Rahab had to make the initial choice.

In Section 1.4, I shall illustrate how a game matrix in which the players make choices in a particular order can be set up.

The problem with such a setup in the present game is that it ignores some crucial steps in the sequence of moves, including the deal struck between Rahab and the spies and the fact that Rahab could still betray the spies after agreeing not to; similarly, they could betray her after she saved them. Also, if Rahab did not hide the spies, they would never have had the opportunity to make a choice of saving her or not, as assumed in the Figure 1.2 outcome matrix.

A more realistic representation of Rahab's game is as an outcome matrix with a nested subgame, as shown in the revised representation in Figure 1.3. In this game, I assume that each player can rank the outcomes from best to worst, where "4" is considered a player's best outcome; "3," next best; "2," next worst; and "1," worst. Hence, the higher the number, the better the outcome. Although these numbers constitute only ordinal ranks (i.e., orderings of outcomes), I shall refer to them as *payoffs*.

In Figure 1.3, the first number in the ordered pair (x,y) refers to Rahab's payoff, the second number to the spies'/Joshua's payoff (assumed to be the same). Because these numbers are ranks and not utilities (to be defined shortly), they do not say, for example, how much more a player prefers its next-best (3) to its next-worst (2) outcome. Later, however, I shall assume these ranks to be utilities to illustrate an expected-utility calculation that incorporates the probability that a player is trustworthy.

In the game, Rahab and the spies must decide whether to offer to barter their lives or not. If neither offers, I assume both players obtain their next-worst outcome (2)—they can at least try to fend for themselves. If one offers and the other does not, I assume that the one who does not still obtains his or her next-worst outcome (2) because no barter is consummated; the one who offers, however—only to be spurned by the other player—receives his or her worst outcome (1).

If both players agree to the barter, the subgame ensues, with payoff (x,y) as yet to be determined. Now Rahab has the first move: she may either keep the agreement or break it. If she keeps the agreement and the spies escape with their lives, they in turn can either save her or kill her by keeping or not keeping their side of the agreement.

If they keep their word, I assume both they and Rahab obtain their best outcome (4); if they betray Rahab, they live but are dishonored for allowing someone to be killed who was loyal to them and had recognized their God as the only true God, which I take to be their next-best outcome (3). Rahab, who is double-crossed, receives her worst outcome (1).

Should Rahab not keep her agreement, the spies would be killed, and the choice would presumably fall on Joshua of whether or not to save

Figure 1.3. Rahab's game revised

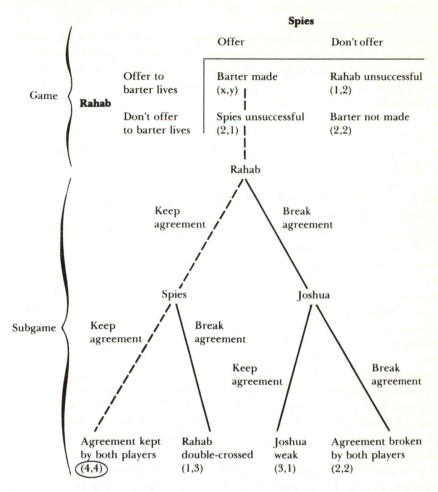

Key: (x,y) = (Rahab, Spies/Joshua); 4 = best; 3 = next best; 2 = next worst; 1 = worst.
Circled outcome is rational.

Rahab (assuming he learned later of their betrayal).[5] If he did not avenge the betrayal of his spies, I assume he would obtain his worst outcome (1), for he would be considered weak for not exacting retribution; Rahab would receive her next-best outcome (3) for living but facing possible later retribution. (The later retribution might come if Joshua learned of her betrayal, because, like everybody else, Rahab and her family would presumably be killed when Jericho was destroyed.) Both players, I assume, would obtain their next-worst outcome (2) if they both broke the agreement, for it would be tantamount to not offering to barter in the first place.[6]

Because the outcome chosen in the subgame determines the rationality of bartering in the game, prudence dictates that each player first determine the rational outcome in the subgame. Inserting this outcome into the matrix in Figure 1.3, the players could then determine a rational strategy choice in the game.

Starting with the bottom choices in the game tree of the subgame in Figure 1.3, the spies would prefer (4,4) to (1,3), and Joshua would prefer (2,2) to (3,1). Working up the tree, between (4,4) and (2,2) Rahab would prefer (4,4), so the rational choice of each player in the subgame is to honor the agreement he or she makes. This, of course, is all rather obvious, but I shall introduce uncertainty into the analysis later that complicates matters.

The next question is: It is rational for the players to make an agreement in the game? Given that the outcome of the subgame will be (4,4), this outcome can be substituted for (x,y) in the matrix defining the game in Figure 1.3. However, while this substitution yields both players their best outcome (4) when they agree to barter their lives, it is not associated with a *dominant,* or unconditionally best, strategy of either player, which neither has in the game after the substitution of (4,4) for (x,y). Thus, for example, while "offer" is better than "don't offer" for Rahab if the spies choose "offer," this is not true if the spies choose "don't offer," for 2 is better than 1 for Rahab in the spies' second column of Figure 1.3.

Define a *superior outcome* to be one preferred by both players to any other outcome in a two-person game, which is necessarily the mutually best outcome. In a game having such an outcome but in which neither player has a dominant strategy, I interpret this to be the rational outcome of the game.

It is, however, rational in a weaker sense than an outcome associated with the dominant strategy of a player. To illustrate this point by the game in Figure 1.3, if one player should act irrationally and either not return the other's offer or not keep his or her side of the agreement, the other player obtains his or her worst outcome (1). (If the other player had a dominant strategy in the game, he or she could obtain at least its next-worst outcome [2].) Nonetheless, in the composite game comprising the game and its subgame, it is rational for both players to barter their lives—and to do so in good faith, sticking to the agreement they make—insofar as they believe in the rationality of their opponent (a probabilistic argument about belief will be developed shortly).

A notion of what constitutes a "just agreement" can be gleaned from Rahab's game. First, it must be voluntarily subscribed to, and second, it must be stable—invulnerable to violation by one or both players. By "invulnerable" I mean that neither player would have an interest in violating an agreement once it is made, because he or she would suffer a worse outcome if one or both players violated it.

In Rahab's game, these conditions for a just agreement are clearly met: it was voluntarily subscribed to; and it was stable because, as the game-tree analysis demonstrates, either player would have done worse if he or she had violated the agreement. In fact, both players would have done worse, because the outcome (4,4), if lost in the subgame because one or both players violates the agreement, also would have been lost in the game.

It is easy to see that if the players in a composite game are rational, their assent to an agreement in the game implies that the agreement, built up in the subgame, is stable. For if it were not, at least one player would have an incentive to violate it; assuming a violation by one player hurts at least one other player, that other player would not give his or her assent to the agreement in the first place. Hence, it is sufficient to define a *just agreement* as one to which rational players would voluntarily subscribe. If they did not, it would be because they anticipate a violation that would hurt them, thereby robbing them of any incentive even to begin negotiation.

Recall that, to secure Rahab's agreement, the spies told Rahab that their barter of lives was conditional on her adhering to their instructions. Indeed, after telling Rahab and her family to stay indoors during the capture of Jericho, the spies repeated their conditions, which Rahab accepted:

> "If you disclose this mission of ours, we shall likewise be released from the oath which you made us take." She replied, "Let it be as you say." (Josh. 2:20–21)

Thus, the agreement in Rahab's game was rendered stable not just by a promise of the spies to keep it but by their intimation of revenge if they were betrayed. By inextricably linking their lives and Rahab's, the spies made it impossible for her to double-cross them with impunity, even though she could have struck the first blow by turning them in to her king.

Of course, the foregoing analysis is predicated on the assumption that Rahab believed that

1. the spies would keep their agreement if she did;
2. Joshua would break the agreement if she did.

But what if Rahab did not have perfect faith in such a quid pro quo arrangement? Suppose, for example, that she thought that the probability of (1) to be p and the probability of (2) to be q.

To explore the implications of this supposition, assume that the *cardinal utilities*—or numerical values, indicating degrees of preference—that Rahab attaches to the outcomes in Figure 1.3 are exactly the same as the ranks. For example, (1,3) means that Rahab receives one unit of utility if this outcome is chosen, which might be measured in terms of money or some other currency of satisfaction. Then if Rahab keeps the agreement (K), her expected utility will be

$$E(K) = 4p + 1(1 - p),$$

or the utilities of each of the two outcomes associated with her selecting the left-hand branch of the tree times the complementary probabilities (p and $1 - p$) that each outcome will occur. Similarly, if Rahab breaks the agreement (B), her expected utility will be

$$E(B) = 3(1 - q) + 2q.$$

$E(K) > E(B)$ if

$$3p + 1 > 3 - q, \text{ or } 3p + q > 2.$$

The solid line given by the equation $3p + q = 2$ is shown in Figure 1.4, with the shaded region above this line defining the area in which $E(K) > E(B)$.

To simplify this relationship, assume $p = q$, which is depicted by the dashed diagonal line in Figure 1.4. Then $E(K) > E(B)$ if

$$4p + 1 - p > 3 - 3p + 2p, \text{ or } 4p > 2,$$

which reduces to $p > \frac{1}{2}$; graphically, points along the diagonal in the shaded region satisfy this inequality. In other words, the chance that the spies and Joshua will be true to their word must be only greater than 50–50 in order for Rahab to do better on average by keeping the agreement than breaking it.

Rahab's trust in her potential benefactors, therefore, need not be profound in order to make it worth her while to be trustworthy herself. To be sure, a different assignment of utilities to the four outcomes would change the threshold probability $p = q$ that induces Rahab to keep her side of the bargain. But my main point is not to argue for a particular assignment but rather to indicate how the basic game-tree model can be

Figure 1.4. Region in which $E(K) > E(B)$

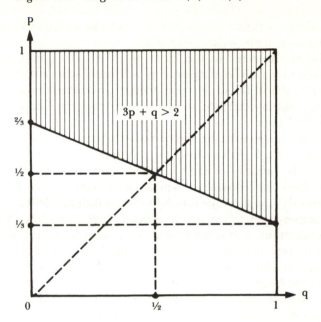

complicated to accommodate uncertainty about the players' trustworthiness in the eyes of each other.

In the present game, I assumed that Rahab might be uncertain about the trustworthiness of the Israelites, but I did not assume uncertainty on the part of Joshua and the spies about Rahab's trustworthiness. More sophisticated calculations that incorporate two-sided uncertainty into games will be introduced in Chapters 2 and 3.

1.4. Solomon's Arbitration: Discovering the Truth

Most of the "wisdom" of the Bible is simply asserted, as in the book of Proverbs, which is filled with advice about proper behavior, admonitions against improper behavior, and miscellaneous sayings and aphorisms meant to be instructive on various matters. Lessons, of course, are meant to be learned from the stories of conflict and intrigue I have already discussed, but the message in these stories is usually less direct and more often subject to different interpretations.

It is a rare story indeed that imbues a character other than God—or one with God at his side—with a soaring intelligence and depth of insight that seem to surpass human bounds. True, most characters act rationally according to their preferences, and a few—like Cain, and Moses in his later years—show by the arguments they present to God that they are superb strategists. It is hard, however, to find human characters who, when pitted against their fellow mortals, emerge as larger-than-life figures by virtue of their godlike wisdom.

The biblical character in the Hebrew Bible who stands out as the striking exception to this statement is Solomon, who ruled as king of Israel after Saul and David. What is usually considered his most breathtaking judgment is described in just twelve verses in Chapter 3 of the First Book of Kings.

This judgment concerns the disposition of a baby for whom two women claimed maternity. I shall model this judgment as a game Solomon devised to test the veracity of the women's claims. Although the game as played involved one woman's moving first, Solomon could have set the rules differently—to allow for simultaneous or independent moves—and still have achieved the same result. Also, I shall show how the concept of "wise arbitration"—to complement the notion of a "just agreement" defined in Section 1.3—can be derived from Solomon's game. Unlike a just agreement, which depends only on the choices that the parties to the agreement make, wise arbitration depends also on the choices of a nonplayer, who arbitrates a settlement between the parties to a dispute.

Solomon's game arises from a dispute between two prostitutes who come before him:

> The first woman said, "Please, my lord! This woman and I live in the same house; and I gave birth to a child while she was in the house. On the third day after I was delivered, this woman also gave birth to a child. We were alone; there was no one else with us in the house. During the night this woman's child died, because she lay on it. She arose in the night and took my son from my side while your maidservant was asleep, and laid him in her bosom; and she laid her dead son in my bosom. When I arose in the morning to nurse my son, there he was dead; but when I looked at him closely in the morning, it was not the son I had borne." (1 Kings 3:17–21)

The other prostitute protested this version of their encounter: "No; the live one is my son, and the dead one is yours!" (1 Kings 3:22). The two women continued arguing in Solomon's presence, while he reflected:

> "One says, 'This is my child, the live one, and the dead one is yours'; and the other says, 'No, the dead boy is yours, mine is the live one.' " So the king gave the order, "Fetch me a sword." (1 Kings 3:23–24)

Solomon's solution was one of dazzling simplicity: "Cut the live child in two, and give half to one and half to the other." (1 Kings 3:25). The

Figure 1.5.   Outcome matrix of Solomon's game

		Impostor	
		Protest order (P)	Don't protest order (P̄)
Mother	Protest order (P)	Baby surely saved (4,2)	Baby perhaps saved; impostor wins favor of Solomon (3,4)
	Don't protest order (P̄)	Baby perhaps saved; impostor loses favor of Solomon (2,1)	Baby surely killed (1,3)

Key: (x,y) = (Mother, Impostor); 4 = best; 3 = next best; 2 = next worst; 1 = worst.

subtlety underlying this solution soon became apparent in the reactions
of the two claimants:

> But the woman whose son was the live one pleaded with the king, for
> she was overcome with compassion for her son. "Please, my lord," she
> cried, "give her the live child; only don't kill it!" The other insisted, "It
> shall be neither yours nor mine; cut it in two!" (1 Kings 3:26)

The story concludes with the following observation:

> When all Israel heard the decision that the king had rendered, they
> stood in awe of the king; for they saw that he possessed divine wisdom
> to execute justice. (1 Kings 3:28)

Thus is Solomon venerated for his exemplary judgment.

The outcome matrix for the game played between the two women,
reacting to Solomon's order to cut the baby in two, is shown in Figure
1.5, with the rankings by the two women that I shall now try to justify.
(These rankings are as they saw the situation; Solomon, of course, saw
things quite differently, but he is not a player.) I assume that the mother's
goal was to save her baby, the impostor's to win Solomon's favor; by
acceding to Solomon's judgment, the impostor indicated absolutely no
interest in the baby's welfare, much less having him for herself.

More specifically, the mother, I believe, would consider the best outcome (4) to be that in which both women protest Solomon's order, because
their combined protest would be most likely to save the baby. If the
mother protested alone, the baby perhaps might be saved, so this would
be the mother's next-best outcome (3).

This latter strategy would lead to the impostor's best outcome (4); she would win Solomon's favor, because the mother's single protest would unequivocally distinguish her (the impostor's) support of the king's order and the mother's nonsupport. The outcome the impostor would next most prefer (3) is that in which neither she nor the mother protested the king's order, because then, although she would not be singled out favorably, she would not be in his disfavor. For the mother, though, this strategy would lead to her worst outcome (1), for the baby would surely die.

I assume that a better outcome (2) for the mother is for her not to protest and the impostor to protest; the baby might be saved, but he would not go to her.[7] In fact, I believe, the mother would be abject for rejecting her baby when the impostor did not, though the possibility that the baby might survive under these circumstances prevents this outcome from being her worst.

For the impostor, on the other hand, this would be an odious outcome (1), because she would lose the favor of the the king by protesting his order while the mother did not. As I previously indicated, the impostor would most prefer that the opposite happen.

Does game theory explain the choices of the mother and the impostor in this arbitration case? The game shown in Figure 1.5 is a *game in normal (or strategic) form,* which is represented by an outcome or payoff matrix. Because the player's strategy choices are assumed to be simultaneous— or, equivalently, made independently of each other—this game does not depict the game that was actually played. This form has been used mainly to describe the four different outcomes that can arise and the preferences of the two players for each of them.

The actual game played was one in which the mother, by protesting the king's order, committed herself first; then the impostor responded. This sequence of moves described in the story can be represented by the game-tree shown in Figure 1.6: the mother first chooses to protest or not protest Solomon's order; only then does the impostor choose to protest or not. The facts that the mother's move precedes the impostor's, and that the impostor is aware of the mother's prior choice, mean the game cannot properly be represented as a 2×2 game (two players, each with two strategies), which is the representation given by the outcome matrix in Figure 1.5. Rather the proper representation in matrix form of this game is as a 2×4 game (mother has two strategies, impostor has four).

This representation is shown in Figure 1.7. The 2×4 game reflects the fact that because the mother made the first choice, she can choose whether to protest or not to protest Solomon's order. The impostor, on the other hand, whose choice occurs only after the mother has made a choice, has four possible choices, depending on what the mother chose.

Figure 1.6. Game tree of Solomon's game

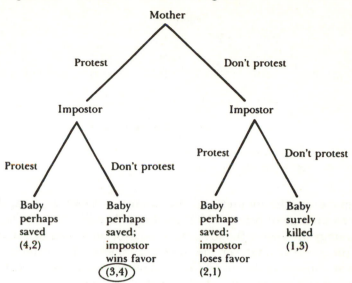

Key: (x,y) = (Mother, Impostor); 4 = best; 3 = next best; 2 = next worst; 1 = worst. Circled outcome is rational.

Thus, the impostor has four strategies, contingent upon the mother's prior choices:

1. P/P: *protest regardless*. Protest if mother does, protest if mother does not.
2. $\overline{P}/\overline{P}$: *don't protest regardless*. Don't protest if mother does, don't protest if mother does not.
3. P/$\overline{P}$: *tit-for-tat*. Protest if mother protests, don't protest if not.
4. $\overline{P}$/P: *tat-for-tit*. Don't protest if mother protests, protest if not.

The 2 × 4 payoff matrix in Figure 1.7 gives the payoffs that each player receives for every pair of strategy choices (two for the mother, four for the impostor) of the two players. Thus, for example, if the mother chooses to protest (P) and the impostor chooses tat-for-tit ($\overline{P}$/P), $P\overline{P}$ is the resultant outcome, for the choice of P by the mother implies the choice of $\overline{P}$ by the impostor under tat-for-tit. As can be seen from Figure 1.6, this yields a payoff of (3,4)—the next-best outcome for the mother, the best for the impostor (in their eyes, anyway)—which is shown in the P row and $\overline{P}$/P column of Figure 1.7.

What are the game-theoretic implications of the preference assump-

Figure 1.7. Payoff matrix of Solomon's game

		Impostor			
		P/P	P̄/P̄	P/P̄	P̄/P
	P	(4,2)	(3,4)	(4,2)	(3,4)
Mother					
	P̄	(2,1)	(1,3)	(1,3)	(2,1)

← Protest dominant

↑
Don't protest regardless dominant

Key: (*x,y*) = (Mother, Impostor); 4 = best; 3 = next best; 2 = next worst; 1 = worst.
Circled outcome is rational.

tions made for the mother and the impostor? Observe, first, that the mother's strategy of protest (*P*) is dominant: her payoffs associated with this strategy are better than her payoffs associated with her strategy of don't protest ($\overline{P}$), whatever the impostor chooses. For example, if the impostor chooses tat-for-tit ($\overline{P}$/*P*), the mother obtains her next-best outcome (3) if she protests (*P*), which is better than her next-worst outcome (2) if she does not protest ($\overline{P}$). Similarly for the impostor's other three strategies, the mother obtains a better outcome by protesting than not.

Thus, *P* is the mother's unconditionally best strategy—not dependent on which strategy the impostor chooses—and presumably the choice that a rational player would make in this game. In fact, define for now a *rational player* to be one who chooses a dominant strategy if there is one.[8]

The impostor also has a dominant strategy: don't protest regardless ($\overline{P}/\overline{P}$) leads to a better outcome than any of her other three strategies, whichever strategy (*P* or $\overline{P}$) the mother chooses. By comparison, neither Rahab nor the spies has a dominant strategy, as shown in Section 1.3.

(The question of whether strategies are dominant or not in a game tree is not quite so straightforward as in a payoff matrix, so the determination of whether Cain or God has a dominant strategy requires a bit more analysis. To illustrate it in the Cain story, observe in Figure 1.1 that God's better choice at the final stage (to kill or to punish Cain) depends on what Cain did at the prior stage: if Cain admitted or denied murdering Abel, God would prefer to kill him; but if Cain defended his morality, God would prefer to punish him. Thus, God's preferred choice at the final stage, and hence at the first stage as well, depends on what Cain does—it is *not* unconditional. Similarly, Cain's best choice depends on anticipating God's subsequent choice, based on His preferences, so Cain also does not have an unconditionally best choice. Consequently, neither player in this story has a dominant strategy.[9])

To return to the Solomon story, the choices of *P* by the mother and $\overline{P}$/

$\bar{P}$ by the impostor result in outcome (3,4), the next-best outcome for the mother and the best outcome for the impostor (again, as they see the situation). Because this is the outcome that would be chosen by rational players, it is defined to be the *rational outcome*. I shall say more about the equilibrium characteristics of such outcomes in later chapters.

This selection can be justified in another way, based on the game-tree representation in Figure 1.6. Applying the same kind of backward reasoning as was discussed in Section 1.2 to the Figure 1.6 game tree, observe that the last-moving player at the bottom of the tree (the impostor) will not protest—whether the mother protests or not—leading either to outcome (3,4) or outcome (1,3). Given the choice of protest regardless by the impostor, the mother would prefer to protest because (3,4) is better for her than (1,3). In this game, then, unlike the earlier games, the rational choices of the players do not depend on their anticipating what the other player will will do, which is precisely what makes their strategies dominant.

This calculation, incidentally, is unaffected if the next-best and next-worst outcomes (2 and 3) of either player are interchanged in Figures 1.6 and 1.7. Because the rational outcome of Solomon's game is insensitive to the precise rankings of the middle two outcomes by the players, it is consonant with other interpretations (one was suggested for the mother earlier) that might be given to the their motives in this story and, therefore, is fairly robust.

In pursuit of the truth, fortunately, Solomon had foreseen the women's true preferences. He correctly gauged that the women would play basically the game as I have modeled it: the mother's highest priority would be saving her baby, even at the cost of losing him to the impostor; the impostor would disdain saving the baby and instead seek to align her position with Solomon's. Thus, Solomon was playing a larger kind of game with the women, in which he read the strategies they chose in the game he devised as evidence of who was telling the truth, which is in the end what he was interested in discovering.

Wise arbitration involves the setup of a game by an arbitrator in such a way as to distinguish truthful from untruthful disputants. That is, the arbitrator designs the rules of the game such that play of the game reveals which player is the deceiver (assuming one disputant's claim is truthful and the other's is not). Such arbitration is "wise" in the sense that it distinguishes honest players from dishonest players by eliciting responses that, when properly interpreted, indicate who is lying and who is truthful.[10]

It is difficult to define "properly interpreted," but one necessary condition is that the players not know the arbitrator's interpretation of their strategy choices. If they did, then presumably the players would play a different game from that which the arbitrator intends, and the arbitrator thereby would not elicit the truth-revealing responses wanted.

For example, assume that the impostor knew that Solomon did not desire her affirmation of his order but instead intended to favor the woman (women) who protested his order. Then it would obviously be in her interest also to protest, and the game would not distinguish her from the mother.

The arbitrator does, of course, want the disputants to play a game, but the structure of their preferences should not be such that one player has to anticipate the other's choice in order to make a rational choice in turn. This point can be illustrated in Solomon's game by noting that because each woman had a dominant strategy in Figure 1.7, it was unnecessary for either to try to predict the other's choice. Whatever the other's choice, each woman's dominant strategy was best against it.

It is easy to show that a slight alteration in the rules of the game would still have elicited truth-revealing responses from the two women. If the women had been in separate rooms when Solomon informed each of his order, they would have played the game shown in Figure 1.5, for neither woman would have been responding to the strategy choice of the other. That is, because each's strategy choice would have been made in ignorance of the other's choice, the game can be modeled as a 2 × 2 game.

In the 2 × 2 game shown in Figure 1.5, both women have dominant strategies—the impostor to agree with the king, the mother to protest. Thus, this game, as well as the 2 × 4 game actually played, wherein the mother reacted to the king's order first and the impostor knew her response, would also have ferreted out the truth.

To carry this kind of analysis one step further, consider a hypothetical game in which the impostor's preferences are the same as the mother's: both most prefer a double protest [(4,4)] and least prefer no protest [(1,1)]; each would next most prefer to protest (3) when the other does not (2). Notice in this new game that the impostor no longer has a dominant strategy of agreeing with the king; instead she has, like the mother, a dominant strategy of protesting, thereby ensuring the mutually best outcome of (4,4).

This game, however, is not one involving deception but rather one in which information about maternity is fugitive. Naturally, if both women have maternalistic preferences, and each protests the order, it would not make things easy for Solomon. But well it should not, for if each woman truly believes she is the mother, and the maternity of the baby cannot be determined from any external evidence, wise arbitration alone will not be sufficient to settle the dispute. No game to ferret out the truth can be constructed, even by a Solomon, if the truth is not there to be ferreted out![11]

1.5. Conclusions

It is probably no accident that the stories that seem to shed the most light on justice and wisdom in the Hebrew Bible involve deception: Cain lies about the whereabouts of Abel; Rahab deceives her king by sheltering the Israelite spies and facilitating their escape; and one of the prostitutes attempts to deceive Solomon into thinking that a baby is hers. It is the element of deception in each of these stories that forces the characters to make difficult strategic choices and ethical decisions:

> 1. Should Cain dissemble about the murder of Abel and attempt to implicate God in the crime? Cain's deception and shift-the-blame strategy is at least partially successful in making God perhaps feel guilt-ridden but more likely commending Cain as an effective spokesman, thereby helping him extract from God protection from those who might try to avenge Abel's murder. God, in turn, presumably gains from Cain's spreading the word about the fair punishment he received.

> 2. Should the spies sheltered by Rahab trust a prostitute who was willing to lie to her king? They do, but they make Rahab, who must show her good faith first, painfully aware that her fate is linked to theirs. This mutual understanding renders her betrayal irrational and thereby makes the agreement they reach just.

> 3. Should Solomon carry out his order to cut the disputed baby in two? His wisdom and perspicacity shine through when he evaluates the responses of the prostitutes to his order, based on the game he surmised they would play, and retracts the order, awarding the baby to the protesting mother. The lesson seems to be that an arbitrator is wise if he deceives those whose dispute he is arbitrating in such a way as to reveal which disputant is being truthful.

These decisions raise an interesting ethical question: Can deception be put to the service of justice and wisdom? A just agreement was consummated between Rahab and the Israelite spies because she deceived her king. Solomon's decision is applauded because he hoodwinked the impostor into thinking that he was looking for affirmation of his order. I have more difficulty seeing what ethical precepts are advanced by the behavior of Cain and God in Abel's murder—except, perhaps, the notion that guilt may be shared.

On the other hand, it might be argued that God incited Cain to slay Abel so that He could make Cain's punishment an unmistakable example to others of His justice. If one believes that people needed such a precedent to understand how to behave properly (after all, this was before the time of the Ten Commandments and other laws), then conceivably God's action can be justified as satisfying His longer-term (loftier?) goals.

In any event, these stories raise difficult philosophical issues concerning the morality of deception, particularly when it is ostensibly linked to a just agreement or wise arbitration. As I noted, Solomon's probity has been universally extolled, but one can well imagine ingenious arbitration games that elicit only half-truths, or do not place the elicited information in a proper context.[12]

Rules of law are supposed to prevent this, but they are of course not perfect. Unscrupulous individuals, without the judicious temperament of a Solomon, may succeed in subverting agreements or undermining institutions. The biblical stories teach us that such problems may be lessened by having a good knowledge of, and a healthy respect for, the strategic weaknesses in situations.

Morality is empty without safeguards to enforce it, which seemed mostly absent in the murder of Abel. Nevertheless, God and Cain were able to negotiate a kind of standoff agreement, which resulted in a serviceable if morally ambiguous outcome.

Rahab and the spies agreed on explicit safeguards against being double-crossed, with minimum reliance on trustworthiness and more reliance on ultimatums and threats. In Solomon's game, the two women, though prostitutes, were evidently not sophisticated enough to see through Solomon's motives. I judge arbitration schemes like Solomon's dangerous, however, because their assumption of a naïveté on the part of the players may sometimes be unwarranted.

The give-and-take of bargaining is most evident in the Cain story. In the other two stories, the focus shifts to the rationality of negotiating agreements with other parties or placing a decision in the hands of an arbitrator trying to coax out the truth.

In the end, however, the exchanges between the parties that produce an agreement or resolve a conflict are successful. Everyone benefits to some degree—except, of course, the impostor, whose mendacity is uncovered in the Solomon story. The fact that Rahab deceives her king, and Cain finds it in his interest to lie to God, illustrate that advanced bargaining skills may go hand in hand with questionable ethics.

Notes

[1] All translations for the Cain and Abel story are from *The Torah: The Five Books of Moses* (1967); for the Rahab and Solomon stories, from *The Prophets* (1978). The subsequent analyses are adapted from Brams (1980) with permission.

[2] A contrary view that Abel's murder was unpremeditated is taken in Sarna (1970, 31).

[3] It might also be read as a challenge to God's omniscience—and His complicity—as suggested by the natural follow-up question: "Why should One who

watches over all creatures ask one, unless He planned the murder Himself?" (Graves and Patai 1963, 92). God's role as an accomplice in the murder is also considered, though rejected, by Wiesel (1977, 58): "Cain could not help but kill: he did not choose the crime; instead the crime chose him." I find this line of reasoning, which says that Cain effectively did not make a choice but was preconditioned to respond, unpersuasive. Cain's response, as I argued earlier, was not an emotional outburst but instead was apparently planned. If this is so, it follows that Cain could anticipate being discovered by God and plan for his defense.

[4]Cain's defense, perhaps, convinces God that Cain is not an ordinary miscreant but one of great intelligence who will convey eloquently the message He wants to send about His brand of justice.

[5]Even if Joshua never learned of Rahab's betrayal, she might simply have been killed like everybody else.

[6]Indeed, it might be worse, if each was now—because of trust in the other— caught off guard. But this alternative ranking has no effect on the rational choices of the players in this game.

[7]If the mother also felt that Solomon would reward her obedience, her 2 and 3 outcomes might be interchanged, whose effects I shall say more about later.

[8]It is easy to show that the expansion of every 2 × 2 ordinal game in which preferences are strict (i.e., whose four outcomes can be ranked from best to worst without ties) to a 2 × 4 ordinal game always results in the second-moving player's having a dominant strategy, whether that player had one or not in the 2 × 2 game. The rationality of choosing dominant strategies is challenged by the Prisoners' Dilemma (see Chapter 4) and, more recently, by "Newcomb's problem," which has theological overtones and whose game-theoretic structure I analyze in Brams (1975b, 1983).

[9]Because this game is one of *perfect information* (i.e., each player, at each stage, knows the choices of the other player up to that point), each can determine the other's rational choices and, on this basis, make best choices throughout the game tree. But if information is imperfect or one's opponent might not be rational— say, God might punish Cain if Cain admits or denies his crime but kill him if he defends his morality—Cain obviously cannot make an unconditionally best set of choices.

[10]Even when both players see a cost in opposing Solomon's order, the mother may calculate that, on balance, it is better to bear this cost and try to save her baby by protesting, whereas the impostor would reach the opposite conclusion. Thereby wise arbitration may also work through "costly signaling" that separates player types. In Section 5.4, I shall give an example in which this does not occur, because one type of player can successfully mimic the behavior of another type in equilibrium.

[11]A recent formalization of the procedure that Solomon used as a multistage mechanism, whereby the players are assumed to attach values to the prize sought, is given in Glazer and Ma (1989), who show that the player who values the prize

most gets it at the unique subgame perfect equilibrium. Problems of indeterminacy in the use of rational-choice mechanisms are stressed in Elster (1989b).

[12]Bok (1978) offers a good analysis of such questions; see also Brams (1977) and Brams and Zagare (1977,1981) for a game-theoretic analysis of deception strategies, which will be developed further in Chapters 4 and 8.

Chapter 2
Bargaining Procedures and the
Problem of Honesty

2.1. Introduction

The *bargaining problem* concerns how to get players in a conflict to reach an agreement that is in their mutual interest when it is in each player's individual interest to hold out for as favorable a settlement as possible.[1] By holding out, however, the players may sabotage the achievement of any agreement. This problem has been called the "toughness dilemma:"

> The tougher (more unyielding) a party acts, the greater its chances for an agreement close to its positions but the greater the chances for no agreement at all, whereas the softer (more yielding) a party acts, the greater the chances are for an agreement but the less the chances for a favorable one (Zartman 1987, 279).

This dilemma has been subjected to a prodigious amount of research in a variety of disciplines, including economics, political science, psychology, management science, and mathematics. Game theorists, in particular, have attacked it by analyzing the incentives that players have to exaggerate their positions in order to influence a possible settlement to their advantage.

In this chapter I focus on the conditions that induce bargainers to be honest about their "reservation prices," which are their minimal demands. In the context of a buyer and a seller, the reservation prices are the maximum that the buyer will pay, and the minimum that the seller will accept, for an object, such as a good or service. Put another way, these are the prices (or other terms for a settlement) at which the buyer and the seller will break even, and hence be indifferent between making an agreement or not.

I shall restrict the analysis to two-person games between a buyer and a seller, but the theoretical results can be extended to other bargaining

29

settings, as I shall illustrate later. Even between a single buyer and a single seller, however, these results are quite involved and, because of the high level of abstraction, may often appear other-worldly. But this makes the results more general, which means that they have potentially wider applicability than those tied to a concrete situation, as in the case of the Bible stories in Chapter 1.

Although the issue of coalition formation is irrelevant in two-person bargaining games, under some of the procedures to be analyzed a third party is introduced to facilitate an agreement between the bargainers. This third party, however, is never a player in the sense of being an actor who has preferences and makes strategic choices, though its actions may be informed (e.g., by certain information) or constrained (e.g., by limited resources or self-imposed restrictions) in certain ways.

A third party can ameliorate the bargaining problem by providing a partial escape from the implications of a result proved by Myerson and Satterthwaite (1983)—namely, that a bargaining procedure cannot be both "incentive-compatible" and "ex-post efficient" without being subsidized by an outside party—which has been extended in Williams (1987) and Satterthwaite and Williams (1989). Roughly speaking, this means that if, under some bargaining procedure, a player cannot do better than be truthful against a truthful opponent (*incentive compatibility*), then this procedure cannot be fully effective in implementing all feasible agreements (*ex-post efficiency*). (Feasible agreements are those in which the bargainers' reservation prices overlap—the buyer's is at least as high as the seller's.) The trade-off between honesty (i.e., being truthful) and efficiency (i.e., consummating all feasible agreements)—at least in the absence of a subsidy by an outside party—will be illustrated by a particular procedure that is well known in the economic bargaining literature.

I then explore ways that a third party can circumvent this dilemma, either

- by helping the bargainers to subsidize their own bargain, or
- by providing an independent appraisal of the value of an object.

The third party, however, is not simply a mediator, who may provide good offices, clarify issues, find areas of agreement, or otherwise aid the parties in hammering out an agreement. Important as mediators are in helping parties resolve conflicts ranging from labor-management disputes over wages to international disputes over territorial boundaries (an example is given in Section 3.10 of Henry Kissinger's mediation of disengagement agreements in the Middle East after the 1973 Yom Kippur War), they do not choose the settlement in the end. By contrast, the third parties in four of the five bargaining procedures I shall analyze are part and parcel of the procedures themselves, in ways I shall preview next.

The first of the procedures, called the *Bonus Procedure*, involves a third party and has been proposed in the literature on incentive compatibility in economics. (Loosely, incentives are "compatible" if they do not interfere with each other; thus, honesty on the part of one player induces honesty on the part of the other.) Under this procedure, there is a unique bonus, which is paid only if there is an exchange, that a third party (e.g., the government) can offer the two bargainers so as to make their strategies of announcing their (honest) reservation prices dominant, or best whatever the other player does.

If the third party is the government, I show that it can assess a tax against the players that recovers, on an expected-value basis, the bonus it pays out. Moreover, even with the imposition of a tax, it is advantageous for the players truthfully to reveal their reservation prices. This is because, with the bonus, the amounts that the buyer pays and the seller receives do not depend directly on their own announcements. Thereby they can "afford" to be honest in order to try to strike a mutually profitable deal.

Honesty under the Bonus Procedure results in a dominant-strategy "Nash equilibrium," which is a type of stable outcome to be defined in Section 2.2. Unfortunately, this honesty equilibrium is vulnerable to collusion. How the bargainers can collude against the government or some other third party, and what might be done to prevent such collusion, will be considered. In particular, I show how an "appraiser," or independent third party—different from the government or another party that might dispense bonuses and collect taxes—can make collusion a risky business and thereby deter the bargainers from trying to exploit the bonus payer.

The bonus procedure with an appraiser is called the *Bonus Appraisal Procedure*. To induce the bargainers to be honest under this procedure requires that the appraiser have the same uncertainty associated with its choice as the buyer and seller do, which I formalize later.

The third procedure for inducing truthful revelation of reservation prices is called the *Penalty Procedure*. The players bargain strictly on their own, without benefit of a government that taxes them and pays out bonuses or an appraiser who makes an independent judgment. The rub is that the offers that the players make to each other, even if they overlap and a settlement is therefore feasible, will not always be implemented. Implementation is probabilistic, based on the amount of overlap, so this procedure is not ex-post efficient: a feasible settlement may not in fact come to fruition.

The harshness of this procedure may be mitigated by interpreting implementation in terms of levels of settlement rather than probabilities. If the amount of overlap in the players' reservation prices can be calibrated with, say, the magnitude or duration of an agreement—and both players desire to make the agreement as large or as long as practicable—then it would be in the interest of the players to be honest not just to increase the likelihood of a settlement but also to increase its level, as measured by its size or the length of a contract.

Just as the Bonus Procedure has an associated appraisal procedure, so does the Penalty Procedure—in fact, it has two. The first I call the *Penalty Appraisal Procedure,* because it is a direct counterpart of the Penalty Procedure. Under this procedure, there is a settlement exactly when the bargainers' offers overlap and the appraisal falls in the overlap interval. Like the Penalty Procedure, this procedure is not ex-post efficient, but its inefficiency can be reduced by an appraiser's "omniscience," or ability to anticipate the possible overlap in the players' reservation prices and situate itself in this interval.

A more distant relative of the Penalty Procedure is the final procedure I shall discuss, called the *Expansive Appraisal Procedure.* Under this procedure, the requirement that the appraisal be acceptable to both players—by being more than the buyer's offer and less than the seller's offer—is weakened: a settlement is implemented whenever the appraisal is acceptable to one, but not necessarily to both, players.

Like the Penalty Appraisal Procedure, the Expansive Appraisal Procedure always induces truthful revelation of reservation prices. In addition, it leads to a higher probability of a settlement than the Penalty Appraisal Procedure, but at the cost of *individual rationality:* an exchange may take place when one player's offer overlaps the appraisal but not the other player's offer, causing the player whose offer does not overlap to suffer a loss when it bids its reservation price.

This possible loss to one player means that the Expansive Appraisal Procedure is not a true bargaining procedure in the sense that every settlement that occurs will satisfy both parties. But neither is it an arbitration procedure (Chapter 3), which by definition always forces a settlement. This is so because there will be no settlement under the Expansive Appraisal Procedure if neither player's offer overlaps the appraisal (and hence neither overlaps the other player's offer). I shall discuss when and how this hybrid procedure, as well as the four other bargaining procedures, might prove to be of practical value.

All the bargaining procedures are modeled as "noncooperative games of incomplete information." In these games, information is *incomplete* because, while the bargainers know their own reservation prices, they do not know either their adversary's reservation price or the proposed settlement of the appraiser. What each player is assumed to know, however, is that these uncertain quantities, or *random variables,* can be described by probability distributions (to be illustrated later).

The games are *noncooperative* because an agreement binding on both sides cannot be imposed; only an agreement from which both bargainers benefit will therefore be made. This is true even of the Expansive Appraisal Procedure: by agreeing to adhere to the rules of this procedure, the players are consenting to its use, even though on occasion one might lose under it. I shall compare the expected balance of gains and losses under this procedure with the expected balance under the other procedures.

According to one dictionary (*Webster's Ninth New Collegiate Dictionary*), a bargain is "an agreement between parties settling what each gives or receives . . . ," suggesting that the agreement depends exclusively on the parties themselves. Insinuating an appraiser into a bargaining procedure, while it does not divorce the bargainers' offers from the settlement, does add a new ingredient to the bargaining process. Thus, under the three procedures with an appraiser, there are well-defined rules that specify under what circumstances one of the bargainers' offers, or the appraiser's offer, will be implemented (if at all). The fact that none of the five procedures *always* produces a settlement distinguishes them from arbitration procedures, to be discussed in Chapter 3.

The bargaining procedures assayed in this chapter all induce the bargainers to be honest in proposing settlements. This catalogue of procedures seems to exhaust those that make truthful revelation a dominant strategy, or one that is *distribution-free:* honesty does not depend on the probability distributions that characterize incomplete information about the bargainers' reservation prices or about the appraisal. However, knowledge of these distributions does enable one to calculate the expected payoffs to the players under the different procedures, the taxes that need to be assessed for the government to break even under the bonus procedures, the position of an appraiser that maximizes the bargainers' payoffs under the appraisal procedures, and the like.

Although the great virtue of the different procedures is that they are honesty-inducing, each has costs as a practical method of dispute resolution. Nonetheless, I suggest in the penultimate section of this chapter that if their rules cannot yet be readily applied, the procedures have heuristic value. Thus, their logic helps to explain why the United States apparently was able to elicit reservation prices from Egypt and Israel to forge the Camp David accords of 1978. How the procedures might be more formally and systematically implemented in different settings needs to be explored further.

2.2. The Honesty Problem

Consider a buyer B and a seller S, whose reservation prices are b and s, respectively. In a single-offer bargaining situation, assume that B offers b_0 and S offers s_0.[2] If $b_0 \geq s_0$, B is willing to pay at least the price at which S is willing to sell. Hence, an exchange is feasible. Assume the exchange price is equal to the mean, $m = (b_0 + s_0)/2$, of the offers. If $b_0 < s_0$, there is no exchange.

Are there circumstances under which B and S will reveal their reservation prices? More specifically, do there exist bargaining rules that make it rational for B to announce $b_0 = b$ and for S to announce $s_0 = s$?

In the bargaining situation just described, the profit P_B to B is

$$P_B = \begin{cases} b - m & \text{if } b_0 \geq s_0, \\ 0 & \text{if } b_0 < s_0, \end{cases} \qquad (2.1)$$

the profit P_S to S is

$$P_S = \begin{cases} m - s & \text{if } b_0 \geq s_0, \\ 0 & \text{if } b_0 < s_0. \end{cases}$$

Thus, if an exchange is feasible, the profit is the difference between each player's reservation price and the exchange price. The profit to each player will be positive if the players' offers overlap or coincide (i.e., $b_0 \geq s_0$), zero otherwise (because there is no exchange).

Assume the players' offers are simultaneous—or, equivalently, independent of each other—in a noncooperative game of incomplete information. Then Chatterjee and Samuelson (1983) show that one pair of Nash equilibrium strategies of the players is not to be honest.

A strategy pair is a *Nash equilibrium* if either player, by departing unilaterally from its choice, cannot improve its payoff and will, in general, do worse (Nash 1951). Hence, neither player will have an incentive to deviate from such an outcome, given that its adversary also does not deviate, rendering it a stable point or equilibrium.

To see what level of dishonesty is stable, assume that B and S both believe that the other player's reservation price is uniformly distributed over $[0,1]$, or the probability density functions are $f_B = f_S = 1$. This means that B thinks that s, and S thinks that b, is equally likely to fall anywhere in the interval between 0 and 1—every number in this interval is equiprobable. In addition, assume that each player knows what the other player thinks, each knows that the other player knows, and so on ad infinitum, which is the usual assumption of *common knowledge* but now quite controversial (Aumann 1988). Then given these assumptions, Chat-

Figure 2.1. Linear symmetric equilibrium strategies of B and S
under Chatterjee-Samuelson procedure

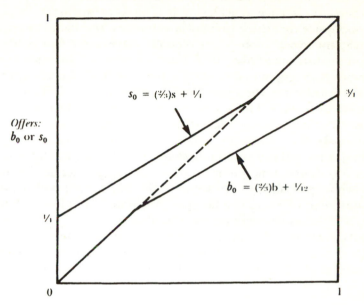

Reservation Prices: b or s

terjee and Samuelson (1983) show that there is a "linear symmetric"
(Bayesian) Nash equilibrium whereby each player may significantly exaggerate its reservation price: B will announce

$$b_0 = \begin{cases} b & \text{if } 0 \leq b \leq \frac{1}{4} \\ (\frac{2}{3})b + \frac{1}{12} & \text{if } \frac{1}{4} < b \leq 1, \end{cases}$$

and s will announce

$$s_0 = \begin{cases} (\frac{2}{3})s + \frac{1}{4} & \text{if } 0 \leq s \leq \frac{3}{4} \\ s & \text{if } \frac{3}{4} < s \leq 1. \end{cases}$$

These strategies are illustrated in Figure 2.1 and demonstrate, among
other things, that if $s > \frac{3}{4}$ or $b < \frac{1}{4}$, there will be no settlement because
$b_0 \leq \frac{3}{4}$ and $s_0 \geq \frac{1}{4}$. More generally, $b_0 \geq s_0$ implies $b \geq s + \frac{1}{4}$. Consequently, at this Nash equilibrium, there will be an exchange iff (if and
only if) B's reservation price exceeds S's by at least $\frac{1}{4}$.

B's understating of the price b_0 it will pay, and S's overstating of the
price s_0 it will sell at, reduce the probability of their agreement from $\frac{1}{2}$
$= 0.50$ (if the players were honest and announced $b_0 = b$ and $s_0 = s$) to

$\frac{9}{32} \approx 0.28$ (at the Nash equilibrium). Dividing the latter probability by the former shows that the Chatterjee-Samuelson procedure is only $\frac{9}{16} \approx$ 56.3 percent effective in achieving feasible agreements.

I emphasize that these numerical values are specific to this example, wherein the reservation prices of both players are independent and uniformly distributed over [0,1]. Note in Figure 2.1 that the larger b is, the more B exaggerates (i.e., the farther b_0 is from the 45-degree line), and the smaller s is, the more S exaggerates (i.e., the farther s_0 is from the 45-degree line). Thus, if $b = 1$, then $b_0 = \frac{3}{4}$, which means that B makes an offer 25 percent less than its reservation price.

Curiously, the players are honest only when they know that, even if truthful, they will not succeed because B is offering too little ($b_0 = b < \frac{1}{4}$) or S is demanding too much ($s_0 = s > \frac{3}{4}$). In fact, in the relatively rare event [probability $= (\frac{1}{4})(\frac{1}{4}) = \frac{1}{16} \approx 0.06$] that both players are truthful, their offers will be far apart, separated by at least a distance of $\frac{3}{4} - \frac{1}{4} = \frac{1}{2}$, so no agreement is feasible.

At the Nash equilibrium in this example, the combined expected profit of B and S is $\frac{9}{64} \approx 0.141$. This figure can be found by calculating the expected profit for each player. Thus, B's *expected profit* is

$$EP_B = P_B \times Pr[b_0 \geq s_0], \text{ summed (i.e., integrated) over all } s \text{ in } [0,1] \quad (2.2)$$

or the sum (technically, the integral, using calculus) of the profit P_B times the probability that $b_0 \geq s_0$ for each value of s in the interval from 0 to 1. As mentioned earlier, in equilibrium the probability that $b_0 \geq s_0$ is zero whenever $b < s + \frac{1}{4}$.

On the other hand, the potential combined expected profit of the players—if they were to reveal their reservation prices truthfully—is $\frac{1}{6} \approx 0.167$, with the settlement probability zero only when $b < s$. Dividing the equilibrium expected profit by the potential expected profit shows that the Chatterjee-Samuelson procedure is $\frac{27}{32} \approx 84.4$ percent efficient at achieving the players' potential expected profit.

The 16-percent loss in expected profit under the Chatterjee-Samuelson procedure (the complement of its 84-percent efficiency) is much lower than its 44-percent forfeiture of feasible agreements (the complement of its 56-percent effectiveness in implementing feasible agreements). The reason for this discrepancy between the profit losses and the agreement forfeitures is that the settlements foregone in this example, while numerous when $b \geq s$ but $b - s < \frac{1}{4}$, generate little expected profit for the players compared with situations in which the players' reservation prices overlap by a greater amount (up to a maximum distance of 1 when $b = 1$ and $s = 0$). In other words, when the players' reservation prices overlap by less than 1/4, they profit relatively little and, therefore, do not sacrifice much in expected profit under the Chatterjee-Samuelson procedure.

Thus, at the Chatterjee-Samuelson equilibrium the players lose relatively little in expected profits (16 percent) when they fail to settle in nearly half (44 percent) of the cases in which $b \geq s$. In fact, it has been proved that there is no bargaining procedure superior to the Chatterjee-Samuelson procedure in maximizing the players' expected profit in equilibrium (Myerson and Satterthwaite 1983).

To be sure, the game in the previous example has other Nash equilibria (Leininger, Linhart, and Radner 1989), but they all are sustained by asymmetric step-function strategies—in which one player captures most of the expected profit—and never involve truthful revelation of reservation prices by either player. Moreover, besides being unfair to one player, they are well below the 84-percent efficiency of the Chatterjee-Samuelson equilibrium. Other distributions over the players' reservation prices lead to different exaggeration strategies, but they do not alter the basic result that, in equilibrium, B generally benefits by understating b and S generally benefits by overstating s.

In short, honesty does not pay. It is rational for B and S to sacrifice some feasible agreements if they desire to maximize their equilibrium expected profits.

If the players' distributions are discrete, so that their reservation prices can take on only a finite set of values, truthful revelation may maximize the players' expected profits under a simultaneous-offer procedure. An example of a discrete distribution in which honesty is an equilibrium strategy is given in Myerson and Satterthwaite (1983, 273); however, Chatterjee (1985, 20–21) shows that when this distribution is made continuous by "spreading out" the density in a particular way, truthful revelation loses its equilibrium status.

Discrete distributions, nonetheless, may enable players to reach an agreement, even if they are not honesty-inducing. Consider a situaton in which S's possible reservation prices are 1 or 2, and B's 2 or 3. In other words, each player may have either a high or low reservation price— with S's high price coinciding with B's low price—and this is common knowledge. Given that the players prefer an agreement with zero profit to no agreement (e.g., for the purpose of promoting better future relations), then it is easy to see that both players will always choose 2, regardless of their reservation prices, under the Chatterjee-Samuelson procedure.

I have said nothing about the probabilities with which the players' high and low reservation prices occur. Consider the following cases.

1. Assume that 3 (for B) and 1 (for S) occur with almost certainty. Then this analysis says that, by lying with almost certainty by announcing

2, B and S will always do better. In this case, then, their lying will never hurt them because there will always be an agreement at 2.

2. Assume that B has S's reservation price (1 or 2) and S has B's (2 or 3), and these are common knowledge. Then it is rational for the players always to be truthful: for B to announce 1 or 2, and for S to announce 2 or 3, according to their reservation prices. The reason is that only when the players simultaneously announce 2 can they benefit (because they reach an agreement that they prefer, even if their profit is zero), so they will seize this opportunity when they can.

3. Assume that the players' reservation prices in the previous case are not discrete but vary continuously between 1 and 2 (B) and 2 and 3 (S). Although their truthfulness is still rational, it is not really beneficial because only with infinitesimal probability will each player's reservation price be at its endpoint 2; for all practical purposes, then, the players will never agree.

Unlike Myerson and Satterthwaite's (1983) and Chatterjee's (1985) example, truthfulness is preserved when the probabilities are spread out (Case 3), but not to the mutual advantage of the players in this case. From their perspective, it is preferable that there be discrete overlapping points (Case 2), which occur with positive probability, even if there are gaps where no agreement can occur.

Indeed, exactly one feasible agreement point (i.e., 2) was the key to induce the players to be honest in Case 2, where $b \geq s$ only at 2. By contrast, in Case 1, where $b \geq s$ generally, 2 was the profit-maximizing— though not generally the truth-inducing—agreement point for the players.

These examples illustrate that while incentives to be honest in bargaining are possible, they will occur only in rather special situations. In those situations modeled by continuous distributions over the players' reservation prices, which either partially or totally overlap, the Chatterjee-Samuelson procedure gives players the greatest expected profit in equilibrium.

On the other hand, sequential procedures, such as those proposed by Brams (1990) for which Nash-equilibrium strategies have yet to be found, better allow players to update their incomplete information about the position of an adversary, even if they are less efficient in maximizing expected profit. I shall return to the question of simultaneous versus sequential procedures for dispute resolution when analyzing different arbitration procedures in Chapter 3, for which there are more definite results on sequential procedures than there are for bargaining in games of incomplete information.

Instead of considering changes in the usual rules of play (e.g., simultaneous versus sequential offers or different information conditions), I shall next consider changes in the players' payoff functions that might induce them to be more honest and thereby consummate feasible agreements more often. Of course, the payoffs to the players are also specified by the rules of a bargaining procedure. The revisions in the payoff functions that I shall analyze, however, seem to affect the nature of bargaining in a more fundamental way than do changes in other rules of play. Accordingly, it is useful to distinguish them from other rule changes that have been analyzed in the bargaining literature.

2.3. The Bonus Procedure

Under the Bonus Procedure, the players' payoff functions are modified so that each player receives a bonus when, and only when, an agreement is reached. Given that an exchange takes place at some price, the bonus changes the selection of a settlement from a *constant-sum game* of splitting the profit—which is assumed to be fixed or constant, so that what one player wins the other loses—into a nonconstant-sum game, wherein both players receive added value, depending on the settlement they reach.

Possible sources of this added value, which will vary with the players' strategy choices, will be considered later. The fact that the bonuses depend on the players' offers, b_0 and s_0, and not on private information, such as their reservation prices b and s, ensures that the procedure can be implemented.

Denote the bonus to B by the function $t_B(b_0,s_0)$. Because a bonus is paid only when an exchange takes place, this function is defined only when $b_0 \geq s_0$. If the exchange price is $m = (b_0 + s_0)/2$, then B's payoff in the resulting bargaining game is

$$Q_B = \begin{cases} b - m + t_B(b_0,s_0) & \text{if } b_0 \geq s_0 \\ 0 & \text{if } b_0 < s_0. \end{cases} \qquad (2.3)$$

S's payoff function, Q_S, is analogous.

Assume, as under the Chatterjee-Samuelson procedure, that B does not know S's reservation price, s, but does know that s is distributed according to probability density function f_S. Then, in a calculation analogous to EP_B in (2.2), one can calculate B's expected profit, EQ_B, under the Bonus Procedure and demonstrate that B's dominant strategy is to offer $b_0 = b$, no matter what the distribution f_S is, if

$$t_B(b_0,s_0) = (b_0 - s_0)/2. \qquad (2.4)$$

In other words, given this particular bonus, B's optimal strategy under the Bonus Procedure is honesty. Moreover, this result does not depend on assuming that S is honest. There is a parallel result for S, which means that truthful revelation is a dominant-strategy Nash equilibrium exactly when $t_B = t_S = (b_0 - s_0)/2$.

When the bonus (2.4) is substituted into (2.3), B's payoff function becomes

$$Q_B^* = \begin{cases} b - s_0 & \text{if } b_0 \geq s_0 \\ 0 & \text{if } b_0 < s_0. \end{cases} \tag{2.5}$$

Notice that (2.5) exhibits a major difference from P_B in (2.1): when $b_0 \geq s_0$, Q_B^* does not depend directly on B's strategy choice, b_0.

This independence, however, does not make B's choice of b_0 irrelevant; rather, the value of b_0 determines whether b_0 equals or exceeds s_0. But given $b_0 \geq s_0$, the payoff to B given by (2.5), $b - s_0$, does not depend on its own offer, b_0. Because of this independence, B can "afford" to be honest under the Bonus Procedure.[3] More generally, the fact that the players' payoffs do not depend directly on their actions is the key to the incentive compatibility of mechanisms independently proposed by Groves (1973), Clarke (1971), and Vickrey (1961).[4]

Bonuses in the form of "incentive payments" are also proposed in Chatterjee, Pratt, and Zeckhauser (1978). Unlike here, however, they are paid independently of whether a settlement is reached; also, they yield dominant strategies for the players only if the offers are successive (e.g., B goes first, S responds), not simultaneous.

The payoff function (2.5) for B, and an analogous payoff function for S,

$$Q_S^* = \begin{cases} b_0 - s & \text{if } b_0 \geq s_0 \\ 0 & \text{if } b_0 < s_0, \end{cases}$$

define the Bonus Procedure, under which truthful revelation (i.e., $b_0 = b$ and $s_0 = s$) is a dominant strategy for both players. It is worth pointing out that B's bonus of $(b_0 - s_0)/2$ given by (2.4) is exactly equal to the profit P_B given by (2.1) under the Chatterjee and Samuelson (1983) procedure when the players choose their honesty strategies and $b_0 \geq s_0$.

Thus, the players' dominant strategies under the Bonus Procedure double the profits they would realize under the Chatterjee and Samuelson (1983) procedure if they bid their reservation prices. This doubling occurs because, instead of splitting the difference at the mean m, each player receives as profit the entire overlap interval, $b_0 - s_0$, when $b_0 \geq s_0$.

The *revelation principle* (Myerson 1979) implies that for any bargaining procedure (indirect mechanism), an equivalent procedure (direct mechanism) can be found in which truthful revelation is a Nash equilibrium. (The bargainers truthfully reveal their reservation prices to some outside party, who computes what the bargainers would have done in equilibrium and then plays the game for them using the direct mechanism.) The Bonus Procedure does more than the direct mechanism: it provides a simple ex-post efficient bargaining mechanism for which truthful revelation by both players is not only a Nash equilibrium but also a dominant strategy for each, making it independent of the players' distributions over their adversaries' reservation prices. This is perhaps the major theoretical advantage of the Bonus Procedure: it induces the players to be honest, whatever "type" their adversary is (i.e., whatever the random variable giving their adversary's reservation price is). In other words, honesty is robust against any adversary.

To illustrate the Bonus Procedure, consider the example used in section 2.1 in which f_B and f_S are uniform over $[0,1]$. If the players choose their dominant strategies of truthful revelation, then it is not hard to show that their expected profits are

$$EQ_B^* = b^2/2 \text{ and } EQ_S^* = (1-s)^2/2. \tag{2.6}$$

B's a priori expected profit (indicated by the double expectation, EE) is

$$EEQ_B^* = EQ_B^*, \text{ summed (i.e, integrated) over all b in } [0,1], \tag{2.7}$$

which gives what B on average will receive, whatever its own type is. In fact, $EEQ_B^* = 1/6$, and similarly for S.

Under the corresponding bargaining procedure with no bonus (i.e., the Chatterjee-Samuelson [1983] procedure), the a priori expected payoffs of B and S for truthfully revealing their reservation prices are each $1/12$. Thus, the Bonus Procedure makes honesty a dominant strategy by giving a $1/6 - 1/12 = 1/12$ subsidy to each player, confirming the earlier calculation that the bonus doubles each player's profit when the players are honest under the Chatterjee-Samuelson (1983) procedure.

Myerson and Satterthwaite (1983, 279) showed in this example that any incentive-compatible bargaining procedure requires a minimum expected subsidy to both players of $1/6$ to achieve ex-post efficiency. This means that the Bonus Procedure induces honesty at minimum cost; moreover, it effects a dominant-strategy Nash equilibrium without additional cost.

Unfortunately, the Bonus Procedure has a major drawback: it is vulnerable to collusion. In particular, the players may realize that they can derive more profit from the government (or any other third party that pays the bonus) than from each other. Specifically, each player, by being as generous as possible to its adversary, can not only recover the cost of its largess in the bonus but also do better than by being honest. Thus in the example, if the players collude, with B's announcing $b_0 = 1$ and S's announcing $s_0 = 0$, they can achieve a *collusion equilibrium* that yields

$$Q_B^* = b - s_0 = b;$$
$$Q_S^* = b_0 - s = 1 - s.$$

It follows from (2.6) that bargainers under the Bonus Procedure in general do better if they collude because $b \geq b^2/2$, which is an equality iff $b = 0$; and $(1 - s)^2/2 \leq 1 - s$, which is an equality if $s = 1$. Manifestly, there are benefits to collusion.

That this collusion equilibrium can be superior to the dominant-strategy equilibrium of truthful revelation may seem bizarre. The logic of the situation can perhaps more readily be understood by considering an example in which only discrete offers are available under the Bonus Procedure, as illustrated in Figure 2.2. If $b = \frac{1}{2}$, then $b_0 = \frac{1}{2}$ is B's *(nonstrictly) dominant strategy*—at least as good, but not always better, than any other strategy for some choices by S. (Strict dominance means always better.) When both sides use their dominant strategies, however, B's payoff may be less than at the collusion equilibrium, $(b_0,s_0) = (1,0)$.

To illustrate this point, assume that s is uniformly distributed—so $s = 0, \frac{1}{4}, \frac{1}{2}, \frac{3}{4},$ and 1, each with probability $\frac{1}{5}$—and that S chooses its dominant strategy $s_0 = s$. If $b_0 = b = \frac{1}{2}$, then B's expected payoff is

$$(\frac{1}{5})[b + (b - \frac{1}{4}) + (b - \frac{1}{2})] = 3b/5 - \frac{3}{20} = \frac{3}{20},$$

which is the sum of B's nonzero payoffs across the row $b_0 = \frac{1}{2}$, each multiplied by $\frac{1}{5}$. By comparison, at the collusion equilibrium B's payoff of $b - s_0 = b = \frac{1}{2}$ is unaffected by its offer, b_0. Likewise for S, its payoff of $b_0 - s = 1 - s$ does not depend on s_0.

It is precisely this feature of the collusion equilibrium, whereby it pays more than the dominant-strategy equilibrium, that saddles it with a serious instability. Because B's offer of $b_0 = 1$ and S's offer of $s_0 = 0$ affect only the *other* player's payoffs, each player has no incentive to play its own collusion strategy, given that its opponent played its collusion strategy. Only if there is "honesty among thieves" do bargainers have reason to stick to their collusive agreement.

But this reputed honesty may not be sufficient if the government or another party that pays the bonus suspects collusion and takes action to counter such strategies (more on this shortly). Suppose that, under threat of such counteraction, S chooses to "play it straight" and announces $s_0 = s$, whereas B selects its collusion strategy of $b_0 = 1$. Then B's expected

Figure 2.2. Discrete bargaining under the Bonus Procedure

B's Offer	S's Offer				
	$s_0 = 0$	$s_0 = \frac{1}{4}$	$s_0 = \frac{1}{2}$	$s_0 = \frac{3}{4}$	$s_0 = 1$
$b_0 = 0$	(b, −s)	(0,0)	(0,0)	(0,0)	(0,0)
$b_0 = \frac{1}{4}$	(b,¼−s)	(b−¼,¼−s)	(0,0)	(0,0)	(0,0)
$b_0 = \frac{1}{2}$	(b,½−s)	(b−¼,½−s)	(b−½,½−s)	(0,0)	(0,0)
$b_0 = \frac{3}{4}$	(b,¾−s)	(b−¼,¾−s)	(b−½,¾−s)	(b−¾,¾−s)	(0,0)
$b_0 = 1$	(b,1−s)	(b−¼,1−s)	(b−½,1−s)	(b−¾,1−s)	(b−1,1−s)

profit in the case of s uniform over $[0,1]$ (continuous case) drops to $b - \frac{1}{2}$; it is easy to ascertain that $b - \frac{1}{2} \leq b^2/2 \leq b$, so B generally does worse than at the honesty equilibrium as well as at the collusion equilibrium. S, on the other hand, continues to receive $1 - s$, exactly as at the collusion equilibrium.

Clearly, there will be an incentive to collude only if the aid that one player offers the other seems likely to foster a reciprocal relationship whereby both players can, in repeated play, enjoy the benefits of their collusion. If, however, one of the two bargainers does not "go along" and make good on its side of the agreement to "soak" the government, then the bargainer who reneges will be unaffected, but the bargainer who does not will suffer from the other's defection.

A failure to stick to an agreement will almost surely undermine attempts at collusion in any future play. Conversely, collusion will be supported if the bargainers (1) see themselves as in a continuing relationship and (2) are able to maximize the bonus without fear of retribution from the government.

The government in this model is not a player with preferences but rather a source that provides the bonus needed to induce truthful revelation of reservation prices by the two bargainers. Despite the government's inertness, one would be naïve to assume that any government will sit idly by and hand out bonuses, especially if there is collusion by the bargainers that is solely designed to fatten their own pockets at the expense of the government.

Given the vulnerability of the collusion equilibrium to untrustworthy adversaries who do not keep their side of the bargain, collusion can probably be made risky for the colluders if it cannot be ruled out altogether. If this is the case, it would seem sensible for the government as the bonus payer to collect taxes to match the expected bonuses it will pay out. These might take the form of a fee it assesses each time the bargainers want to use its services.

Can the government tax the bargainers so as to recover, on an expected-value basis, the amount it pays out and still induce the players to be honest? In the earlier example, the bargainers would have to be assessed the amount $\frac{1}{12}$ each time they bargain using the Bonus Procedure. Nonetheless, bargaining would still be profitable for the bargainers because each would earn an expected profit of $\frac{1}{6}$, netting $\frac{1}{12}$ after being taxed; furthermore, the government would break even with such a tax. In a similar vein, Groves and Loeb (1975, 1979) and d'Aspremont and Gérard-Varet (1979) show that there exist special incentive-compatible mechanisms that are also budget balancing, but in general such mechanisms are not possible (Groves and Ledyard 1987, 65).

Note that the tax must be charged even if there is no settlement. In fact, the tax must be charged before the bargainers learn their reservation prices, b and s, because otherwise there will be some occasions (low values of b or high values of s) when B and S will be certain that their profit at the honesty equilibrium will be less than the tax. Consequently, they will have no motivation to pay the tax. For this reason, the Bonus Procedure with a tax does not satisfy Myerson and Satterthwaite's (1983, 268) *interim* individual-rationality condition, though it does satisfy their *a priori* individual-rationality condition. That is, whereas it is in each bargainer's interest to play the game over a sufficiently long series of trials, in any single trial a bargainer may find it unprofitable because the low profit it will receive from a settlement will be more than offset by the tax it will be charged to use the procedure.

The rationality of paying a tax, then, rests on an expectation over a series of plays, on some of which the players will benefit but on others of which they will not. In fact, even if $b < s$, and there is therefore no settlement and zero profit to the players, the tax must still be paid. Yet the strategy of honesty remains dominant even after the tax is charged, because a constant tax of $\frac{1}{12}$ subtracted from EQ_B or EQ_S does not affect their maximization.

It is not hard to generalize the Bonus Procedure tax calculation to prior distributions other than the uniform. With an appropriate tax, the government can always break even, in the long run, providing there is no collusion.

Even without collusion, however, there may be significant practical difficulties in determining an appropriate tax and implementing the Bonus Procedure. For example, the probability distribution(s) over the players' reservation prices, assumed as common knowledge in the model, may not be known or agreed to by the players. In this situation, perhaps, a trial-and-error taxing procedure could be used to determine an appropriate tax. Presumably, what the government takes in—minus its costs of administering the Bonus Procedure—should be paid back in bonuses to the players.

Adjustments in the tax may have to be made from time to time, especially if there is collusion between B and S. Given some experience with a series of settlements, for example, the government might decide it needs to raise the future tax to break even. The bargainers, knowing this possibility might arise—and perhaps facing severe sanctions if caught colluding—would presumably have little incentive to try to deceive the government, as least in principle.

2.4. The Bonus Appraisal Procedure

The Bonus Appraisal Procedure and other appraisal procedures I shall describe later introduce into the bargaining an outside party whose role is different from that of the bonus payer. This outside party determines an exchange price if there is to be an exchange. Such a person, whom I call the *appraiser*, provides an independent *appraisal* (valuation) of the object over which the players bargain.

The appraisal is an informed and independent evaluation of some good or service whose value is in dispute. Appraisals, which are sometimes used in bargaining, are far more common in insurance contracts and tax assessments.

Assume that B and S simultaneously submit their offers of b_0 and s_0 to the appraiser (A), whose choice of an exchange price is a. Furthermore, assume that it is common knowledge that b, s, and a are all chosen from the same distribution. Because A is not a player, I assume that A has no reason not to be truthful about its appraisal (preferred settlement).

As under the Bonus Procedure, if $b_0 < s_0$, there is no settlement. If $b_0 \geq s_0$, there is a settlement, which depends on where a lies in relation to b_0 and s_0. There are three possibilities, and for each of these I indicate below, by underscoring either a or s_0 on the interval over which the distribution ranges, the price B would pay to S to buy the good or service:

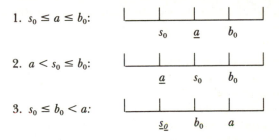

1. $s_0 \leq a \leq b_0$: s_0 $\underline{a}$ b_0

2. $a < s_0 \leq b_0$: $\underline{a}$ s_0 b_0

3. $s_0 \leq b_0 < a$: $\underline{s_0}$ b_0 a

Note that in Cases 1 and 2, where $a \leq b_0$, it is A's choice that prevails; in Case 3, a is not feasible as an exchange price because it is greater than B's offer, so s_0 is made the settlement. In no case does B ever have to pay

b_0, which renders the exchange price for B independent of its offer. (However, the ordinal position of b_0—whether it is greater or less than a—determines whether the settlement is a or s_0.) Analogously, define the exchange price for S in the three cases to be (1) a, (2) b_0, and (3) a, also independent of its offer s_0.

In two of the three cases for each player, a is the exchange price. Only in Case 1, however, where a falls between s_0 and b_0, is a the *common* exchange price—the same for both players. When paid by B to S, each player profits from this settlement.

By contrast, in Case 2, where a is less than what S finds acceptable, S receives b_0 (and B pays a); in Case 3, where a is more than what B finds acceptable, B pays s_0 (and S receives a). Because S receives more than what B pays in Case 2, and B pays less than what S receives in Case 3, this procedure obviously requires a bonus payer.

As under the Bonus Procedure, assume that a third party (e.g., the government) closes these gaps by paying, in the form of a bonus,

- in Case 1, 0 to both players because there is a common exchange price of a;
- in Case 2, $b_0 - a$ to S so that B can buy at price a and S can sell at b_0;
- in Case 3, $a - s_0$ to S so that B can buy at price s_0 and S can sell at a.

These particular bonuses define the Bonus Appraisal Procedure; to see their relationship to the Bonus Procedure, compare the payoffs to the players between the former and latter procedures in the three cases:

1. Both players do worse under the Bonus Appraisal (a) than the Bonus (b_0 for S and s_0 for B) Procedure;
2. B does better under the Bonus Appraisal (a) than the Bonus (s_0) Procedure; S does the same (b_0) under both;
3. S does better under the Bonus Appraisal (a) than the Bonus (b_0) Procedure; B does the same (s_0) under both.

Insofar as the losses of both players under the Bonus Appraisal Procedure in Case 1 are exactly offset by the gains in Case 2 (to B) and Case 3 (to S), the two procedures will "balance out" in the three cases.

It is not difficult to show that a sufficient condition for the matching of gains and losses under the two procedures is that the players' incomplete information about a be the same as their incomplete information about each other's reservation prices, b and s—that is, that $f_A = f_B = f_S$. Then B's expected payoff is maximized when it chooses $b_0 = b$, and similarly $s_0 = s$ is S's maximizing choice.

As under the Bonus Procedure, the players' strategies of honesty are dominant, making $(b_0, s_0) = (b,s)$ a dominant-strategy Nash equilibrium. Subject to the condition that the probability distributions describing a, b, and s are the same, therefore, B and S will always consummate an agreement whenever $b > s$, making the Bonus Appraisal Procedure ex-post efficient.

This procedure obviates a major potential problem that encumbers the Bonus Procedure—namely, the latter procedure's vulnerablity to collusion. The reason that collusion by the players against the bonus payer is not an effective strategy under the Bonus Appraisal Procedure is the presence of A. Thus, if the players in the example used earlier to illustrate collusion under the Bonus Procedure chose the endpoints of $[0,1]$, they would ensure that Case 1 is operative. Hence, the settlement would be at a.

But if a in this case is either greater than b or less than s, one or both players suffers a loss from the settlement. Such a loss can never occur when the players choose their dominant strategies of honesty because, given $b \geq s$, a settlement is reached that is, in general, profitable; otherwise $(b < s)$, there is no settlement and, therefore, no loss.

The earlier illustrative calculation showing that a tax of $\frac{1}{12}$ would enable the government to break even, and still give each player an expected profit of $\frac{1}{12}$, applies to the Bonus Appraisal Procedure as well as the Bonus Procedure. Indeed, the bargainers might have more of a motivation to participate under the Bonus Appraisal Procedure than under the Bonus Procedure if A were more likely to choose a compromise settlement near the median of the postulated probability distribution.

This fact would not upset the honesty incentive of the Bonus Appraisal Procedure as long as Cases 2 and 3 remained equiprobable, with a as likely to be less than s_0 (Case 2) as greater than b_0 (Case 3) by the same amount. For example, if a were uniform over $[\frac{1}{4}, \frac{3}{4}]$, but b and s were uniform over $[0, 1]$, A's greater average proximity to the median of $\frac{1}{2}$ would still induce B and S to be truthful about their reservation prices. The issue of a truncated probability distribution for A will be explored again for the Penalty Appraisal Procedure in section 2.6.

Both bonus procedures yield truthful revelation as a dominant strategy, thereby ensuring a settlement if the reservation prices of the two players overlap. This property renders them ex-post efficient, but both require the payment of subsidies by a bonus payer. The chief reason for incorporating A into the bargaining process under the Bonus Appraisal Procedure is to prevent collusion by B and S against the bonus payer. Whereas the players cannot by themselves guarantee a particular outcome under the Bonus Appraisal Procedure, they can under the Bonus

Procedure. A's presence, therefore, is significant, effectively undercutting the collusion equilibrium under the Bonus Procedure.

On the other hand, the Bonus Appraisal Procedure requires a strong assumption to ensure its equivalence to the Bonus Procedure—that all three probability distributions are the same, or at least share certain symmetry properties (e.g., should f_A be truncated). Because the Bonus Procedure did not require any assumptions about the nature of the density functions f_B and f_S, it is distribution-free in a way that the Bonus Appraisal Procedure is not.

Because A plays a somewhat different role under the Penalty Appraisal Procedure, the distribution of a is not consequential under this procedure, as I shall show later. First, however, I shall describe the Penalty Procedure without an appraiser.

2.5. The Penalty Procedure

Both the Bonus Procedure and the Bonus Appraisal Procedure, in order to be financed, require a third party to collect taxes and then return them in the form of bonuses. The difficulty of determining such a break-even tax raises the question of whether a different kind of payoff function, which eliminates the need for a third party like the government to play a broker role, can be used to induce B and S to be honest.

The answer is "yes," but, paradoxically, it may lead to a cancellation of the benefits that accrue to the parties when their reservation prices overlap. Like the two bonus procedures, the Penalty Procedure is a bargaining procedure in which the players' profit functions are modified to make truthful revelation a dominant strategy. Specifically, each player's payoff, given for B by (2.1), is reduced by a factor that is based on the players' offers. Again, private information, such as the players' reservation prices, is not used so as to ensure implementability.

Denote the proportion of B's payoff remaining after the reduction by $r_B(b_0,s_0)$. Of course, $r_B(b_0,s_0)$ need only be defined when $b_0 \geq s_0$, because there is nothing to reduce when no exchange takes place. Assume that the exchange price is again $m = (b_0 + s_0)/2$. Then B's payoff in the bargaining game is

$$R_B, = \begin{cases} (b - m)r_B(b_0,s_0) & \text{if } b_0 \geq s_0 \\ 0 & \text{if } b_0 < s_0, \end{cases} \tag{2.8}$$

and S's payoff function, R_S, is analogous.

As before, assume S's reservation price is distributed according to probability density function f_S. Then, in a calculation analogous to EP_B in (2.2), one can calculate B's expected profit, ER_B, under the Penalty

Procedure and demonstrate that B's dominant strategy is to offer $b_0 = b$, no matter what the distribution f_S, iff

$$r_B(b_0,s_0) = (b_0 - s_0)c_B, \tag{2.9}$$

where c_B is a positive constant. Later I show that the factor $r_B(b_0,s_0)$ may be interpreted either as the proportion of profit that remains after the reduction or as the probability that B realizes all its profit.

Given $b_0 \geq s_0$, $r_B(b_0,s_0)$ is a function of the amount of overlap in the players' offers, or their reservation prices when they choose their dominant strategies of truthful revelation. In effect, the Penalty Procedure makes honesty attractive by enabling the players to keep more of their profit—or realize it more often—the greater the overlap, $(b_0 - s_0)$, in their offers. Just as Q_B^* given by (2.5) is the unique "additive" payoff function that makes truthful revelation a dominant strategy under the Bonus Procedure, R_B^* (defined below) is the unique "multiplicative" payoff function under the Penalty Procedure to induce honesty. Under this procedure, the profit, P_B, is multiplied by a discount factor rather than having a bonus added to it.

Substituting (2.9) into (2.8), B's payoff becomes

$$R_B^* = \begin{cases} [b(b_0 - s_0) - (b_0^2 - s_0^2)/2]c_B & \text{if } b_0 \geq s_0 \\ 0 & \text{if } b_0 < s_0. \end{cases} \tag{2.10}$$

R_B^* and its analogue for S,

$$R_S^* = \begin{cases} [(b_0^2 - s_0^2)/2 - s(b_0 - s_0)]c_s & \text{if } b_0 \geq s_0 \\ 0 & \text{if } b_0 < s_0, \end{cases}$$

define the Penalty Procedure. Under the Penalty Procedure, as under the two bonus procedures, truthful revelation ($b_0 = b$, $s_0 = s$) is a dominant strategy for both players. While (2.10) is not as readily interpretable as (2.5) for the Bonus Procedure, it is is easy to show that $b_0 = b$ maximizes R_B^*, and $s_0 = s$ maximizes R_S^*.

The constants, c_B and c_S, do not affect the maximization. To interpret the payoff functions, assume that the density functions f_B and f_S are defined over [0,1], or possibly over a shorter interval of length less than 1, ensuring that $r_B(b_0,s_0) = r_S(b_0,s_0) \leq 1$. Then the proportionate reduction given by (2.9) can be interpreted as the probability that a feasible settlement is actually implemented. In other words, the Penalty Procedure can be put into effect by carrying out a feasible exchange (i.e., when $b_0 \geq s_0$) with probability $r_B(b_0,s_0)$, and not carrying one out with complementary probability $1 - r_B(b_0,s_0)$.

To illustrate the effect of this interpretation, assume f_B and f_S are uniform over [0,1], and choose $c_B = c_S = 1$. When B and S select their dominant strategies of $b_0 = b$ and $s_0 = s$ under the Penalty Procedure, B's a priori expected payoff, EER_B^* (analogous to EEQ_B^* given by [2.7]), is $\frac{1}{24}$. This is half of B's a priori expected payoff of $\frac{1}{12}$ if there were no penalty and the players were honest. In other words, half of B's expected profit is foregone under the Penalty Procedure.

Myerson and Satterthwaite (1983) show that no bargaining procedure that induces truthful revelation can be both budget-balancing and ex-post efficient. The Bonus Procedure induces truthful revelation and is ex-post efficient, but it requires a subsidy from a third party. By comparison, the Penalty Procedure induces truthful revelation and is budget-balancing, but it is not ex-post efficient. In fact, it is only 50 percent efficient in the case in which both players have uniform distributions over [0,1].

Instead of interpreting (2.9) as a probability, assume it is the proportion of B's profit, P_B, that B gets to keep whenever $b_0 \geq s_0$. If the government collects the remaining proportion, $1 - (b_0 - s_0)c_B$, as a tax, then a feasible settlement will always be implemented under this interpretation, but it will simply be reduced by the proportion $(b_0 - s_0)c_B$. In the previous example, the players will receive on the average half their profit when $c_B = 1$.

The Penalty Procedure, under this interpretation, will always result in a settlement provided $b \geq s$. Moreover, the average tax of $\frac{1}{24}$ collected by the government in this particular example could in principle be returned to the players, so they would receive their full a priori expected profit of $\frac{1}{12}$ each. Alternatively, the choice of $c_B = 2$ would guarantee that the players' a priori expected profits after taxation would equal $\frac{1}{12}$ each, exactly as if there were no tax.

The problem with this interpretation is that the value of b in (2.8) is known only to B, making it impossible for the government to ascertain B's profit, $(b - m)$, so as to tax the fraction, $[1 - (b_0 - s_0)c_B]$, of it away. As an alternative formulation, consider the following payoff function, where known quantity $(b_0 - m)$—instead of unknown quantity $(b - m)$—is taxed at rate $[1 - (b_0 - s_0)c_B]$:

$$T_B = \begin{cases} (b - m) - [1 - (b_0 - s_0)c_B](b_0 - m) & \text{if } b_0 \geq s_0 \\ 0 & \text{if } b_0 < s_0. \end{cases}$$

When $b_0 \geq s_0$, the first term on the right-hand side is B's profit, and the second term is the government's tax. When $b_0 = b$, $T_B = R_B^*$.

Unfortunately, when the payoff is T_B, B does not have a dominant strategy of announcing $b_0 = b$. As under the Chatterjee-Samuelson procedure, B will understate its reservation price, at least against an honest adversary. Thus, honesty is not a Nash equilibrium.

In the context of bargaining over a single object, there does not seem to be an interpretation of the penalty under the Penalty Procedure other than as a probability of nonimplementation. But in another context, in which more than one object might be exchanged, a different interpretation of the Penalty Procedure is possible. The overlap factor $(b_0 - s_0)$ might be used to determine, say, the duration of an agreement or the volume (e.g., number of items) that will be contracted for in an exchange. If both bargainers desire a longer and larger agreement (up to some practicable limit), they will have an incentive to make the overlap in their bids, $(b_0 - s_0)$, as great as possible, which means announcing their reservation prices.

Thus, the Penalty Procedure may introduce opportunities into the bargaining process rather than just the risk of forfeiture. If the $(b_0 - s_0)$ factor in (2.9) is tied not to the probability of implementation but instead to the length or size of the settlement, players who prize longer and larger settlements will not only state their positions honestly but also, given $b \geq s$, settle at an optimal level.

Of course, relating settlement levels to the players' interests is not an easy task, but this nonprobabilistic interpretation of $(b_0 - s_0)$ could facilitate settlements by encouraging truthful revelation of reservation prices. It may provide a way to link the nonconstant-sum aspects of a settlement (e.g., volume and duration) to its constant-sum aspects (e.g., exchange prices) to ensure that a feasible settlement will be implemented at optimal levels.

2.6. The Penalty Appraisal Procedure

Under the Bonus Procedure and the Penalty Procedure, I assumed that if the players' offers overlap, the exchange price is the arithmetic mean, $m = (b_0 + s_0)/2$. Analogous procedures could be designed that make b_0, s_0, or any weighted arithmetic mean the exchange price without materially affecting the need for a subsidy under the Bonus Procedure, or the need to forfeit some feasible trades under the Penalty Procedure (if interpreted probabilistically).

In addition to b_0 and s_0, the exchange price under the Bonus Appraisal Procedure will sometimes be A's appraisal a. By comparison, under the Penalty Appraisal Procedure (to be discussed next), the players' offers never directly determine the exchange price, which is always a if there is an exchange.

As under the Bonus Appraisal Procedure, B and S simultaneously submit their offers, b_0 and s_0, under the Penalty Appraisal Procedure; A

independently offers a valuation, *a*, of the object. There is an exchange only if $b_0 \geq s_0$, but, even in this circumstance, no exchange takes place unless *a* lies between the two offers (i.e., $b_0 \geq a \geq s_0$), which is Case 1 under the Bonus Appraisal Procedure (Section 2.4). If these conditions are met, the exchange does indeed take place, and *a* is the exchange price.

Thus, under the Penalty Appraisal Procedure, *B*'s payoff function is

$$U_B = \begin{cases} b - a & \text{if } b_0 \geq a \geq s_0 \\ 0 & \text{otherwise,} \end{cases}$$

and *S*'s payoff function is analogous. Notice that *B*'s offer, b_0, does not directly affect the payoff. Like the Bonus Procedure, the players' offers serve only to determine whether or not an exchange is possible.

Like the Bonus Appraisal Procedure, *B* and *S* are assumed to know the probability distributions that describe *s* and *b*, respectively, and also to have a common belief about the distribution of *a*. However, unlike the Bonus Appraisal Procedure, I do not assume that $f_A = f_B = f_S$. In fact, no restrictions are put on these density functions, so they could all be different. Truthful revelation by *B* and *S* ($b_0 = b$, $s_0 = s$) is a dominant-strategy Nash equilibrium under the Penalty Appraisal Procedure.[5]

This procedure is analogous to the Penalty Procedure and duplicates its properties: whereas it induces truthful revelation and is budget-balancing, it is not ex-post efficient. But unlike the Penalty Procedure, the *source* of the penalty under the Penalty Appraisal Procedure is not the probability that a settlement might not be implemented when $b \geq s$. Instead, it is the possibility that *A*'s appraisal *a* might not fall in the interval [*s*,*b*].

This is the price exacted by the Penalty Appraisal Procedure for its honesty-inducing property. As under the Penalty Procedure, the greater the overlap in reservation prices when the players choose their dominant strategies, the greater the probability that *a* will fall between *b* and *s* and *a* will thereby be realized as the settlement.[6]

The Penalty Appraisal Procedure is equivalent to "posted-price bargaining" (Hagerty and Rogerson 1987). Under *posted-price bargaining*, an exchange price is given exogenously—posted—and the bargainers settle at that price iff both agree to do so.[7] Clearly, the bargainers have a dominant strategy of agreeing to trade iff the posted price is more favorable to each than their reservation prices.

As with posted-price bargaining, the appraisal under the Penalty Appraisal Procedure—as the bargainers view the situation before *a* is revealed—is not a specific price but instead a random variable. Even given this uncertainty about *a*, *B* and *S* will still be motivated to reveal their reservation prices. Although the Penalty Appraisal Procedure may fail to attain many feasible settlements because a does not fall between s and b, if $b \geq s$, it may be more efficient than the Penalty Procedure at effecting exchanges for an interesting practical reason.

Call A *omniscient* if he or she somehow knows the reservation prices, b and s, of the bargainers. Given $b \geq s$, A can then ensure a settlement by choosing a in the interval $[s,b]$. Furthermore, the players' knowledge that A is omniscient does not alter the honesty-inducing character of the Penalty Appraisal Procedure.

If A is omniscient, all feasible settlements will be achieved without the need for an external subsidy. Typically, of course, A will not be omniscient. Nonetheless, savvy appraisers may, by uncovering feasible settlements, be able to engineer exchanges under the Penalty Appraisal Procedure even when the overlap between the players is small. Insofar as appraisers are not omniscient, they still may wish to concentrate their choices in some truncated interval—say, around the mean of the (common) distribution of b and s—where there is a greater likelihood that there will be an overlap interval in which a will fall. Thus, they may be able to increase the players' expected payoffs without sacrificing the ability of the procedure to induce honesty.

2.7. The Expansive Appraisal Procedure

As under the Penalty Appraisal Procedure, the exchange price under the Expansive Appraisal Procedure is always a. However, A's appraisal is determinative more often than under the Penalty Appraisal Procedure—hence, the nomenclature—though the conditions under which an exchange takes place still depend on the offers of B and S.

The motivation for the Expansive Appraisal Procedure is illustrated by Figure 2.3. Interpreting $s_0 \leq a$ as "a is acceptable to S," and $a \leq b_0$ as "a is acceptable to B," the Penalty Appraisal Procedure implements an exchange only when a is acceptable to *both* bargainers (Region I).

By contrast, the Expansive Appraisal Procedure is less stringent: it effects a settlement whenever a is acceptable to at least one bargainer. When in fact only one bargainer views a as acceptable (Region II)—S in the upper left ($s_0 \leq a$ and $b_0 < a$) and B in the lower right ($b_0 \geq a$ and $s_0 > a$)—the other bargainer will be aggrieved. Never can both bargainers be aggrieved (Region III: $b_0 < a < s_0$), however, because the procedure does not force a settlement when both bargainers deem it unacceptable (this assumption is changed for the arbitration procedures in Chapter 3).

Because one player may be forced to settle at a price less favorable than what it offers, the Expansive Appraisal Procedure is not a true bargaining procedure. Still, this procedure is not an arbitration proce-

Figure 2.3. Settlement regions for Penalty Appraisal Procedure and Expansive Appraisal Procedure: B's view

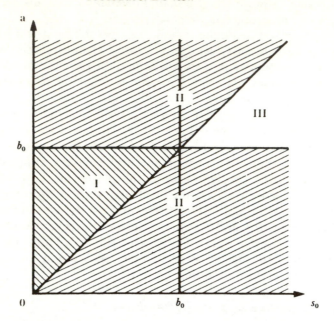

Key: Region I: $s_0 \leq a \leq b_0$ (both procedures); Region II: $s_0 \leq a$ and $b_0 < a$ or $b_0 \geq a$ and $s_0 > a$ (Expansive Appraisal Procedure only); Region III: $b_0 < a < s_0$ (no settlement).

dure, either, because there is the possibility (Region III) that no settlement will be reached. Nonetheless, there are reasons why this hybrid procedure may be useful in practice, not the least of which is its relatively high probability of effecting a settlement. Furthermore, it inherits from the Penalty Appraisal Procedure the property of being honesty-inducing.

Under the Expansive Appraisal Procedure, B's payoff function is

$$V_B = \begin{cases} b - a & \text{if } b_0 \geq a \text{ or } a \geq s_0 \\ 0 & \text{if } b_0 < a < s_0, \end{cases}$$

and S's payoff function is analogous. Again, notice that B's offer b_0 does not directly affect its payoff. The offers of both players serve only to determine whether they obtain nonzero payoffs. As under the earlier procedures, however, truthful revelation is a dominant strategy for the players.[8]

The Expansive Appraisal Procedure has no equivalent bonus or penalty procedure (without an appraiser), unlike the other two appraisal procedures. Nevertheless, like the Penalty Appraisal Procedure, it is honesty-inducing and budget-balancing, but it is not ex-post efficient. Also, it may fail to be interim incentive-compatible because it sometimes forces a player to settle at a price less favorable than its reservation price.

To illustrate both the costs and benefits of the higher probability of settlement that the Expansive Appraisal Procedure entails, consider again the example in which f_A, f_B, and f_S are density functions uniformly distributed over [0,1]. Then the probability of a settlement under the Expansive Appraisal Procedure is ⅚, which is the sum of the following component probabilities:

- ⅙ that a settlement is feasible and found by the Penalty Appraisal Procedure;
- ⅓ that a settlement is feasible and found by the Expansive but not the Penalty Appraisal Procedure;
- ⅓ that an settlement is imposed by the Expansive Appraisal Procedure, to the disadvantage of one player.

Left out is the ⅙ probability that there is no settlement under either of these two appraisal procedures.

Each player's expected profit under the Expansive Appraisal Procedure is ¹⁄₂₄, the same as under the Penalty Appraisal Procedure. This means that the average net gain from the additional settlements under the Expansive Appraisal Procedure—both forced and unforced—is zero. (This difference will not generally be zero; it is particular to the example.) Also, a player tends to do better under the Expansive Appraisal Procedure if its reservation price is extreme in its favor—as b approaches 1, or s approaches 0—because it, alone, can dictate a (highly probable) settlement from which it, but not necessarily its adversary, will benefit. (Of course, the more B offers, the more likely that S also benefits, whereas B benefits the less S offers.)

This result, of course, is hardly surprising. For example, when $a = 0$, b will overlap a with certainty, ensuring a settlement at 0. In this manner, A can always ensure a favorable settlement for B—or for S by choosing 1—so the Expansive Appraisal Procedure is vulnerable to a bias that A might have, which may favor either player. More likely, though, A would be reluctant to choose extreme values near either 0 or 1, hoping to minimize the possibility of expected losses by either player.

If this is the goal of an (unbiased) A, then one might ask how A should restrict its choices to ensure that B and S will, on average, benefit. It turns out in this example that if A limits its choices to some randomly chosen *a* between .430 and .570 on the unit interval, it can guarantee that neither player will, on average, suffer a loss. In other words, by exercising some self-restraint in the selection of a settlement, *A* can, on average, please *both* players under the Expansive Appraisal Procedure.

Appraisers may well desire to choose compromise settlements that minimize the possibility of *expected* losses by both players. (Under the Expansive Appraisal Procedure, both players can never lose in a single instance because, by assumption, the player who overlaps at least breaks even.) By restricting themselves to choices in the range $0.50 \pm .07$, appraisers can still exercise an independent judgment—albeit over a truncated range—and at the same time prevent the players from incurring expected losses. This calculation, while specific to this example, can obviously be generalized. Indeed, it suggests why it might be realistic to define f_A as having a smaller domain than both f_B and f_S in the calculation of the players' expected payoffs.

Finally, if one compares the expected payoffs of the Penalty and Expansive Appraisal Procedures, they are the same for the players (i.e., $\frac{1}{16}$) when $a = \frac{1}{2}$. If $a < \frac{1}{2}$, *B* receives a higher expected payoff from the Expansive Procedure, whereas if $a > \frac{1}{2}$, the Penalty Procedure is more advantageous to *B*; the opposite is true for *S*.

Given any *a*, therefore, there is a natural conflict between *B* and *S* as to the preferred procedure. If *a* is low, *B* will prefer the Expansive Appraisal Procedure because it makes more likely a low settlement, which *B* favors. On the other hand, *B* will prefer the Penalty Appraisal Procedure if *a* is high for the opposite reason—it makes less likely a high settlement, which *B* does not favor. Because *S*'s preferences are diametrically opposed, the choice between the Expansive and the Penalty Appraisal Procedures would seem to be a difficult one to resolve in any particular conflict, given *a* is known.

By assumption, however, *a* is a random variable for both players, so the choice of the Expansive versus the Penalty Appraisal Procedure will depend on the perceived need to reach settlements. Patently, these are rendered more likely by the Expansive Procedure. Moreover, insofar as *A* tends to choose compromise settlements near the mean of the players' distribution (if it is a common one), both players can rest assured of positive expected payoffs under the Expansive Procedure.

Some conflicts, it is generally agreed, cannot be left unresolved. When the public is significantly affected, as in the case of strikes by firefighters or the police, full-fledged arbitration is often used. But as pointed out earlier, an appraiser is not an arbitrator who can dictate a settlement—not even under the Expansive Procedure (if $b < a < s$). (Here the interpretation might be that *b* is the [low] wage proposal of the government, and *s* is the [high] proposal of the public employees.) For this reason, different arbitration procedures for forcing settlements—when the disputants' offers overlap neither each other nor the appraiser's—will be analyzed in Chapter 3.

To revise the Expansive Appraisal Procedure to force settlements at the appraiser's valuation, when neither player overlaps a, means that the players' payoffs do not depend on their offers—the settlement is always a. This fact undermines the dominance of truthful revelation because it robs the players of an incentive to be honest in their offers, which ultimately do not matter. My focus in analyzing arbitration procedures, therefore, will shift from the question of honesty to that of convergence of the players' offers.

2.8. Camp David: The Logic of the Procedures Applied

It is hard to conceive of an unmotivated benefactor simply entering a dispute between two parties and making up the difference between their offers, $(b_0 - s_0)$, given that $b_0 \geq s_0$. Such a third party must, it would seem, also derive some benefit—tangible or intangible—from the settlement of the dispute.

Benefits may take different forms. A government, as I suggested earlier, could tax the players so as to break even, or at least not lose too much. But it would be vulnerable to collusion unless there were norms or sanctions that prevented its exploitation by the disputing parties, or there were an appraiser acceptable to both sides who could offer an independent judgment. Private organizations or even entrepreneurs might also play the role of benefactor, but they would surely have to charge fees for their services unless they possessed considerable wealth as well as more than a modicum of altruism.

Generally speaking, altruism alone will not be sufficient to motivate the dispensing of rewards, especially if the bonuses that might have to be paid are great. It was hardly altruism or pure good will, for example, that motivated Jimmy Carter in September 1978 to make expensive promises to both Israel and Egypt at Camp David in return for accords that led to Israel's withdrawal from the Sinai, which it had occupied since the 1967 Arab-Israeli War (Dayan 1981). By Carter's reckoning, neutralizing conflict if not encouraging peace between the two major antagonists in the Middle East would not only benefit the United States but also be a public good for many others (a notable exception was the more radical Arab states).

The billions of dollars in military and economic aid, and the numerous security guarantees that the United States promised to both sides in return for their cooperation, were major inducements that led to the Camp David agreement. These may plausibly be interpreted to have made up the difference in the two sides' reservation prices, which seemed far apart in the beginning.

Equally plausible is the interpretation that the two sides agreed in principle—beginning with Anwar Sadat's dramatic meeting with Menachem Begin in Jerusalem in November 1977, ten months before Camp David—on the need for and value of Israeli withdrawal with security guarantees, and Egyptian recognition of Israel, so their reservation prices actually overlapped. However, the two sides did not have the wherewithal to make their agreement in principle a practical reality, and this is where the United States stepped in with the necessary support.

In effect, the United States paid bonuses to each side that turned an agreement in principle (except, notably, on the Palestinian problem) into one that the two sides believed, in the end, could actually be implemented to their mutual advantage—and to that of the United States, as well. Indeed, the United States may have been willing to pay dearly precisely to learn the two sides' reservation prices, and, therefore, whether an agreement was even feasible.

Still a third interpretation of the rationale behind the Camp David agreement is that the two sides, while agreeing in principle, saw the chances of an actual agreement as very slim in the beginning. Thus, following the logic of the penalty procedures, they could afford to be honest because an agreement did not appear to be in the cards. But then the more each side was willing to concede, the more the United States offered in support (Raiffa 1982, 213)—increasing the likelihood of an agreement—with maximum support coming only if an agreement was signed. Consequently, $(b_0 - s_0)$ increased as overlap in principle was translated into practical overlap, raising the probability or value of an agreement until, finally, it was assured. (A formal peace treaty was not signed, however, until March 1979, after a number of difficulties were resolved in the six months following the agreement on "Frameworks" at Camp David.)

To be sure, neither the Bonus Procedure nor the Penalty Procedure was formally applied at Camp David, but the logic of each seems in part to have been operative. These extremely difficult and delicate negotiations over thirteen days were on the verge of collapse more than once. Not only did Sadat and Begin refuse to speak with each other after the third day, but on several occasions each side threatened to walk out.

This seems *prima facie* evidence that the logic of the procedures elicited both sides' reservation prices. In fact, if both sides in the end had been less than forthcoming and not gone to their "bottom lines," most observers agree that there almost surely would have been no settlement.

Jimmy Carter's role as an appraiser in the bargaining process seems to have been crucial. Almost from the beginning, Sadat "would give Carter in advance a series of concessions to be used at appropriate moments in the negotiations" (Quandt 1986, 222), presumably on the supposition that Carter would use this information judiciously (otherwise, Sadat would have been irrational in being truthful). The consequence was that "Carter was inclined to disregard the Egyptian proposal and to believe that Sadat could be persuaded to make concessions whenever a stalemate was reached" (Quandt 1986, 223). Begin, by contrast, "had no intention of telling Carter what his fallback position really was" (Quandt 1986, 225). Thus, in terms of the analysis of Section 2.6, Carter had one-sided omniscience.

With the two sides at an impasse after ten days, "Carter was very rough with Sadat," but at the same time he "assured him that Egypt would not be held to its concessions if Begin proved to be recalcitrant" (Quandt 1986, 239). In this way, Carter took on more and more the role of an active player rather than just an appraiser, skillfully shepherding a final agreement step by arduous step. (Henry Kissinger had behaved similarly in multilateral negotiations a few years earlier; I shall interpret his behavior in terms of a sequential arbitration model in Section 3.10.) But while successful in getting Begin to relinquish the airfields and settlements in the Sinai, he was not successful in persuading Begin, who agreed to a three-month moratorium on building new settlements in the West Bank and Gaza, to give up sovereignty of these occupied territories. Quandt concludes: "Begin could not be made to budge. Sadat, whom he [Carter] genuinely liked and admired, would. That perception, as much as any other, influenced the final outcome" (Quandt 1986, 258).

Thus, it seems, Carter did not so much choose what he thought was an authentic compromise outcome—as would an appraiser, at least in principle—but was forced to give more to Begin, who "was no doubt the most able negotiator at Camp David" (Quandt 1986, 255). Still, Carter, more than anyone else, was not only the architect of the final accords but also the person who wheedled the disputants into accepting numerous compromises. As Quandt remarks, Carter's role was "central" (Quandt 1986, 256); the possibility that the two parties could forge an agreement by themselves was practically inconceivable.

In this manner, bargaining with an appraiser/player—especially one who has been informed of the fallback position of one side—led to one of the most significant international agreements since World War II. True, the process by which it was achieved is quite far removed from the bargaining models. Nevertheless, it does seem to indicate both (1) the importance of (partial) omniscience under the Penalty Appraisal Procedure and (2) the crucial role of rewards under the Bonus Appraisal

Procedure. Carter, without being quite clairvoyant, was able not only to find common ground for an agreement but also to enrich it with promises of aid and other support.

2.9. Conclusions

The idea of giving players bonuses—so that a buyer can buy at price s, and a seller can sell at price b—has an appealing simplicity to it. But the Bonus Procedure is vulnerable to collusion; introducing an appraiser, however, converts this procedure to the Bonus Appraisal Procedure, which is collusion-proof but requires additional assumptions about the appraiser's distribution. A possible practical problem with the latter procedure may be in finding a person that both sides agree is fair: Jimmy Carter seems to have been that person at Camp David.

The switch from the Bonus Procedure to the Bonus Appraisal Procedure is paralleled by the switch from the Penalty Procedure to the Penalty Appraisal Procedure. Unlike the Bonus Procedure, collusion by the players under either penalty procedure is ineffective, for the simple reason that there is no bonus payer against whom to collude.

Rather than preventing collusion, the main advantage of the Penalty Appraisal Procedure and the Expansive Appraisal Procedure over the Penalty Procedure lies in providing the players with the possibility of a settlement selected by an independent and neutral party. The incorporation of such a person's judgment into the bargaining process highlights the appraisal as a possible compromise solution. Its choice is made more likely by the Expansive Appraisal Procedure, because only one player's offer must overlap the appraiser's choice in order that the latter becomes the settlement.

In summary, the big trade-off in two-person bargaining games of incomplete information—at least as far as eliciting reservation prices is concerned—is between bringing in a third party to pay a bonus and suffering a loss in efficiency. Without an appraiser, one can get full efficiency out of the Bonus Procedure, but it is vulnerable to collusion and requires a tax collector/bonus payer; or one can get collusion-proofness out of the Penalty Procedure, but it is inefficient unless the ($b_0 - s_0$) factor can be given a nonprobabilistic interpretation that ties the nonconstant-sum aspects of a settlement to its constant-sum aspects.

Appraisers may help under both kinds of procedures— especially the Bonus Procedure—by cutting out, under the Bonus Appraisal Procedure, the incentive to collude. The Penalty Appraisal Procedure and the Expansive Appraisal Procedure may also facilitate settlements difficult to reach under the Penalty Procedure. This seems particularly true of the Expansive Penalty Procedure because a settlement does not require that both players overlap each other.

Players will tend to favor this procedure over the Penalty Appraisal Procedure if their reservation prices are relatively generous to their adversaries, thereby making it easier for them to implement profitable agreements by themselves. Players whose prices are less generous, by comparison, will prefer not to be stuck with an unfavorable settlement, which can happen under the Expansive Appraisal Procedure. Moreover, the Expansive Appraisal Procedure is vulnerable to bias because the appraiser can essentially dictate a settlement by choosing an outcome extremely favorable to one side.

This is not the case under the Penalty Appraisal Procedure, because both players must overlap the appraiser. Under this procedure, however, there may be a settlement that is mutually profitable (i.e., $b > s$) but not implemented because the appraisal does not fall in the overlap interval. This problem can be "solved" if the appraiser is omniscient; more realistically, it will be alleviated if the appraiser selects compromise settlements in a restricted range.

Manifestly, there are trade-offs among the five procedures, which seem to exhaust the possibilities for making honesty a dominant strategy. None is unequivocally best, but each may be practicable in different situations. Moreover, their logic may be discerned even in relatively unstructured bargaining situations, like those at Camp David, that have led the bargainers to make major concessions that, evidently, approached their reservation prices.

Whether the logic of the different procedures can be applied more explicitly and systematically is an open question. Successful negotiations with momentous consequences, like those at Camp David, are rare, but the same calculus may induce truthful revelation in more mundane, yet still consequential, negotiations. At the least, the bargaining models demonstrate that there are multiple paths to wringing honesty out of bargainers, which may lead to ageements that might otherwise not be realized.

How best to apply the insights of the various procedures in different settings will require much more thought and reflection. But the fact that there are five distinct approaches to inducing honesty in bargaining, and perhaps clinch agreements that might otherwise elude the disputants, is, I think, encouraging. The different approaches, with or without an appraiser, each have serious limitations of both a practical and theoretical nature. But knowledge of their existence should put to rest the notion that bargaining inevitably requires endless posturing, constant maneuvering, and occasional outright deception.

Notes

[1]This chapter is adapted from Brams and Kilgour (1989). Some of the procedures have been renamed, and one new procedure has been added (the Bonus Appraisal Procedure). Whereas mathematical proofs underlying most of the results reported in this chapter are given in Brams and Kilgour (1989), more informal arguments and examples are given here. The application of the basic logic of the procedures to the Camp David agreement is new to this chapter.

[2]Bargaining models that do not assume single but instead sequential offers by the players are described in the edited collections by Roth (1985) and Binmore and Dasgupta (1987). Some of these models are based on games of complete information (e.g., Rubinstein 1982, has been an influential model that permits alternating offers by the players); a relatively accessible overview of several models can be found in Elster (1989a, chap. 2). More generally, applications of game theory to economics can be found in Shubik (1982, 1984), Friedman (1986), Tirole (1988), Rasmusen (1989), Binmore (1990), Osborne and Rubinstein (1990), and Kreps (1990), among other places, that echo the kind of analysis to be developed in this chapter.

[3]The optimality of $b_0 = b$ is not difficult to demonstrate formally. B gains $b - s_0$ when there is an exchange and 0 when there is not. Obviously, B would prefer an exchange iff $b > s_0$. By picking $b_0 < b$, B gains $b - s_0$ when $s_0 \leq b_0 < b$ but misses out on some profitable exchanges when $b_0 < s_0 < b$. On the other hand, if $b_0 > b$, B effects every profitable exchange (when $s_0 < b$) but loses on other exchanges (when $b < s_0 < b_0$). Thus, when b_0 deviates from b in either direction, B loses profit, so $b_0 = b$ is optimal.

[4]These mechanisms have usually been interpreted in the context of public-goods pricing or the transmittal of messages and the transfer of goods within a firm. The more recent formulations, beginning with d'Aspremont and Gérard-Varet (1979) and Ledyard (1978, 1979), have been as noncooperative games of incomplete information. These mechanisms have been summarized and synthesized in Green and Laffont (1979), Groves and Ledyard (1987), and Moulin (1988); they have been specifically related to two-person bargaining in Radner (1986, 12–13).

[5]To demonstrate this for B, fix a and consider B's choice of b_0. If $s_0 > a$ (Case 2 in section 2.4), B's choice does not affect the outcome because s_0 does not overlap a, so there is no exchange. If $s_0 \leq a$ (Cases 1 and 3), B's choice does matter. If $b_0 < b$, then B may prevent a possible settlement in the interval $[b_0, b]$, where it would always profit if $b_0 < a < b$ (Case 3). If $b_0 > b$, then B allows for a possible settlement in the interval $[b, b_0]$, where it will always lose if $b < a \leq b_0$ (Case 1). Only the strategy of $b_0 = b$ always ensures a profit for B (if $b \geq s$) and always prevents a loss (if $b < s$), so it dominates any strategy $b_0 \neq b$.

[6]The degree of inefficiency of the Penalty Appraisal Procedure depends on the appraisal density function, f_A. To illustrate this point, if f_A is, like f_B and f_S, uniformly distributed over [0,1], and B and S choose their dominant strategies of honesty, then a feasible trade is implemented with probability ⅓, and each player

receives an a priori expected profit of $\frac{1}{24} \approx .0417$, the same as under the Penalty Procedure. On the other hand, if a is concentrated around $\frac{1}{2}$, then a feasible trade is implemented with a probability approaching $\frac{1}{2}$, and each player's a priori expected profit approaches $\frac{1}{16} = .0625$. Finally, the a that maximizes B's a priori expected profit is $\frac{1}{3}$, and that which maximizes S's a priori expected profit is $\frac{2}{3}$, with B and S realizing a priori expected profits of $\frac{2}{27} \approx .0741$ at their respective maxima.

[7]In effect, the probability that the appraisal a takes on a particular value is all concentrated at a single point—that is, the posted price. In fact, this price need not be posted in advance but could be revealed after the players make their offers—making f_A a degenerate density function.

[8]To demonstrate this, fix a and consider B's choice of b_0. If $s_0 \leq a$ (Cases 1 and 3 in section 2.4), B's choice does not affect the outcome because s_0 overlaps a, which is sufficient to make a the settlement. If $s_0 > a$ (Case 2), B's choice does matter. But unlike Case 2, assume $b_0 < a$:

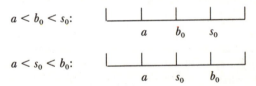

$b_0 < a < s_0$:

                b_0 a s_0

If $b_0 < b$, B may preclude a possible settlement in $[b_0, b]$, where it would always profit if $b_0 < a < b$. On the other hand, assume $b_0 > a$, for which there are two possibilities when $s_0 > a$:

$a < b_0 < s_0$:

                a b_0 s_0

$a < s_0 < b_0$:

                a s_0 b_0

If $b_0 > b$, B may preclude a possible settlement in the interval $[b, b_0]$, where it would always lose if $b < a < b_0$. Only the strategy of $b_0 = b$ always ensures a profit for B (if $b > a$) and always prevents a loss (if $b < a$), so it dominates any strategy $b_0 \neq b$.

Chapter 3
Arbitration Procedures and the Problem of Convergence

3.1. Introduction

Arbitration is defined to be "the hearing and determination of a case in controversy by a person chosen by the parties or appointed under statutory authority" (*Webster's Ninth New Collegiate*).[1] By this definition, not only do the parties to a dispute submit their differences to the judgment of an arbitrator, but there is also the "determination" of an outcome: the dispute does not end in impasse; there is a resolution that both parties are obliged to accept. This was true in biblical times, too:

> If a case is too baffling for you to decide, be it a controversy over homicide, civil law, or assault—matters of dispute in your courts—you shall promptly repair to the place which the LORD your God will have chosen, and appear before the levitical priests, or the magistrate in charge at the time, and present your problem. . . . you shall carry out the verdict that is announced to you. (Deut. 17: 8–10)

Thus does arbitration have a venerable history.

This is not the case in bargaining, even with an appraiser, as I showed in Chapter 2. For example, a dispute is not settled under the Penalty Appraisal Procedure unless both players overlap the appraiser (and necessarily each other); it is not settled under the Expansive Appraisal Procedure unless at least one player overlaps the appraiser. If both players overlap each other (i.e., $b \geq s$) but not the appraiser (either $a > b$ or $a < s$) under the Penalty Appraisal Procedure, or neither player overlaps the appraiser ($b < a < s$) under the Expansive Procedure, there is no settlement.

Arbitration always forces a settlement, even when the arbitrator's choice is more than the buyer is willing to pay and less than the seller is willing to accept, causing both to suffer a loss. This difference between arbitration and bargaining renders the players' reservation prices somewhat beside the point: they will have to live with the settlement, even if they both lose. Because the question no longer is whether a settlement will be consummated, the honesty of the players in their bargaining is also not an issue. Rather, the convergence of the players' offers under different arbitration procedures becomes the new focus as the players strive to make the (inevitable) settlement as favorable to themselves as possible.

The subsequent analysis will be restricted to arbitration between parties that have different "interests," as opposed to "grievance" or "rights" arbitration that involves the interpretation of the privileges or rights allowed the parties under an existing contract. As in the bargaining models in Chapter 2, I assume that disputes involve only two parties, which in fact constitute the great bulk of cases settled by interest arbitration.

Although the dictionary definition of arbitration is silent on how a settlement is determined, traditionally the arbitrator is free to render any judgment. Presumably, once a dispute has reached a certain stage, either the parties to a conflict will be willing to have a third party step in and make a judgment they hope will be equitable, or the law dictates that a settlement will be imposed that puts an end to the dispute. The usual rationale for such laws is that the external costs (i.e., those to parties not involved) of, say, a strike by police officers or firefighters are so great that imposing a settlement is preferable to jeopardizing public safety.

Under the most commonly used form of interest arbitration, an arbitrator acceptable to both sides of a dispute specifies a settlement that is binding on the parties. I will refer to this procedure as *Conventional Arbitration*. It would appear to work well when the arbitrator is knowledgeable about issues and impartial, so any judgment he or she renders is considered fair.

In practice, however, Conventional Arbitration suffers from several disadvantages (Neale and Bazerman 1987). The most important is that the arbitrator's judgment may not be independent of the two sides' positions. Insofar as the arbitrator tends to split the difference between these positions, each side will have an incentive to make extreme demands and not budge from them.

Such behavior obviously has a chilling effect on the negotiation process, even if, as is usually the case, arbitration is used only as a last resort when bargaining fails to produce a settlement. For the very prospect of ending up in arbitration may encourage early posturing and derail a negotiated settlement. The extent to which an arbitration procedure promotes convergence toward a settlement is one criterion I shall use in evaluating different procedures.

There is a certain arbitrariness to arbitration; its possible bias seems especially severe in the case of Conventional Arbitration. Because the parties to a dispute do not resolve the conflict on their own but rather must acquiesce in someone else's judgment, one or both parties may end up quite dissatisfied.

By comparison, players can avoid losses under most of the procedures discussed in Chapter 2. This is certainly the case under the Penalty Appraisal Procedure, because the players' offers must overlap each other as well as the appraiser's proposal.

Under the Expansive Penalty Procedure, one player can suffer a loss (if it does not overlap the arbitrator when the other player does), but the appraiser can preclude either player from suffering an *expected* loss (over a long enough series of plays) by choosing compromise settlements sufficiently near the mean of the probability distribution that characterizes the appraiser's choice. Even if there is no appraiser, I suggested in Section 2.5 how certain incentives relating to the nature of a contract can be incorporated into the Penalty Procedure to render it more efficient.

In the case of the bonus procedures, the players by definition can never lose, though taxes presumably would have to be assessed to make these procedures practicable. In arbitrated disputes, on the other hand, there may be no way of avoiding losses to the players. For example, if $b < s$, even when the arbitrator makes a compromise choice a (i.e., $b < a < s$), it will not satisfy the players simply because there is no profit to be had.

3.2. Different Arbitration Procedures

With reservation prices excluded, I shall compare arbitration procedures that take account of both the players' offers and the arbitrator's choice of a settlement to produce a "reasonable" resolution to a dispute. In an attempt to minimize players' dissatisfaction with a settlement, new forms of arbitration that give the disputants greater control in the determination of the settlement have been proposed.

One procedure that has gained widespread attention and has, in addition, been used in both the public and private sectors is called *Final-Offer Arbitration* (FOA). Stevens (1966) proposed this strikingly simple procedure some twenty-five years ago, though it had been discussed informally earlier (Stern et al. 1975, 113, fn. 7). Under FOA, each party submits its final offer for a settlement to an arbitrator, who must choose one final offer or the other. The offer chosen by the arbitrator determines the settlement. Unlike Conventional Arbitration, the arbitrator is not permitted to split the difference, or compromise the offers of each side in any other way. One side or the other "wins" by getting its offer chosen.

Ostensibly there is a game that, it seems, will force the two players to converge and eliminate the need for a settlement imposed by the arbitrator, as under Conventional Arbitration. Here is how one analyst described the reasoning underlying the convergence argument:

> If the arbitrator or panel was permitted to select only one or the other of the parties' final offers, with no power to make a choice anywhere in between, it was expected that the logic of the procedure would force negotiating parties to continue moving closer together in search of a positon that would be most likely to receive neutral sympathy. Ultimately, so the argument went, they would come so close together that they would almost inevitably find their own settlement. (Rehmus 1979, 218)

Of course, if the two sides do not converge, or come close to converging, the arbitrator will be forced to pick between two possibly extreme offers. Hence, the value of FOA depends in this case on the claim that it can induce a negotiated settlement by drawing the parties together. One purpose of this chapter will be to test this logic by describing a game-theoretic model of FOA and comparing its theoretical consequences with empirical data on the usage of both FOA and Conventional Arbitration.

I shall not limit the analysis, however, to just these two procedures. Recently, several variations on FOA have been proposed that appear to possess a number of desirable properties:

1. *Bonus FOA* posits that the winner under FOA receives a bonus, equal to the gap between the two final offers, for having its offer accepted by the arbitrator. (This bonus is purely for winning, above and beyond the value of the settlement, and is paid to the winner by the loser.) Bonus FOA provides a greater incentive than does FOA for the parties, under certain conditions, to come together, but it does not necessarily lead to their convergence with identical offers.

2. *Combined Arbitration* mixes Conventional Arbitration and FOA in such a way that both sides have an incentive to converge completely under rather general conditions. On occasion, however, it may require that the arbitrator's judgment be imposed.

3. *Two-Stage and Multistage FOA. Two-Stage FOA* allows the initial loser under FOA to respond with a counteroffer. If closer to the arbitrator's judgment, the loser's counteroffer is combined with the winner's original offer and becomes the settlement; if the winner's original offer remains closer than the counteroffer, then the original offer becomes the settlement. *Multistage FOA* is similar to two-stage FOA, except that the sequence of offers and counteroffers is not limited to two stages but continues until one side wins twice in a row. Like Two-Stage FOA, Multistage FOA induces partial convergence and tends to produce less extreme settlements than FOA. Although Two-Stage FOA is simpler

and seems to perform as well as Multistage FOA in many situations, it lacks the give-and-take aspect of bargaining in many real-life situations. This aspect is a virtue insofar as protracted negotiations may produce settlements that could not be achieved otherwise.

I examine one case of protracted negotiations later—Henry Kissinger's shuttle diplomacy in the Middle East—which resulted in disengagement agreements between Israel and its neighbors, Egypt and Syria, after the 1973 Yom Kippur War. Kissinger was both more and less than an arbitrator; his involvement is at least suggestive of how Multistage FOA may encourage convergence. (Admittedly, Multistage FOA is quite far removed from these diplomatic negotiations; nevertheless, these negotiations illustrate the potential value of arbitration procedures that allow for extended exchanges.) I also consider the use of arbitration in public-employee disputes, major league baseball, and, implicitly, in treaty interpretation.

3.3. Trade-Offs and Implicit Arbitration

FOA and its variants all aim at moving the parties toward each other under the threat of a settlement more beneficial to the other party. In effect, the two parties play a guessing game with each other about where the arbitrator stands, trying to offer a settlement favorable to themselves that will at the same time not deviate too much from the judgment of the arbitrator. A number of analysts have modeled these trade-offs, which I will discuss presently.[2] First, however, I describe some of the basic modeling assumptions I will make.

Both Conventional Arbitration and FOA and its variants can all be modeled as two-person games, wherein each party tries to beat the other with a more competitive offer. Indeed, the games (with one minor exception) are all constant-sum, because gains by one side are exactly balanced by losses of the other, making the sum of the payoffs to both sides a constant.

This is not the case in bargaining if the players' reservation prices overlap. Because *both* players can benefit from an agreement and lose from nonagreement, winning for one does not imply losing for the other.

I shall not model Conventional Arbitration here, except to illustrate how this procedure rewards grossly exaggerated claims if the arbitrator is likely to split the difference between the parties. The game, if there is one, is to ask for the moon without sounding preposterous about it, presumably because arbitrators will devalue offers that seem outlandish (Bazerman and Farber 1985). Even so, many critics have charged that

Conventional Arbitration robs the parties of any incentive to reconcile their differences.

In the case of FOA and its variants, I assume that the players have only incomplete information about what the arbitrator, who is assumed to make an independent judgment, thinks is a fair settlement. As with the bargaining models, this assumption can be operationalized in terms of a probability distribution, but over the arbitrator's preferences rather than the appraiser's.

The incomplete information is assumed to be common knowledge—both players possess it. To simplify the analysis, I will focus on the uniform distribution, as in Chapter 2, to illustrate how the optimal strategies of the two parties can be computed under the different FOA-related procedures. In addition, I assume that the players begin by making simultaneous offers that do not affect the arbitrator's choice, and the dispute is over a single quantifiable issue.

The analysis indicates that there is no perfect procedure: trade-offs are inevitable. Thus, for example, there is no procedure that simultaneously induces the parties to converge on their own (so an arbitrated settlement need never be imposed), mirrors the settlement preferred by the arbitrator (which presumably helps to ensure its fairness), and forecloses the possibility of an extreme settlement (by encouraging both sides to compromise if not converge).

That trade-offs are inevitable under FOA and related procedures is perhaps not surprising. Far more interesting and less apparent are the quantitative dimensions of the trade-offs—specifically, the detailed effects that the different procedures have on the disputants' optimal strategies, the degree of convergence of these strategies, and the point or points to which they converge. The design of better procedures, I contend, cannot be intelligently undertaken without modeling such strategic effects.

But good design also requires empirical testing and normative evaluation. At this stage, comparison of the theoretical predictions of the models with experience is possible only for Conventional Arbitration and FOA; all the other procedures are untried.[3] On the other hand, controlled experiments with the other procedures are possible. As I shall indicate, some preliminary experimental data on Multistage FOA seem supportive of the modeling results (Neale and Bazerman 1987), which reflect the back-and-forth movement of real-life negotiations.

Apart from the theory and practice of arbitration, I shall recommend certain procedures, based on criteria that I believe a good arbitration procedure should satisfy. With the exception of Conventional Arbitration, all the arbitration procedures force the disputants to compromise between attempting to match the arbitrator's judgment and pushing for their own best offers. But they do this in varying degrees; Two-Stage FOA, for example, by giving the loser a second chance, attenuates the consequences of losing initially by being too extreme.

To what extent should a procedure force the disputants to try to mimic the arbitrator's judgment? This question cannot be answered by theoretical or empirical analysis alone. It can be clarified, however, by examining the strategic consequences that the different procedures have on the disputants' behavior.

Some procedures, as I shall demonstrate, induce the disputants to home in on the arbitrator's preferred settlement, whereas others either do not promote such convergence or induce convergence to some other point. In general, it seems, only the threat of an unfavorable settlement can reduce posturing and get the parties to make concessions and offers that converge; yet convergence may not be to the arbitrator's position.

What one considers desirable, from a normative perspective, depends on the kind of behavior that one believes an arbitration procedure should encourage or prescribe in the settlement of disputes. In the concluding section I offer some judgments, based on different criteria, about possible trade-offs.

Before commencing the more formal analysis, it is worth noting that arbitration may occur in settings in which the mechanism for dispute resolution seems quite far removed from any prescribed arbitration procedure. Consider the interpretation of a treaty between two countries with different languages, for which there are two official versions of the treaty written in the language of each country. Because even expert translations may leave room for different interpretations of the treaty in the two languages, it is sometimes mandated that there be a third official version of the treaty in a different language. In the event of a dispute over interpretation, this third version is authoritative (Barston 1988, 219).

This approach seems more akin to rights arbitration, whereby the third language is, in effect, the arbiter of the right, than interest arbitration. But the fact that the third language is authoritative does not imply an end to a dispute, even if this language eliminates bargaining about which country's language should take precedence.

The neutral party who makes a judgment about the interpretation of the authoritative version may be thought of as an arbitrator. Assume the authoritative version permits an interpretation between the claimed interpretations of the two countries. From the perspective of these two countries, what claims should they make? Under Conventional Arbitration, each side would be well advised to make an extreme claim if the arbitrator is likely to split the difference. But if the dispute involves a qualitative issue, such as which country holds the right to some indivisible property, the arbitrator will be forced to side with one claim or the other, as under FOA. Then the strategic question for each country will be whether to demand an exclusive right, or to soften its claim to make it more acceptable as a compromise choice for the arbitrator and, therefore, more likely to be selected.

If the rules permit counterclaims—a rebuttal to the other side's legal brief might be filed, in which one's old claim is revised—the arbitration procedure might resemble one with multiple stages. In this manner, an arbitration procedure might be *implicit* either in the nature of the dispute (e.g., whether there can be a split-the-difference resolution) or in the rules for making claims (e.g., whether the claims can be revised). Indeed, I shall indicate later, using Kissinger's shuttle diplomacy as an example, how a mediator, who has no formal powers to resolve a dispute, may take on aspects of the role of arbitrator as he or she persuades, cajoles, or bullies two parties into a settlement.

3.4. Final-Offer Arbitration (FOA)

FOA is used to settle labor disputes involving certain classes of public employees in ten states (as of 1981; see Freeman 1986), salary disputes in major league baseball (Chass 1988, 1990), and bidding competitions on U.S. Defense Department contracts (Carrington 1988; Halloran 1988). I shall say more about experience with FOA later in this section and in Section 3.5.

To model FOA, let a and b denote the final offers of a "low" bidder A and a "high" bidder B, respectively. A, for example, might be management, which wants to keep the wage scale as low as possible, and B labor, which wants higher wages. I make the simplifying assumption that the dispute is over a single quantifiable issue, such as a wage scale or cost-of-living adjustment, but models of FOA have been developed that allow for more than one issue (Wittman 1986).

Let x denote the arbitrator's preferred settlement. Under FOA, if x is closer to a, the settlement is a; if x is closer to b, the settlement is b; if x is equidistant from a and b, the settlement is the average, $(a + b)/2$; and if $a = b$, the settlement is the common value. I assume that the players do not know x but only that the players' beliefs about the position of x are common knowledge and can be represented by some probability density function f.

For example, assume the density function is uniform, as was assumed of b with respect to S's beliefs, of s with respect to B's beliefs, and of a with respect to both players' beliefs in the bargaining models in Chapter 2. In the case of the arbitration models, this assumption means that the players think that the position of the arbitrator x is equally likely to fall anywhere in a specified interval. Management and labor might agree, for example, that the arbitrator would prefer a wage increase x of between 4 percent and 8 percent, and that every value x in that interval has the same chance of occurring. For convenience, I assume that the endpoints of the interval are 0 and 1, so that the density function is $f(x) = 1$, $0 \leq x \leq 1$.

On the other hand, one might assume that the arbitrator is more likely to be closer to the midpoint of the interval, 1/2, than the endpoints, 0 or 1. I shall illustrate such density functions later. Because the uniform density function is very easy to work with, however, I use it here and subsequently to illustrate the calculation of the optimal strategies of the players.

To do this, begin by defining the expected settlement, $F(a,b)$, which may be interpreted as the payoff that A wants to minimize and B wants to maximize. If $a \geq b$ so that the final offers converge or crisscross (i.e., the minimizer's offer equals or exceeds the maximizer's offer), the settlement is simply equal to the converged-upon offer, or the offer closer to the arbitrator. Henceforth I assume for FOA and other procedures that this is not the case and concentrate on the expected settlement in the case of nonconvergence.

In the latter case,

$$F(a,b) = a(Pr[x \text{ is closer to } a]) + b(Pr[x \text{ is closer to } b]),$$

where Pr indicates "probability that." As illustrated in Figure 3.1, a will be closer to x if x is between 0 and $(a + b)/2$, which will occur with probability $(a + b)/2$. (This probability is simply the area of the rectangle, extending from 0 to the midpoint of the offers of A and B, with height equal to the value of the density function, 1, between these points.) Likewise, b will be closer to x with probability $1 - (a + b)/2$. Hence,

$$F(a,b) = a[(a + b)/2 - 0] + b[1 - (a + b)/2]$$
$$= (a^2 + 2b - b^2)/2.$$

It is easy to show using calculus that A minimizes $F(a,b)$ by choosing $a = 0$; similarly, B maximizes $F(a,b)$ by choosing $b = 1$. These strategy choices simultaneously minimize (for A) and maximize (for B) the expected settlement and constitute the solution of this two-person constant-sum game. These strategy choices imply that $F(0,1) = \frac{1}{2}$, which is the *value* of the game, or the settlement that the players can ensure for themselves.

Moreover, this value is the best possible for each player in the sense that, if $a = 0$, $F(0,b) \leq \frac{1}{2}$, so the minimizer guarantees the settlement is never more than $\frac{1}{2}$ (*minimax*); and if $b = 1$, $F(a,1) \geq \frac{1}{2}$, so the maximizer

Figure 3.1. Final offers of *A(a)* and *B(b)* for uniform distribution

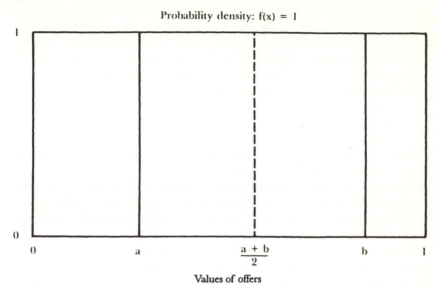

Probability density: f(x) = 1

Values of offers

guarantees the settlement is never less than ½ (*maximin*). If either player deviates from these optimal strategies, it cannot do better and runs a genuine risk of doing worse, making these strategies dominant, or best whatever the other player does.

For example, if *A* chooses $a = 0$, but *B* chooses $b \neq 1$, $F(a,b) < \frac{1}{2}$, so *B*, who wants to maximize $F(a,b)$, is hurt by this choice. Consequently, *B* would have no incentive to depart from $b = 1$, making the solution a *saddlepoint* (von Neumann and Morgenstern 1953) that provides the guarantees mentioned in the previous paragraph. The saddlepoint is also a Nash equilibrium, or an outcome from which neither player would depart unilaterally because it would do worse if it did.[4]

It may seem strange that it is the endpoints, 0 and 1, of the interval that are the optimal strategies of *A* and *B*, respectively. After all, these strategies are divergent, contrary to the view expressed earlier that FOA will induce each side to approach its adversary in order to maximize the chances of having its offer selected.

The flaw in this reasoning is that, although each player increases the probability that its offer will be chosen by moving toward the midpoint of the distribution, this gain in probability is more than offset by the loss in potential payoff it suffers by compromising its final offer. The net effect is to push the players to the extremities of the distribution, not to pull them toward the center.

But what if there were "more probability" in the center—say, the density function were unimodal (i.e., had one peak or mode) and symmetric (i.e., had the same shape on each side of the mode)? Under certain conditions, the concentration of area around the center helps, but rarely by very much. For example, the optimal strategies of A and B for the well-known normal distribution are more than two standard deviations apart (2.51, to be exact), which means that 80 percent of the area under this density lies between the optimal positions of A on the left and B on the right (Brams and Merrill 1983).

For other distributions, a player's optimal strategy may not even lie inside the interval of possible values of x, resulting in an even greater divergence of offers than was illustrated for the uniform distribution. Optimal strategies for still other distributions—including discrete distributions, in which the number of possible offers is finite—may be "mixed" (involving randomized choices between two "pure," or specific, strategies) or may not exist.

Necessary and sufficient conditions have been found for the existence of different kinds of optimal strategies, which tend to be quite sensitive to the specific distribution assumed over the arbitrator's preferences (Brams and Merrill 1983). But for no nondegenerate continuous distributions is there ever convergence of the optimal final offers (e.g., to the median). Quite the contrary: optimal final offers tend more to be divergent than convergent, often separated by two or more standard deviations.

But is this necessarily bad? According to Stern et al. (1975, 3), the tendency of final offers to diverge under FOA "increases the pressure on the parties to take realistic bargaining positions and to settle their disputes through direct negotiations without use of arbitration." Consider major league baseball, in which FOA has been used since 1975 to settle salary disputes between the teams and players. Of the 111 major league players who filed for arbitration in 1988, 93 (84 percent) negotiated contracts before FOA was actually used (Chass, 1988). As one baseball arbitrator put it: "I'm starting to feel like the atomic bomb. The deterrent effect of me as an arbitrator is enough" (Cronin 1989, quoting Stephen B. Goldberg).

Thus, divergent final offers put pressure on the disputants to settle on their own, discouraging the actual use of FOA. (Because there has been no use of Conventional Arbitration in major league baseball, however, I cannot compare the proportion of negotiated settlements under the two different procedures.) On the other hand, an arbitration procedure that induces convergence may also be good, because it facilitates the closing of the final gap that might separate two sides.

Curiously, then, both the divergence and convergence of offers under an arbitration procedure may lead to settlements. Out of fear of implementing the procedure, divergence may induce serious bargaining before its use. Convergence of offers may lead directly to a settlement—or something close to it, from which the bargainers can negotiate a settlement on their own.

In practice, it turns out, FOA tends to lead to more negotiated settlements than Conventional Arbitration in public-employee disputes as well as baseball (Freeman 1986). But if two sides end up in impasse and FOA is then used, settlements by their very nature will tend to be one-sided. This is especially true if one side places greater value on winning, as I shall next show.

3.5. FOA in Practice: The Importance of Winning

Before looking at further experience with FOA, I need to introduce some additional theory. Suppose that one or both players under FOA derives value from winning per se (i.e., having its offer chosen), in addition to the gain from the settlement that the arbitrator selects. To model the situation in which winning adds value to the settlement under FOA, assume that the final offer selected by the arbitrator is more valuable to the player who proposed it than were the same final offer proposed by the other party and selected by the arbitrator.

It certainly seems reasonable that some bargainers might simply prefer winning to losing, whatever the value of the settlement. To model this phenomenon, assume that the "perceived" settlement is adjusted downward if A wins and upward if B wins. Call this adjustment a *bonus*. A labor negotiator in a wage dispute, for example, may be more satisfied with, say, a 5 percent raise in the pay rate—if that settlement is his or her own final offer—than if the same settlement is achieved but represents management's final offer. Such bonuses for winning—above and beyond the value of the settlement—may accrue to both parties in a dispute and need not be equal.

There are several reasons why labor's bonus might exceed management's, although our subsequent conclusions in no way depend on such a relationship. The rank and file, on whose votes labor leaders depend, tend to identify with the euphoria of winning and the frustration of losing a settlement. A string of losses may be fatal to a labor negotiator's position as a union leader. Management negotiators are likely to have less personal stake in the appearance of victory and focus more on the possible long-run consequences of appearing weak. Labor negotiation is only one, albeit an important one, of the concerns of management.

Assume as before that A and B believe that the preferred position x of the arbitrator is equally likely to fall anywhere in the interval between 0 and 1, so $f(x) = 1$, $0 \leq x \leq 1$. In addition, assume that A and B perceive themselves to receive bonuses of S_A and S_B, respectively, for winning an FOA decision per se. Furthermore, these bonuses are known to each player—and hence they are common knowledge, as is other information about the game. Then A will seek to minimize the payoff function,

$$G_A(a,b) = (a - S_A)[(a + b)/2] + b[1 - (a + b)/2]$$
$$= b - (b - a + S_A)[a + b)/2].$$

Note that the bonus S_A is subtracted from A's offer when it wins, because A is the minimizer and wants a settlement as low as possible. A will win with probability $(a + b)/2$; similarly, with complementary probability B's offer will win and A will receive no bonus.

B will seek to maximize the payoff function,

$$G_B(a,b) = a[(a + b)/2] + (b + S_B)[1 - (a + b)/2]$$
$$= (b + S_B) - (b - a + S_B)[(a + b)/2)].$$

Unlike FOA, in which there was a common expected payoff that A sought to minimize and B sought to maximize, the different bonuses that the players receive introduce an asymmetry into their optimization problem. In fact, the game is no longer constant-sum, because what one player receives from winning the other player does not lose; the game is constant-sum only if the bonuses are equal.

Using calculus, it is not difficult to show that A minimizes $G_A(a,b)$ by choosing $a = S_A/2$, and B maximizes $G_B(a,b)$ by choosing $b = 1 - S_B/2$ (provided $S_A + S_B \leq 2$, i.e., S_A and S_B are not too large). Note that when there are no bonuses (i.e., when $S_A = S_B = 0$), the optimal strategies of the players are $a = 0$ and $b = 1$, as I demonstrated in Section 3.4.

The bonuses for winning have the effect of inducing the players to moderate their final offers in the uniform case. Writing the gap or distance between the two final offers as

$$d = b - a,$$

convergence of the final offers is obtained when $d = 0$, or

$$(1 - S_B/2) - S_A/2 = 0,$$

which implies that $S_A + S_B = 2$.

In other words, to induce convergence, the sum of the values of the bonuses must be equal to twice the gap of 1 between the optimal final offers without the bonuses. Thus, if the bonuses are equal, *each* must be equal to the gap in order for the parties to be motivated to close it. (If the total bonuses are larger than twice the gap, the optimal final offers would crisscross, in which case the settlement would be the offer closer to the arbitrator.)

For reasons given earlier, the bonuses may not be equal. For example, B (labor) may perceive a positive bonus S_B, whereas A (management) does not ($S_A = 0$). For convergence to occur in this case, B would need to gain twice as much from the bonus ($S_B = 2$) as the gap of 1 that separates A's final offer from B's without the bonus.

Unfortunately for B, the point of convergence would then be A's optimal final offer of $a = 0$ without the bonus. This means that B must capitulate, agreeing to accept the endpoint of the distribution favoring A, for there to be convergence. This lopsided outcome, $(a,b) = (0,0)$, is a Nash equilibrium in the uniform case.

More generally, when one player (say, A) but not the other (B) derives a bonus from winning—and both players are aware of the different added values they place on winning—then A will be forced toward the position of B. Similarly, Wittman (1986) showed that a risk-averse player, who prefers moderate settlements to risky lotteries, will move toward its adversary. To be risk-averse, in fact, is another way of saying that winning less with greater certainty provides a player with a bonus.

For distributions different from the uniform, a bonus of 2 may not be sufficient to ensure convergence of the parties, but, under fairly general conditions, a bonus for either player causes the gap between the equilibrium offers to decrease or stay the same. Furthermore, in most cases either both of the two offers move in the same direction, or the bonus receiver's moves and the adversary's remains fixed (Brams and Merrill 1989).

In analyzing "optimum retorts," Raiffa (1982, 114–15) showed that the best response of one player to another's shift toward the center was to move farther away. In other words, concessions by one player do not elicit concessions by the other. Quite the opposite: both players move leftward or rightward together.

In this manner, both players' strategies are affected by knowledge of the bonus that one party receives. Clearly, it would be in the interest of the party deriving the bonus to hide its bonus—if that were possible—to induce movement by the adversary toward its position rather than away from it.

Such attempts at cover-up are surely made ("we will never surrender"), but they, like bonuses, are difficult to detect. Nevertheless, it may still be possible to infer, from the positions two parties take and some estimate of where the arbitrator stands, which party derives the bonus.

To illustrate this calculation, I turn to a study by Ashenfelter and

Bloom (1984) of 423 arbitration cases involving salary disputes between police unions and local governments in New Jersey over the period 1978–80. Of these cases, 324 were conducted under FOA and 99 under Conventional Arbitration. Of the 324 FOA settlements, more than two-thirds (69 percent) were awarded to labor. Ashenfelter and Bloom (1984) argue that not only were the FOA decisions impartial but also that the arbitrators used the same standards as under Conventional Arbitration. They indicate, however, that under FOA

> the parties may not typically position themselves equally distant from, and on opposite sides of, the arbitrator's preferred award. This might happen either because unions have a more conservative view of what arbitrators will allow, or because unions may be more fearful of taking a risk of loss than are employers. (Ashenfelter and Bloom 1984, 123)

Brams and Merrill (1989) suggested that one way to account for the more conservative behavior of labor is to postulate that labor, but not management, perceived itself to receive a bonus from winning. Indeed, the data strongly indicate that labor final offers under FOA, which averaged 7.9 percent (expressed as a percent increase in total compensation), more closely approximated arbitrator preferences (7.5 percent under Conventional Arbitration) than management final offers, which averaged 5.7 percent.

Using Ashenfelter and Bloom's (1984) estimates for the mean and standard deviation of this distribution (based on a statistical method called "probit analysis"), Brams and Merrill (1989) computed labor and management's equilibrium final offers, both with and without a labor bonus. The hypothesis that labor received no bonus was shown to be untenable. On the other hand, a hypothesized bonus equivalent to 3.8 percent—the gap between the estimated equilibrium offers of 6.1 and 9.9 percent without a bonus—worked well to explain the actual final offers (see Figure 3.2).

Ashenfelter and Bloom (1984, p. 123) observed that labor pays dearly for enhancing its probability of winning by decreasing the expected value of the settlement. To be more precise, if each party wins half the time with its estimated equilibrium offer, the average settlement is 8.0 percent. By comparison, the actual average settlement was 7.4 percent under FOA and 7.5 percent under Conventional Arbitration, which are, respectively, 8 and 6 percent less than the 8.0 percent labor would have achieved without the hypothesized bonus.

The tables, interestingly enough, are turned between management and labor in major league baseball. The scorecard reads 165 FOA victories for the teams and 138 for the players from 1975 to 1989 (only in 1981 and

Figure 3.2. Gap with and without the bonus under FOA

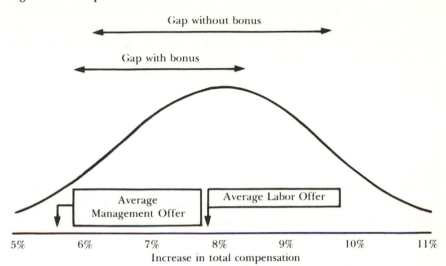

1989 did the players come out ahead) (Chass 1990, B14). I speculate that the difference lies in the fact that players, unlike labor union leaders, have only themselves to worry about. Even in losing, the players who chose FOA made remarkable gains in 1989, averaging an incredible 110 percent average salary increase over 1988. By contrast, the FOA winners averaged 135 percent increases, whereas those who negotiated their salaries (84 percent of the total, the same as in 1988) had increases of 98 percent (Chass 1990, B14). Evidently, the players who used FOA had stronger cases for big increases than those who negotiated settlements.

3.6. Bonus FOA

So far I have assumed that the bonuses of the two parties for winning are *internal:* they accrue to the winner of FOA from the pride or satisfaction of winning. Now suppose that the rules of FOA are modified and the bonus is made *external:* the winner is awarded a bonus equal in value to the gap between the final offers, to be paid by the loser.

Call this procedure, in which the payoffs do not depend on internal rewards but are built into the procedure itself, *Bonus FOA.* Players using Bonus FOA may also derive internal rewards, but I shall not assume these in the subsequent analysis.

More precisely, given final offers a and b, if A wins, A receives a payoff not of a but of $a - (b - a)$; thereby management (under the previous interpretation) benefits by having to pay labor less. The situation is reversed if labor wins: B does not receive b but $b + (b - a)$. It turns out that this escalation of the stakes narrows the gap between equilibrium final offers by a factor of 3. Using calculus, one can show that the Nash equilibrium is $(a,b) = (\frac{1}{3}, \frac{2}{3})$, which minimizes for A, and maximizes for B, the expected settlement.

Unlike internal bonuses that are each equal to the gap, $b - a$, between the equilibrium final offers without the bonus, external bonuses equal to the gap do not induce convergence. This is so because, as each party moves toward the center, the external bonus $b - a$ diminishes, reducing the expected payoff relative to that of an internal bonus, which remains fixed. Hence, an external bonus is not as powerful an incentive to convergence as an internal bonus.

There is, nonetheless, a considerable closing of the gap separating the final offers under Bonus FOA as compared with FOA. However, the outcomes under Bonus FOA when players choose their Nash equilibrium strategies are exactly the same as under FOA. For example, the equilibrium strategies under FOA in the uniform case are 0 and 1; under Bonus FOA, they are $\frac{1}{3}$ and $\frac{2}{3}$. Yet when the external bonus of $\frac{1}{3}$ separating these final offers is awarded to the winner and paid by the loser, Bonus FOA, like FOA, results in equilibrium outcomes of 0 or 1, respectively.

Bonus FOA, therefore, has no effect on the one-sidedness of outcomes under FOA. Nevertheless, it has the virtue of moving the two parties much closer together, from where they may be able to close the gap on their own before arbitration is used. As I shall show in Section 3.7, however, there is another procedure that has even stronger convergence properties, but at the price of sometimes forcing the parties to accept the arbitrator's judgment.

A natural generalization of Bonus FOA is to assume that the winner wins (and the loser loses) an amount proportional to the gap, say $p(b - a)$, where p is the proportion. When this is so, the equilibrium strategies are symmetric, with the equilibrium gap $b - a$ equal to $1/(2p + 1)$ in the uniform case. Convergence of the final offers is obtained only asymptotically—that is, as the proportion p approaches infinity.

Whereas $p = 1$ corresponds to Bonus FOA, $p = 0$ corresponds to FOA. A settlement defined by (exactly) splitting the difference at the mean of the two final offers, as under Conventional Arbitration, is equivalent to a negative bonus of $-(b - a)/2$. In this situation, the "reward" for winning is for each player to *pay* half the gap, although there is no winner or loser as such when the mean is chosen.

Setting the negative bonus of $-(b - a)/2$ equal to $p(b - a)$ implies $p = -\frac{1}{2}$. Unhappily for the parties, as p approaches $-\frac{1}{2}$, the equilibrium gap $b - a = 1/(2p + 1)$ approaches infinity, which implies that the equilibrium final offers diverge. This fact helps to explain why an arbitrator, likely to split the difference under Conventional Arbitration, simply encourages extreme posturing and outrageous demands by each side, as Farber (1981) showed using a different model.[5]

Although Bonus FOA does not in theory produce complete convergence, the near-convergence it induces may, in practical terms, be sufficient to persuade the two parties to come together on their own—given that they are allowed to negotiate before the arbitrator announces a decision and Bonus FOA is actually implemented. I shall have more to say about amending the rules to allow for such a penultimate stage when I discuss Combined Arbitration in Section 3.7, to which a prior negotiation stage is even more applicable.

In summary, by converting the arbitration process into a high-stakes gamble, Bonus FOA has the potential to draw closer together two parties that may not be motivated by internal bonuses. However, it may render more difficult the task of convincing the disputants to accept Bonus FOA in the first place, especially if they are risk-averse.

3.7. Combined Arbitration

A combination of Conventional Arbitration and FOA, called *Combined Arbitration,* has a remarkable property under certain plausible conditions: it induces both sides, in order to maximize their expected payoffs, to choose the median of the arbitrator's probability distribution (Brams and Merrill 1986, Brams 1986). Combined Arbitration's advantage over FOA and Bonus FOA is that it leads to complete convergence; its advantage over Conventional Arbitration is that the two sides, not the arbitrator, make the choice, at least in theory.

This hybrid procedure works as follows (one emendation will be made later to allow for a penultimate stage before the rules take effect):

1. The rules of FOA apply if the arbitrator's choice of a fair settlement falls *between* the two final offers. If they converge or crisscross (i.e., the minimizer's [A's] is greater or equal to the maximizer's [B's]), the converged-upon offer, or the offer closer to the arbitrator's position in the overlap region—as under FOA—is chosen.

2. The rules of Conventional Arbitration apply if the arbitrator's choice of a settlement falls *outside* the two final offers, unless they converge or crisscross, as noted in Rule 1 above. Thus, when the arbitrator's choice is either higher or lower than both final offers, it is chosen and binding on the two sides.

These rules are illustrated in Figure 3.3 for a hypothetical probability distribution of the arbitrator's choice of a fair settlement. The final offers of the two parties, on each side of the median, are shown.

Figure 3.3. Use of Conventional Arbitration and FOA under Combined Arbitration

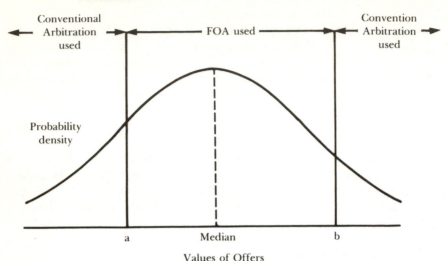

Values of Offers

It is Rule 2 of Combined Arbitration that is most controversial, because it leads to a settlement more extreme than the final offers of either side.[6] I shall now justify informally this aspect of Combined Arbitration.

The reason that FOA proved insufficient to induce the two sides to converge is that, by departing from the arbitrator's median (up to a point), each player on the average received more "value" than it lost in "probability"—from being closer to the arbitrator—in its expected-value calculation. Although Bonus FOA ameliorates this problem, an external bonus is not sufficient to induce absolute convergence, though internal bonuses under FOA can, if they are sufficiently large, close the gap.

Combined Arbitration offers a different kind of incentive to converge. Because of Rule 2, each side is "protected," in a strange way, should the arbitrator's choice be more extreme than its own final offer. For when the side favored by the arbitrator makes a (more reasonable) compromise final offer—closer to the opponent's than the arbitrator's position is—it is, paradoxically, the arbitrator's position that will prevail because of Rule 2.

The protection offered to each player by Rule 2—though it would seem to lead to more extreme settlements on occasion—is sufficiently great that the two sides will always be motivated to converge to the arbitrator's median, provided that the arbitrator's probability distribution is continuous, unimodal, and symmetric about the median. In this seem-

Figure 3.4. Final offers of *A(a)* and *B(b)* for triangular distribution

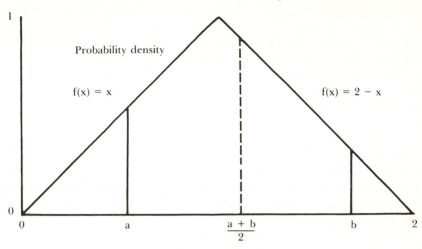

ingly probable situation, therefore, the threat of Conventional Arbitration implicit under Combined Arbitration *obviates the need ever to use it—* again, at least in theory.

Whereas the uniform distribution is continuous and symmetric, it is not unimodal. Another simple density function—that for a triangular distribution, where $f(x) = x$ for $0 \leq x \leq 1$ and $f(x) = 2 - x$ for $1 < x \leq 2$—is unimodal and illustrated in Figure 3.4.

For this distribution, it is not difficult to show that any deviation by either player from the median strategy choice of $a = b = 1$ is nonoptimal, making the median a saddlepoint. By contrast, in the case of the earlier uniform distribution (Figure 3.1), the expected payoff to the players is the same whatever their choices of a and b, so they have no incentive to converge to the median of $a = b = \frac{1}{2}$ in Figure 3.1. If, however, the uniform distribution were slightly perturbed so as to make the arbitrator's probability of choosing the median slightly greater than that of making nonmedian choices, then this perturbed distribution *would* motivate both A and B to make $\frac{1}{2}$ their final offers, leading to their convergence at the median.

If A and B have different unimodal densities f_A and f_B over the arbitrator's notion of a fair settlement—with, say, the median of f_A to the left of the median of f_B—then obviously they will not converge to a common median because there is none. On the other hand, if they are aware of their differences and use this information to construct an "average" density, and if the different densities are close enough so as to make the average density also unimodal, then A and B will converge to the median of the average density.

If the different densities are separated by more than a "critical distance" (Brams and Merrill 1986), however, the average density will not be unimodal and, consequently, A and B will not converge. Thus, the parties' perceptions about where the arbitrator stands cannot be too discrepant. Put another way, the parties will find a settlement if *their* views of the *arbitrator's* views of what is fair are sufficiently congruent.

I see nothing sinister or prejudicial about using the parties' perceptions of the arbitrator's views to help them align their offers, given that the arbitrator's views are based on a reasonably objective reading of the facts of a case and, in addition, are viewed by the parties as helpful in guiding them to a settlement. Although the parties' own arguments and evidence help to determine the "facts," the arbitrator's impartiality is supported by empirical studies (Ashenfelter and Bloom 1984; Farber and Bazerman 1986). Moreover, it is reinforced in particular situations by giving the parties some voice in the selection of an arbitrator, most often by allowing them to eliminate unacceptable candidates from a list.

Under Combined Arbitration, unlike FOA and Bonus FOA, the arbitrator not only offers guidance or orientation but may also select the settlement. Ideally, of course, this person will not have to impose a settlement, or even choose between final offers, because the parties will be motivated to converge on their own. In practice, however, independent convergence by the parties, even if they share the same basic perception of the arbitrator's distribution, may be too much to ask for or even expect.

Accordingly, Brams and Merrill (1986) proposed that, unlike FOA (as used today)—under which an arbitrator makes his or her decision after receiving the two final offers—the arbitrator under Combined Arbitration indicates his or her preferred settlement at the same time that the two sides submit their final offers. Especially when the arbitrator's proposed settlement is not between the two final offers, and therefore is the one to be implemented, it would be more difficult to challenge the arbitrator's integrity if his or her proposed settlement were submitted in a way independently of the two final offers.

The point, of course, in allowing the proposal of the arbitrator to be implemented, under certain conditions, is to induce the two sides to come together on their own. But if they do not, the two sides' final offers would be made public before the arbitrator's judgment is revealed. If they converge or crisscross, there is no problem; if not, then the two sides would be given an opportunity to negotiate with each other and, if possible, come to an agreement on their own. Only if they were unable to work out a settlement in such a penultimate stage would Combined Arbitration be implemented.

Given the strong convergence properties of this procedure, it seems likely that the two sides will normally be sufficiently close that they can forge their own settlement. This will be especially true if each side fears that the arbitrator's judgment may fall outside the final offers and, in addition, is as likely to favor its adversary as itself. If this turned out to be the case, then the side not favored by the arbitrator would, paradoxically, do even worse than if it had accepted the *other* side's final offer before the arbitrator's judgment was revealed.

Such a resolution, after the fact, would be hard for a party to justify to its supporters, particularly if it had been adamant in the negotiations preceding revelation of the arbitrator's judgment. For this reason, I believe, the two sides will very much be in a negotiating mood before they are ready to submit to the possible imposition of a settlement by the arbitrator.

Clearly, the threats implicit under Combined Arbitration, even more than under FOA or Bonus FOA, are what motivate the two sides to come together initially, or at least be willing to negotiate their differences before the arbitrator's judgment is revealed. The pressure on the two sides is greater under Combined Arbitration than FOA or Bonus FOA because the settlement can be more extreme than the final offers, which is never the case under the latter procedures.

It is worth repeating that Combined Arbitration has, as suggested here, a penultimate stage that FOA does not. By giving the parties a "second chance" to settle their differences—after their final offers are made public but before the arbitrator's judgment is revealed—compromises will be encouraged. The inducement to compromise, however, is not simply a product of appeals to fairness, which often go unattended, but the significant risk of being hurt by an imposed settlement of the arbitrator.

Despite the appealing convergence property of Combined Arbitration, it has, arguably, two shortcomings: (1) it allows for the possibility of an imposed settlement, as under Conventional Arbitration (even though in theory this should never happen if the conditions of the model are met); and (2) convergence is to the median of the arbitrator's distribution. Although the median coincides with the arbitrator's expected settlement over a long series of trials (because the median is the mean for a symmetric distribution), the median/mean will not in general be the arbitrator's preferred settlement in any particular instance.

I shall next consider a fourth arbitration procedure—actually, a class of procedures—that avoids the imposition of the arbitrator's preferred settlement but instead moves the parties toward the arbitrator's own position in stages. This position will not necessarily be the median, as under Combined Arbitration; but neither is it likely to be a relatively extreme offer, as under FOA, unless the arbitrator is extreme.

3.8. Two-Stage and Multistage FOA

I have shown that Combined Arbitration may create incentives for its *non*use either before offers are made or after they are made but before the arbitrator's choice is revealed. Under *Two-Stage FOA* (Brams, Kilgour, and Weber 1989), the arbitrator's preferred settlement is "felt," as under FOA and Bonus FOA, but it never prevails, as can happen under Combined Arbitration. Indeed, the purpose of introducing additional stages in FOA is to give feedback to the players about the position of the arbitrator and to allow them to make appropriate adjustments in their offers.

In reading the rules of Two-Stage FOA, it will be helpful to refer to the following first-stage and second-stage strategies of the players (and averages):

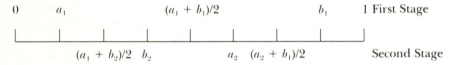

The rules are as follows:

1. All offers are public, but the arbitrator's choice is private.

2. A and B make simultaneous initial offers, a_1 and b_1, respectively. If they crisscross, the settlement is the average, $(a_1 + b_1)/2$. Otherwise, the winner (say, A) is the player whose offer is closer to the arbitrator's position, x (not shown); his or her offer (a_1) is made public.

3. The loser (B) is then permitted a second chance. If B's second offer (b_2) is still farther from x than A's initial offer (a_1), a_1 is the settlement.

4. If b_2 is closer to x than a_1, then the settlement is $(a_1 + b_2)/2$—or the average of A's winning *first* offer and B's winning *second* offer—unless b_2 "overshoots" x.

5. If b_2 overshoots x, b_2 and a_1 are both to the left of x. In this case, the offer closer to x becomes the settlement. In fact, this will always be b_2, because B will never have an incentive to overshoot a_1—this could only lower B's expected payoff.

6. If B is the initial winner, the settlement will be either b_1 (if B wins

again in the second stage), $(a_2 + b_1)/2$ (if A wins in the second stage and does not overshoot x), or a_2 (if A overshoots x in the second stage).

7. If the players are equidistant from x at either stage, the settlement is the average of the players' offers at this point.

I shall later discuss an extension of Two-Stage FOA that does not necessarily terminate in two stages; indeed, it continues as long as there is a new winner at each successive stage. The rationale of stopping at two stages is not only that limiting the procedure to two stages makes it quite simple but, in addition, it *seems* fair: if the initial winner (say, A) does not prevail at the second stage, B's second offer, if winning, is diminished by its being averaged with A's first offer—unless B is so accommodating as, by overshooting x, to offer more than the arbitrator thinks fair.

These rules, it would appear at first blush, would give both players an incentive to be competitive at the first stage. Thereby they increase their chances of winning initially and, possibly, subsequently without having to compromise. But if they give away too much trying to win initially, they may squander their payoffs, whether they (1) win again at the second stage, (2) are forced to average, or (3) lose by drawing their adversary to their side of the arbitrator.

Given this subtle mix of incentives, what are the optimal strategies of the players? For the uniform distribution, A should begin by selecting $a_1 = 0$ and B $b_1 = 1$. Assume B is the initial winner. Then A knows that x is somewhere to the right of $\frac{1}{2}$. His or her second-stage optimal strategy is to select $a_2 = \frac{2}{3}$. By the same token, if A is the initial winner, B's optimal second-stage strategy is to select $b_2 = \frac{1}{3}$. Thus it is easy to show that there are six possible outcomes, each of which occurs with the probability of $\frac{1}{6}$: 0, $\frac{1}{6}$, $\frac{1}{3}$, $\frac{2}{3}$, $\frac{5}{6}$, and 1.

For example, if x is between $\frac{1}{6}$ and $\frac{1}{3}$, which will occur with probability $\frac{1}{6}$, A will win initially by selecting $a_1 = 0$ when B selects $b_1 = 1$. At the second stage, when B selects $b_2 = \frac{1}{3}$, B will become the new winner, so the settlement will be the average of these offers, or $\frac{1}{6}$.

If, after winning at the first stage, A or B had the opportunity to deviate from $a_1 = 0$ or $b_1 = 1$, respectively—rather than simply stand pat in response to the other player's second-stage strategy—then it can be shown that neither player would do so: these first-stage strategies remain optimal at the second stage for the initial winner. Thus, Rule 2 of Two-Stage FOA, which permits only the initial loser a second chance, in no way constrains the optimal behavior of the initial winner in the second stage. In fact, the stand-pat strategy of the initial winner, and the strategy of the initial loser to move $\frac{2}{3}$ of the distance toward the winner, constitute optimal strategies for the players in this two-stage game.

Plainly, Two-Stage FOA moderates the all-or-nothing impact of FOA.

In the uniform case, only 33 percent of the time will the settlement be 0 or 1 when the players select their optimal strategies; 67 percent of the time the settlement will be a less extreme ⅙ or ⅚, or a still-more-centrist ⅓ or ⅔, depending on the position of the arbitrator as revealed in the first stage. Indeed, Two-Stage FOA ensures in the uniform case that the settlement will be a distance of no more than ⅙ from the arbitrator's position.

In effect, Two-Stage FOA is a procedure that induces the two sides to home in on the arbitrator's position without imposing it; the parties' choices in the end determine the settlement. This procedure not only alleviates the harshness of extreme—and possibly unfair, at least as viewed by the loser—settlements under FOA and Bonus FOA but also induces near-convergence of strategies, comparable to that of Bonus FOA.

Unlike Bonus FOA, however, this is not necessarily convergence close to the median. Unlike Combined Arbitration, it is not convergence to the median itself (at ½ if the distribution is unimodal and symmetric about ½). Instead, there is *near-convergence to the position of the arbitrator*. Thus, if the arbitrator is relatively extreme, this fact will be mirrored in the settlement under Two-Stage FOA, whereas it will not be under the other procedures. In effect, the arbitrator is able to influence the outcome, but this influence is indirect: his or her choice of a settlement can never be imposed, as under Combined or Conventional Arbitration.

To illustrate Two-Stage FOA, consider how it might work in major league baseball, where T = team (assumed to have a female owner), P = player (assumed to be male), and A = arbitrator (for balance, here we leave open the question of gender):

1. T proposes a salary of $1M and P proposes $1.3M; both offers are made public. A thinks $1.1M is fair, but this choice is not announced. (It may be recorded for later reference so as to be able to check, after the arbitration, that A made choices consistent with his or her judgment about what is fair.)

2. A selects T as the *initial winner* because she is closer to A's ideal of $1.1M than P is.

3. P gets a second chance, after being told that T is the initial winner. Knowing that A's ideal must be between $1M and $1.15M (because T's $1M is closer to A's ideal than P's $1.3M), P makes a counteroffer of $1.15M, which is made public.

4. P becomes the *new winner* because his counteroffer of $1.15M is now closer to A's ideal of $1.1M than is T's winning original offer of $1M. The settlement under Two-Stage FOA is the average of the initial and new winning offers: ($1M + $1.15M)/2 = $1.075M.

Note that P's counteroffer in (3) is not optimal if A's distribution is uniform between \$1M and \$1.3M. Instead, P should have responded with an offer of \$1.1M, ⅔ of the distance from his initial offer, which is exactly A's ideal point. Then the settlement would have been \$1.05M, so P, anomalously, would have done worse by behaving "optimally."

The rub is that optimality, as I have used the term, is determined by expected payoffs, based on probabilistic assumptions about the behavior of the arbitrator. Hence, only "on the average" will an optimal strategy be better; in any single play of a game, a deviation from such a strategy may yield a player a higher payoff.

I shall return to this example later, but next I ask: Why limit sequential FOA to just two stages? Why not allow FOA to proceed indefinitely, with the loser at any stage replacing the winner at the next stage—if he or she is closer to, but does not overshoot, the arbitrator—until one side wins twice in a row? This procedure, proposed by Neale and Bazerman (1987) and labeled "progressive approximation" FOA, is what Brams, Kilgour, and Weber (1989) call *Multistage FOA* to distinguish it from Two-Stage FOA. (They also analyze multistage procedures intermediate between these two.) At first glance, it would appear likely to bring the players closer to the position of the arbitrator than Two-Stage FOA and, additionally, eliminate the need for averaging at the second stage.

With no fixed number of stages under Multistage FOA, I assume that there are two ways in which play can terminate:

- If one player overshoots the arbitrator, the player who overshoots will be closer to the arbitrator and have his or her offer chosen as the settlement—except at the first stage if the players crisscross, in which case their offers will be averaged;

- If one player wins twice in a row, this two-time winner, who stood pat after winning initially, will have his or her offer chosen as the settlement.

Although this game has no *definite* termination point, Brams, Kilgour, and Weber (1989) show that by making a certain symmetry assumption, it is not difficult to calculate the optimal strategies of players in the uniform case.

On round 1, A and B will choose the endpoints of the unit interval, $a_1 = 0$ and $b_1 = 1$, as under FOA and Two-Stage FOA. If B wins on the first round, the *current interval*—where the arbitrator must lie at that stage—is $(.5, 1)$, and A offers $a_2 \approx .586$. If A wins on the second round, the current interval is $(.586, .793)$, and B offers $b_3 \approx .758$. If B wins on the third round, the current interval is $(.672, .758)$, and A offers $a_4 \approx .686$. If A wins on the fourth round, the current interval is $(.686, .723)$, and B

offers $b_5 \approx .716$. And so the current interval is quickly narrowed, with the two offers approaching each other.

If the arbitrator's position is $x = 1/\sqrt{2} \approx .707$, the process continues indefinitely and approaches this value in the limit, making it the *point of convergence* if B wins initially. If A wins initially, the point of convergence is $1 - 1/\sqrt{2} \approx .293$.

As play continues under Multistage FOA, the length of the current interval after $k \geq 3$ rounds is reduced by a factor of approximately $(.4142)^{k-2}$ relative to the first round. We require $k \geq 3$ because, on Round 1, the players make their simultaneous offers. On Round 2, the loser responds with a revised offer, at which point there is a better than even chance (.5858) that the initial loser will overshoot x, or that the initial winner will be closer to x; the game will terminate in either case. Hence, only as of Round 3 does the question of whether the game terminated earlier arise.

The reduction in the length of the interval also defines the probability that the game continues at least $k \geq 3$ rounds. It is not difficult to show that the probability that the game lasts at least k rounds is approximately

$k =$	3	4	5	6	7	8	12
Prob. =	.4142	.1718	.0711	.0294	.0122	.00505	.00015

Thus, with probability .4142 the game continues to Round 3. Then there is only about one chance in 200 that the game goes to Round 8, and one chance in 7,500 that the game reaches Round 12.

Patently, when the players make optimal choices, they have little to fear that the game will be interminable, or even continue very long. The points of convergence, where play would go on forever if they were the arbitrator's position, are a theoretical curiosity, not a practical reality. Closer to reality, in a series of experiments that approximate Multistage FOA, Neal and Bazerman (1987) found that the disputants did tend to move toward each other and reach a settlement more often than under FOA.

They also validated experimentally that players tend to start from extreme positions. Thus, Multistage FOA does not deprive the parties in a dispute of the opportunity to do some initial posturing—in fact, it makes it optimal—which may be good for public relations purposes. Thereby the parties can demonstrate to their supporters that they will make stiff demands of an adversary, backing off only when compelled to do so by the arbitrator.

To return to the baseball example, I pick up the action after T's initial winning offer of \$1M and P's counteroffer of \$1.15M, which yielded a settlement of \$1.075M under Two-Stage FOA. Under Multistage FOA, it would still be true that

4. *P* becomes the *new winner* because his counteroffer of $1.15M is now closer to *A*'s ideal of $1.1M than is *T*'s winning original offer of $1M.

But instead of there being a settlement on this round, as under Two-Stage FOA, under Multistage FOA *T* would now have an opportunity to make her own counteroffer—knowing that *P* won (temporarily) with his counteroffer of $1.15M—and the process might unfold as follows:

5. *T* makes a counteroffer of $1.06M, which is closer to *A*'s $1.1M than *P*'s $1.15M, so *T* becomes the new winner.

6. *P* responds with a new counteroffer of $1.12M, which is closer to *A*'s $1.1M than *T*'s $1.06M.

7. *T* responds with a new counteroffer of $1.07M, which is *not* closer to *A*'s $1.1M than *P*'s $1.12M. Hence, *P*'s $1.12M becomes the settlement because he won twice in a row.

By comparison with the settlement under Two-Stage FOA ($1.075M), the settlement of $1.12M under Multistage FOA is slightly closer to *A*'s ideal of $1.1M in this hypothetical example.

The degree of convergence of Multistage FOA will depend on the number of rounds before one player loses twice in a row. The longer play continues, the closer on average the players will be to the arbitrator, as the optimality calculations carried to five rounds that we gave earlier illustrated. Thus, in the fifth round, the current interval is (.686, .716); if *A* becomes the two-time winner in this round because his or her offer of .686 is closer to the arbitrator's than *B*'s, *B* can be a distance of at most $.716 - .686 = .030$ from the arbitrator, which is only three percent of the original interval.

3.9. Is Convergence in Stages Desirable?

The question I raise in this section would seem to have an obvious answer: insofar as the arbitrator is capable of choosing a fair settlement, convergence to this settlement seems unobjectionable. But then, one might ask, why not use Conventional Arbitration? This kind of arbitration would absolutely eliminate any discrepancy between the settlement and the arbitrator's position.

The apparent reason for using FOA or a variant is that it induces the players to converge on their own. Consequently, the settlement is not imposed, although the players' convergence—or lack thereof—is very much driven by the position of the arbitrator.

If convergence means forcing two parties to accept a settlement contrary to their interests, it would not seem to be a laudable goal. However, when the lack of a settlement in, say, a public-employee strike jeopardizes public health or safety, one might reasonably argue that public consequences should take precedence and arbitration be able to override any impasse in the negotiations.

In private disputes, if two parties (1) can mutually benefit from a settlement but (2) cannot reach it by bargaining on their own—at least, not in a speedy fashion—then an arbitrated settlement has evident appeal. This is so even when the parties' interests are diametrically opposed, because it saves them the costs of a continuing impasse.

It would seem preferable, nevertheless, that the parties reach an agreement on their own, even if driven to do so by an arbitration procedure, than have an arbitrator impose it on them. Judging from the high number of agreements reached in major league baseball without resorting to FOA, the threat of implementing FOA seems to foster negotiated settlements.

Compared with FOA, which induces no convergence at all in the uniform case, the settlement under the sequential procedures I have examined (Two-Stage and Multistage FOA) are certainly less likely to be one-sided. Thus, for example, Two-Stage FOA leads to a nonextreme settlement (i.e., not at 0 or 1) with probability .67, more than any other sequential procedure (Brams, Kilgour, and Weber 1989). By comparison, Multistage FOA leads to a nonextreme settlement with probability .59.

These results for the sequential procedures assume that the preferred settlement of the arbitrator is uniformly distributed between 0 and 1. However, this equiprobability assumption may not be descriptive of many arbitration situations, wherein the arbitrator is more likely to take a centrist than an extremist position. A unimodal distribution, with the mode (peak) at or near the mean or median, draws the players toward the center under FOA (Brams and Merrill 1983), and probably more quickly under multistage extensions, than does the uniform distribution.

Which sequential procedure is best? To force a quick resolution and avoid what might be an unduly long process, I would recommend Two-Stage FOA. Moreover, because a settlement in the uniform case is equally likely at $\frac{1}{6}$ intervals between 0 and 1— except at the midpoint of $\frac{3}{6} = \frac{1}{2}$—Two-Stage FOA is not biased against outcomes anywhere on the unit interval, except near $\frac{1}{2}$.

Outcomes under Multistage FOA are not equiprobable across the unit interval; the endpoints, 0 and 1, are most favored and have probabilities of about .21 each. On the other hand, Multistage FOA better replicates the give-and-take of bargaining and, if the process lasts more than a very few rounds, will bring the players extremely close to the arbitrator (and to each other).

These are the trade-offs that need to be considered in selecting a sequential arbitration procedure. Whereas a sequential procedure provides one possible way to reduce the likelihood of an extreme settlement, it should be remembered that the very lack of a procedural incentive to compromise (under FOA or Bonus FOA) may encourage the players to bargain on their own, without resorting to arbitration, to reach a settlement. Insofar as they do, FOA and Bonus FOA can be said to have a desirable effect.

If Two-Stage FOA is simpler than Multistage FOA, the saving grace of the latter procedure is that, after two rounds, it permits greater learning of, and movement toward, the position of the arbitrator. This feature, along with its approximation of the give-and-take of bargaining (without an arbitrator), may be beneficial in many disputes.

Indeed, Multistage FOA seems to be implicitly the procedure "mediators with muscle" (Straus 1981, 261–62) follow, just as I showed earlier how disputes over treaty interpretation may mirror different arbitration procedures. But instead of the arbitrator's assuming a fixed position, he or she may, along with the disputants, become somewhat of a moving target in the search for a compromise settlement. This process is known as "med-arb," wherein the mediator arbitrates a settlement only if mediation fails (Kochan 1981, 133).

3.10. Kissinger's Shuttle Diplomacy: A Case of Multistage Negotiations

A person who seemed both a mediator and an arbitrator—insofar as he was able to draw the disputants toward his position, even if he could not impose a solution on them—was U.S. Secretary of State Henry Kissinger in his role as bridge-builder between Israel and the Arab countries after the October 1973 Yom Kippur War. Different facets of his role have been explored in the several contributions to Rubin (1981), on which, along with other sources, I rely. Here I emphasize how Kissinger acted as a magnet, like the arbitrator under Multistage FOA, drawing the different sides together.

Kissinger's overarching goal in the Middle East was to enhance United States influence by excluding the Soviet Union (Fischer 1981, 96–97). More immediately, he sought to avoid another war by effecting a separation and withdrawal of forces after the war, principally between Israel on the one hand and Egypt and Syria on the other. To achieve this goal, Kissinger practiced shuttle diplomacy not only between these countries but also with several others, notably Saudi Arabia, whose oil wealth gave it considerable leverage over Israel's main Arab antagonists. His efforts, which lasted nearly two years (from October 1973 to August 1975), took him on over a dozen major missions, covered more than 300,000 miles, involved thousands of hours of negotiations, and resulted in two disengagement agreements between Israel and Egypt and an interim political settlement between Israel and Syria.

I cannot retrace the step-by-step movement toward settlement on each of these agreements, but the following features of the extended negotiations indicate that Kissinger assumed many of the trappings of an arbitrator:

- He had strong views about procedures, favoring a step-by-step approach to negotiations that sustained momentum. In Kissinger's words, "What's important is the process itself—to keep negotiations going, to prevent them from freezing" (Sheehan 1981, 73)—and he manipulated the process toward this end. In December 1973, for example, Kissinger advised against promulgating Israeli Defense Minister Moshe Dayan's proposal to disengage immediately in the Mitla and Giddi passes—in exchange for an Egyptian commitment to reopen the Suez Canal—so that Israel could better maintain an appearance of strength. The rationale, according to Quandt (1977, 221), was for "the Arabs to see that it was difficult for the United States to influence Israel, otherwise their expectations would soar." Likewise, in May 1974, Israeli leaders discussed with Kissinger a number of concessions they would be willing to make to Syrian president Hafez Assad on disengagement in the Golan Heights. Kissinger disclosed some of these concessions to Assad but withheld others for future trips in order "to avoid whetting Assad's already substantial appetite for Israeli concessions, while at the same time being able to show continued progress" (Quandt 1977, 241).

- Kissinger structured the substance of the interchange between the parties, primarily by pursuing "a series of relatively workable bilateral disengagements . . . by deferring the more difficult problems for a later time" (Rubin 1981, 30). On occasion, he would even present "proposals of each side as if they were his own, thereby making compromises more palatable" (Hopmann and Druckman 1981, 215).

- Timing was important. Kissinger once told a friend: "I never treat crises when they're cold, only when they're hot. This enables me to weigh the protagonists one against the other, not in terms of ten or two thousand years ago but in terms of what each of them merits at this moment" (Sheehan 1981, 46). He also said, "Stalemate is the most propitious condition for settlement" (*New York Times*, October 12, 1974). In applying these principles, Kissinger often spoke of the dire consequences of failure to follow his counsel (Zartman 1981, 156). For example, he said to the Israelis in March 1975, "It's tragic to see people dooming themselves to a course of unbelievable peril."

Sheehan (1976, 79) reports that Prime Minister Yitzhak Rabin's wry reply was: "This is the day you visited Masada."

- Kissinger's personality and style made him more than a neutral go-between: "no . . . secretary of state had displayed such warmth" (Sheehan 1981, 50), and this personal charm facilitated agreements. Kissinger's bargaining was laced with humor, often self-deprecating (Pruitt 1981, 141–42), which he used to defuse the disputants' anger. But he was also "a highly directive and aggressive mediator" (Kochan 1981, 131), continually trying to move negotiations forward.

- Kissinger was not averse to using threats and sanctions to try to push the disputants toward a resolution. For example, in May 1974 he twice threatened Assad that he would suspend negotiations and return to Washington unless Syria changed its position on disengagement (Touval 1982, 256). In the spring of 1975, there was a "reassessment" of U.S. policy toward Israel, accompanied by delays in the delivery of promised military supplies, following Israel's failure to be as forthcoming as Kissinger desired in the second set of disengagement talks with Egypt (Touval 1982, 263–64). Promises of economic and military aid were also made to various parties (Hopmann and Druckman 1981, 216–17) to maintain momentum.

While granting Kissinger's prodigious intelligence and powers of persuasion as a mediator, my contention is that he transcended this role by significantly influencing the negotiation procedure used, the nature of the agreements pursued, the timing and sequencing of concessions, and the devices used to wring these out of the disputants and turn them into an agreement. In a sense, these qualities made Kissinger more than an arbitrator, but he was also less because he could not make an agreement binding on the parties without their consent.

He was, in short, a bargainer himself, not impartial, driven to orchestrate an agreement using whatever tactics seemed effective. Yet he was not a full-fledged partisan, which can be ruinous for a mediator (Touval and Zartman 1985), but rather somebody the disputants thought they could use to their own advantage (Touval 1982).

This role resembles that of the arbitrator under Multistage FOA, at least insofar as it induces give-and-take between the disputants. But there are two major qualifications. The first is that as the parties moved toward the agreements that Kissinger himself helped to fashion, they were drawn to each other less by a fear of losing twice in a row and more by a fear that Kissinger (and the United States) would abandon the mediation process, leaving them stuck in impasse. Second, Kissinger's position was not fixed from the start. Rather, he was able continually to adjust the center of gravity of the negotiations in response to the concessions made, and those likely to be made, to engineer an agreement. As he put it: "We have no peace plan of our own. It's easy to make specific proposals—the important thing is to take practical steps" (Sheehan 1981, 61).

Probably the closest fit of the empirical situation to the arbitration models is the assumption that the disputants' beliefs can be construed as a probability distribution over Kissinger's position. Continually being adjusted, this position became very elusive in their eyes.

This "application" of an arbitration procedure may strike the reader as more a metaphor than a model to explain why Kissinger succeeded—to the extent that he did—in the so-called med-arb (I would add bargaining, too, or med-arb-bar) process. While I would not disagree, I think one value of linking a real-life case to an abstract model is to show what effective arbitration might entail.

In the case of hammering out the disengagement agreements, the process required protracted and sensitive negotiations with constant feedback. This example suggests the need for sequential procedures, which home in on the mediator-arbitrator-bargainer's (possibly changing) position. Furthermore, to secure agreements on complex and difficult issues may take considerable time and energy as well as careful calculation.

A procedure that allows for this—and, in the process, learning something about the other side—may be necessary in many negotiations. Two-stage FOA and Multistage FOA represent stylized versions of such procedures and, therefore, may benefit negotiators who are unwilling or unprepared to make single final offers without the opportunity of feedback and constant revision.

3.11. Conclusions

If a compulsion to agree is built into a procedure, what should the point of agreement be? With the exception of Conventional Arbitration, all the procedures I have discussed force the parties to make some compromises, lest thay be hurt by demanding too much. Conventional Arbitration is the exception because it provides, as I showed, a negative rather than a positive bonus to compromise. Insofar as the arbitrator is likely to split the difference, the disputants will make outrageous demands, leading to divergence rather than convergence.

Among the remaining procedures, FOA is the least satisfactory in inducing convergence, unless the parties derive internal bonuses from winning independent of the value of the settlement itself. But if only one party derives an internal bonus from winning, and both parties are aware of it, the party receiving the bonus is hurt in the settlement because its greater receptivity to compromise induces its adversary to toughen its stance and concede less.

The upshot is that the more compromising party, while enhancing its chances of having its offer selected under FOA, does so at the expense of lowering its expected payoff when the parties choose their equilibrium strategies. As seen in the police arbitration disputes in New Jersey, the unions were the exploited party, getting an average of eight percent less in pay increases than they might have achieved with less conservative final offers, even though they won most of the settlements under FOA. By contrast, in major league baseball the teams have won more FOA cases than the players, but I suggested that this is because the players represent only themselves and do not have to worry, like labor leaders, about satisfying constituents. I also showed how disputes over treaty interpretation may make implicit use of FOA and other arbitration procedures.

Externalizing the internal bonuses under FOA defines a new procedure (Bonus FOA). Because the settlement price under Bonus FOA includes the gap between the final offers, which is paid by the loser to the winner, the stakes for the parties are raised. With the costs of losing significantly greater, the two sides are motivated to narrow their FOA final offers by a factor of ⅔.

All these results are based on the assumption that the players' uncertainty about the arbitrator's position can be characterized by a probability distribution, which was illustrated by the uniform distribution between 0 and 1 in most of the calculations. This distribution reflects the equal likelihood of all arbitrator choices in this interval; in the case of FOA, the equilibrium final offers are 0 and 1, whereas they are ⅓ and ⅔ under Bonus FOA.

The possible settlements under Bonus FOA—as opposed to offers—remain the same as under FOA, namely 0 and 1. Thus, while forcing the players to make significant compromises in their final offers, Bonus FOA in no way alters the extreme settlements that occur under FOA. The considerable convergence in final offers, however, may give the parties an impetus to bridge the remaining gap separating them, especially if they are allowed to negotiate their differences before the judgment of the arbitrator is revealed and thereby prevent one or the other of the final offers from being implemented.

Such a penultimate stage makes even more sense under Combined Arbitration, wherein convergence is absolute if the distribution is symmetric and unimodal (illustrated by a triangular distribution in the calculations). Even if convergence does not occur under Combined Arbitration, the distance separating the two parties is likely to be small, because each party is protected by an increasing probability that the arbitrator's choice will favor it as it moves toward the center. By virtue of being the arbitrator's choice, however, its imposition smacks of Conventional Arbitration.

Yet recall that it is precisely the possibility of such an outcome under Combined Arbitration that is supposed to rule out its actual occurrence. In practice, to be sure, convergence may not result. Nevertheless, it seems quite likely that a settlement will be negotiated by the two parties in the penultimate period provided them—if only to wrap up an agreement on their own rather than have one of the final offers, or perhaps the arbitrator's judgment, imposed.

Despite Combined Arbitration's strong convergence properties, one may question whether convergence to the median of the arbitrator's putative distribution is what should be encouraged by an arbitration procedure. After all, the arbitrator will typically not be at the median, or even very close to it, unless the distribution is strongly unimodal. Moreover, if the arbitrator's judgment epitomizes a fair settlement—as attested to by his or her selection by both parties—a case can be made that the arbitrator's position, not the median, is the proper point of convergence.

Unlike Combined Arbitration, Two-Stage and Multistage FOA encourage near-convergence to the arbitrator's position. Although Two-Stage FOA is simpler, Multistage FOA better simulates the round-by-round concessions that two parties might make in bargaining. This was illustrated by Kissinger's shuttle diplomacy, although his role as a combination mediator-arbitrator-bargainer deviated in major respects from that of the arbitrator in Multistage FOA. Compared with FOA and Bonus FOA, settlements far removed from the arbitrator's choice are eliminated under the sequential procedures, but some divergence is still possible, especially when the arbitrator's position is extreme.

Given that some kind of convergence benefits both parties, the issue in choosing an arbitration procedure boils down to what kind of convergence is most desirable. If it is convergence to what the two parties see as the center of the arbitrator's distribution (i.e., his or her median position), then Combined Arbitration seems best equipped to move them there. If it is convergence to what the arbitrator considers fair, then Two-Stage or Multistage FOA tends to move them toward that point, even if it is a position different from the median of the arbitrator's distribution (as the players perceive it).

One's faith in the perceived median as a compromise, versus one's faith in the arbitrator's judgment, will be the determinant of whether one regards Combined Arbitration, or either Two-Stage or Multistage FOA, as the better arbitration procedure(s) for settling disputes. The choice between these alternatives may be summarized in the following fashion:

- Combined Arbitration, more than any other procedure, compels the parties themselves to bargain, possibly in a penultimate stage; the arbitrator's distribution provides them with an orientation, and its median becomes a focal point for agreement.

- Two-stage and Multistage FOA, more than any other procedures, tend to draw the parties toward the arbitrator in successive stages, but never at the cost of imposing the arbitrator's judgment upon them (as can occur under Combined Arbitration if the parties fail to converge).

These are the two sets of procedures I find most attractive in fostering convergence. But I leave unresolved which is more equitable because this determination rests on a normative judgment about what kind of convergence—to the median or the arbitrator's position—one seeks to foster. A case can be made, I think, for each kind.

At the same time, I stress, FOA and Bonus FOA have certain advantages. The fact that both may lead to extreme settlements tends to encourage serious bargaining and negotiated settlements before they are used, as has been the case with FOA in major league baseball. But when negotiated settlements are harder to reach, as has been true in public-employee disputes, the procedures with more convergence-inducing properties deserve to be considered.

They are, to be sure, untried, but their attractive theoretical properties commend them for experimentation, especially in situations in which Conventional Arbitration or FOA are no longer viewed as last resorts. When even FOA fails to stimulate serious bargaining and becomes regularly invoked, arbitration procedures like Combined Arbitration and Two-Stage and Multistage FOA seem called for to promote convergence.

Notes

[1] This chapter is adapted from Brahms, Kilgour, and Merrill (1990), which will appear in Young (1991).

[2] See, for example, Farber (1980); Chatterjee (1981); Crawford (1982); Brams and Merrill (1983, 1986); and Wittman (1986). For a model of both conventional and final-offer arbitration, wherein the arbitrator seeks to maximize his or her expected utility, based on the offers of the two sides and inferences about their private information (e.g., reservation prices), see Gibbons (1988). In modeling FOA, Samuelson (1989) also assumes the players possess private information in a game of incomplete information; McCall (1990) assumes that the union negotiator has information superior to that of the rank and file in a principal-agent model of FOA.

[3] Still other procedures have been proposed but, generally speaking, they have not been formally analyzed. Here, for example, is one procedure that I have not

seen proposed before but which would appear to have some desirable properties: each player submits two final offers; the arbitrator *eliminates* one offer and *chooses* one player, who in turn chooses one of the three remaining offers. Presumably, the arbitrator will eliminate the most "extreme" offer and choose the player who, in the arbitrator's judgment, will select the most reasonable of the remaining offers. (A possible restriction on the arbitrator's choice: he or she must select the player whose offer was eliminated and who, therefore, has only one offer remaining.)

One rationale for this procedure is that players will have an incentive not to make extreme offers, lest one be eliminated. Another rationale is that it will be a player, not the arbitrator, who makes the final choice, though it would be partially determined by the arbitrator. Also, insofar as the players are better informed than the arbitrator, this procedure has the advantage—over those discussed in the text—of putting the selection of a settlement more in the hands of those who may be most knowledgeable about it and who, additionally, will have to live with it. Finally, because arbitrators have less control, less blame can be pinned on them for an unfair settlement, making it more likely they will be employed again.

[4] For the uniform distribution, the solution is a dominant-strategy Nash equilibrium, because both players' strategies associated with this outcome are dominant, or unconditionally best. (This need not be the case for other distributions.) Under the different bonus and penalty procedures discussed in Chapter 2, recall that honesty is also a dominant strategy for both players.

[5] In letting p approach $-\frac{1}{2}$, one gives up the assumption, used to model FOA and Bonus FOA, that the arbitrator's position is instrumental in the determination of a winner and loser. As indicated in the text, there is no winner and loser because both players pay equally for the gap.

[6] Under Rule 2 *alone,* Combined Arbitration is equivalent to the Expansive Appraisal Procedure (Section 2.7), with the arbitrator an appraiser who cannot force settlements when its choice falls between the two final offers. In effect, Rules 1 and 2 *together* turn bargaining into arbitration: the players' offers now directly matter in a constant-sum game, in which there is always a settlement. By comparison, under the Expansive Appraisal Procedure, the players' offers do not directly affect the settlement but instead determine only if there is a settlement (because at least one player overlaps the appraiser). The independence of the players' offers and the settlement under the Expansive Appraisal Procedure is what makes this and the other bargaining procedures honesty-inducing.

Chapter 4
Superpower Crisis Bargaining and the Theory of Moves

4.1. Introduction

In this chapter, I shift the focus somewhat, putting more emphasis on applications. To be sure, the theory in Chapter 2 was supplemented by a discussion of the incentives that pushed Begin and Sadat to accept an agreement at Camp David skillfully engineered by Jimmy Carter. And the predictions of some of the arbitration models of Chapter 3 were compared with data on labor-management settlements.

New theory is introduced in this chapter, in part through two case studies. The first case is the well-known Cuban missile crisis of 1962, the second the less well-known crisis between the superpowers that erupted in 1973. The latter crisis was precipitated by Richard Nixon's decision to put U.S. military forces on worldwide alert in an attempt to forestall Soviet intervention on the side of Egypt, and bring about a cease-fire, in the so-called Yom Kippur War.

Both crises were resolved peacefully, but they generated much tension between the superpowers, especially the 1962 crisis. How the superpowers—or, more accurately, their leaders—managed these crises has been described in great detail, but this scrutiny has involved little in the way of formal and systematic strategic analysis. I hope not only to make strategic choices in these crises perspicuous, using game theory, but also to explore how classical game theory can be revised so as to elucidate the flow of moves by players over time. This revision I call the "theory of moves"; its central concept is that of a "nonmyopic equilibrium," which is a more farsighted and dynamic concept of stability than a Nash equilibrium.

In fact, the founders of game theory recognized that their theory was a static one (von Neumann and Morgenstern 1953, 44–45). By reformulating assumptions of this theory, I shall show how the sequential calculations of players, as they look ahead and try to anticipate consequences of their actions, can be modeled.

101

Much of this chapter, therefore, will be theoretical, though I hope not so large a portion that the modeling of the two crises, and how the two sides successfully negotiated with each other through their words and deeds, will be lost to the reader. An important lesson of such empirical analysis, I believe, is that there is generally no single "correct" view of a situation. In fact, alternative perspectives will be presented on each crisis to illuminate different plausible interpretations.

The theory developed in this chapter differs in fundamental ways from the mostly probabilistic and utility-based theory of the previous two chapters. Although it enables one to analyze more completely the dynamics of ordinal games like those discussed in Chapter 1, at the same time it glosses over expected-payoff calculations that players might make in real-life games. In later chapters, I shall return to these probabilistic and quantitative considerations in the game-theoretic analysis.

Before introducing the cases, I shall briefly analyze two infamous games. These games are the only two 2 × 2 games that have nonmyopic equilibria that are not also Nash equlibria. One figures prominently in the analysis of the first crisis and the other in the analysis of the second crisis.

4.2. Prisoners' Dilemma and Chicken

The 2 × 2 games of Prisoners' Dilemma and Chicken, in which two players can rank the four outcomes from best to worst, are illustrated in Figure 4.1. In Sections 4.3 and 4.6 I shall briefly recount the stories that give each game its colorful name.

Because the players do not order any two outcomes the same in these games—that is, there are no ties between ranks—they are *strict* ordinal games. As in the biblical games of Chapter 1, I do not assume that players can assign numerical values, or cardinal utilities, to the outcomes, as was the case in the bargaining and arbitration games in Chapters 2 and 3.

The players in Prisoners' Dilemma and Chicken are assumed to be able to choose between the strategies of cooperation (C) and noncooperation ($\overline{C}$). The choices of a strategy by each player lead to four possible outcomes, ranked by the players from best (4) to worst (1). Again as in the biblical games, the first number in the ordered pair that defines each outcome is assumed to be the ranking of the row player, the second number the ranking of the column player. Thus, the outcome (3,3) in both games is considered to be the next best for both players, but no presumption is made about whether this outcome is closer to each player's best (4) or next-worst (2) outcome.

The shorthand verbal descriptions given in Figure 4.1 for each outcome are intended to convey the qualitative nature of the outcomes,

Figure 4.1. Prisoner's Dilemma and Chicken

		Prisoner's Dilemma				Chicken	
		Column				**Column**	
		c	*c̄*			*c*	*c̄*
Row	*c*	(3,3) Compromise	(1,4) Column wins	**Row**	*c*	(3,3) Compromise	(2,4) Column advantaged
	c̄	(4,1) Row wins	(2,2) ← Dominant Conflict strategy ↑ for row Dominant strategy for column		*c̄*	(4,2) Row advantaged	(1,1) Disaster

Key: (x,y) = (rank of row, rank of column); 4 = best; 3 = next best; 2 = next worst; 1 = worst; C = cooperation, C̄ = noncooperation. Circled outcomes are Nash equilibria.

based on the players' rankings, in each game. Both of these games are *symmetric:* the two players rank the outcomes along the main diagonal the same, whereas the ranks of the off-diagonal outcomes are mirror images of each other. Because of the symmetry of the games, each of the two players faces the same problems of strategic choice.

In both games, each player obtains its next-best outcome by choosing C if the other player also does ("compromise" outcome), but both have an incentive to defect from this outcome to obtain their best outcomes of 4 by choosing C̄ when the other player chooses C. Yet, if both choose C̄, they bring upon themselves their next-worst outcome ("conflict") in Prisoners' Dilemma, their worst outcome ("disaster") in Chicken.

These games are nonconstant-sum, or *variable-sum,* because the sum of payoffs (or ranks) at every outcomes is not constant but variable. Hence, what one player "wins" the other does not necessarily "lose," so both players can simultaneously do better at some outcomes (e.g., *CC*) than others (*C̄C̄*). These games are also *games of partial conflict*—as opposed to (constant-sum) *games of total conflict,* in which the benefits that redound to one player invariably hurt the other.

The dilemma in Prisoners' Dilemma is that both players have a dominant strategy of choosing C̄: whatever the other player chooses (C or C̄), C̄ is better; but the choice of C̄ by both leads to (2,2), which is *Pareto-inferior* to, or worse for both players, than (3,3).[1] In addition, (2,2) is a Nash equilibrium because neither player has an incentive to deviate unilaterally from this outcome because it would do worse by doing so.[2]

For example, if row switched from $\overline{C}$ to C but column stuck to $\overline{C}$, the resulting outcome would be (1,4), which is obviously worse for row. By contrast, (3,3) is not stable in this sense, or—in the terminology of Chapter 1—is "vulnerable": by switching from C to $\overline{C}$, row can induce (4,1); the fact that this is a preferred outcome for row, and (1,4) is a preferred outcome that column can induce, renders (3,3) vulnerable and therefore unstable.

Presumably, rational players would each choose their dominant, or unconditionally best, strategies of $\overline{C}$, resulting in the Pareto-inferior (2,2) Nash equilibrium. Because of its stability, and despite (3,3)'s being a better outcome for both players, neither would be motivated to depart from (2,2). Should (3,3) somehow manage to be chosen, however, both players would be tempted to depart from it to try to do still better, rendering it unstable. Put another way, mutual cooperation would seem hard to sustain because each player has an incentive to double-cross its opponent.

In Chicken there are two Nash equilibria in pure strategies, (4,2) and (2,4), both of which are *Pareto-superior* because there are no other outcomes better for *both* players. But each player, in choosing its strategy $\overline{C}$ associated with the Nash equilibrium favorable to itself [(4,2) for row, (2,4) for column], risks the disastrous (1,1) outcome (should the other player also choose $\overline{C}$).

The fact that neither player has a dominant strategy in Chicken means that the better strategy choice of each (C or $\overline{C}$) depends on the strategy choice of the other player. This interdependence gives each player an incentive to *threaten* to choose $\overline{C}$, hoping that the other will concede by choosing C so that the threatener can obtain its preferred Nash equilibrium. As in Prisoners' Dilemma, the compromise (3,3) outcome is unappealing because, should it be chosen, it is not stable.

It is hard to say which game poses more obdurate problems for the players. As a model of bargaining between the superpowers during the Yom Kippur War, Prisoners' Dilemma will be used to explain why the the United States and the Soviet Union did not come to blows themselves—but by using a different equilibrium concept from that of Nash. An alternative game-theoretic representation of this crisis will also be discussed. As a model of strategic moves in the Cuban missile crisis, Chicken is one of three possible games I shall consider as a possible explanation of why the superpowers were willing to flirt with nuclear war in 1962.

4.3. The Cuban Missile Crisis as a Game of Chicken

The most dangerous confrontation between the superpowers ever to occur is known as the Cuban missile crisis by the United States and the Caribbean crisis by the Soviet Union. It was precipitated by a Soviet

Figure 4.2. Cuban missile crisis as a game of Chicken

| | | **Soviet Union** | |
		Withdrawal (w)	Maintenance (M)
	Blockade (B)	(3,3) Compromise	(2,4) Soviet victory, U.S. defeat
United States			
	Air strike (A)	(4,2) U.S. victory, Soviet defeat	(1,1) Nuclear war

Key: (*x,y*) = (rank of United States, rank of Soviet Union); 4 = best; 3 = next best; 2 = next worst; 1 = worst.

attempt in October 1962 to install in Cuba medium-range and intermediate-range nuclear-armed ballistic missiles capable of hitting a large portion of the United States.[3]

After the presence of such missiles was confirmed on October 14, the Central Intelligence Agency estimated that they would be operational in about ten days. A so-called Executive Committee of high-level officials was convened to decide on a course of action for the United States, and the Committee met in secret for six days. Several alternatives were considered, which were eventually narrowed to the two that I shall discuss.

The most common conception of this crisis is that the two superpowers were on a collision course. Chicken, which derives its name from a "sport" in which two drivers race toward each other on a narrow road—or both approach a cliff—would at first blush seem an appropriate model of this conflict.

In this gruesome story, each player has the choice between swerving, and avoiding a head-on collision, or continuing on the collision course. As applied to the Cuban missile crisis, with the United States and the Soviet Union the two players, the alternative courses of action, and a ranking of the players' outcomes in terms of the game of Chicken, are shown in Figure 4.2.[4]

The goal of the United States was immediate removal of the Soviet missiles, and United States policy-makers seriously considered two alternative courses of action to achieve this end:

1. A naval blockade (*B*), or "quarantine" as it was euphemistically called, to prevent shipment of further missiles, possibly followed by stronger action to induce the Soviet Union to withdraw those missiles already installed.

2. A "surgical" air strike (A) to wipe out the missiles already installed, insofar as possible, perhaps followed by an invasion of the island.

The alternatives open to Soviet policy makers were:

1. Withdrawal (W) of their missiles.
2. Maintenance (M) of their missiles.

Needless to say, the strategy choices and probable outcomes as presented in Figure 4.2 provide only a skeletal picture of the crisis as it developed over a period of thirteen days. Both sides considered more than the two alternatives I have listed, as well as several variations on each. The Soviets, for example, demanded withdrawal of American missiles from Turkey as a quid pro quo for withdrawal of their missiles from Cuba, a demand publicly ignored by the United States. Furthermore, there is no way to verify that the outcomes given in Figure 4.2 were the most likely ones, or valued in a manner consistent with the game of Chicken. For example, if the Soviet Union had viewed an air strike on their missiles as jeopardizing their vital national interests, the AW outcome may very well have ended in nuclear war between the two sides, giving it the same value as AM. Still another simplification relates to the assumption that the players chose their actions simultaneously, when in fact a continual exchange of messages, occasionally backed up by actions, occurred over those fateful days in October.

Nevertheless, most observers of this crisis believe that the two superpowers were on a collision course, which is actually the title of one book describing this nuclear confrontation.[5] Most observers also agree that neither side was eager to take any irreversible step, such as one of the drivers in Chicken might do by defiantly ripping off his or her steering wheel in full view of the other driver, thereby foreclosing the option of swerving.

Although in one sense the United States "won" by getting the Soviets to withdraw their missiles, Premier Nikita Khrushchev at the same time extracted from President John Kennedy a promise not to invade Cuba, which seems to indicate that the eventual outcome was a compromise solution of sorts. Moreover, even though the Soviets responded to the blockade and, therefore, did not make the choice of their strategy independently of the American strategy choice, the fact that the United States held out the possibility of escalating the conflict to at least an air strike indicates that the initial blockade decision was not considered final—that is, the United States considered its strategy choices still open after imposing the blockade.

Truly, this was a game of sequential bargaining, in which each side

Figure 4.3. Payoff matrix of alternative representation of the Cuban missile crisis

		Soviet Union	
		Withdrawal (w)	Maintenance (M)
United States	Blockade (B)	(3,3) Compromise	→ (1,4) Soviet victory, U.S. capitulation
		⇑	⇓
	Air strike (A)	(2,2) "Dishonorable" U.S. action, Soviets thwarted	← (4,1) "Honorable" U.S. action, Soviets thwarted

Key: (x,y) = (rank of United States, rank of Soviet Union); 4 = best; 3 = next best; 2 = next worst; 1 = worst. Arrows indicate rational moves of United States (vertical) and Soviet Union (horizontal); double arrows signify moving power of United States (see text).

permitted itself a recourse should the other side fail to respond in a manner considered appropriate. Representing the most serious breakdown in the deterrence relationship between the superpowers that had persisted from World War II until that point, each side was gingerly feeling its way, step by ominous step.

Before the crisis, the Soviets, fearing an invasion of Cuba by the United States and also the need to bolster their international strategic position, concluded that it was worth the risk of installing the missiles; confronted by a *fait accompli,* the United States, in all likelihood, would be deterred from invading Cuba and would not attempt any other severe reprisals (Garthoff 1989). Presumably, the Soviets did not reckon the probability of nuclear war to be high (Avenhaus et al. 1989), thereby making it rational for them to risk provoking the United States.

Although this thinking may be more or less correct, there are good reasons for believing that United States policy-makers viewed the game as not Chicken at all, at least as far as they ranked the possible outcomes. In Figure 4.3, I offer an alternative representation of the Cuban missile crisis,[6] retaining the same strategies for both players as given in the Chicken representation (Figure 4.2) but assuming a different ranking of outcomes by the United States (the arrows in this figure will be explained later). These rankings may be interpreted as follows:

1. *BW:* The choice of blockade by the United States and withdrawal by the Soviet Union remains the compromise outcome for both players—(3,3).

2. *BM:* In the face of a U.S. blockade, Soviet maintenance of their missiles leads to a Soviet victory (their best outcome) and U.S. capitulation (their worst outcome)—(1,4).

3. *AM:* An air strike that destroys the missiles that the Soviets were maintaining is an "honorable" U.S. action (their best outcome) and thwarts the Soviets (their worst outcome)—(4,1).

4. *AW:* An air strike that destroys the missiles that the Soviets were withdrawing is a "dishonorable" U.S. action (their next-worst outcome) and thwarts the Soviets (their next-worst outcome)—(2,2).

Even though an air strike thwarts the Soviets in the case of both outcomes (2,2) and (4,1), I interpret (2,2) to be a less damaging outcome for the Soviet Union. This is because world opinion, it may be surmised, would severely condemn the air strike as a flagrant "overreaction"—and hence a "dishonorable" action of the United States—if there were clear evidence that the Soviets were in the process of withdrawing their missiles, anyway. On the other hand, given no such evidence, a U.S. air strike, perhaps followed by an invasion, would probably be viewed by U.S. policy makers as a necessary, if not "honorable," action to dislodge the Soviet missiles. [If one did not view *AM* as the best outcome for the United States, as indicated in Figure 4.3, but instead as the next-best—as (3,1), with the compromise outcome (4,3) viewed as best—the subsequent analysis of deception possibilities in this game in Section 4.4 would be unaffected.]

Before analyzing these possibilities, however, I shall offer a brief justification—mainly in the words of the participants—for the alternative ranking and interpretation of outcomes. The principal protagonists, of course, were President Kennedy and Premier Khrushchev, the leaders of the two countries. Their public and private communications over the thirteen days of the crisis indicate that they both understood the dire consequences of precipitous action and shared, in general terms, a common interest in preventing nuclear war. For the purpose of the present analysis, however, what is relevant are their specific preferences for each outcome.

Did the United States prefer an air strike (and possible invasion) to the blockade (and its eventual removal), given that the Soviets would withdraw their missiles? In responding to a letter from Khrushchev, Kennedy said:

> If you would agree to remove these weapons systems from Cuba . . . we, on our part, would agree . . . (a) to remove promptly the quarantine measures now in effect and (b) to give assurances against an invasion of Cuba. (Allison 1971, 228)

This statement is consistent with the alternative representation of the crisis [because (3,3) is preferred to (2,2) by the United States] but not consistent with the Chicken representation [because (4,2) is preferred to (3,3) by the United States].

Did the United States prefer an air strike to the blockade, given that the Soviets would maintain their missiles? According to Robert Kennedy, a close adviser to his brother during the crisis, "If they did not remove those bases, we would remove them" (Kennedy 1969, 170). This statement is consistent with the alternative representation [because (4,1) is preferred to (1,4) by the United States] but not consistent with the Chicken representation [because (2,4) is preferred to (1,1) by the United States].

Finally, it is well known that several of President Kennedy's advisers felt very reluctant about initiating an attack against Cuba without exhausting less belligerent courses of action that might bring about the removal of the missiles with less risk and greater sensitivity to American ideals and values. As Robert Kennedy put it, an immediate attack would be looked upon as "a Pearl Harbor in reverse, and it would blacken the name of the United States in the pages of history" (Sorensen 1965, 684). This statement is consistent with the United States's ranking the outcome *AW* next worst (2)—a "dishonorable" U.S. action in the Figure 4.3 representation—rather than best (4)—a U.S. victory in the Figure 4.2 representation of Chicken.

If Figure 4.3 provides a more realistic representation of the participants' perceptions in the Cuban missile crisis than does Figure 4.2, it still offers little in the way of explanation of how the compromise (3,3) outcome was achieved and rendered stable. After all, as in Chicken, this outcome is not a Nash equilibrium; but unlike in Chicken, no other outcome in the Figure 4.3 game is stable either.

The instability of outcomes in this game can be seen most easily by examining the cycle of preferences, indicated by the arrows (ignore the distinction between single and double arrows for now) between all pairs of adjacent outcomes. These arrows show that, at each outcome, one player always has an incentive to move to another outcome—in the same row or column—because it can do better by such a move: the Soviets from (3,3) to (1,4); the United States from (1,4) to (4,1); the Soviets from (4,1) to (2,2); and the United States from (2,2) to (3,3).

Because one player always has an incentive to move from every outcome, none of the outcomes in the Figure 4.3 game is a Nash equilibrium, as (4,2) and (2,4) are in Chicken. Moreover, neither player has a dominant strategy: as in Chicken, each player's best strategy depends on the strategy choice of the other player. Thus, for example, the United States prefers *B* if the Soviets choose *W*, but *A* if they choose *M*.

How, then, can one explain the choice of (3,3) in the Figure 4.3 game, given this is a plausible reconstruction of the crisis? I shall suggest in Section 4.4 two qualitatively different sorts of explanation, one based on deception by the Soviet Union and the other based on the exercise of two different kinds of power by the United States. Then, in Section 4.5, I shall present a game-tree reconstruction of sequential choices in the crisis that better mirrors its bargaining aspects, with everything quite fluid until the end.

4.4.   Deception and Power in the Cuban Missile Crisis

Define a player's *deception strategy* to be a false announcement of its preferences to induce the other player to choose a strategy favorable to the deceiver.[7] For deception to work, the deceived player must

> (1)   not know the deceiver's true preference ranking (otherwise the deceiver's false announcement would not be believed, as seen in the Solomon story in Section 1.4).

In fact, I interpret this assumption to mean that the deceived has *no* information—not just incomplete information (as assumed in Chapters 2 and 3)—about the deceiver. Hence, the deceived has no basis for mistrusting the deceiver, unless there is contrary evidence because the deception is revealed (discussed in Section 8.7). I also assume the deceived does

> (2)   not have a dominant strategy (otherwise the deceived would always choose it, whatever the deceiver announced its own strategy to be).

Given that conditions (1) and (2) are met, the deceiver, by pretending to have a dominant strategy, can induce the deceived to believe it will always be chosen. Anticipating this choice, the deceived will then be motivated to choose its strategy that leads to the better of the two outcomes associated with the deceiver's (presumed) dominant strategy.

Before illustrating the possible use of deception by the Soviets in the Figure 4.3 game, consider the sequence of communications that led to a resolution of the crisis. First, as the crisis heightened, the Soviets indicated an increasing predisposition to withdraw rather than maintain their missiles if the United States would not attack Cuba and pledge not to invade it in the future. In support of this shift in preferences, contrast two statements by Khrushchev, the first in a letter to the the British pacifist, Bertrand Russell, the second in a letter to Kennedy:

If the way to the aggressive policy of the American Government is not blocked, the people of the United States and other nations will have to pay with millions of lives for this policy. (Divine 1971, 38)

If assurances were given that the President of the United States would not participate in an attack on Cuba and the blockade lifted, then the question of the removal or destruction of the missile sites in Cuba would then be an entirely different question. (Divine 1971, 47)

Finally, in an almost complete about-face, Khrushchev, in a second letter to Kennedy, all but reversed his original position and agreed to remove the missiles from Cuba, though he demanded the quid pro quo alluded to earlier (which was ignored by Kennedy in his response, quoted earlier):

We agree to remove those weapons from Cuba which you regard as offensive weapons. . . . The United States, on its part, bearing in mind the anxiety and concern of the Soviet state, will evacuate its analogous weapons from Turkey. (Divine 1971, 47)

Khrushchev, who had previously warned (in his first letter to Kennedy) that "if people do not show wisdom, then in the final analysis they will come to clash, like blind moles" (Divine 1971, 47), seemed, over the course of the crisis, quite ready to soften his original position. This is not to say that his later statement misrepresented his true preferences—on the contrary, his language evoking the fear of nuclear war has the ring of truth to it. Whether he actually changed his preferences or simply retreated strategically from his earlier pronouncements, there was a perceptible shift from a noncooperative position (maintain the missiles regardless) to a conditionally cooperative position (withdraw the missiles if the United States would also cooperate).

Perhaps the most compelling explanation for Khrushchev's modification of his position is that there was, in Howard's phrase, a "deterioration" in his original preferences in the face of their possibly apocalyptic game-theoretic consequences (Howard 1971, 148, 199–201). By interchanging, in effect, 3 and 4 in the Soviet ranking of outcomes in Figure 4.3, Khrushchev made W appear dominant, thereby inducing the United States also to cooperate (choose B). The resulting (3,4) outcome is next best for one player, best for the other, and renders BW a Nash equilibrium in this putative game.

Whether Khrushchev deceived Kennedy or actually changed his preferences, the effect is the same in inducing the compromise that was actually selected by both sides. Although there seems to be no evidence that conclusively establishes whether Khrushchev's shift was honest or deceptive, this question is not crucial to the analysis. True, I have developed the analysis in terms of rational deception strategies, but it could as well be interpreted in terms of genuine changes in preferences, given that preferences are not considered immutable.

Could the United States have deceived the Soviets to induce (3,3)? The answer is "no": if the United States had made *B* appear dominant, the Soviets would have chosen *M*, resulting in (1,4); if the United States had made *A* appear dominant, the Soviets would have chosen *W*, resulting in (2,2). Paradoxically, because the United States, as a deceiver, could not ensure an outcome better than its next worst (2)—whatever preference it announced—it was in *its* interest to be deceived (or at least induced) so (3,3) could be implemented.

More generally, in five of the 78 strict ordinal 2×2 games (a listing of 57 "conflict" games will be given in Chapter 5), at least one player can do better as the deceived than the deceiver. Thus, it may be profitable not only that the deceived not know the preferences of the deceiver but also for the deceiver to know that the deceived does not know, and so on ad infinitum (Brams 1977). For this set of five games, the odd notion that "ignorance is strength"—or "ignorance is bliss"—seems well founded.

Is there any way that the United States, on its own, could have engineered the (3,3) outcome? One possible means would be to play it safe by chooosing its *security-level strategy*. (A player's *security level* is the best outcome or payoff it can ensure for itself, whatever strategy the other player chooses, which in this case is the United States's next-worst outcome of 2.) The choice of such a strategy to avoid its worst outcome (l) means choosing *A*; if the Soviets also choose their security-level strategy (*W*), the resulting outcome would be (2,2), which is Pareto-inferior to (3,3).

If it is reasonable to assume that, because the conflict occurred in the Caribbean in the U.S. sphere of influence, the United States could exercise greater power than the Soviet Union, then there are means by which the United States can induce (3,3). Indeed, three kinds of power defined for 2×2 games—moving, staying, and threat—can all be used to implement (3,3) (Brams 1983), but here I shall illustrate only the use of moving and threat power. (Staying power will be illustrated in section 4.10.)

Moving power is the ability of a player to continue moving in a game that cycles, like that in Figure 4.3, when the other player must eventually stop (Brams 1982). The source of this ability may be superior resources, better leadership skills, greater resolve, or the like. Assume that the United States has moving power, which I indicate by the vertical double arrows in Figure 4.3. This means that the United States will be able to hold out longer than the Soviet Union in the move-countermove cycle shown in Figure 4.3.

Eventually, then, the Soviet Union must break the cycle when it has the next move—at either (3,3) or (4,1), from which the single arrows emanate. Because the Soviets prefer (3,3), this is the moving-power outcome the United States can eventually implement.

The threat power the United States has in the Figure 4.3 game is of the deterrent variety. Informally, *threat power* gives a player greater ability to endure a Pareto-inferior outcome than its opponent; by prevailing, it can induce the choice of a Pareto-superior outcome, which is, of course, better for both players. (A formal development of this concept will be given in Chapter 5.) In the Figure 4.3 game, by threatening to choose *A*, which includes the Soviet Union's two worst outcomes, the United States can induce the Soviets to choose *W* when the United States chooses *B*, resulting in (3,3). Even though the Soviets have an incentive to move from (3,3) to (1,4), as indicated by the top horizontal arrow, they would be deterred from doing so by the threat that if they did, the United States would choose its strategy *A* and stay there, inflicting upon the Soviets an outcome Pareto-inferior to (3,3)—presumably (2,2), their better outcome in this row. Given that the United States has threat power, then it is rational for the Soviets to accede to this threat, making it possible for the United States to implement (3,3).

It turns out that if the Soviet Union had moving or threat power in the Figure 4.3 game, it, too, could implement (3,3). Similarly, the possession of staying power by either player would also lead to the implementation of (3,3) (Brams and Hessel 1983).

Because (3,3) can be implemented in the Figure 4.3 game whichever player has any of the three kinds of power, such power is said to be *ineffective*—it does not make a difference who possesses it. However, though ineffective, its impact certainly is salutary in allowing the players to avoid a worse outcome [e.g., (2,2)] in a game in which neither player has a dominant strategy, there are no Nash equilibria, and, consequently, there is no indubitably rational choice.

Thus, as with being deceived, being influenced into choosing an outcome in a thoroughly unstable game, like that in Figure 4.3, may not be unrewarding. On the contrary, one player's ability to deceive (or induce) the other player may be critical in effecting a compromise outcome like (3,3).

4.5. A Sequential View of the Cuban Missile Crisis

Whether any of these forces was instrumental in resolving the Cuban missile crisis is hard to say with certitude. In fact, a much simpler calculation might have been made, as illustrated by the game tree and payoff matrix in Figure 4.4. Here I have slightly altered the preferences of the players once again so that, for example, the United States is

Figure 4.4.   Game tree and payoff matrix of sequential choices in the Cuban missile crisis

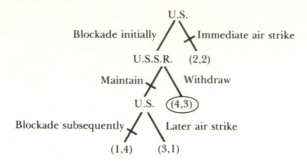

	U.S.S.R.	
	Withdraw	Maintain
Immediate air strike	(2,2)	(2,2)
Blockade subsequently (if U.S.S.R. maintains)	(4,3)	(1,4)
Later air strike (if U.S.S.R. maintains)	(4,3)	(3,1) ← Dominant strategy

U.S. labels the three rows.

Key: (x,y) = (rank of United States, rank of Soviet Union); 4 = best; 3 = next best; 2 = next worst; 1 = worst. Circled outcome in game tree is rational outcome (following path of uncut branches, starting at top); circled matrix outcome is a Nash equilibrim.

assumed most to prefer (4) that the Soviets withdraw after being blockaded, but if they are resistant, next most (3) to carry out an air strike against the missiles.[8]

Starting at the top of the tree, the United States can choose between a blockade initially and an immediate air strike (the later air-strike option is considered only if the Soviets do not cooperate by maintaining their missiles). If the United States chooses blockade, the Soviets can choose, as before, between maintaining and withdrawing their missiles. Finally, if they choose not to cooperate by maintaining their missiles, then the United States can choose between no escalation by continuting the blockade (blockade subsequently) or escalation (to later air strike), assuming it had previously demurred.

I introduced informally the notion of *backward induction* in Chapter 1 whereby the players, working backward from the bottom to the top of the game tree, anticipate each other's subsequent rational choices. Somewhat more formally, start at the bottom of the tree and note that the United States would prefer "later air strike" to "blockade subsequently" should play of the game reach this point. Consequently, cut the "blockade subsequently" branch to indicate it will not be chosen and that (3,1) would be the outcome at this point.

Comparing, at the next-higher level, (4,3) with (3,1), which, as I showed in the previous paragraph, the United States would choose at the bottom, the Soviets would prefer (4,3), so cut the "maintain" branch. Finally, at the top of the tree, comparing (4,3)—the result of the preceding analysis—with (2,2), the United States would prefer (4,3).

To ascertain the rational choices of the players from the top down, reverse the backward-induction process. Starting at the top of the tree, the players would follow the uncut branches: the United States would blockade initially; and the Soviets would subsequently choose to withdraw. This is precisely what happened in the crisis.

A somewhat abbreviated normal-form representation of this game tree, in which some nonessential strategies have been eliminated, is shown at the bottom of Figure 4.4. Note that the United States has a dominant strategy, but the Soviets do not; anticipating the United States's dominant choice—blockade initially, then air strike if the Soviets maintain (indicated by "later air strike" in Figure 4.4)—the Soviets would prefer (4,3) to (3,1) and hence would choose to withdraw.

The resulting (4,3) outcome is the same rational choice that was deduced from the previous game-tree analysis (as it should be). The difference is that in the normal or matrix form, strategies describe complete plans of action for all contingencies that may arise, whereas in the extensive or game-tree form only single choices of the players are indicated at each branch.

Whichever representation of the Cuban missile crisis in this and the preceding sections one finds most congenial, together they illuminate different aspects of player choices in the crisis and problems that might have arisen in achieving a rational stable outcome. The compromise reached—if that is what it was—has remained more or less intact for a generation, which perhaps testifies to its durability.

Although the United States has had subsequent conflicts with the Soviet Union over Cuba as well as with Cuba itself, none has involved a confrontation with the Soviet Union on nearly the scale that occurred in 1962. As a result of this crisis and the apprehension and fear it aroused, a "hot line" was established linking the heads of state in Washington, D.C., and Moscow, which has on occasion been used to try to prevent displays of brinkmanship from carrying the parties again so close to the threshold of nuclear war. One indication of the gravity of the Cuban missile crisis is that President Kennedy, at the height of the crisis, estimated the chances of war to be between one-third and one-half (Sorensen 1965, 705).

Threats may be either explicit or implicit, as in the Figure 4.4 game tree, wherein I assumed the Soviets could anticipate a later air strike unless they responded to the blockade by withdrawing their missiles. Whatever form they take, they seem to have been part and parcel of the bargaining calculations of the protagonists in the Cuban missile crisis. Indeed, Sorensen described this "game-tree" thinking when he reflected on American deliberations:

> We discussed what the Soviet reaction would be to any possible move by the United States, what our reaction with them would have to be to that Soviet reaction, and so on, trying to follow each of those roads to their ultimate conclusion. (quoted in Holsti, Brody, and North 1964, 188)

In the next international crisis that I shall discuss, the hot line was used and probably facilitated the two sides' pulling back from the brink instead of overstepping it. Undoubtedly, what has been called the "delicate balance of terror" persists,[9] at least to a degree; the intellectual challenge now is to find ways not to disturb it.

4.6. The 1973 Alert Decision

On October 25, 1973, President Richard Nixon ordered U.S. military forces put on a worldwide "precautionary alert," which is one of only about half a dozen documented incidents in which the United States employed nuclear threats (the Cuban missile crisis was an earlier case).[10] This was in response to a veiled threat by the Soviet Union to intervene in the Yom Kippur War that pitted Israel against Egypt and Syria.

Armed with Soviet weapons, Egypt and Syria had launched a coordinated surprise attack against Israel on October 6 during the Jewish religious holiday of Yom Kippur. Although Israel suffered initial losses, a week later she launched a counteroffensive after a promise from the United States of a massive airlift of war matériel.

Egyptian and Syrian forces were quickly thrown back; on October 22, with these forces facing imminent disaster, a cease-fire was called for by the U.N. Security Council. But fighting continued, and Nixon received a note from Soviet Communist Party General Secretary Leonid Brezhnev accusing Israel of flouting the cease-fire arrangement and warning that

> if you find it impossible to act together with us in this matter, we should be faced with the necessity urgently to consider the question of taking appropriate steps unilaterally. Israel cannot be allowed to get away with the violations. (*New York Times*, April 10, 1974, p. 9)

Nixon responded by ordering that United States forces be put on a worldwide alert, or Defense Condition (DEFCON) 3, warned Brezhnev of "incalculable consequences" if the Soviets took unilateral action, but also indicated a willingness to cooperate with the Soviets in promoting peace.[11] In addition, he delivered an ultimatum to the Israelis demanding that they permit the Egyptian Third Army, encircled by Israeli forces, to be resupplied with nonmilitary equipment, food, and water.

With the passage of a Security Council resolution on October 25 establishing a U.N. Emergency Force to enforce the October 22 cease-fire, Nixon rescinded the alert order. The superpower crisis, as well as the prospect of further fighting in the Middle East, abated.

Zagare (1983) summarizes the choices facing the superpowers on October 24, and their preferences regarding the consequences of these choices, in the payoff matrix of Figure 4.5. The Soviets had to choose between trying to save the vulnerable Egyptian Third Army through diplomatic means or accepting Egyptian President Anwar Sadat's invitation to send a military contingent to protect it and the political position of his government. United States policy-makers had to decide whether to cooperate with the Soviets to help extricate Sadat from his extremely precarious position or to try to frustrate any Soviet diplomatic or military initiative.

Zagare argues that, with the imposition of the alert, each side's *perceptions* of each other's preferences were as shown in Figure 4.5. Had the alert not been called, however, the United States believed that the Soviet perception of this game would have been different. Specifically, the Soviets would have viewed U.S. preferences for Outcomes *C* and *D* in Figure 4.5 to have been reversed: *D* would have been seen as worst (1) and *C* next worst (2), as I have indicated by the "interchange without alert" arrow between these two U.S. rankings in Figure 4.5.

Nixon believed that Soviets misperceived U.S. preferences because of the "crisis of confidence" brought on by the Watergate affair (discussed in part in Chapter 6). For the alert crisis followed less than a week after the notorious "Saturday Night Massacre," in which Nixon fired the Watergate Special Prosecutor, which immediately led to the resignation of the attorney general and his deputy in protest. Indeed, some critics of the Nixon administration suggested that "the alert might have been prompted as much perhaps by American domestic requirements as by the real requirements of diplomacy in the Middle East" (*New York Times*, October 26, 1973, p. 18).[12]

There may be some truth to these charges. The alert seems to have been designed, at least in part, to indicate to the Soviets the U.S. intention of coming to Israel's rescue (Outcome *D*) rather than acquiesce in unilateral Soviet intervention (Outcome *C*). To prevent a misinterpretation of

Figure 4.5. Payoff matrix of cease-fire game

Soviet Union

	Seek diplomatic solution	Intervene in war
United States — Cooperate with Soviet initiative	A. Compromise; Egyptian Third Army resupplied; cease-fire of Oct. 22 re-established; political resolution of Middle East conflict attempted. (3,3)	C. Soviet victory; possible joint Soviet-American peace-keeping force; Soviet military presence in Middle East reintroduced. (①,4)
Frustrate Soviet initiative	B. Israeli victory; possible occupation of Egypt, Syria, Jordan. (4,1)	D. Superpower confrontation. (②,2)

Interchange without alert

← Dominant strategy (with alert)

Dominant strategy

Key: (x,y) = (rank of United States, rank of Soviet Union); 4 = best; 3 = next best; 2 = next worst; 1 = worst.
Source: Frank C. Zagare, "A Game-Theoretic Evaluation of the Cease-Fire Alert Decision of 1973," *Journal of Peace Research* 20, no. 1 (1983): 75 and 77 (Figures 1 and 2).

the American position, Nixon claimed that because "words were not making our point, we needed action" (Nixon 1978, 938).

The transformation of the game occasioned by the alert decision has a clear effect on the stability of outcomes. Without the alert, Outcome *C*, perceived by the Soviets as (2,4), is the unique Nash equilibrium. Obviously, they would have no incentive to defect from this outcome, their best; and the United States would have no incentive to move to *D*, resulting in (1,2), its worst outcome.

With the alert, however, the game would be seen as Prisoners' Dilemma, whose unique Nash equilibrium is Outcome *D*. Because (2,2) is next worst for both players, one might presume that the Prisoners' Dilemma perception on the part of the Soviets would make them somewhat reluctant to choose their strategy of intervention associated with it.

But this strategy is dominant, with or without the alert. In the Soviet view, the only thing that changes with the alert is that the United States would then have a dominant strategy of frustrating the Soviet initiative, leading to Pareto-inferior Outcome *D*.

In fact, however, both sides cooperated in the end, choosing Outcome *A*. How can this action be explained, given that (3,3) in Prisoners' Dilemma is the product of *dominated strategies*—strategies that result in a worse outcome for each player, whatever the choice of the other player— and not a Nash equilibrium?

The difficulties of cooperation in this game can perhaps best be driven home by recounting the story that gives Prisoners' Dilemma its name, attributed to A. W. Tucker. Two persons suspected of being partners in a crime are arrested and placed in separate cells so that they cannot communicate with each other. Without a confession from *at least one* suspect, the district attorney does not have sufficient evidence to convict them of the crime. In an attempt to extract a confession, the district attorney tells each suspect the following consequences of their (joint) actions:

1. If one suspect confesses and the other does not, the one who confesses can go free (gets no sentence) for cooperation with the state, but the other gets a stiff 10-year sentence—equivalent to (4,1) and (1,4) in Figure 4.1.
2. If both suspects confess, both get reduced sentences of 5 years— equivalent to (2,2) in Figure 4.1.
3. If both suspects remain silent, both go to prison for 1 year on a lesser charge of carrying a concealed weapon—equivalent to (3,3) in Figure 4.1.

What should one do to save one's skin, assuming that neither suspect has any compunction against squealing on the other? Observe first that if either suspect confesses, it is advantageous for the other suspect to do likewise to avoid the very worst outcome of 10 years in prison. The rub is that the idea of confessing and receiving a moderate sentence of 5 years is not at all appealing, even though neither suspect can be assured of a better outcome. Moreover, if one's partner does not confess, it is better to turn state's evidence by confessing and, therefore, going scot free.

Thus, both suspects' strategies of confessing strictly dominate their strategies of not confessing, though the choice of the former strategy by both suspects leads to a worse outcome (5 years in prison for each) than maintaining silence and getting only 1 year in prison. But without being able to communicate with one's partner to coordinate a joint strategy—much less make a binding agreement—one could, by not confessing, set oneself up for being double-crossed. Because both players will be tempted to defect from the "cooperative" outcome of not squealing, this outcome is unstable.

One might think that if Prisoners' Dilemma were played repeatedly, perspicacious players could in effect communicate with each other by establishing a pattern of previous choices that would reward the choice of the cooperative strategy. But if the game ends after n plays, and the final round is therefore definitely known, it clearly does not pay to cooperate on this round since, with no plays to follow, the players are in effect in the same position if they played the game only once. If there is no point in trying to induce a cooperative response on the nth round, however, such behavior on the $(n-1)$st round would be to no avail either because its effect could extend only to the nth round, where cooperative behavior has already been ruled out. Carrying this reasoning successively backwards, it follows that one should not choose the cooperative strategy on any play of the game.

In Section 5.4 I shall explore this line of reasoning further in a different game and suggest that, in certain situations, it is unpersuasive. Next, however, I will show how, even in the single play of games like Chicken and Prisoners' Dilemma, cooperation can be justified by changing the rules of play.

4.7. Nonmyopic Equilibria and the Theory of Moves: A Digression

From the foregoing analysis of Prisoners' Dilemma, it seems either that the superpowers in the cease-fire game foresook their rational choices leading to the stable outcome or that the concept of stability needs to be redefined. I shall take the latter tack in this and later sections, introducing a new notion of equilibrium that not only rationalizes cooperation in Chicken and Prisoners' Dilemma but also provides a foundation for the dynamic analysis of all games.

This notion, based on new rules of play, distinguishes short-term stable outcomes, or "myopic equilibria," from long-term stable outcomes, or "nonmyopic equilibria." By myopic equilibria, I mean Nash equilibria, which say, in effect, that a player considers only the *immediate* advantages and disadvantages of switching its strategy. If neither player in a game can gain immediately by a unilateral switch, the resulting outcome is stable, or a Nash equilibrium.

By contrast, Wittman and I (Brams and Wittman 1981), in defining a nonmyopic equilibrium, assume that a player, in deciding whether to depart from an outcome, considers not only the immediate effect of its actions but also the consequences of the other player's probable response, its own counterresponse, and so on. I shall refer to this process as *nonmyopic calculation*. When neither player perceives a long-term advantage from departing from an initial outcome, this outcome is called a nonmyopic equilibrium:

> The [intuitive] idea is that players look ahead and ascertain where, from any outcome in an outcome matrix, they will end up if they depart from this starting outcome. Comparing the final outcome with the starting outcome, if they are better off at the starting outcome (taking account of their departures, possible responses to their departures, and so on), they will not depart in the first place. In this case, the starting outcome will be an equilibrium in an extended, or nonmyopic, sense. (Brams and Wittman 1981, 42–43)

This new equilibrium concept presupposes a set of rules different from that assumed in classical game theory. Because a "game" is sometimes defined to be the sum-total of the rules that describe it, these rules, in fact, define a new game, which I call a "sequential game" (Brams 1983, 75). Although I shall continue to refer to games like Chicken and Prisoners' Dilemma by their original names, it should be borne in mind that it is the sequential versions that will be analyzed subsequently.

Rule 1, given below, is usually the only rule that the classical theory of games posits to govern the play of normal-form, or matrix, games. The *theory of moves*, on the other hand, postulates three additional rules that define a *sequential game:*[13]

1. Both players simultaneously choose strategies, thereby defining an *initial outcome*.[14]
2. Once at an initial outcome, either player can unilaterally switch its strategy and change that outcome to a subsequent outcome in the

> row or column in which the initial outcome lies. Call the player who switches Player 1.[15]
>
> 3. Player 2 can respond by unilaterally switching its strategy, thereby moving the game to a new outcome.
>
> 4. The alternating responses continue until the player whose turn it is to move next chooses not to switch its strategy. When this happens, the game terminates, and the outcome reached is the *final outcome*.

Note that the sequence of moves and countermoves is *strictly alternating:* first, say, the row player moves, then the column player, and so on, until one stops, at which point the outcome reached is final. A fifth "stopping rule" will be specified later to define a nonmyopic equilibrium.

How does a rational player determine whether it should move at each stage? I assume that this player performs a backward-induction analysis, based on the game tree of possible moves that would ensue if it departed from the initial outcome. I shall develop this analysis in terms of row and column as the players, who make choices—according to the theory of moves—based on Rules 1 through 4 and another rule to be discussed later.

In the remainder of this section, I illustrate this theory with the game of Chicken (Figure 4.1). This is a digression from the previous analysis of the 1973 cease-fire game, but I shall return to this case in Section 4.8. The reason for this digression is not only to illustrate the theory of moves but also to show its effects in Chicken, the game used to model the Cuban missile crisis in Section 4.3. The theory's consequences are somewhat different in Prisoners' Dilemma, which I shall pick up again in Section 4.8 when I resume the analysis of the 1973 alert decision.

To illustrate the theory, assume that each of the players chooses its compromise C (cooperation) strategy initially in Chicken (Figure 4.1), resulting in (3,3). If row then departs from this initial outcome and moves the process to (4,2), column can move it to (1,1), and row in turn can respond by moving it to (2,4). These possible moves, and the corresponding "stay" choices at each node, are illustrated in Figure 4.6.

To determine rational choices for the players to make at each node of the game tree, starting at (3,3), it is necessary to work backward up the game tree in Figure 4.6, as shown in Section 4.5. Consider row's choice at (1,1). Since row prefers (2,4) to (1,1), I indicate "stay" at (1,1) would *not* be chosen by cutting its branch, should the process reach the node at (1,1). Instead, outcome (2,4) would be chosen, which can be mentally substituted for the endpoint, "Row at (1,1)."

Working backward again, compare (4,2) at the prior "stay" branch with (2,4) at the "move" branch (given the previous substitution). Because column prefers (2,4), the "stay" branch at this node is cut, and (2,4) moves

Figure 4.6. Game tree of moves, starting with row, from (3,3) in Chicken

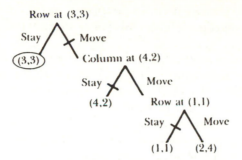

Key: (x,y) = (rank of row, rank of column); 4 = best; 3 = next best; 2 = next worst; 1 = worst. Circled outcome is rational outcome (following path of uncut branches, starting at top).

up to a final comparison with (3,3) at the top node. At this node row prefers (3,3), so the "move" branch at the top node is cut, and (3,3) is therefore the final outcome that "survives" the cuts.

In other words, there would be no incentive for row, anticipating the rational choices of players at subsequent nodes in the game tree of Figure 4.6, to depart from (3,3). Similarly, because of the symmetry of the game, there would be no incentive for column to depart from (3,3) in Chicken. When the final outcome coincides with the initial outcome, as it does in the case of (3,3), it is a *nonmyopic equilibrium.*[16]

The existence of a nonmyopic equilibrium depends on a termination condition, or *stopping rule:*

5. There exists a node in the game tree such that the player with the next move can ensure its best outcome by staying at it. If this node is reached in the move-countermove process, play will terminate at it.

The outcome (2,4) at the bottom of the game tree in Figure 4.6 is such a node, because column, the player with the next move, achieves its best outcome by staying at it rather than returning to (3,3). Note that even if another possible move were given at the bottom of the tree that allowed column at (2,4) either to stay at (2,4) or move to (3,3), backward induction at this point would preclude it because column receives its best outcome at (2,4).

If a game contains no node that is the best outcome for the player with the next move, Rule 5 does not apply, and cycling will continue indefinitely. This is true in the alternative representation of the Cuban missile crisis (Figure 4.3): it is always rational for players to move in the direction of the arrows because no player, at its turn to move, ever receives its best outcome. Hence, this game does not contain a nonmyopic equilibrium.

It should be emphasized that Rule 5 does not say that play will necessarily terminate at an outcome best for a player with the next move (if one exists). In fact, the move-countermove process may terminate before any moves are made at all. In Chicken, for example, row never departs from (3,3) because, once this departure occurs, Rule 5 implies that play will then terminate at (2,4)—no matter how far the game tree is extended— and this outcome is inferior for row to (3,3).

For the other three outcomes in Chicken, there is no corresponding incentive for both players to stay at them, should any be the initial outcome of the game. For example, a game-tree analysis, starting at (1,1), reveals that row would have an incentive to depart to (2,4) and column to (4,2). After either departure, the process would terminate because the player with the next move—column at (2,4), row at (4,2)—would obtain its best outcome. But if (2,4) or (4,2) were the initial outcomes, rational departures by row from (2,4) and column from (4,2) would carry the process to (1,1), whence it would go to (4,2) if row departed initially, (2,4) if column departed initially, and stay for the reason just given.

But there is a complication with starting at (1,1). Clearly, row would prefer that column depart first from (1,1), yielding (4,2), and column would prefer that row depart first, yielding (2,4). Since one cannot say a priori which player would be able to hold out longer at (1,1), and force the other to move first, call the final outcome, starting at (1,1), "(2,4)/ (4,2)"—either (2,4) or (4,2) is possible.

It is easy to show that if (2,4) is the initial outcome, the final outcome according to the game-tree analysis would be (4,2), and (2,4) if (4,2) were the initial outcome. This is because the player obtaining its next-worst outcome (2), by moving the process to (1,1), can force the other player to move to the outcome best for itself [(4,2) for row, (2,4) for column]. In either case, the player obtaining its best outcome (4) at (2,4) or (4,2) would seem to have no incentive to depart to the inferior outcome, (3,3).

But an objection can be raised to this reasoning: the player who obtains 4 initially, knowing it will be reduced to 2, would have an incentive to move the process to (3,3) first, whereby it obtains its next-best outcome rather than its next-worst. Moreover, once at (3,3), the process would stop there since a subsequent move by, say, row to (4,2) would then move the process to (1,1), and thence to (2,4), which is inferior for row to (3,3).

This countermove to (3,3) by the player obtaining its best outcome at (2,4) or (4,2) would appear to introduce a new kind of rational calculation into the analysis—what the other player will do if one does not seize the initiative. True, I implicitly assumed earlier that each player, separately, would ascertain the final outcome only for itself; yet it seems reasonable that each player would consider not only the consequences of departing from an outcome itself but also the consequences of the other player's departure. Because each player could do better by holding out at, say, (1,1), each presumably would strive to delay its departure, hoping to force the other player to move first.

The situation, starting at (2,4) or (4,2), is the reverse for the players. Although the game-tree analysis shows that, say, row should not move from (4,2) to (3,3), row's recognition of the fact that column can move the process to (2,4) would induce row to try to get the jump on column by moving first to (3,3). In contrast, at (1,1) each player has an incentive to hold out rather than scramble to leave the initial outcome first.

In either event, a rational choice is dictated not only by one's own game-tree analysis but by that of the other player as well, which may cause one to override one's own (one-sided) rational choice. Henceforth, I assume that a final outcome reflects the *two-sided* analysis that both players would make of each other's rational choices, in addition to their own.

In the case of outcomes (2,4) and (4,2), it is impossible to say a priori which player would be successful in departing first. Accordingly, as in the case of (1,1), it seems best to indicate a *joint* outcome of "(4,2)/(3,3)" starting from (2,4), and of "(2,4)/(3,3)" starting from (4,2).

In summary, the final outcomes of Chicken, given that the players make rational choices—according to a two-sided game-tree analysis and the four rules specified previously—are as follows for each initial outcome:

Initial Outcome	Final Outcome
(3,3)	(3,3)
(1,1)	(2,4)/(4,2)
(4,2)	(2,4)/(3,3)
(2,4)	(4,2)/(3,3)

If one substitutes the final outcomes for the intial outcomes in the payoff matrix of Figure 4.1, the new game shown in Figure 4.7 results. The outcomes of this game may be thought of as those that would be obtained if the four rules of sequential play specified earlier, coupled with rational choices based on a two-sided game-tree analysis, were operative.

In the preliminary analysis of this game, assume that each of the two outcomes in the joint pairs is equiprobable.[17] Then, in an expected-value sense, C dominates $\overline{C}$ for each player. If column, for example, chooses

Figure 4.7. Revised Chicken, with final outcomes

		Column	
		C	$\overline{C}$
Row	C	(3,3)	(4,2)/(3,3)
	$\overline{C}$	(2,4)/(3,3)	(2,4)/(4,2)

Key: (x,y) = (rank of row, rank of column); 4 = best; 3 = next best; 2 = next worst; 1 = worst; C = cooperation; $\overline{C}$ = noncooperation. Circled outcome is a Nash equilibrium.

C, (3,3) is better for row than (2,4)/(3,3), which half the time will yield (2,4); if column chooses $\overline{C}$, (4,2)/(3,3) is better for row than (2,4)/(4,2) because, though the (4,2)s "cancel each other out," (3,3) is preferred to (2,4) half the time.

Strictly speaking, however, for C to dominate $\overline{C}$ in *every play* of the game for row, it is necessary to make two assumptions:

1. Whenever column chooses $\overline{C}$, if $\overline{C}$ for row yields (4,2) as a final outcome, so does C for row;
2. There is some possibility, however small, that the choice of $\overline{C}C$ by the players yields (2,4).

In this manner, row's choice of C is always at least as good as, and sometimes better than, $\overline{C}$.

Assumption 1 is the crucial assumption. It says, in effect, that whenever column chooses $\overline{C}$ in Chicken, and row can hold out longer at (1,1) if it chooses $\overline{C}$ itself—forcing the final outcome to be (4,2)—row can preempt column at (2,4) if it chooses C, yielding the final outcome (4,2). In other words, if row is the "stronger" player at (1,1), it is also the "quicker" player at (2,4), because it is able to move the process to (1,1) before column moves it to (3,3).

The guarantee of dominance provided by Assumptions 1 and 2 seems as plausible as the expected-value assumption, which says, given the equiprobability of the two outcomes in the joint pairs, that C dominates $\overline{C}$ "on the average." Either way, rational players in Chicken, anticipating the final outcomes shown in Figure 4.7, will each choose their dominant strategy C. Thereby the four rules of sequential play specified earlier induce the compromise (3,3) outcome in Chicken, which is circled in Figure 4.7.

In situations of nuclear deterrence, it seems implausible that players would consider actually moving through the (1,1) outcome—though they might threaten to do so—whereas in situations of conventional deterrence such punishing behavior might be considered appropriate to bolster one's reputation for "toughness" and thereby enhance one's future credibility. "The *reputation* of nations," as David Hartley wrote Benjamin Franklin in 1782, "is not merely a *bubble*. It forms their real security" [italics in original]. The effects of threats and reputation in 2 × 2 ordinal games will be analyzed more systematically in Chapter 5.

4.8. Stability in the Cease-Fire Game

The justification of the (3,3) outcome as stable in the cease-fire game with the alert in Figure 4.5, which is a Prisoners' Dilemma, relies on different comparisons, according to the theory of moves, than does the (3,3) outcome in Chicken. This game is shown as the initial-outcome matrix in Figure 4.8, with the game tree of sequential moves from (3,3) shown at the bottom.

An analysis of this game tree demonstrates that, thinking ahead, neither player would be motivated to depart from (3,3), because if it did [say, if row moved to (4,1)], the other player (column) would countermove to (2,2), where subsequent moves would terminate.

This is so because if row moved from (2,2) to (1,4), column would stay since by doing so it could implement its best outcome. But since row can anticipate that the process would end at (2,2) if it departed initially from (3,3), it would have no incentive to depart from (3,3) in the first place. Thereby (3,3) is the rational outcome when Prisoners' Dilemma is played according to the sequential rules.

The two-sided analysis I illustrated in the case of Chicken in Section 4.7, when applied to Prisoners' Dilemma, shows that from initial outcomes (4,1) and (1,4) the process would move to final outcome (3,3). At (4,1), for example, it would be in *both* players' interest that row move to (3,3) before column moves to (2,2), where the process would stop, as I indicated in the previous praragraph. Because there is no incentive for row to move to (1,4) or column to move to (4,1) from (2,2), it, like (3,3), is stable in a nonmyopic sense.

Thus, were (2,2) initially chosen by the players, it would be the final outcome, whereas all other outcomes would be transformed into (3,3). Altogether, the final-outcome matrix of Prisoners' Dilemma given in Figure 4.8 shows only the upper-left (3,3) Nash equilibrium to be the product of dominant strategy choices by the players and, presumably,

Figure 4.8. 1973 cease-fire game (with alert) as Prisoners' Dilemma

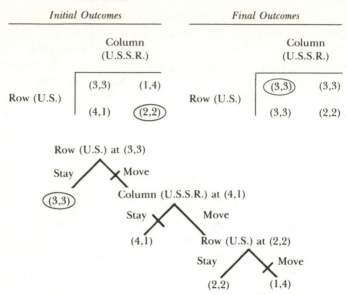

Key: (x,y) = (rank of row, rank of column); 4 = best; 3 = next best; 2 = next worst; 1 = worst. Circled matrix outcomes are dominant-strategy Nash equilibria; circled outcome in game tree is rational outcome (following path of uncut branches, starting at top).

the outcome that would be chosen. Note that it coincides with the (3,3) outcome in the initial-outcome matrix; the other two (3,3) outcomes in the final-outcome matrix are Nash equilibria, but they are not ones associated with the players' dominant strategies.

Thus, as in Chicken, the sequential rules lead to the cooperative (3,3) outcome in Prisoners' Dilemma, but, unlike in Chicken, the implementation of this outcome does not depend on one player's being stronger and quicker than the other. Not only does the dominance of strategies associated with (3,3) in the final-outcome matrix require no special assumptions, but the dominance of the players' other strategies, associated with (2,2) in the initial-outcome matrix, is reversed.

Thereby, starting at (3,3), it would not be advantageous for either player in the cease-fire game, looking ahead, to switch strategies. Had the status quo been the (2,2) outcome, however, this outcome, because it is nonmyopically (as well as myopically) stable, would have prevailed and the (3,3) compromise outcome would have remained unreachable by alternating moves. This is perhaps why the (2,2) outcome, once reached, is so hard to break out of; but if farsighted players can avoid this trap from the beginning, there is no reason they should fall prey to it later— if they are truly farsighted.

Had Nixon not ordered the alert, U.S. preferences in the game would have been interchanged, as indicated in Figure 4.5. In this game, (3,3) is not a nonmyopic equilibrium, and a full game-tree analysis is not needed to show why.

From the Soviet perspective, if they move to what they perceive to be (2,4), the United States would not move to (1,2). The reason is that if the United States did, the Soviets would terminate play there, knowing that if they moved to (4,1), the United States, obtaining its best outcome— and inflicting upon them their worst—would stop, according to Rule 5 in section 4.7. Knowing, therefore, that the Soviets would not move to (4,l), the United States would not move from (2,4) to (1,2), so (2,4) is the nonmyopic equilibrium in this game without the alert.

As I indicated in Section 4.6, this equilibrium is also the Nash equilibrium in this game. Remarkably, of the 37 (out of 78) 2 × 2 strict ordinal games that have nonmyopic equilibria, *only in Chicken and Prisoners' Dilemma are the (3,3) nonmyopic equilibria not also Nash equilibria*. This may in part explain why these two harrowing games have received so much attention in the game theory literature. Theorists' abiding interest in them seems to stem from an intuitive recognition that mutual cooperation can somehow be justified. But how? Nonmyopic equilibria that allow for the possibility of sequential moves and countermoves in dynamic play offer one justification.

This equilibrium in the cease-fire game *with* the alert would, according to the theory of moves, have robbed the Soviets of an incentive to intervene militarily, whereas the (2,4) nonmyopic equilibrium in the cease-fire game without the alert would have encouraged them to intervene. In either case, these equilibria are associated with the U.S. strategy of cooperating with the Soviet initiative.

Thus, what the United States gains with the alert, according to the theory of moves, is not a new rational strategy for itself; rather, the use of the alert introduces a new rational strategy for the Soviets. In imparting nonmyopic stability to (3,3) by stressing its commitment to Israel, the United States makes it rational for the Soviets to seek a diplomatic solution.

This distinction is not made by classical game theory: (3,3) is not a Nash equilibrium in either version of the cease-fire game. The effect of the alert, according to this theory, is to render (2,2) a Nash equilibrium, and the U.S. strategy of frustrating the Soviet initiative a dominant one.

Since the United States did not choose this strategy, the applicability of the classical theory is cast in doubt. It seems, instead, that both superpowers acted on the basis of a longer-term dynamic view of the situation.

Whether Nixon's decision to put U.S. forces on alert status was crucial in preserving the (3,3) status quo is impossible to verify empirically since the situation without the alert never occurred. But the sequential game-theoretic analysis certainly suggests that, at least based on the apparent perception of the crisis by the players, Nixon had good reason to order the alert to deter possible military intervention by the Soviets.

Brezhnev's warning to Nixon quoted in Section 4.6 lends credibility to this assessment. For had the Soviets sent troops to the Middle East to try to rescue the Egyptian army and save Sadat, and had the United States responded by intervening militarily in support of Israel, the two superpowers would, Nixon believed, have been plunged into an arena with "an extremely dangerous potential for great power rivalry" (Nixon 1978, 938).

The alert may well have averted this situation and the potentially serious risk of nuclear war. Yet, raising the stakes with the alert is what Zagare (1983, 81) calls "a very dangerous game indeed." Even Secretary of State Henry Kissinger described it as "deliberate overreaction" (quoted in Zagare 1983, 82), which leads Zagare to consider an alternative game-theoretic formulation that puts the United States in the role of "honest broker."

4.9. Was There an Alternative to the Alert?

Zagare bases his analysis on Glassman's contention that there was a more prudent and less provocative course of action that might also have deterred Soviet intervention:

> Rather than declaring a meaningless alert and putting pressure on Israel, a better response to the Russian threat might have been a diplomatic statement that the United States was also concerned with implementing a cease-fire and that we would seek to convince Israel of the necessity of such a move. (Glassman 1975, 65)

In game-theoretic terms, Glassman's call for an American declaration of its desire to promote compromise (Outcome A in Figure 4.5, without the alert) rather than an Israeli military victory (Outcome B) leads to the cease-fire game, with the United States as honest broker, shown in Figure 4.9.

Zagare (1983, 82) argues that the preferences depicted for the United States, in which the previous U.S. preferences for B over A are now

Figure 4.9. Cease-fire game, with United States as honest broker

Soviet Union

		Seek diplomatic solution	Intervene in war	
United States	Cooperate with Soviet initiative	A. Compromise (4,3) →	C. Soviet victory (2,4)	← Dominant strategy
		↑	↓	
	Frustrate Soviet initiative	B. Israeli victory ← (3,1)	D. Confrontation (1,2)	
			↑	
			Dominant strategy	

Key: (x,y) = (rank of United States, rank of Soviet Union); 4 = best; 3 = next best; 2 = next worst; 1 = worst. Arrows indicate rational moves of United States (vertical) and Soviet Union (horizontal). Circled outcome is a Nash equilibrium.

Source: Frank C. Zagare, "A Game-Theoretic Evaluation of the Cease-Fire Alert Decision of 1973," *Journal of Peace Research* 20, no. 1 (1983): 82 (Figure 5).

reversed, were probably true preferences, making its two sets of pre-viously described preferences false and hence deceptive (as possibly the Soviets' were in the Cuban missile crisis, discussed in Section 4.3). But if U.S. preferences were perceived as those in Figure 4.9 by the Soviets, would the compromise (4,3) outcome in this game have been the rational choice of the two superpowers?

There are sound reasons to think not, despite the fact that this out-come's ranking is raised for the United States, and not lowered for the Soviets, over the previous (3,3) compromise outcome. First, both players have dominant strategies, as shown in Figure 4.9, which—unfortunately for the United States—results in the choice of the unique Nash equil-brium, (2,4). This outcome is a clear Soviet victory, best for them but only next worst for the United States. Second, as in the Figure 4.3 representation of the Cuban missile crisis, preferences cycle, as indicated by the arrows in Figure 4.9 emanating from every outcome.

To be sure, the moves from (2,4) to (1,2) by the United States, and from (1,2) to (3,1) by the Soviets, would appear to be irrational switches because they lead immediately to inferior outcomes for the player who changes strategies. I assume they will still be made, however, because the stopping rule (Rule 5 in Section 4.7) is never invoked in this game— no outcome is ever reached that is best for the player with the next move. Ultimately, the first-moving player, by moving according to the theory of moves, seeks to induce its opponent to countermove to a still better outcome for itself, the first-moving player.

This long-term perspective means that the process will never come to rest. The Figure 4.9 game, therefore, contains no nonmyopic equilibrium. Nevertheless, outcome (4,3) is an "absorbing outcome," to which, Hessel and I (Brams and Hessel 1982) suggest, the players would be expected to converge if the possibility of indefinite cycling were precluded.

In fact, the 41 (out of 78) 2 × 2 strict ordinal games without nonmyopic equilibria all have absorbing outcomes, which are based on less demanding rationality criteria than nonmyopic equilibria. They would seem satisfactory solutions to these games if cycling is ruled out as too costly, or otherwise inimical, to the players.

For this reason, Zagare (1983, 83) contends that the two superpowers might possibly have settled on the compromise (4,3) outcome in the Figure 4.9 game if the Nixon Administration had tried more to promote a policy of détente instead of *Realpolitik* in this crisis. Of course, it is impossible to offer incontrovertible evidence that this would indeed have been the case, though Nixon for one saw "Soviet behavior during the Mideast crisis not as an example of the failure of détente but as an illustration of its limitations—limitations of which I had always been keenly aware" (Nixon 1978, 941). Apparently, he was unwilling to attempt the Glassman strategy, stripped, as it were, of *Realpolitik*.

4.10. The Possible Effects of Power in the Cease-Fire Game

There is another perspective one can take, grounded in the theory of moves, in searching for a (hypothetical) solution to the Figure 4.9 game. Given that the United States had greater moving, staying, or threat power in this game, it could have used any of these three different kinds of power to implement (4,3) (Brams 1983).

In Section 4.4 I discussed the use of moving and threat power in the Figure 4.3 version of the Cuban missile crisis. In the present game, the United States, with moving power, could have forced the Soviets to choose between (4,3) and (1,2)—if the United States had shown itself to be (more or less) indefatigable—and clearly the Soviets as well as the United States would have preferred the former outcome.

Similarly with threat power, the United States could have threatened the Soviets that unless they chose their first (cooperative) strategy, they (the United States) would choose their second strategy, thereby visiting upon the Soviets their two worst outcomes associated with this strategy. Since (4,3) is better than either of these alternative outcomes for the Soviets (as well as for the United States), it would have been rational for them to compromise.

Staying power allows the player who possesses it to hold off making a strategy choice until the player without this power does. Thereafter, moves alternate, according to the theory of moves, starting with the player without staying power, with a "rational termination" condition postulated that prevents cycling (Brams and Hessel 1983). This condition specifies that the player without staying power, who does not want the process to return to the initial outcome—from which it will repeat itself—will act to halt this process before this point is reached.

Assume that the Soviets had chosen their dominant strategy of intervention initially. If the United States had responded with its frustration strategy, resulting in (1,2), rational moves and countermoves would carry the process to (4,3), where it would stay. For if the Soviets moved subsequently to (2,4), the United States would return to (1,2). Because I assume the onus is on the player without staying power to prevent such cycling so the game will terminate, the Soviets would not have moved from (4,3) if the United States had had such power.

On the other hand, if the Soviets had chosen their cooperative strategy initially, a similar comparison, which can be formalized by analyzing a game tree of possible moves, demonstrates that rational termination would again occur at (4,3). Thus, all three kinds of power induce the most favorable outcome for the United States.

By comparison, if the Soviets possessed greater moving, staying, or threat power, they would have been able to implement (2,4), their best outcome. Thus, lacking a nonmyopic equilibrium, the outcome of this game hinges on which player has the greater power (as I have defined these different kinds of power in 2 × 2 ordinal games).

The Figure 4.9 game illustrates a case when power is *effective,* or makes a difference—depending on who possesses it—on what outcome is implemented. Recall from Section 4.4 that the exercise of power in the Figure 4.3 Cuban missile crisis game was ineffective because, whichever player possessed it, the same (3,3) outcome would have been induced.

The effectiveness of power in the Figure 4.9 cease-fire game, with the United States as honest broker, makes it much more difficult to predict the outcome likely to be implemented. The player that obtains its best outcome in this game is the player that can continue moving when the other player must eventually stop (moving power), that can delay making an initial choice longer (staying power), or that has the more effective and credible threat (threat power).

Fortunately, no test of strength that might have ignited superpower conflict was required. Because power is ineffective in the Prisoners' Dilemma created by the alert, whichever player had moving, threat, or staying power, the (3,3) outcome induced is the same. Hence, being perceived as the more powerful player would not have improved one's outcome compared with the other players' being so perceived.

Games in which power is ineffective probably lend themselves to more amicable resolutions. For this reason, Nixon and Kissinger may be applauded for upping the ante in the cease-fire game, by ordering an alert, so as to generate a Prisoners' Dilemma. But manufacturing a high-stakes game to deter an opponent has its own perils, which certainly must be weighed against the risks of not demonstrating resolve. Zagare offers the following assessment:

> It is not surprising, then, that the Nixon Administration decided not to place its faith in détente (or Soviet self-restraint), but instead chose to rely on a strategy rooted in the venerable tradition of Realpolitik, even though this strategy entailed certain risks. Game-theoretically speaking, the Administration's decision was sound and understandable. The long-term stability of the status quo in the game induced by the alert order [Figure 4.5] does not depend on either wishful thinking or the benevolence of Soviet leaders, but rather depends upon Soviet recognition of their own interests. (Zagare 1983, 83)

Coincidentally, in an earlier analysis of the 1967 Middle East war, Zagare (1981) also found a Prisoners' Dilemma, played between the superpowers over intervention, to have some of the earmarks of their 1973 game. Although there is no indication that the United States tried to misrepresent its preferences to the Soviets, President Lyndon Johnson did put the Strategic Air Command on alert after an Israeli attack on the *USS Liberty*, an American intelligence ship monitoring communications off the Israeli coast that appeared at first to have been attacked by the Soviets. When this turned out not to be the case, the Soviets were quickly informed via the hot line that the alert was no cause for alarm, and the crisis cooled down.

4.11. Conclusions

Because the language of much of this chapter has been about different kinds of equilibria and power, it is fitting, and perhaps a bit eerie, to discover that Nixon echoed these game-theoretic concerns with stability and strength in his own evaluation of the 1973 events in the Middle East: "Any equilibrium—even if only an equilibrium of mutual exhaustion—would make it easier to reach an enforceable settlement" (Nixon 1978, 921). This statement, I believe, not only epitomizes Nixon's view of power politics but also is the major theme that emerges from the foregoing game-theoretic analysis of bargaining in the two superpower crises analyzed.

There are several subthemes worth mentioning, including the importance, yet difficulty, of identifying different players' preferences in the real-world games studied. The three different representations given of the Cuban missile crisis, and one (with two hypothetical variations) of the 1973 cease-fire game that led to the alert decision, testify to the need to ponder these strategic conflicts from different perspectives that take as much account of the perceptions of players as of their true preferences.

In the fashion of *Rashomon* (a Japanese movie that portrays four different versions of a rape), each perspective gives new insights. It is especially instructive to see how sensitive rational outcomes are to the different reconstructions on which each is based and the relationship of these to the actual outcome.

A discrepancy between one's preferences and the perception of these by an opponent highlights another subtheme. Lack of complete information in a game may induce one player to try to deceive the other. There is evidence in both of the crises analyzed in this chapter that deception strategies were tried and possibly successful in abetting compromises in each case.

Another subtheme is the need for looking at conflicts as dynamic events that unfold over time that help to establish the terms of a settlement. I suggested that the theory of moves, and the nonmyopic equilibria based on this theory, may enable one not only to explain the moves but also to uncover stability in certain games that classical game theory hides or places elsewhere.

Related to this theory is the potential importance of power in different games. In the fields of political science and international relations, power has proved to be a very elusive concept indeed, even at a theoretical level (see Chapter 8 for a further discussion of power). But definitions that tap different aspects of power—moving, staying, and threat in this analysis—come to the fore naturally in sequential games in which players can make rational moves and countermoves.

Different constraints on such moves can provide different measures of power. I have not attempted in this chapter to explore the full dimensions of the constraints that one player can impose upon another, for I have dealt with this topic elsewhere (Brams 1983). Rather, my purpose here has been to try to give certain strategic insights into bargaining in two superpower crises to demonstrate the power that formal analysis can bring to the study of cases (Achen and Snidal 1989).

To return to the Nixon quotation, I believe he correctly identified the importance of "equilibrium" in any enforceable settlement. But what is its basis, and how is it enforced? I believe the theory of moves and its ancillary concepts, whose application to the events of 1962 and 1973 I have illustrated in this chapter, provide some answers.

Among other things, this theory enables one to probe certain strategic structures in depth, as they play out over time, and clarify the consequences of farsighted behavior. In Chapter 5 I turn to a more systematic development of the part of this theory most germane to explicating moves in bargaining where one's reputation is at stake.

Notes

[1]Recall that having a dominant strategy in the bargaining and arbitration models of Chapters 2 and 3 meant having a strategy against an adversary, whatever the adversary's reservation price or the judgment of the appraiser (i.e., that person's type in a game of incomplete information), that was better than any other strategy. Likewise, a player in Prisoners' Dilemma always does better choosing $\overline{C}$, regardless of the adversary's strategy.

[2]I consider here equilibria only in pure strategies, which involve choosing single (nonprobabilistic) courses of action; in Section 4.7 I shall contrast these equilibria with "nonmyopic equilibria."

[3]This section and the next are drawn from Brams (1977) with permission. I have also drawn on material in Brams (1985b) with permission in these and subsequent sections.

[4]Henceforth I shall assume in this crisis, as in the 1973 alert decision, that the superpowers can be considered unitary actors, though this is an obvious simplification. It is rectified in part by constructing other models that emphasize different features, as Allison (1971) has done.

[5]Pachter (1983). Other books on this crisis include Abel (1966); Weintal and Bartlett (1967); Kennedy (1969); Allison (1971); Divine (1971); Chayes (1974); Dinerstein (1976); Detzer (1979); and Brune (1985). Books that take account of recent revelations from the Soviet side include Blight and Welsh (1989) and Garthoff (1989).

[6]Yet another 2×2 game is proposed in Snyder and Diesing (1977, 114–16); an "improved metagame analysis" of the crisis is presented in Fraser and Hipel (1982–83).

[7]Brams (1977); Brams and Zagare (1977, 1981); Zagare (1979); Muzzio (1981). A useful compilation of material on deception, both in theory and practice, is Daniel and Herbig (1982).

[8]This game was suggested in a personal communication with Philip D. Straffin, Jr. (1976).

[9]Wohlstetter (1959) coined this term. On the basis of a dynamic model of a missile war from which they derive conditions for stable deterrence, Intriligator and Brito (1984) argue that the chances of the outbreak of major war have, paradoxically, been reduced because of the U.S.-Soviet quantitative arms race (at least until recently). For a critique and response to their article, see Mayer (1986) and Intriligator and Brito (1986). A formal model relating factors that affect the probability of nuclear war is developed in Avenhaus, Brams, Fichtner, and Kilgour (1989).

[10]Blechman and Hart (1982, p. 132). For an analysis of more than two hundred instances in which the United States used military force to try to achieve political ends since World War II, see Blechman and Kaplan (1978). A number of detailed case studies of superpower conflict are given in George and Smoke (1974) and George et al. (1983).

[11]There seems little doubt that by October 24, when the alert was given, the Soviets were making military preparations to intervene unilaterally on the side of Egypt within twenty-four hours (Blechman and Hart 1982, 139); the text of Nixon's message to Breshnev is given on p. 141.

[12]Nixon's concerns about the effects of Watergate on Brezhnev's perceptions are discussed in Muzzio (1982, 89, 94).

[13]For a full development of this theory, see Brams (1983).

[14]By "strategy" I mean here a course of action that can lead to any of the outcomes associated with it, depending on the strategy choice of the other player; the strategy choices of both players define an outcome at the intersection of their two strategies. Although the subsequent moves and countermoves of players could also be incorporated into the definition of a strategy—meaning a complete plan of responses by a player to whatever choices the other player makes in the sequential game—this would make the normal (matrix) form of the game unduly complicated and difficult to analyze. Hence, I use "strategy" to mean the choices of players that lead to an initial outcome, and "moves" and "countermoves" to refer to their subsequent sequential choices, as allowed by Rules 2 through 4.

[15]There may be a problem of timing if both players want to switch simultaneously, a situation I discuss later in this section.

[16]Brams and Wittman (1981); see also Kilgour (1984, 1985) and Zagare (1984, 1987) for extensions of, and revisions in, the concept of a nonmyopic equilibrium. It is related to the notion of "subgame perfect equilibrium" (Selten 1975), in which players also look ahead to determine future choices and reject those, in particular, that are conditioned on threats that it would be irrational for them to carry out in some subgame. The effects of such threats in repeated games, wherein it may be rational to carry out threats and incur temporary losses in order to bolster one's reputation in future play, will be analyzed in Chapter 5.

[17]The equiprobability assumption is not crucial; it is made to illustrate the calculation of expected values and is contrasted with other assumptions given in the next paragraph.

Chapter 5
Threats and Reputation in Bargaining

5.1. Introduction

A new concept of equilibrium, in which the rules of play allow for sequences of moves and countermoves after initial strategy choices are made in normal-form or matrix games, was introduced in Chapter 4. The analysis of sequential play reflects the view that most real-life games are ongoing and do not necessarily terminate after the players make their initial strategy choices. In fact, if these choices leave a player in a position that it could improve upon, either by itself or by inducing subsequent moves by other players, then the rules of (nonsequential) games seem unduly restrictive. They preclude the analysis of some commonly recognized empirical phenomena, such as jockeying for a favorable position in the early phase of extended negotiations so as to be in a more advantageous position later.

True, nonmyopic equilibria are based upon farsighted calculations that fully anticipate the sequence of moves and countermoves that players might make in a game. However, these calculations presuppose the single play of a game; while permitting sequential moves and countermoves by the players *within* a game after they make their initial strategy choices, they do not assume that the game is repeated.

Hessel and I (Brams and Hessel 1984) altered this assumption to permit repeated play of sequential games, which will be the main focus of this chapter. Repeated play, as I shall show, affects not only nonmyopic equilibria but also allows players to make threats, which are rendered credible by being enforceable in later games. As Moulin (1986, 248) put it, "No threat is meaningful when there is no tomorrow."

To be sure, if the threat is nuclear, there may be no tomorrow once the threat is carried out. Thus, as I have argued elsewhere (Brams 1985b, chap. 1), the credibility of nuclear threats must rest on the perception that they will be carried out with a sufficiently high probability. If there may be no tomorrow, this perception requires that the threatener precommit itself to command and control procedures that ensure retaliation will occur sufficiently often.

By contrast, in this chapter I assume that the players, after a threat has been carried out, live to see another day (in the repeated game) in which the threatener, by virtue of its action, has enhanced its credibility in future play. In the language to be used later, the threatener is perceived to have "threat power," which is the ability to carry out threats. This power, if correctly perceived, obviates the need actually to carry out threats; it was illustrated in Sections 4.4 and 4.10 but not defined formally.

By retaining the previous rules of sequential play in individual games, but permitting the games themselves to be repeated, one can analyze both the stability of outcomes in repeated play and the effectiveness of threats. Thus, the ability of players to "stretch out" their calculations in anticipation of playing future games may destabilize outcomes stable in the single play of a sequential game, much as myopically stable outcomes like Nash equilibria may be rendered unstable when the rules allow moves and countermoves from initial outcomes. Likewise, outcomes unstable in the single play of a sequential game may be rendered stable when the game is repeated, because players—anticipating its recurrence—change their rationality calculations (in ways to be made precise shortly).

Although repeated play of (nonsequential) games, or *supergames* if repeated infinitely, has been extensively analyzed (see Brams and Wittman [1981] for citations), there is no comparable supergame analysis of sequential games. Yet play under these rules seems ubiquitous, and repeated play under these rules may be just as common. The willingness of parties, for example, to accept prolonged stalemates, to refuse to negotiate at all, or to resort to the use of force—all at a considerable cost—can often only be explained by their expectation of possibly having to face the same situation over and over again. In this context, setting a precedent of implacable firmness may, though costly at the moment if challenged, more than pay for itself later by deterring future untoward actions of opponents.

In international politics, for example, a superpower might anticipate that it will be continually engaged in the same kind of dispute with several small countries, but each small country anticipates it will have only one encounter of this kind with the superpower. If this is the case, the superpower must worry about its bargaining reputation, whereas the small country has no such concern because its stake is not continuing.[1]

Call the continuing player (superpower) the *threatener*, and the noncontinuing player (small country) the *threatenee*. The threatener can make its threat credible by ignoring what it would lose in the short run if it were forced to carry out its threat. Incidentally, I assume that there is always a cost to the threatener (as well as the threatenee) when the threatener carries out its threat. If this were not the case, there would be no need to threaten an action—it would be rational simply to carry it out.

Although carried-out threats *may* enhance the credibility of the threatener's future threats in repeated play of a game, this is not always the case. In fact, most of the analysis of this chapter is devoted to showing what kinds of threats in what games produce what kinds of effects.[2] This analysis is also applicable to situations in which both players can threaten each other, but one has a greater ability to hold out against threats—should they be carried out—and both players recognize this greater ability on the part of one.

It should be noted that "repeated play of a game" may involve the threatener against either the same or different threatenees (as in the superpower-small country example). Whether both players are the same or different in repeated play, I assume that both know that the threatener is willing and able to carry out its threats to establish its future credibility.

Insofar as the threatener establishes credibility by carring out threats, this credibility is likely to extend to repeated play of *different* games. Thus, a threatener who has built up a reputation for "toughness" by taking reprisals against opponents who have not met its terms can be assumed to be a qualitatively different player from one who is out to ensure its best possible outcome in any single play of a sequential game. Similarly, the threatenee, aware of the threatener's reputation, will also be a different player.

Put another way, each player will have goals different from those assumed in the single play of a sequential game. This requires that one specify each player's rational calculus, given the assumption of repeated play for one player (i.e., the threatener) and knowledge by the other player (the threatenee) of the threatener's concern for credibility in future play.

In Section 5.2, I define the basic concepts that provide the building blocks for the analysis of credible threats, giving conditions under which a player has a threat strategy. Threat outcomes, which may be "compellent" or "deterrent," are analyzed in Section 5.3 when one or both players have threat strategies. Those games in which threat power is "effective" are distinguished from those in which it is not when both players in a game have threat strategies.

Although the focus of this chapter is on 2×2 sequential games, some propositions are given for general two-person games in Section 5.3. Additionally, comparisons are made of threat power with other kinds of power—moving and staying, as discussed in Chapter 4—in (nonrepeated) sequential games; the unique effect of threats in Chicken is noted. In Section 5.4, a "sequential-primary game," in which a repeated game is decomposed, vividly illustrates a paradox of repeated play in which the backward-induction argument suggests a different solution from a forward-induction argument. The mixed effects of threats, sometimes in undermining and sometimes in reinforcing cooperative outcomes, are summarized in Section 5.5, where some concluding observations are offered.

5.2. Repeated Play of a Sequential Game

Assume that one of the two players in a sequential game defined by Rules 1 through 4 (Section 4.7) faces repeated play of the game. Call this player T (threatener). The other player, $\overline{T}$ (threatenee), is concerned with only single play of the game; $\overline{T}$ is aware, however, of T's continuing involvement in repeated play of the game.

As noted earlier, recurrence of a game may make it rational for T to threaten $\overline{T}$ *and* carry out its threat, even if it results in a worse payoff for both players when the game is played only once. To analyze the effect of repeated play of a game on the stability of the game's outcome, make the following assumption about T's *threat behavior:* T will stay at, or move to, a strategy disadvantageous to itself (as well as $\overline{T}$) in a single play of a sequential game iff this choice enables it to establish the credibility of its threats in future play of games (ultimately leading to more desirable outcomes for T). "Credibility," along with other concepts I shall discuss informally here, will be formally defined later in this section.

T's credibility, I assume, prevents $\overline{T}$ from moving toward a final outcome in a game that is advantageous to $\overline{T}$ but disadvantageous to T. Should $\overline{T}$ contemplate such a move, T's threat will be to terminate the game at a (final) outcome disadvantageous to both players.

T's capability and will to carry out threats I call its *threat power.* This is the power to hurt (Schelling 1966; Aumann and Kurz 1977), which T may threaten to use, but will actually use, only if its threats are ignored. These threats are given force by threat power, which enables T to terminate a game at a mutually disadvantageous outcome. Although such termination is irrational for T (as well as $\overline{T}$) in any single play of the game, it becomes rational if T's involvement in a game continues and a carried-out threat deters future challenges.

To illustrate these concepts, consider Chicken in Figure 5.1. If neither player is engaged in repeated play of this game, the game has a unique nonmyopic equilibrium, (3,3) as demonstrated in Section 4.7. Now suppose that row is T, so it can outlast column at any outcome disadvantageous to both, and both players know this. In particular, row can move from (3,3) to (4,2), and then threaten column with *not* moving from (1,1) should column move there. This threat will induce column, given that it

Figure 5.1. Moves in Chicken and
Prisoners' Dilemma

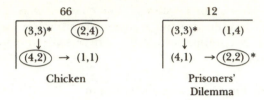

Key: Arrows indicate possible moves by row and
column, starting with a move by row from
the upper left outcome and followed by a
move by column from the lower left outcome. Circled outcome is a Nash equilibrium; starred outcome is a nonmyopic equilibrium.

knows row is engaged in repeated play of the game and has threat power,
to remain at (4,2). Because column knows that row can endure the
mutually worst outcome, (1,1), longer, column will not challenge row's
threat power by moving to (1,1). However, should row lack credibility,
column's move to (1,1) will terminate the game, providing an object
lesson to column (as well as future—perhaps different—players) about
the futility of challenging row in Chicken.

By the symmetry of payoffs in Chicken, if column is the more powerful
player (i.e., with threat power), it can obtain its best outcome (4) in this
game. Whoever T is, then, if T is credible, it can, by choosing its second
strategy initially, induce $\overline{T}$ to choose its first strategy, resulting in the best
outcome for T and the next-worst for $\overline{T}$. If T is not credible, and $\overline{T}$ also
chooses its second strategy initially, T can, by holding out at (l,l), force $\overline{T}$
to move away first, which has the same effect (except for the damage
caused) as $\overline{T}$'s choosing its first strategy initially. In either event, the
nonmyopic equilibrium (3,3) is rendered vulnerable by one player's readi-
ness to engage in repeated play and use threats that, if necessary, it can
and will carry out.

Clearly, repeated play of Chicken commits T not to swerve (i.e., choose
its second strategy) if, in the usual interpretation of this game, it is on a
collision course with $\overline{T}$, who also chooses its second strategy. But $\overline{T}$'s
reckless behavior will be deterred if it recognizes T's threat as credible,
forcing $\overline{T}$ to "chicken out."

Curiously, the possession of threat power does not always help one
player to defeat an opponent but may instead help both to extricate
themselves from an uncomfortable situation. Consider Prisoners' Di-

Figure 5.2. Ordinal 2 × 2 outcome matrix

(a_{11},b_{11})	(a_{12},b_{12})
(a_{21},b_{21})	(a_{22},b_{22})

lemma in Figure 5.1. Played once, this game has two nonmyopic equilibria, (2,2) and (3,3), as I showed in Section 4.8.

Repeated play of Prisoners' Dilemma undermines the stability of (2,2) at the same time that it confers on (3,3) the status of the "threat outcome." Assume, for example, that row is T, and the initial outcome is (3,3). If row announces to column, "should you move to (1,4), I will move to (2,2) and not switch from my second strategy," this threat will be credible: row's second strategy leads to column's two worst outcomes, one of which [presumably (2,2)] column would be stuck with if it departed from (3,3). Moreover, not only would column prefer (3,3), but so would row.

At the same time, row (as T) would have no incentive to move to (4,l), because this would simply induce column to move to (2,2), from which row would not depart. Furthermore, row can prevent C from choosing its second strategy *initially* by saying, "if you choose this strategy, I'll move to, and stay at, my own second strategy." Thereby both players will be motivated to choose (3,3) initially and not depart from this outcome.

As I shall show later, although one player's threat power singles out the Pareto-superior nonmyopic equilibrium as *the* outcome that would be chosen by rational players in Prisoners' Dilemma, there are two 2 × 2 games in which a player's threat power undermines the unique (Pareto-superior) nonmyopic equilibrium. Hence, this kind of equilibrium, even when it is not Pareto-inferior—as is (2,2) in Prisoners' Dilemma—may be vulnerable to threat power.

Manifestly, T's ability to use threats effectively—that is, to ensure a better outcome than is possible without them— depends on the preferences of *both* players and their ability to implement desirable outcomes, according to Rules 1 through 5, in any single play. To explore this interdependence more systematically, consider the 2 × 2 outcome matrix in Figure 5.2, in which each player is assumed to be able to rank the four outcomes from best to worst. (This matrix is not needed to follow the subsequent analysis; however, it may be useful to substitute the numerical subscripts in the matrix for the lettered ones in the text to illustrate the analysis.)

Assume that T desires to implement an outcome in row i and column j, (a_{ij},b_{ij}), for some $i = 1$ or 2 and for some $j = 1$ or 2, as the final outcome of the game, but it thinks that $\overline{T}$ might move from (a_{ij},b_{ij}) Suppose, further, that to deter $\overline{T}$ from making this move, T threatens to force the termination of the game at some outcome $(a_{mn},b_{mn}) \neq (a_{ij},b_{ij})$. Call T's threat *real* (against $\overline{T}$) iff, when carried out, it worsens the outcome for $\overline{T}$. T's threat is *rational* (for itself) iff, when successful in deterring $\overline{T}$, it improves T's own outcome over what it would be if $\overline{T}$ moved from (a_{ij},b_{ij}). A threat that is both real and rational is *credible* if it satisfies certain additional conditions.

To determine the conditions under which T has credible threats, suppose, without loss of generality, that row is T. Suppose, further, that row threatens terminaton of the game at (a_{mn},b_{mn}) in order to prevent column from moving from (a_{ij},b_{ij}). Clearly, this implies that $b_{ij} < 4$—that is, (a_{ij},b_{ij}) is not column's best outcome, for if it were, column would have no incentive to depart from it, making R's threat superfluous. Now R's threat is real iff

$$b_{mn} < b_{ij}; \tag{5.1}$$

it is rational iff

$$a_{mn} < a_{ij}. \tag{5.2}$$

Combining inequalities (5.1) and (5.2), a necessary (but not sufficient) condition for row's threat to be credible is that there exists a Pareto-inferior outcome

$$(a_{mn},b_{mn}) < (a_{ij},b_{ij}), \tag{5.3}$$

which means that the outcome on the left-hand side of the inequality is worse for both players than that on the right.

If T has a credible threat, $\overline{T}$ would not move from (a_{ij},b_{ij}) only to accept Pareto-inferior outcome (a_{mn},b_{mn}) as the final outcome. For this reason, call (a_{mn},b_{mn}) T's *breakdown outcome:* it forces $\overline{T}$ to comply with T's threat to avoid such an outcome, from which T will not depart. Instead, $\overline{T}$ is encouraged to stay at Pareto-superior outcome (a_{ij},b_{ij}), which is called T's *threat outcome;* T's strategy associated with this outcome is called T's *threat strategy*. By contrast, T's strategy associated with its breakdown outcome is its *breakdown strategy*.

Because T would not move from breakdown outcome (a_{mn},b_{mn})—even though it is worse for both players than threat outcome (a_{ij},b_{ij})—it is necessarily the final outcome should $\overline{T}$ depart from (a_{ij},b_{ij}). The cost to T of suffering a breakdown outcome, I assume, is the price it is willing to pay in any single play of a game to ensure that its threat will not be viewed as empty (i.e., a bluff) and will be credible in future games. Henceforth, I assume that T's possession of a credible threat implies that it is *non-*

empty — *T* will exercise it by moving to, or not moving from, its breakdown strategy.

Two qualitatively different kinds of credible threats may be distinguished, one requiring no move on the part of *T* (assumed to be row in the subsequent analysis), and the other requiring that *T* switch strategies:

1. *Row would stay: threat and breakdown strategies coincide.* When $m = i$, row's threat strategy and breakdown strategy are the same. Hence, row can threaten to stay at the Pareto-inferior outcome (a_{in}, b_{in}) should column move there. Inequality (5.3) becomes

$$(a_{in}, b_{in}) < (a_{ij}, b_{ij}), \qquad n \neq j, \tag{5.4}$$

so the existence of an outcome Pareto-inferior to the other outcome in the same row is sufficient for row to have a credible threat. Note also that row can always implement its threat outcome by choosing its threat strategy initially.

Chicken in Figure 5.1 illustrates this case. As I showed earlier, row can implement its threat (and most-preferred) outcome, (4,2), by choosing its second strategy initially and threatening not to move from (1,1), row's breakdown outcome, should column choose its second strategy.

2. *Row would move: threat and breakdown strategies diverge.* When $m \neq i$, row's threat and breakdown strategies are different. In this case, row can threaten to move to its breakdown strategy should column move from (a_{ij}, b_{ij}). Because column can move subsequently, it can choose as the breakdown outcome, (a_{mn}, b_{mn}), the better of its two outcomes associated with row's breakdown strategy. Necessarily, then, $b_{mn} \geq 2$. But I showed earlier that $b_{ij} < 4$, and from inequality (5.3), $b_{ij} > b_{mn}$. Taken together, these inequalities imply $b_{ij} = 3$ and $b_{mn} = 2$. Hence b_{mk} ($k \neq n$), column's ranking of the *other* outcome associated with row's breakdown strategy, must be 1. In other words, column's two worst outcomes are associated with row's breakdown strategy m.

Thus, in Case 2, row can threaten, should column move from its strategy associated with (a_{ij}, b_{ij}), to force column to choose between its next-worst and worst outcomes by switching to its breakdown strategy m. As in Case 1, row can always implement its threat outcome by choosing its threat strategy initially; unlike Case 1, however, the Pareto-inferior outcome that establishes the credibility of row's threat is associated with row's other (i.e., breakdown) strategy. In sum, whereas breakdown and threat strategies are coincidental in Case 1, they are not in Case 2, necessitating a move on the part of row in Case 2 to demonstrate that its credible threat is nonempty.[3]

Game 55 in Figure 5.3 illustrates Case 2.[4] Because column's two worst

Figure 5.3. Game illustrating a deterrent threat of row

55

$$\begin{array}{cc} \boxed{(2,4)} & (4,3) \\ (1,1) & (3,2) \end{array}$$

Key: Circled outcome is a Nash equilibrium.

outcomes are in row 2, this is a breakdown strategy with which row can threaten column. Moreover, row has reason to do so: not only does row prefer its better outcome in row 1, (4,3), to column's better outcome in row 2, (3,2), but row also prefers (4,3) to (2,4) in row 1, whereas the reverse is the case for column. Thus, (3,2) is row's breakdown outcome, and (4,3) its threat outcome. As T, then, row can implement (4,3) under threat that if column moves to (2,4), row will move to (1,1) and not move from row 2, its breakdown strategy. Although column can escape its worst outcome by moving to (3,2), clearly it (as well as row) would prefer (4,3).

In Schelling's terms, Case 1 reflects a *compellent threat: T* compels $\overline{T}$ to accept the threat outcome by saying that it will not abandon its threat/ breakdown strategy should $\overline{T}$ challenge its threat (i.e., depart from the threat outcome and move to the breakdown outcome) (Schelling 1966). Case 2 reflects a *deterrent threat: T* deters $\overline{T}$ from moving from the threat outcome by saying that it will retaliate by switching to its breakdown strategy should $\overline{T}$ challenge its threat. The two types of threats are not mutually exclusive and, indeed, may yield different threat outcomes in the same game. I shall show shortly that whenever the two threat outcomes differ, T will prefer the one associated with its deterrent threat, assuming both threats are credible.

The previous analysis allows one to state some propositions about threat strategies and outcomes in 2×2 ordinal games. First, it follows immediately from inequality (5.3) that:

1. *If a game contains only Pareto-superior outcomes, neither player has any threat strategies. In particular, neither player can credibly threaten its opponent in a total-conflict (zero-sum) game.* Thus, the Pareto-inferiority of at least one outcome is necessary for the effective exercise of threat power in a game. Providing that the sufficient conditions given under Cases 1 and 2 are met, the Pareto-inferior outcomes become breakdown outcomes for T.

Furthermore, as indicated for each case,

2. T *can always implement its threat outcome*. Recall that by initially choosing its threat strategy, T can force $\overline{T}$ either to choose between T's threat outcome and its breakdown outcome (Case 1) or to risk T's choosing its breakdown stratetgy, containing $\overline{T}$'s two worst outcomes, unless $\overline{T}$ accedes to T's threat outcome (Case 2). In either event, T's threat outcome is Pareto-superior to its breakdown outcome, so $\overline{T}$ will, if rational, choose its strategy associated with T's threat outcome at the start.

Finally, it is not difficult to establish that

3. *If* T's *compellent and deterrent threat outcomes differ*, T *will always prefer its deterrent threat outcome*. To see this, note that if deterrent and compellent threat outcomes are different, they must appear in different rows (or columns) of the outcome matrix. It follows immediately that the compellent threat outcome must be the breakdown outcome of the the deterrent threat; consequently, inequality (5.3) requires that it must be Pareto-inferior to the deterrent threat outcome.

There is exactly one game (55 in Figure 5.3) in which a player has different (credible) compellent and deterrent threat outcomes. This player is row, and its deterrent threat outcome, (4,3), is Pareto-superior to its compellent threat outcome, (3,2). By contrast, (4,2) is row's compellent threat outcome in Chicken in Figure 5.1; (3,3) is not, however, a deterrent threat outcome for row because (4,2) is not a breakdown outcome—it is better, not worse, for row than (3,3).

Before examining the outcomes induced by these different types of threats, I state two additional propositions that extend the previous analysis to $m \times n$ games larger than 2×2. They both give sufficient conditions for the implementation of T's *best outcome*. Here is the first:

4. *If* T *has a "junk" strategy—all of whose outcomes are Pareto-inferior to its best outcome associated with any other strategy—then* T *can induce the choice of its best (Pareto-superior) outcome with a deterrent threat*. Clearly, T would prefer its best outcome to any outcome associated with the junk strategy; so would $\overline{T}$ because this outcome is Pareto-superior and hence better for it, too. Moreover, T can ensure this outcome under threat of switching to its junk strategy.

Brinkmanship, as commonly interpreted in superpower confrontations, might be thought of as a junk strategy. It is extremely dangerous, of course, to threaten destruction of the world with nuclear weapons, but it would not necessarily be irrational if T thought it could survive and thence maintain supremacy over $\overline{T}$ in future confrontations (if there are any!).

A compellent threat may also be used to cow an opponent in an $m \times n$ game:

> 5. *If* T *has a "carrot-and-stick" strategy, one of whose outcomes is best for* T *and Pareto-superior to all other outcomes associated with this strategy, it can induce this outcome with a compellent threat.* A carrot-and-stick strategy differs from a junk strategy in having exactly one Pareto-superior outcome. If this outcome is best for T, T's compellent threat will induce its choice. An example of such a strategy might be one in which T threatens to punish $\overline{T}$ severely (at a cost to T as well) unless $\overline{T}$ makes certain concessions.

Note, however, that with a junk strategy, T can ensure its best outcome *whatever* other strategy it is associated with (i.e., wherever it lies in the outcome matrix). With a carrot-and-stick strategy, by contrast, T's best outcome must be the unique Pareto-superior outcome (the "carrot") associated with this strategy in order to guarantee its choice with a compellent threat. Thus, the possession of a junk strategy is, in a sense, a more powerful weapon than a carrot-and-stick strategy, because T can use it to implement its best outcome, wherever it lies in the outcome matrix, with a deterrent threat.

5.3. Threat Outcomes in Repeated Play of a Game

Of the 78 2×2 strict ordinal games, 21 are *no-conflict games* that contain a mutually best (4,4) outcome. I shall not consider these games further because the choice of (4,4) would appear to be unproblematic— no threats by the players would be necessary to implement this outcome. The following algorithm can be used to determine whether a particular 2×2 ordinal game has one or more threat outcomes, (a_{ij}, b_{ij}), for row, and, if so, what they are:

1. Select i and j such that $a_{ij} = 4$.
2. If $b_{ij} = 4$, stop: no threats are necessary to implement (a_{ij}, b_{ij}).
3. If $b_{ij} = 1$, go to (8): no threats can induce (a_{ij}, b_{ij}).
4. Select (a_{mn}, b_{mn}) that satisfies (5.3). If none exists, go to (7).
5. If $m = i$, (a_{ij}, b_{ij}) is row's compellent threat outcome.
6. If $m \neq i$, and $b_{mn} = 2$, stop: (a_{ij}, b_{ij}) is row's deterrent threat outcome.
7. If $a_{ij} = 3$, stop: row has no threat outcomes.
8. Select i and j such that $a_{ij} = 3$. Go to (2).

Figure 5.4. Category 1 games in which neither player has a threat strategy

7		8		9		10	
(3,3)*	(4,2)	(3,3)*	(4,2)	(3,3)*	(4,1)	(2,3)*	(4,2)
(2,4)	(1,1)	(1,4)	(2,1)	(1,4)	(2,2)	(1,4)	(3,1)

11		45		46		73	
(2,3)*	(4,1)	(3,2)	(4,1)	(3,2)	(4,1)	(2,4)	(4,1)
(1,4)	(3,2)	(2,3)	(1,4)	(1,3)	(2,4)	(3,2)	(1,3)

74		75		76	
(2,4)	(3,1)	(2,3)	(4,1)	(2,3)	(3,1)
(4,2)	(1,3)	(3,2)	(1,4)	(4,2)	(1,4)

Key: Circled outcome is a Nash equilibrium; starred outcome is a nonmyopic equilibrium.

With the *a*'s and *b*'s interchanged, the same algorithm can be used to obtain column's threat outcomes.

Of the 57 2 × 2 *conflict games,* there are:

1. 11 in which *neither* player has a threat strategy;
2. 26 in which *one* player has a threat strategy;
3. 20 in which *both* players have a threat strategy.

As shown in Figure 5.4, five of the 11 games (7 through 11) in Category 1 have a nonmyopic equilibrium that is also a Nash equilibrium; games 45 and 46 have only a Nash equilibrium, (3,2). None of the other four games contains either a Nash or a nonmyopic equilibrium.

The threat outcomes that column can implement as *T* in the 26 Category 2 games are shown in Figure 5.5. (In the classification scheme of Rapaport and Guyer [1966], it so happens that row never has a threat strategy in any of these games, but the players could be interchanged so as to make row *T*.) Because only one player has threat power, all the Category 2 games are necessarily asymmetric.

T obtains its best outcomes in 22 of the games, its next-best outcomes in four. Moreover, in the latter games (42, 43, 53, 54), the threat outcomes are all (3,3), so *T* never does worse than $\overline{T}$. Thus, if only one player has a threat strategy, the threat outcome it can implement—given that it has threat power—will rank at least as high for it as for its opponent.

The threat outcomes in eight of the 26 Category 2 games (31 through

Figure 5.5. Category 2 games in which one player has a threat strategy

13

$(3,4)^{c1}$ ⃝	$(4,2)$
$(2,3)$	$(1,1)$

14

$(3,4)^{c1}$ ⃝	$(4,2)$
$(1,3)$	$(2,1)$

15

$(3,4)^{c1}$ ⃝	$(4,1)$
$(2,3)$	$(1,2)$

16

$(3,4)^{c1}$ ⃝	$(4,1)$
$(1,3)$	$(2,2)$

17

$(2,4)^{c1}$ ⃝	$(4,2)$
$(1,3)$	$(3,1)$

18

$(2,4)^{c1}$ ⃝	$(4,1)$
$(1,3)$	$(3,2)$

31

$(3,4)^{*c1}$ ⃝	$(2,2)$
$(1,3)$	$(4,1)$

32

$(3,4)^{*c1}$ ⃝	$(2,1)$
$(1,3)$	$(4,2)$

33

$(3,4)^{*c1}$ ⃝	$(1,2)$
$(2,3)$	$(4,1)$

34

$(3,4)^{*c1}$ ⃝	$(1,1)$
$(2,3)$	$(4,2)$

35

$(2,4)^{*c1}$ ⃝	$(3,2)$
$(1,3)$	$(4,1)$

36

$(2,4)^{*c1}$ ⃝	$(3,1)$
$(1,3)$	$(4,2)$

37

$(3,4)^{*c1}$ ⃝	$(2,3)$
$(1,2)$	$(4,1)$

38

$(3,4)^{*c1}$ ⃝	$(1,3)$
$(2,2)$	$(4,1)$

40

$(3,4)^{c1}$ ⃝	$(4,1)$
$(2,2)$	$(1,3)$

41

$(3,4)^{c1}$ ⃝	$(4,1)$
$(1,2)$	$(2,3)$

42

$(3,3)^{c1}$ ⃝	$(4,1)$
$(2,2)$	$(1,4)$

43

$(3,3)^{c1}$ ⃝	$(4,1)$
$(1,2)$	$(2,4)$

47

$(2,3)$ ⃝	$(4,1)$
$(1,2)$	$(3,4)^{c2}$

48

$(2,2)$ ⃝	$(4,1)$
$(1,3)$	$(3,4)^{c2}$

51

$(3,4)^{c1}$ ⃝	$(4,2)$
$(1,1)$	$(2,3)$

52

$(3,4)^{c1}$ ⃝	$(4,2)$
$(1,1)$	$(2,3)$

53

$(3,3)^{c1}$ ⃝	$(4,2)$
$(2,1)$	$(1,4)$

54

$(3,3)^{c1}$ ⃝	$(4,2)$
$(1,1)$	$(2,4)$

57

$(2,3)$ ⃝	$(4,2)$
$(1,1)$	$(3,4)^{c2}$

70

$(3,4)^{c2}$	$(2,1)$
$(4,2)$	$(1,3)$

Key: c = outcome column can implement; 1 = outcome induced by compellent threat; 2 = outcome induced by deterrent threat. Circled outcome is a Nash equilibrium; starred outcome is a nonmyopic equilibrium.

38) are nonmyopic equilibria. Because these outcomes are stable, even in the absence of power asymmetries, it can be argued that threat power in these games is redundant—the outcome would be the same without it.

Figure 5.6. Five Category 3 games in which both players have a threat strategy and power is ineffective

12	
$(2,2)^*$	$(4,1)$
$(1,4)$	$(3,3)^{*c2,r2}$

Prisoners' Dilemma

71	
$(3,3)^{c2,r1}$	$(2,1)$
$(4,2)$	$(1,4)$

72	
$(3,2)$	$(2,1)$
$(4,3)^{r2}$	$(1,4)$

77	
$(2,2)$	$(4,1)$
$(3,3)^{c1,r2}$	$(1,4)$

78	
$(2,2)$	$(3,1)$
$(4,3)^{c1,r2}$	$(1,4)$

Key: c = outcome column can implement; r = outcome row can implement; 1 = outcome induced by compellent threat; 2 = outcome induced by deterrent threat. Circled outcome is a Nash equilibrium; starred outcome is a nonmyopic equilibrium.

In only 5 of the 20 Category 3 games in which both players have threat strategies do threats lead to the same outcome, whether row or column is T. These games are shown in Figure 5.6. In each, the power asymmetry induces a (3,3) or (4,3) "cooperative" outcome. In these games, threat power is *ineffective,* because it does not make any difference on the outcome induced which player has it. Thus, it is impossible to determine from the outcome which player is T, for either can claim to have induced the (common) threat outcome.

Of the five games in which threat power is ineffective, only one, Prisoners' Dilemma (Game 12 in Figure 5.6), contains nonmyopic equilibria. Prisoners' Dilemma is also unique in being the only game that is symmetric and in which each player, as T, can implement the threat outcome, (3,3), with a deterrent threat. Indeed, as I argued earlier, the threat power of either player induces the cooperative (3,3) nonmyopic equilibrium, relegating the noncooperative nonmyopic equilibrium to oblivion, so to speak.

Threats, in other words, offer a kind of resolution of the dilemma in Prisoners' Dilemma that is very different from the trust that some theorists have argued is necessary, in the absence of a binding and enforceable contract, to induce cooperation in this well-nigh intractable game. By comparison, it is simply not rational to be either trusting or trustworthy in the nonsequential play of this game (i.e., when moves and countermoves are not allowed), at least when it is not repeated.[5]

When play is sequential, however, as assumed here, threat power enables the implementation of the Pareto-superior (cooperative) nonmyopic equilibrium. Threat power, therefore, even if ineffective, may still be important in singling out one outcome as *the* outcome that will be induced if both players have threat strategies but a power asymmetry elevates one to the role of threatener.

The consequences of this asymmetry are salutary not only in Prisoners' Dilemma but also—by ensuring at least the next-best outcome for both players—in the other four games in Figure 5.6, in which threat power is ineffective. By stabilizing the (3,3) or (4,3) outcomes in these games, which lack Nash and nonmyopic equilibria, the common threat outcome seems to offer a satisfactory resolution of the fundamental long-term instability that would otherwise plague these games.

In 15 of the 20 Category 3 games in which both players have threat strategies, each player's threat strategy—whether compellent or deterrent—induces a different threat outcome. These games, which are given in Figure 5.7, illustrate threat power that is *effective:* each player, as *T*, can implement a better outcome for itself than were the other player *T*; consequently, each would prefer to be *T*.

In one game (Game 55), discussed in Section 5.2 and shown in Figure 5.3, there is a conflict between the compellent and deterrent threat outcomes for row. Because the deterrent threat outcome, (4,3), is better for row than the compellent threat outcome, (3,2), I assume it is *the* threat outcome that row would implement.

Only two of the 15 games (39 and 66) in Figure 5.7 have nonmyopic equilibria; Game 66, as already noted, is Chicken. While the (2,4) nonmyopic equilibrium in Game 39 coincides with the threat outcome for one player (column), the cooperative (3,3) nonmyopic equilibrium in Chicken—unlike the (3,3) outcome in Game 39—is not a threat outcome for either player.

Threat strategies of one or both players, then, may undermine nonmyopic equilibria in games in which threat power is effective [(2,4) in Game 39 and (3,3) in Chicken] as well as ineffective [(2,2) in Prisoners' Dilemma].[6] This is not a problem in Prisoners' Dilemma because the nonmyopic equilibrium that is lost is Pareto-inferior; and it is not a serious problem in Game 39 because row's threat strategy ensures the compromise outcome, (3,3). In Chicken, however, it is this very outcome that row's compellent threat transforms into (4,2), and column's into (2,4). Thus, threat power subverts compromise *only* in Chicken, an ominous finding to which I shall return in Section 5.5.

On the positive side, *all* threat outcomes, whether only one player has a threat strategy (Figure 5.5) or both do—and, in the latter case, whether threat power is ineffective (Figure 5.6) or effective (Figure 5.7)—are Pareto-superior. Hence, *T* can never abandon the outcome it implements without hurting itself, $\overline{T}$, or both.

How do the outcomes induced by threat power in repeated sequential games compare with the outcomes that moving power (Section 4.4) and

Figure 5.7. Fifteen Category 3 games in which both players have a threat strategy and power is effective

19

(3,4)ᶜ¹	(4,3)ᶜ²
(1,2)	(2,1)

20

(3,4)ᶜ¹	(4,3)ᶜ²
(2,2)	(1,1)

21

(2,4)ᶜ¹	(4,3)ᶜ²
(1,2)	(3,1)

39

(2,4)*¹	(3,3)ᶜ²
(1,2)	(4,1)

44

(2,4)¹	(4,1)
(1,2)	(3,3)ᶜ¹

19

(3,4)ᶜ¹	(4,3)ᶜ²
(2,1)	(1,2)

50

(3,4)ᶜ¹	(4,3)ᶜ²
(1,1)	(2,2)

55

(2,4)ᶜ¹	(4,3)ᶜ²
(1,1)	(3,2)

56

(2,4)ᶜ¹	(4,2)
(1,1)	(3,3)ᶜ¹

64

(3,4)ᶜ¹	(2,1)
(1,2)	(4,3)ʳ¹

65

(2,4)ᶜ¹	(3,1)
(1,2)	(4,3)ʳ¹

66

(3,3)*	(2,4)ᶜ¹
(4,2)ᶜ¹	(1,1)

Chicken

67

(2,3)	(3,4)ᶜ¹
(4,2)ʳ¹	(1,1)

68

(2,2)	(3,4)ᶜ¹
(4,3)ʳ¹	(1,1)

69

(2,2)	(4,3)ᶜ¹
(3,4)ᶜ¹	(1,1)

Key: *c* = outcome column can implement; *r* = outcome row can implement; 1 = outcome induced by compellent threat; 2 = outcome induced by deterrent threat. Circled outcome is a Nash equilibrium; starred outcome is a nonmyopic equilibrium.

staying power (Section 4.10) induce in nonrepeated sequential games?[7] To allow meaningful comparisons, I consider only those games in which the possession of power by the players is effective. Surprisingly, perhaps, whereas threat power is effective in 15 games, moving power is effective in 18 and staying power in 20, but the larger categories do not completely overlap the smaller or each other: each kind of power is effective in some different games.

The overlap of threat-power games with moving- and staying-power games, for example, is as follows: 7 of the 15 threat-power games coincide with moving-power games, and 13 of them coincide with staying-power games. Moreover, even when the games overlap, the outcomes induced by each kind of power are not all the same.

The two games in which threat power *alone* is effective are 39 and 66 (Chicken), the only two games in Figure 5.7 with nonmyopic equilibria. Chicken is doubtless the more interesting, and its prominence in the literature seems well-earned: it is not just a suggestive game, useful in ad hoc illustrations of credibility and deterrence,[8] but also the only game in which threats undermine a "cooperative" nonmyopic equilibrum. This dismaying fact stems from the assumptions about repeated play and the ability of T to exploit the recurrence of a game. Time, as Chicken demonstrates, may not heal all wounds; instead, it may exacerbate them.

Fortunately, the nonmyopic equilibrium in Chicken was the choice of the players in the Cuban missile crisis—if this was indeed the game that was played—though some believe that the United States "won" (Section 4.3). In the two cases to be presented in Chapter 6, threat power seems to have been effective in undermining the nonmyopic equilibrium in one (the Polish crisis of 1980–81), but neither player's threat power in the other (the Watergate tapes case) could be used because of problems of timing, credibility, and commitment.

To illustrate the role of threats in repeated games, I next give a hypothetical example that unpacks details not made explicit in the 2 × 2 games, including information on the number of players and the number of rounds played in component subgames. This game dramatically underscores why a threatener might be willing to suffer (temporary) losses to build up a reputation that serves him or her well in the future.

5.4. The Sequential-Primary Game

The one hurdle that all serious presidential aspirants face in the United States is to gain the nomination of one of the two major political parties. At least in recent times, this has usually necessitated that an aspirant enter a series of state primary elections (or caucuses) to establish his or her popular appeal among party voters in different states (Bartels 1988). If successful, this candidate usually has a better chance of winning his or her party's nomination at its national convention.[9]

Sometimes a person will enter a state primary with no serious hope or intention of capturing his or her party's presidential nomination. Instead, this person's purpose is to deny a state's convention votes to a major candidate—at least on the first ballot of the convention—or slow down or stop an incipient bandwagon that has the potential to sweep the major candidate onto subsequent primary victories and the convention nomination.

The person most frequently cast into the "spoiler" role is a prominent state politician, often the governor, who runs as a so-called favorite son in his state. (As of this writing, there have been no "favorite daughters," but this could change; I shall assume "sons" in the subsequent discussion to keep the language simpler, but even this category has hardly been visible in recent presidential elections—though candidates with strong regional identification have been prominent.) Whether the favorite son's purpose in running is to deny his party's presidential nomination to a particular candidate or—as is often claimed—to maximize his state's later influence in the party convention, he does this by withholding, at the early stages of the convention proceedings, his state's convention votes from all the major candidates at the party convention. After observing how support develops for the various candidates and assessing their prospects for eventually winning the presidential nomination, he is in a better position to throw his support to one candidate at a crucial stage and thereby augment his importance in the decision-making process— and perhaps maximize his own later rewards.[10]

The game I envision is one in which there is a single major party candidate who announces her intention to enter all the state primaries. (Henceforth I assume the major candidate is female, as contrasted with the favorite sons.) Imagine that her vote-getting power has not been well established in different parts of the country (perhaps because of gender, religion, or race), and the primary campaign is designed to demonstrate her nationwide appeal. This was John Kennedy's strategy in his 1960 presidential bid; his Catholicism was the big unknown that he wanted to prove would not impede his chances of winning in the general election if he was nominated by his party.

Assume that the only opposition the leading candidate, designated player A, faces is from favorite sons possibly running against her in each of the state primaries.[11] Concretely, assume that there are 20 primaries, numbered from 1 to 20, each occurring on a different day.[12] Designate the potential favorite sons in each primary as players k, $k = 1, 2, \ldots, 20$, where Player 1 is the potential favorite son in the first primary to occur, 2 is the potential favorite son in the second primary to occur, and so forth. There are thus 21 players in this game, the leading candidate A and the 20 potential favorite sons k.

The game proceeds as follows. After candidate A announces her intention to enter all 20 primaries, each of the 20 potential favorite sons in each state faces the following decision: to run against A in his state (*in*) or not to run (*out*). (This is why I refer to favorite sons as "potential.") Each of the potential favorite sons, however, does not make his decision until his state primary comes up in the sequence of primaries. In particular, except for Player 1, each player k awaits the results of the races (if any) in the $k - 1$ primaries preceding his.

Player A faces the following decisions. If k chooses *out*, she runs unopposed. In this case, she does not have to choose a campaign strategy. If

Figure 5.8. Game tree in one primary election

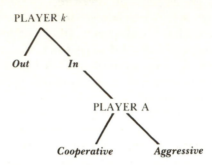

k chooses *in,* *A* must choose between two campaign strategies: *cooperative* or *aggressive,* which I shall describe further later. She faces this choice in the case of each *k* who chooses *in.* In Figure 5.8 I summarize in a game tree the sequence of choices that all players *k,* and Player *A,* make in every primary election.

Although the game runs over all 20 primaries in a definite sequence, I shall not try to specify the payoffs to all players after each primary. Instead, I indicate in the payoff matrix in Figure 5.9 the payoffs in cardinal utilities to *A* and *k,* associated with each of their strategy choices, *as if* the game were played between two players in only one primary.

Naturally, new players will enter the game over the sequence of 20 primaries. And, depending on the outcomes of the previous primaries, the payoffs to *A* will accumulate, which is why utilities and not ranks are assumed. *A*'s payoff is the sum of her utilities across the 20 primaries.

The consequences of the strategy choices of *A* and *k* in each primary can be summarized as follows:

1. If *k* is *out,* he receives a payoff of 1.
2. If *k* is *in,* he does better than had he not entered if *A* is *cooperative* (payoff of 2), worse if *A* is *aggressive* (payoff of 0).
3. *A* does best when *k* is *out* (payoff of 5), less well if k is *in* and she is *cooperative* (payoff of 2), and worst if *k* is *in* and she is *aggressive* (payoff of 0).

Cooperative and *aggressive* refer to how vigorously *A* pursues her campaign against *k.* Underlying the payoffs associated with these campaign strategies is the assumption that an *aggressive* campaign—perhaps with negative advertising, which most voters find distasteful if not abhorrent—is costly not only to *A,* who wages it, but also to *k,* who must respond to it.

Figure 5.9. Payoff matrix in one primary
election (Player A weak)

Player A

		Cooperative	Aggressive
	In	(2,2)	(0,0)
Player *k*			
	Out	(1,5)	(1,5)

↑
Dominant strategy

Key: Circled outcomes are Nash equilibria.

Consequently, both players fare worse, even if the election results are unaffected, when *A* is *aggressive.* They do somewhat better when *k* is *in* and *A* is *cooperative,* because both spend less and do not risk making fatal errors and disaffecting voters with their aggressiveness (e.g., by using smear tactics).

If *k* is *out,* a *cooperative* or *aggressive* campaign makes no difference in the payoffs to both players (see Figure 5.9). In this case, therefore, the nature of *A*'s campaign is irrelevant. This may be interpreted to mean, consistent with the game tree shown in Figure 5.8, that *A* makes effectively no choice—at least not one that results in different consequences for the players—when any *k* is *out.*

I make two assumptions, one about information and one about communication, in the sequential-primary game. First, *k*'s decision to enter or not to enter his primary, when his turn comes up in the sequence, is immediately made known to all the other players. If *k* is *in,* the players are also informed of whether *A* chooses a *cooperative* or *aggressive* strategy in her campaign. In particular, the potential favorite sons who have yet to decide whether to enter their primaries will be informed of the kind of campaign that *A* waged in the primaries preceding their own.

The second assumption is that although all players have knowledge of the choices made at each stage of the game (*perfect information*), and the resulting payoffs to the participants as well as the rules of play (*complete information*), they cannot make agreements with each other that are enforceable. This latter assumption does not preclude their bargaining with each other—in particular, that the favorite sons try to make deals to stop *A*—but I assume that there is no mechanism that can make an agreement binding on them in a cooperative game.

To solve this game, consider the twentieth primary. If the last potential favorite son chooses *out,* he gets a payoff of 1. Of course, he could do better (payoff of 2) if he chooses *in* and *A* chooses her *cooperative* strategy.

But he may also end up with a payoff of 0 if *A* wages an *aggressive* campaign.

Consider this primary from the vantage point of *A*. Because there are no primaries to follow, *A* does not have to be concerned with how her behavior in this primary might influence the choices of possible opponents in future primaries. If the twentieth potential favorite son is *in*, therefore, *A* need be concerned only with how to maximize her payoff in this primary. This *A* accomplishes by choosing her *cooperative* strategy, which gives *A* a payoff of 2 rather than 0 if she wages an *aggressive* campaign. On the other hand, if the twentieth potential son is *out*, *A*'s strategy has no effect on her payoff, making her *cooperative* strategy (nonstrictly) dominant.

Given that it is in the interest of *A* always to be *cooperative* in the last primary, it is also in the interest of the twentieth potential favorite son, knowing this, to run in his primary and also realize a payoff of 2. Thus, although the circled (1,5) outcome in Figure 5.9 is a Nash equilibrium, (2,2) is the unique dominant-strategy Nash equilibrium in the twentieth-primary game.

Having settled on *in* and *cooperative* as their mutually advantageous strategies in the twentieth primary, what strategies should *A* and Player 19 choose in the nineteenth primary? Clearly, they can ignore any possible effects that their choices will have on the twentieth primary because, as I have argued, *the optimal choices in this primary (the twentieth) do not depend on the primaries which preceded it (including the nineteenth).* Thus, the nineteenth primary can be treated as if it were the last primary, and the previous reasoning applied. This would dictate once again the choices of *in* and *cooperative* by Players 19 and *A*, respectively.

Carrying this reasoning successively backward, *all* players *k* should choose *in*, and *A* should *always* respond with her *cooperative* strategy. The payoff to each *k* would then be 2, and the payoff to *A*, summed across the sequence of twenty primaries, would be (20)(2) = 40.

Note that this is the same argument that was used in the case of repeated play of Prisoners' Dilemma to justify the suspects' always choosing their noncooperative strategies (Section 4.6). It may strike one as puzzling that, with a change in the game but not the logic, one can now make the case for cooperation. But just as the noncooperative strategy is dominant for both suspects in Prisoners' Dilemma, the cooperative strategy for *A* in one election of the sequential-primary game is dominant. Extending play of these games over time does not affect the desirability of the respective dominant strategies.[13]

But something seems amiss, at least in the case of the sequential-primary game. Is it really in the interest of *A* always to cooperate in each primary—and realize a payoff of only 2—when she can more than double her payoff (to 5) by inducing potential favorite sons to drop out?

Although the backward-induction argument supporting the *in* and *cooperative* strategies of Players 1, 2, . . . , 20 and Player A, respectively, is logically unassailable, its weakness is that the assumptions on which it is built are, in reality, probably untenable. The crux of the argument is the assumption, stated in the foregoing analysis of the nineteenth and twentieth primaries, that "optimal choices in [one] primary do not depend on the primaries which preceded it." In effect, considering one primary *de novo*—as if it were a single game—does not admit the history of previous play in the sequence.

But this history may be just as important for predicting *A*'s actions as her "rational" choice on the last round, looking to the future. Because there is no future play, the problem with determining what constitutes a rational choice is, by the induction argument, reduced to a trivial question: What constitutes the best choice for players if the game is played only once?

Because the game as defined encompasses a sequence of primaries, and the players have perfect information about the choices made in each primary over the course of play, it seems unbelievable that they would ignore this information. Yet, this is exactly what the induction argument asks one to do. Indeed, if the players had no information about the strategy choices of the players who preceded them, the induction argument could be applied to the twentieth primary, and recursively to preceding primaries, just as before.

In fact, however, the players *do* have perfect information, and it is this information that *A* can exploit. By assuming an aggressive posture initially, she can easily suffer the consequences of payoffs of 0 in several early primaries and still come out ahead in the end.

It is unclear how many primaries it would take for potential favorite sons to become convinced that they almost certainly will lose more than they will gain if they enter their primaries. In fact, *A* could afford to campaign aggressively in as many as the first twelve primaries, and succeed in deterring potential favorite sons from running in only the remaining eight primaries, for her payoff,

$$(12)(0) + (8)(5) = 40,$$

to match that which she would obtain if all potential favorite sons ran and she responded with her cooperative strategy in each case [giving her a payoff of $(20)(2) = 40$].

It seems unlikely that it would take as many as twelve primaries for *A* to establish the credibility of her aggressive response. More likely, six or fewer primaries would suffice—especially if they were strung together in the beginning of the sequence—to discourage future challengers. Assuming this to be the case, A would come out substantially better off by punishing, rather than appeasing, all challengers (except Player 20). This, of course, is the logic of deterrence, which can be applied not only to the analysis of political competition but also to business pricing policies (Selten's example), national-security questions (Brams 1985b; Brams and Kilgour 1988), and many other recurring conflicts.

To tie the sequential-primary game to the analysis of threats in 2×2 games, consider play in the former game to have reached, say, $k = 10$, and assume that the first nine small players entered. Moreover, assume that A was aggressive in each of these games. Then k might well conceive of his choices and their consequences to resemble those of playing Chicken, wherein his opponent, A, has threat power.

Thus, if k is the row player, choosing *in* is tantamount to selecting (1,1) in Chicken, because k has every reason to believe that A will continue to be *aggressive*. On the other hand, choosing *out* will give him (2,4). Hence, if k believes A's threat is credible, the outcome will be next worst for k and best for A.

What the sequential-primary game highlights that repeated play of Chicken does not is the *basis* of A's threat power. In essence, A can communicate, through actions in the course of the game, that she will not be "suckered" into choosing a *cooperative* strategy that allows k to obtain his best outcome (and results in a less-preferred outcome for A). Thereby A is able to signal her intentions through a pattern of repeated choices within the game, whereas in the Cuban missile crisis—modeled as a game of Chicken—the communication of intentions was not explicitly made part of the game structure.

Nevertheless, there is a problem with grounding rational choices on a history of prior choices, rather than individual incentives, because players can arguably enforce almost any outcome in an iterated game. In the sequential-primary game, the incentive problem for being *aggressive* shows up most starkly in the twentieth primary. There is simply no incentive for A to be *aggressive,* and ignore her dominant strategy, on this round. Likewise, it makes no sense for $k = 20$ to base his choice on A's previous behavior: the twentieth primary is a single-shot game, and k can anticipate that A, acting rationally, will choose her dominant strategy. His rational response is to enter this primary, resulting in the (2,2) outcome.

But how far back can one carry this reasoning? Kreps and Wilson (1982a) and Milgrom and Roberts (1982) approach this problem by introducing uncertainty into the game, thereby making it one of incom-

Figure 5.10. Payoff matrix in one primary election
(Player A strong)

Player A

Cooperative   Aggressive

	Cooperative	Aggressive
In	(0,0)	(−1,2)
Out	(1,5)	(1,5) ← Dominant strategy

Player k

↑
Dominant strategy

Key: Circled outcome is a Nash equilibrium.

plete information. They define *sequential equilibria* in this new game, which are Nash equilibria that are rational with respect to the beliefs of the players (Kreps and Wilson 1982b).

To illustrate sequential equilibria, suppose that the (2,2) outcome in Figure 5.9 has some chance of being (0,0): a *cooperative* campaign definitely hurts both A and k when k is *in*, presumably because A's votes are diminished, and her reputation for toughness is damaged, by treating k's entry lightly in any single primary; likewise, k is hurt by a placid campaign. Suppose, further, that the (0,0) outcome in Figure 5.9 has some chance of being (−1,2): k suffers even more than previously from an aggressive campaign waged by A; A, on the other hand, benefits from an aggressive campaign. These changes in A's payoffs are indicated in the payoff matrix of Figure 5.10, wherein A has a dominant strategy of being *aggressive*, and k of choosing *out*, making lower-right (1,5) entry the dominant-strategy Nash equilibrium.

Call the A player of the Figure 5.10 game *strong*, and the A player of the Figure 5.9 game *weak*. These are the only two types of players assumed in this game of incomplete information,[14] as contrasted with the continuum of types assumed for the buyer, seller, and appraiser in Chapter 2, and the arbitrator in Chapter 3.

Suppose the players believe that the probability is $p < 1/2$ that A is weak. Then the following strategies are in equilibrium if A is, in fact, weak:

- $k = 1$ chooses *out*; $k = 2, \ldots, 20$ chooses *in* if A has selected *cooperative* on any previous round, *out* otherwise;
- A chooses *aggressive* on every round $1, \ldots, 17$ on which k selects *in*, *cooperative* on every round 18, 19, 20 on which k selects *in*.

For these strategies, the sequential equilibrium is that all players $k = 1$, ..., 20 choose *out*. The reason is that $k = 1$ is *out;* because A's choice is *aggressive* on every round 1, ..., 17 if k selects *in*, $k = 1$, ..., 18 remains *out*. But now $k = 19$ and then $k = 20$ will also remain *out*—because a weak A never selects *cooperative* (or *aggressive*) as long as k continues to remain *out*—so A never needs to make a choice on these final rounds.

Thus, although it would be rational for a weak A to switch to *cooperative* on the last three rounds if k were to choose *in*, k will not do so because A's history of *aggressive* responses on rounds 1, ..., 17 is unforgiving. None of the players can increase its expected payoff by deviating from these strategies. For example, assume $k = 18$ chooses *in*, deviating from its equilibrium strategy because A would then, following its own equilibrium strategy, choose *cooperative*. Clearly, this deviation would benefit $k = 18$. It would also benefit $k = 19$ and $k = 20$, who—following their equilibrium strategies—will also choose *in*, inducing A to be *cooperative* on these rounds.

The problem with this deviation is that the benefits accrue only if A is weak. But there is, by assumption, a better than even chance that A is strong. In this case, A's best response to k's choice of *in* is to be *aggressive* in each primary, because A's payoff increases from 0 to 2.

Only if A is weak is it rational for her to be *cooperative* near the end of the sequence. But k does not know what type A is. Given this uncertainty, no k can increase his *expected* payoff by choosing *in* on any round. This is true even though $k = 18, 19, 20$ can unequivocally do better on the last three rounds if A is weak.

Thereby, introducing some uncertainty into the game—in the form of two possible types for Player A—justifies a deviation of A and each k from their backward-induction strategies of *in* and *cooperative* on each round. The game of incomplete information yields a very different equilibrium outcome, consistent with the intuition developed earlier about the utility of A's building a reputation for toughness.

In effect, a weak A can mimic a strong A to discourage every k's entry, even though a weak A would in fact capitulate to k's entry in the final three rounds. Before reaching these rounds, however, even a weak A will do better by being *aggressive*, trading off short-run gains for the long-run effect on her reputation. In this manner, the game with incomplete information explains *why*, from a rational-choice perspective, A is credible and deters all entrants.

To be sure, this game is different from the original sequential-primary game with complete information. To circumvent the implausible backward-induction equilibrium required introducing a different and richer model—one with uncertainty—of the strategic situation. Still other models have been constructed to resolve Selten's chain-store paradox (Friedman 1986; Rasmusen 1989), but the rational foundations on which to build sequential models in extensive-form games, and select different equilibria, remain controversial (Binmore 1990).

5.5. Conclusions

In the threat analysis for 2×2 ordinal games, I assumed that only one player, the threatener, had continuing involvement in a game, but this is not the only possible motivation one might assume for exercising threat power. Both players (e.g., the two superpowers today) might play the same or similar games over and over again, with the threatener being the player who can hold out longer at a mutually disadvantageous outcome. This might, for example, be one superpower in one kind of situation, the other in another kind. In fact, in conflicts involving the superpowers, the "game" seems often to be one of establishing credibility when one superpower is not recognized to be clearly superior.

The analysis demonstrates that one or both players have threat power in the large majority (46) of the 57 conflict games without a mutually best outcome. The 26 games in which only one player has a threat strategy (and the power to back it up) invariably enables this player to obtain an outcome of the same or higher rank than the player without a threat strategy.

In only 5 of the remaining 20 games is power ineffective. The common outcome that each player's threat power induces is (3,3) or (4,3) in all these games, which include Prisoners' Dilemma, in which (3,3) is also a nonmyopic equilibrium. In the other 4 games with a common threat outcome, threat power seems especially useful in singling out a "compromise" outcome, which is neither a Nash nor a nonmyopic equilibrum.

The 15 games in which both players have effective threat strategies have, with only two exceptions, no nonmyopic equilibria. Threat power always helps the player who possesses it obtain a better outcome than were the other player to possess it. Chicken is special in being the only game in which the possession of threat power by either player undermines the (3,3) nonmyopic equilibrium.

This is a blow to cooperation in Chicken, which—perhaps more than any other game—epitomizes confrontation situations in which the players appear to be on a collision course. By comparison, cooperation is sustained by both moving and staying power in the nonrepeated play of this game. The vulnerability of Chicken to threats in repeated play underscores how unequal power, and the unequal resources that underlie it, may undermine long-run conflict resolution if the more powerful player can inflict unacceptable damage on the weaker player.

The effects of threats are not limited to two-person repeated games, as the 21-person sequential-primary game illustrated. This game also indicates how the backward-induction argument, which suggested that Player A should always cooperate, may fly in the face of common sense. In particular, because this argument takes account only of what could happen in the future, it neglects a history of behavior that A's actions might establish. Because the players are assumed to have perfect information about all moves made in the game, it seems eminently reasonable that potential favorite sons will be deterred from entering their primaries if A's behavior is consistently aggressive in the beginning. Although waging aggressive campaigns may not work to A's short-run benefit, it seems likely to prove profitable in the long run.

How best to circumvent the backward-induction equilibrium, however, remains an open question. Introducing uncertainty into a game via sequential equilibria, whereby a weak type might imitate a strong type to induce the acquiescence of an opponent, is one means to capture the effects of reputation that deters entry.

This kind of model rationalizes the role that threats may play in games. Chicken notwithstanding, one surprising conclusion I would draw from the analysis of 2×2 games is that the use of threats may lead to the moderation, rather than the aggravation, of conflict. This may occur either through the clarification of intentions, which seems to have led to a cooperative solution in the Cuban missile crisis after each side communicated its tit-for-tat retaliatory policy and accepted the fact that the other side held to a similar policy; or it may occur through a series of actions that communicate this intent more explicitly, which is the lesson I draw from the analysis of the sequential-primary game.

In the realm of international relations, the policy of nuclear deterrence, pursued by both superpowers since World War II, has been justified in similar terms. If the so-called balance of terror has prevented World War III, however, it has not prevented the superpowers from trying to maintain the credibility of their threats through the use of conventional military forces and subversion in many parts of the world.

This, regrettably, may be the price each side pays to avoid an erosion in its alliance commitments. For threats, by their very nature, may on occasion have to be backed up by a show of force. Needless to say, the effects of force will not be benign for all parties.

The apparent contradiction in the use of force to prevent its usage on a more massive scale (e.g., in a nuclear war) creates a dilemma. Once players abandon a policy of appeasement that involves giving in to the threats of an opponent to avoid war, they must choose among riskier alternatives. But precisely because they are riskier, these choices must be made credible, which implies some measure of retribution if certain threats are ignored. In the case of the superpowers, this creates a real quandary: preserving their reputations may require risking war that could escalate to the nuclear level, which they want to avoid at all costs.

So far, it seems, this quandary has been settled in favor of trying to maintain the nuclear balance, and, at the same time, selectively employing nonnuclear options—as in Vietnam for the United States and Afghanistan for the Soviet Union, both of which they abandoned in the end. There seems no easy way out of this quandary for the superpowers or other actors caught in it. Yet, at the very least, it deserves to be better understood, even if the problem is insoluble.

The primary purpose of this chapter has been to show the consequences of having threat power in 2×2 ordinal games. The catalogue of possibilities for the 57 games of conflict are given in the figures, which I hope might be useful for reference purposes—for example, in determining the vulnerability of a particular conflict to compellent or deterrent threats. This analysis can be extended to larger games in which there are more players and/or more strategies, as illustrated by the propositions on junk and carrot-and-stick strategies. But I forego theoretical extensions now and turn, instead, to empirical applications in Chapter 6.

Notes

[1]In the Bible, the continuing player is, of course, God. That He is obsessively concerned with His reputation, which is cemented by threats that He frequently makes and carries out (Brams 1980), is strongly related to His immortality (Brams 1983). Thus, God made Cain a marked man because He wanted to convey a particular message that He thought would serve Him well in the future, as I argued in Chapter 1. A number of analysts have proposed game-theoretic models that take account of bargaining reputations; these models are reviewed in Wilson (1985, 1989), and one is illustrated in Section 5.4. An interesting game-theoretic analysis of "stability by threats" and deterrence, which mirrors some ideas developed here, is given in Moulin (1986, chap. 10); on two-person games, see Moulin (1981). Ho and Tolwinski (1982) develop a leader-follower model of an infinitely repeated game, in which the leader, as the threatener, establishes credibility by carrying out threats against the follower. Because this model is probabilistic, it is rational for the leader to carry out threats in some but not all instances, which is also a major conclusion of the national-security models developed in Brams and Kilgour (1988). Cioffi-Revilla (1983) offers a probabilistic model of credibility, and others (Allan 1982; Maoz 1983) have incorporated the related concept of "resolve" in their models. My interest, by contrast, is not in how players establish their credibility but, given that one player can make credible threats (defined precisely later), what, if any, advantages this ability confers on that player. Thus, a player's goal is not to be credible as such but to achieve its best possible outcome in games; depending on the game, credible threats may or may not be helpful.

[2]This information seems especially important in international politics. As Bald-

win (1989, 57) observes, "The lack of a science of threat systems is both intellectually undesirable and political dangerous . . . to world peace."

[3]While it is possible to provide formal conditions under which row has a reason to threaten column, they are not very enlightening. Their significance is mostly algorithmic, and they can easily be deduced from the algorithm for determining threat outcomes given in Section 5.3.

[4]The numbers of the games to be described next are based on Rapoport and Guyer's classification of the 78 distinct 2×2 games. Chicken and Prisoners' Dilemma are Games 66 and 12, respectively, in their classification scheme (see Figure 5.1). The 78 games are distinct in the sense that no interchange of rows, columns, or players can transform one of these games into any other.

[5]Conditions under which repeated play of (nonsequential) Prisoners' Dilemma leads to cooperation are discussed in Axelrod (1984), Majeski (1984), Taylor (1987), and Axelrod and Dion (1988), among other works.

[6]Rapoport and Guyer (1966) discuss the vulnerability of Nash equilibria to threats.

[7]Brams (1983, 174–77) gives figures showing the coincidence of the different power-induced outcomes in the 57 2×2 ordinal games that contain no mutually best outcome. The compellent threats of column in games 72 and 78 are not indicated in these figures or in Brams and Hessel (1984, 34) but are correctly identified in Figure 5.6 here.

[8]This is disputed by Zagare (1985, 1987), who claims that Prisoners' Dilemma is *the* prototypical example of deterrence. Because Zagare does not assume repeated play in his analysis of deterrence, he argues, in effect, that a threatener would be unwilling to carry out the "incredible" threat that brings the players to (1,1) in Chicken. But, of course, this is true only in a single-play game; if play is repeated, there is nothing irrational about suffering a (temporary) loss if the long-run gain from deterring future opponents more than offsets this loss (Wagner 1982). Zagare's analysis takes account of the long-run gain without revealing why a short-term loss may be necessary to achieve it. To be sure, if the short-term losses for both players incurred at (1,1) are devastating (e.g., nuclear war), the assumption of repeated play makes little sense. On the other hand, the *threat* of nuclear war, as in the Cuban missile crisis, can and has been repeated, though I am by no means recommending nuclear brinkmanship as a policy but simply trying to explain its continued use. Extensions of the ordinal bargaining models, based on the theory of moves, to cardinal-utility models of deterrence, based on Chicken-type games, are given in Brams (1985b) and Brams and Kilgour (1988).

[9]There are exceptions. Estes Kefauver racked up a string of victories in Democratic primaries in 1952 but lost the nomination to Adlai Stevenson. Since 1952, however, no presidential candidate of either major party, except an incumbent president or vice-president (e.g., Hubert Humphrey in 1968), has won his party's nomination without entering and winning in the primaries first.

[10]For a mathematical model of this process, see Brams and Garriga-Picó (1975).

[11]The game described next is based largely on Selten (1978). My adaptation of Selten's ingenious example from a business to a political context, which was presented in an earlier incarnation in Brams (1976, 126–30) and is adapted with permission, retains the game's essential features, but my analysis of its paradoxical aspects in Section 5.5 differs somewhat from Selten's and my own earlier treatment. Selten's example has been extended to games of incomplete and imperfect information, which are analyzed in Trockel (1986) and will be illustrated later.

[12]In the 1988 presidential election, there were 39 Democratic primaries and 35 Republican primaries, but they did not all occur on different days. Quite the contrary: there were 16 Democratic primaries and 15 Republican primaries on "super Tuesday" (March 8); still, the Democrats and Republicans each held presidential primaries on 17 separate dates, with most involving only one state (Pomper et al. 1989).

[13]There is, of course, a difference between playing a game a number of times against a single player, as in repeated play of Prisoners' Dilemma, and playing against different players, as in the sequential-primary game. In the former, players may be able to establish from their pattern of choices the conditions under which they will cooperate, which in some Prisoners' Dilemma experiments has engendered a significant amount of cooperation (Axelrod 1984). When playing against different players in independent trials, however, the cooperative strategy in Prisoners' Dilemma is inherently riskier, and hence the cooperative solution is more difficult to achieve. This would seem to reinforce the reasoning—developed subsequently in the text—that Player A should always campaign aggressively, since no interpersonal relationship between two players, based on repeated play, can evolve.

[14]This game is drawn from Friedman (1986, 138–39). In his Table 4.2 (p. 138), there are errors in the players' payoffs for both outcomes associated with player k's *in* strategy, but these will be corrected in a new edition of the book; the correct payoffs are as given here.

Chapter 6
Threats in Two Domestic Crises

6.1. Introduction

In this chapter I shall analyze two domestic crises that can be modeled by games vulnerable to the use of threat power. In one, threats seem to have "worked" according to the theory of threats developed in Chapter 5. In the other, the threat by one player was more implicit than explicit, though in the end it had an effect. Unfortunately for the players, its effect was the opposite of what was intended—it backfired, hurting both sides.

Its failure, in my opinion, is cogently explained by game theory, just as is the success of threats in the first game. The key to understanding both the success and failure of threats in bargaining lies in the proper modeling of the game being played. Thus, the threat analysis is not helpful in the second game because this game is neither 2 × 2 nor is it covered by the more general propositions (4 and 5) in Section 5.2.

Recall that the third representation of the Cuban missile crisis (Figure 4.4) was also not 2 × 2. Not all strategic situations match this mold, and it is a mistake to try to fit them into it.

Nevertheless, the basic dimensions of many conflicts—if not all their subtleties—can be captured in 2 × 2 ordinal games. A case in point is the conflict between the Polish Communist party and Solidarity in the perilous 1980–81 period. Solidarity was successful in asserting its influence early, but then the party recouped its dominant position. Each protagonist also sought to deter future challenges to its position by seizing the upper hand, even when this proved temporarily costly. Indeed, the Polish conflict not only illustrates the difference between compellent and deterrent threats but also how each kind came into play at different times.

The second case arose out of Richard Nixon's refusal in 1974 to release tapes of his conversations relating to the Watergate break-in and its aftermath. Somewhat ambiguously, he said at the time that he would abide by a "definitive decision" of the Supreme Court on the matter.

168

Taking this as a veiled threat, the Court ruled unanimously against Nixon, forcing his resignation. After showing how this threat created a trap, I suggest why Nixon uttered it in the first place.

6.2. The Use of Threat Power in Poland, 1980–81

The conflict between the leadership of the independent trade union, Solidarity, and the leadership of the Polish Communist party/government/state (assumed to be the same for present purposes) in 1980–81 was rife with threats and counterthreats.[1] I shall model this conflict as a game pitting Solidarity against the party and stress the use of threats by both sides.

Although the threat of Soviet intervention was certainly a factor in the Polish game, I will not introduce the Soviet Union as a separate player. It is not clear to what extent Polish Communist party preferences differed from Soviet ones—that is, to what extent the party's preferences would have been changed if the Soviet influence, whether real or perceived, had been absent. If it is true that Soviet preferences essentially paralleled those of the Polish Communist party, then the Soviets are modeled not as a separate player but instead as a force on the side of the party that affected the balance of power in the game and, hence, the eventual outcome.

Each of the two sets of leaders may be treated as if it were a single decision maker. Of course, internal divisions within Solidarity and the party led to certain intra-organizational games; however, these subgames generally concerned not strategic choices on broad policy issues but rather tactical choices on narrow operational questions. Focusing on the main game has the advantage of highlighting the most significant political-military choices each side considered, the relationship of these choices to outcomes in the game, and the dependence of these outcomes on threats and threat power.

The two players faced the following choices:

1. *Party.* Reject or accept the limited autonomy of plural social forces set loose by Solidarity. Rejection would, if successful, restore the monolithic structure underlying social organizations and interests; acceptance would allow political institutions other than the party to participate in some meaningful way in the formulation and execution of public policy.

2. *Solidarity.* Reject or accept the monolithic structure of the state. Rejection would put pressure on the government to limit severely the extent of the state's authority in political matters; acceptance would significantly proscribe the activities of independent institu-

tions, and Solidarity in particular, to narrower nonpolitical matters, with only minor oversight over certain state actitivities.

Designate these strategies of both sides as "rejection" and "acceptance," and label them R and A, respectively. These strategies might also be designated "confrontation" and "compromise," but I prefer the former, more neutral labels because the disagreements were generally over specific proposals rather than general postures that the two sides struck.

The two strategies available to each side give rise to four possible outcomes:

1. A-A. Compromise that allows plural institutions but restricts their activities to nonpolitical matters, with negotiations commencing on the sharing of political power.

2. R-R. Possibly violent conflict involving the entire society, opening the door to outside (mainly Soviet) intervention.

3. A (Solidarity)-R (Party). Status quo ante, with tight restrictions on all activities of Solidarity and its recognition of the supremacy of party/state interests.

4. R (Solidarity)-A (Party). Authorization of independent political activity, and a corresponding gradual reduction of the party/state role in implementing public policy decisions made collectively.

These four outcomes represent what may be considered the four major scenarios pertinent to the Polish situation. Each of these scenarios can accommodate differences in details, but these differences seem more tactical than strategic. The four outcomes, and the rankings I assign them, are shown in the payoff matrix of Figure 6.1.

The party leadership repeatedly emphasized the unacceptability of any solution that would constrain its political power, which implies that its two worst outcomes are those associated with Solidarity's choice of R. Commenting on the Polish events, Bialer (1981, 530) wrote, "Some [Party] leaders are more conservative and some more reformist; none, to our knowledge, questions the need to preserve the Party's monopoly." The Eleventh Plenary Meeting of the Central Committee of the Polish United Workers Party (PUWP) was explicit on this point:

> The Central Committee of PUWP unequivocally rejects . . . concepts of abandoning the leading role of the Party, of reducing this role to the ideological sphere and dispossessing the Party of the instruments of political power. This is the main danger. (*Nowy Dziennik*, June 17, 1981, p. 2)

Figure 6.1. Payoff matrix of Polish game, 1980–81

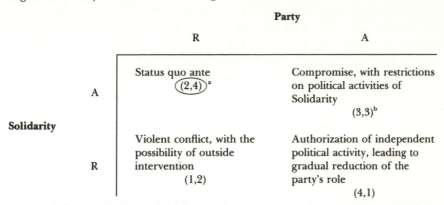

Party

		R	A
Solidarity	A	Status quo ante (2,4)[a]	Compromise, with restrictions on political activities of Solidarity (3,3)[b]
	R	Violent conflict, with the possibility of outside intervention (1,2)	Authorization of independent political activity, leading to gradual reduction of the party's role (4,1)

Key: (x,y) = Solidarity, party); 4 = best; 3 = next best; 2 = next worst; 1 = worst; A = acceptance; R = rejection.
[a]Party's compellent threat outcome.
[b]Solidarity's deterrent threat outcome.
Circled outcome is a Nash and nonmyopic equilibrium.

In fact, the available evidence indicates that the party preferred an all-out confrontation (R-R) to relinquishing its supremacy [R (Solidarity)-A (Party)]. Speaking at the Ninth Congress of PUWP, Deputy Prime Minister Mieczyslaw Rakowski announced: "To the enemies of socialism we can offer nothing but a fight, and not merely verbal at that" (*Nowy Dziennik,* July 21, 1981, p. 2). A later declaration of the Politburo reiterated that challenge: "We shall defend socialism as one defends Poland's independence. In this defense the state shall use all the means it deems necessary" (*Nowy Dziennik,* September 22, 1981, p. 2). Finally, between its two best outcomes associated with Solidarity's choice of A, the party clearly preferred the status quo [A (Solidarity)-R (Party)] to compromise (A-A).

As for Solidarity, there is considerable evidence that it preferred the party's capitulation [R (Solidarity)-A (Party)] most, and violent conflict (R-R) least. In between, it preferred a compromise solution (A-A) to its own capitulation [A (Solidarity)-R (Party)]. Solidarity statements echoed this sentiment. Its chairman, Lech Walesa, said: "We don't want to change the socialist ownership of the means of production, but we want to be real masters of the factories. We were promised that many times before" (*Time,* September 8, 1980, p. 34). Jacek Kuron, one of Solidarity's advisers, further clarified where the line on party activities should be drawn: "The Party's leading role means the monopoly of power over the police forces, the army and foreign policy. All other matters must be open to negotiations with society" (*Time,* December 29, 1980, p. 29). In short, Solidarity preferred not to try to rob the party of its most significant functions, hoping to gain the party's acquiescence and thereby at least Solidarity's next-best outcome (*A-A*).

The reason for Solidarity's preference is evident. Solidarity was aware of the unacceptability of its best outcome [*R* (Solidarity)-*A* (Party)] to its adversary:

> From the start, the Polish workers understood [that] to think of over-throwing the Party in Poland was madness, for it would inevitably lead to Soviet invasion and the destruction of all liberties gained in the past ten or even twenty-five years. (Ascherson 1982, 18–19)

Addressing Solidarity members, Walesa said: "Our country needs internal peace. I call on you to be prudent and reasonable" (*Time,* December 29, 1980, p. 20). On another occasion he said, "[There are] fighters who want to fight at every opportunity; but we must understand that both the society and the union have had enough of confrontation . . . we ought not to go to the brink" (*Solidarność,* April 10, 1981, p. 1). Kuron (1981) concurred: "The goals of the government and of the democratic movement are completely opposite. But the struggle between the two tendencies, the totalitarian and the democratic one, are to be fought exclusively by peaceful means." Thus, Solidarity preferred *R* only if the party chose *A*; if the party chose *R*, it preferred *A*.

The payoff matrix in Figure 6.1 that results from these preferences corresponds to Game 39 in Figure 5.7. Viewed statically (i.e., as a nonsequential game, in which players make simultaneous strategy choices according to Rule 1 in Section 4.9), the party has a dominant strategy of *R*, better for it whatever Solidarity chooses. Anticipating this strategy choice of the party, Solidarity would prefer *A* to *R*, leading to (2,4), the unique Nash equilibrium in this game.

Played according to Rules 1 through 5, (2,4) is also a nonmyopic equilibrium in the sequential game, indicating that this outcome is stable in the long as well as the short run. Given that neither side enjoys any power advantage over the other, (2,4) is therefore the apparent solution of this game in the sense that neither player can, by unilaterally departing from this outcome, ensure a better outcome for itself, whether this departure results in subsequent (rational) moves or not. Because this solution is the best outcome for the party, and only next worst for Solidarity, the game seems to be inherently unfair to Solidarity.

Solidarity, however, can undermine the nonmyopic equilibrium in this game if it possesses threat power. In fact, it can induce (3,3) by a deterrent threat: choosing *A*, it can threaten *R*, and the party's two worst outcomes, unless the party accepts Solidarity's threat outcome, (3,3). Solidarity's breakdown outcome, (1,2), however, is also the breakdown outcome for the party if it is the player with threat power. The party's threat is compellent and is implemented by its choosing, and staying at, R, forcing Solidarity to choose A and the party's threat outcome, (2,4).

Thus, with confrontation (R-R) being the common breakdown outcome, the game turns on who (if either player) holds the balance of power. If Solidarity is the more powerful of the two players, or is at least perceived as such, it can implement (3,3). Otherwise, (2,4), as the Nash and nonmyopic equilibrium, would presumably obtain—and be reinforced should the party possess threat power. Note that Solidarity can implement its threat outcome, (3,3), by choosing its "soft" strategy A, relegating its "hard" strategy R to a (deterrent) threat. This, of course, is the proverbial "speak softly and carry a big stick" policy, with the big stick being used only if necessary.

In contrast to Solidarity, the party always does at least as well as Solidarity [(3,3), if it does not have threat power], and sometimes better [(2,4) if it does, or neither player does], at least in terms of the comparative rankings of the two players. Thus, a power asymmetry unfavorable to itself is not as serious for the party as for Solidarity, based on a comparative ranking of the two threat outcomes. Moreover, because the party's threat is compellent, it can implement its best outcome simply by choosing and then maintaining its hard strategy R, whereas Solidarity must first take a soft position and then threaten escalation to its hard position, putting the onus for breakdown and subsequent disruption on itself.

This game-theoretic analysis based on threat power offers meaningful insights into the actual unfolding of events in Poland in 1980–81. Clearly, the party was stunned by the quick pace of developments and the widespread support for Solidarity after the August 1980 Lenin shipyard strike in Gdansk, which are events that I take as the starting point of the analysis and do not attempt to explain. Whatever set off the crisis, the party did in fact consider Solidarity to be more powerful during the last part of 1980 and into the beginning of 1981. Reluctantly, it followed its acceptance strategy, A; Solidarity, for its part, repeatedly emphasized the nonpolitical character of its demands (A) while threatening R, for the union's very existence was "based on adversary relations, not on a partnership" (Szafar 1981, 79). As the economic situation worsened, however, the instability of the (3,3) compromise outcome became evident, setting the stage for a test of strength between Solidarity and the party.

In March 1981, for the first time, the government used force against Solidarity. Although the force was limited in scope, its use can be interpreted as an attempt to switch to the party rejection strategy R. Yet Solidarity chose to avoid confrontation, and the game remained at (3,3).

Although "the game was to leave the authorities with a semblance of power but to take its substance away" (Watt 1982, 11), the events of March 1981 began to split Solidarity, strengthening proponents of the rejection strategy. But the moderate leadership of Solidarity, and Walesa in particular, kept pointing to society's unwillingness to support the rejection strategy.[2] In doing so, the leadership cast doubt upon the viability of Solidarity's breakdown strategy, thereby undermining the union's power.

In December 1981 the party, apparently believing that the balance of power had shifted, switched decisively to *its* rejection strategy R, moving the game to its threat outcome, (2,4), by imposing martial law and jailing many Solidarity leaders in a massive crackdown. The relative stability of this outcome until 1989 seemed to validate the party's assessment that the balance of power favored it in Poland—or at least demonstrated that Solidarity's power was not greater than its own.

Although Solidarity showed no appetite to switch to R, by 1989 the catastrophic economic situation led the party to take a much more accommodationist position. (I have not tried to model how this situation evolved.) In eight-week roundtable talks in March and April 1989 between the party and Solidarity, an agreement was reached to hold elections in June, in which Solidarity was allowed to compete for 35 percent of the seats in the lower house, and all the seats in the upper house, of parliament. In an embarrassing turn of events, Solidarity not only won virtually all the contested seats, but many party members failed to win majority support even in uncontested elections.

The negotiated compromise and election results can perhaps be viewed as a return to the (3,3) outcome. It was not so much provoked by threats of violent conflict but rather a recognition by both sides that the (4,2) outcome after the December 1981 crackdown had, because of severe economic problems, degenerated to something probably approaching (1,2). Faced with a disastrous economy, both sides saw benefit in trying to reach a modus vivendi.

The Polish game, at least in the 1980–81 period, illustrates when threat power is effective: it makes a difference—depending on whether Solidarity or the party possesses it—on what outcome is implemented. When one player can, by using its power, implement for itself an outcome superior to that which an adversary can achieve using its power, then there will be good reason for the players to vie for influence.

By contrast, the exercise of threat (as well as moving) power in the Figure 4.3 version of the Cuban missile crisis is ineffective because, whichever player possesses it, the same (3,3) outcome is induced. Similarly, power is ineffective in the Prisoners' Dilemma version of the cease-fire game (Figure 4.5) because (3,3) is the moving, staying, and threat outcome in this game, whichever player (if any) possesses such power. Games in which power is ineffective probably better lend themselves to amicable solutions than games in which power is effective—given that one player possesses such power and can thereby ensure implementation of the (same) outcome that each player's power guarantees.

In the White House tapes game (to be described next), power was ineffective. Even so, the common threat-power outcome that either player with threat power could have induced was not implemented. The reason, curiously enough, was due in part to the prior threat of one player and also to the timing of choices, which made it impossible for the threatened player to switch to its deterrent threat strategy, effectively emasculating its threat power.

6.3. The White House Tapes Case: The Players and Their Preferences

The drama of "Watergate" held the American people in thrall for several months in 1973–74, culminating in the resignation of Richard Nixon, the only person ever to resign from the U.S. presidency. Nixon's downfall originated with one of the "dirty tricks" of his 1972 presidential campaign against George McGovern—the break-in to Democratic national party campaign headquarters in the Watergate complex in Washington, D.C.

An attempt to hide the complicity of Nixon campaign officials—and eventually the president himself—in covering up this crime was recorded on White House tapes. The U.S. Supreme Court decision ordering release of certain of these tapes was the most immediate cause of Nixon's resignation.

On July 24, 1974, the Court unanimously ruled to end Nixon's efforts to withhold the tapes from Special Prosecutor Leon Jaworski in the so-called Watergate cover-up case. That same day the president, through his attorney, James St. Clair, announced his compliance with the ruling—he would release the White House tapes the special prosecutor sought. Fifteen days later the Nixon presidency ended in ruins, a direct result of the Court's action.

This case is of special interest because optimal strategies in the game played over the release of the tapes, as I shall reconstruct it, led to a paradoxical consequence—a *trap*, somewhat akin to that in Prisoners' Dilemma in which all the players suffer—that seems to challenge the rationality of the players' choices.[3] But perhaps even more intriguing is the role that a particular threat played in structuring the game. As a bargaining tactic, it had the perverse effect of undermining the possibility of a "settlement" favorable to both players.

The history of the White House tapes decision began on March 1, 1974, when a grand jury indicted seven former White House and campaign aides for attempting to cover up the Watergate scandal (*United States v. Mitchell et al.*). On April 16 the special prosecutor petitioned Judge John Sirica to subpoena tapes and documents of 64 presidential conversations with John Dean, H. R. Haldeman, John Erlichman, and Charles Colson; the subpoena was issued on April 18.

On May 1 the president's attorney, James St. Clair, announced that the president would refuse to submit the subpoenaed materials, and St. Clair sought an order quashing the subpoena. After hearing arguments, Judge Sirica confirmed the subpoena order on May 20. On May 24, St. Clair filed an appeal in the Court of Appeals, which, it seemed, would probably result in the postponement of the cover-up trial.

The prosecutors moved quickly to prevent delay. On the day the appeal by St. Clair was filed in the Court of Appeals, Jaworski, using a seldom-invoked procedure, went to the Supreme Court and sought a writ of *certiorari before judgment* that would leapfrog the appeals process. Citing the imminent cover-up trial date, Jaworski also noted the necessity to settle expeditiously an issue that was paralyzing the government. He requested the Court not only to issue the writ but also, because of the "imperative public importance" of the case, to stay in session into the summer (Lukas 1976, 495). This way the case could be decided in sufficient time that the tapes could be used as evidence at the trial—should Judge Sirica's ruling be upheld. The Supreme Court agreed on May 31 and heard oral arguments on July 8.

When the justices went into conference on July 9, each of the eight who were to consider the case had basically two choices—decide for or decide against the president. (Associate Justice William Rehnquist withdrew from the case, evidently because of his previous service at the Justice Department under Attorney General John Mitchell, though he never publicly stated a reason for disqualifying himself.) It appears from the available record that six of the justices reached an early consensus against the president on all three of the major issues: (1) whether the Court had jurisdiction in the case—standing to sue—since Jaworski was an employee of the executive branch; (2) whether executive privilege was absolute; and (3) whether Jaworski had demonstrated a sufficient need for the subpoenaed materials.

Justices Warren Burger and Harry Blackmun, while concurring with the majority on limiting executive privilege, believed that the special prosecutor lacked legal standing to sue the president. For this reason, it appears, they voted originally against granting the case *certiorari* (Totenberg 1975).

Burger and Blackmun are conceived of as one player. This is because it was almost axiomatic that Blackmun voted with Burger: in the first five terms (1970–74) that Burger and Blackmun served together on the Court, they agreed on 602 of the 721 cases they both heard (83.5 percent), which is the highest agreement level of any pair of justices who served over these five terms.[4] They were referred to as the "Minnesota Twins" by the Supreme Court staff.

As deliberations developed, Burger and Blackmun had a choice of two strategies:

1. To decide against the president, joining the other six justices to create a unanimous decision;
2. To decide for the president, forming a minority to create a 6–2 "weak" decision.

Nixon's possible response to an adverse Supreme Court ruling was long a matter of doubt—and one that, it will be argued here, Burger and Blackmun could not afford to ignore. On July 26, 1973, White House Deputy Press Secretary Gerald Warren stated that Nixon would abide by a "definitive decision of the highest court." Nixon, at a news conference on August 22, 1973, endorsed the Warren formulation, but neither he nor White House spokesmen would expand on the orginal statement (*New York Times*, July 25, 1974, p. 22).

These statements were made in reference to the president's refusal to obey a subpoena from the first special prosecutor, Archibald Cox, for nine White House tapes. That case never reached the Supreme Court. The Court of Appeals ruled against the president, who, after a delay of eleven days, agreed to submit the tapes—but not before he had dismissed Cox. The question of what "definitive" meant then became moot.

The issue arose again on May 24, 1974, when Jaworski filed his appeal with the Supreme Court. On July 9 St. Clair made it clear that the president was keeping open the "option" of defying the Court. The question of compliance, he stated, "has not yet been decided" (*New York Times*, July 10, 1974, p. 1). Because the expectation at the time was that the Court would rule against the president (*Newsweek*, July 22, 1974, p. 18; *Time*, July 22, 1974, pp. 15–17), Nixon had two choices:

1. Comply with an adverse Court ruling;
2. Defy an adverse Court ruling.

Several factors help to explain Nixon's refusal to make a definite commitment concerning his response to a Court decision. If he stated that he would not comply, his statement might be used as a ground for impeachment. If he stated that he would comply, then the House Judiciary Committee might argue that the president would either have to comply with its subpoenas, too, or be impeached (*New York Times*, July 10, 1974, p. 1).

More important, though, the president's refusal to assure his compliance with an adverse decision was designed to threaten the Court and lead the justices to render either a favorable decision or, at worst, a closely divided adverse split decision that he could claim was insufficiently "definitive" for a matter of this magnitude. Evans and Novak (1974) reported at the time, "The refusal of St. Clair to say Nixon would obey an adverse decision has disturbed the judicial branch from the high court on down." But perhaps more than giving his supporters on the Court "encouragement" that he might side with them against the majority, or even that the majority should not risk a constitutional crisis by ruling against him, I believe that Nixon was really attempting to prepare the public for a possible confrontation, about which I shall say more in Section 6.4.

If the president's intent was to threaten the Court, the threat backfired. Why? To explain why Burger and Blackmun departed from their apparent personal preferences and eventually sided with the Court majority, I shall next describe the game they and Nixon played. The probable outcomes of the four possible strategy choices of the two players are presented in the outcome matrix in Figure 6.2. As a justification for these outcomes, first consider the consequences associated with Nixon's defiance of an adverse Supreme Court ruling.

Unquestionably, if the president defied the Court, his defiance would represent a direct assault on the Supreme Court's constitutional place as the "principal source and final authority of constitutional interpretation" and thereby threaten the very structure of the American politial system (Stephenson 1975, 292). Indeed, it seems highly probable that Nixon would have plunged the country into its deepest constitutional crisis since the Civil War. No previous president had ever explicitly defied an order of the Supreme Court, though such action had apparently been contemplated (Scigliano 1971, chap. 2).

At the time of the decision in *United States v. Nixon*, it appeared that the result of presidential defiance would be impeachment by the House of Representatives on the ground of withholding evidence from the special prosecutor or of violation of the principle of separation of powers. While the outcome in the Senate was less certain than that in the House, a unanimous adverse decision by a Court that included three conservative Nixon appointees (Burger, Blackmun, and Lewis Powell, Jr.) would preempt charges that the president was the victim of what presidential counselor Dean Burch called a "partisan lynch mob" (Lukas 1976, 510).

Figure 6.2. Outcome matrix of White House tapes game

| | | **Nixon** | |
		Comply with Court	Defy Court
Burger and Blackmun	Decide for president; create a "weak" 6-2 decision	I . Constitutional crisis averted; Nixon not impeached for non-compliance; majority-rule principle preserved	II . Constitutional crisis; Nixon impeached but conviction uncertain
	Decide against president; create a unanimous 8-0 decision	IV. Constitutional crisis averted; Nixon not impeached for non-compliance; majority-rule principle possibly weakened	III. Constitutional crisis; Nixon impeached and conviction certain

(I do not include Powell as a Court player because he originally favored granting *certiorari;* also, he "demonstrated the highest level of independence within the Nixon Bloc" [*New York Times,* July 1, 1974, p. 10] and was described as "one of the least predictable of the eight and most flexible of the Nixon appointees" [*Time,* July 22, 1974, p. 16].) Not surprisingly, then, on the day of the decision St. Clair warned the president that he would be surely impeached and swiftly convicted if he were to defy the unanimous ruling of the Court (Lukas 1976, 519).

On the other hand, Jaworski believed that "if the vote against [the president] was close he would go on television and tell the people that the presidency should not be impaired by a divided Court" (Jaworski 1976, 164). A "weak" decision from which at least some of the more conservative Nixon appointees dissented would also allow the president to continue his "one-third plus one" strategy in the Senate to avoid conviction and removal from office (by a two-thirds or greater majority).

Consider now the consequences associated with Nixon's compliance with an adverse Supreme Court decision. Clearly, compliance would avert a constitutional crisis, and Nixon would thereby avoid immediate impeachment in the House for not complying with the Court. However, compliance posed problems for the president; he had reason to believe that the subpoenaed materials, if released, would prove damaging and might even lead to his eventual impeachment by the House. In fact, upon hearing of the Court's decision, Nixon, who was at his San Clemente,

California, home, telephoned White House special counsel Fred Buzhardt in Washington. "There may be some problems with the June 23
tape," Nixon said (*Washington Post,* September 9, 1974, p. A1).

Although the revelation of this tape ultimately forced his resignation,
Nixon apparently did not fully realize at the time the incriminating
nature of the recorded conversations. In *The Final Days,* Woodward
and Bernstein (1976, 176) report that Buzhardt felt that the tape was
"devastating." Nixon, by contrast, felt that Buzhardt was "overreacting,"
that it was "not that bad." Even as late as August 5, in his statement
accompanying the public release of the tape transcripts, Nixon reflected
his mixed evaluation of the tape's impact:

> I recognize that this additional material I am now furnishing may further
> damage my case. . . . I am firmly convinced that the record, in its entirety,
> does not justify the extreme step of impeachment and removal from
> office. (*New York Times* staff, 1974)

Compliance—or, more accurately, the announcement of compliance—
would allow the president to fall back on his long-used strategy of delay,
though it would not necessarily remove the threat of impeachment and
ultimate conviction, especially if the Court were unanimous in its judgment. For Burger and Blackmun, who had voted originally against granting the case review, supporting and enlarging the majority (possibly
against their convictions) to counter a presumed threat to the Court's
authority might possibly weaken the majority-rule principle that *any*
majority is sufficient for a decision.[5] But voting their convictions would
be hazardous should the president use a divided decision as a pretext to
defy the Court.

I shall now attempt to combine these conflicting considerations into a
ranking of the four outcomes by the two players. As in previous games,
I shall not try to assess how much each player preferred one outcome
over another.

Clearly, Nixon preferred the *risk* of conviction and removal to its virtual
certainty. Thus, the president would prefer to defy a weak decision
(Outcome II in Figure 6.2) than to defy a unanimous decision (III), which
I indicate by the (partial) preference ranking (II,III), or II preferred to
III. For the same reason, he would prefer to comply with any adverse
decision (I or IV) than to defy a unanimous decision (III)—his worst
outcome—so (I-IV,III), where the hyphen indicates indifference between I and IV (for now).

Defying a weak decision (II) is considered preferable to complying
with any adverse decision (I or IV), for such defiance would forestall the
release of potentially devastating evidence and at the same time present

Nixon with the possibility of avoiding conviction and removal for non-compliance; hence (II,I-IV). Between the two compliance outcomes (I and IV), I assume that the president "preferred" to comply with a weak decision (I) over a unanimous decision (IV), so (I,IV). A weak decision with some justices dissenting would leave the issue confused and subject to interpretation; a weak decision would also leave room to maneuver for partial compliance.[6]

Putting the partial preference rankings together, the president's presumed ranking of the four outcomes is: II preferable to I preferable to IV preferable to III, or (II,I,IV,III). Given these rankings by the president, what are the corresponding rankings of Burger and Blackmun?

Although I previously suggested that Burger and Blackmun would have preferred to decide for the president on at least one of the strictly legal questions (standing to sue by the special prosecutor), there is no doubt that the justices believed that compliance by the president with any adverse Court ruling (I or IV) would be preferable to defiance (II or III); hence, their partial preference scale is (I-IV,II-III). Indeed, in the Court's opinion, which Burger drafted, the chief justice quoted Chief Justice John Marshall in *Marbury v. Madison* (1803): "It is emphatically the province and duty of the Judicial department to say what the law is."

It also seems reasonable to assume that if the president complied, the justices would prefer to decide for him (I) rather than against him (IV); hence (I,IV). After all, the notion that the Court must be unanimous or close to it to make a decision credible, and thereby induce compliance, is an abhorrent restriction on the Court's authority and might establish an unhealthy precedent. Finally, I assume that the justices "preferred" that the president defy a unanimous decision (III) rather than a weak decision (II)—on which his chances of eventual success would be higher—so (III,II).

Putting the partial preference rankings together, the justices' presumed ranking of the four outcomes is: I preferable to IV preferable to III preferable to II, or (I,IV,III,II). The resulting rankings of the four outcomes in the Figure 6.2 outcome matrix are shown in the Figure 6.3 payoff matrix.

6.4. The White House Tapes Case: The Trap

Because the players in the White House tapes game did not make simultaneous choices in ignorance of each other, the payoff matrix in Figure 6.3 does not provide an accurate representation of this game. In fact Burger and Blackmun—and the rest of the Court—acted first. Only then did Nixon have to make a strategy choice, as represented in the revised 2 × 4 payoff matrix shown in Figure 6.4, wherein Burger and

Figure 6.3. Payoff matrix of White House tapes game

		Nixon	
		Comply with Court	Defy Court
Burger and Blackmun	Decide for president	I. (4,3)	II. (1,4)
	Decide against president	IV. (3,2)	III. (2,1)

Key: (x,y) = (Burger and Blackmun, Nixon); 4 = best; 3 = next best; 2 = next worst; 1 = worst.

Blackmun have two strategies while Nixon has four, contingent on the justices' prior choice of "decide for president" (*F*) or "decide against president" (*A*). Alternatively, as illustrated in the the Solomon game (Figure 1.6) or the sequential version of the Cuban missile crisis (Figure 4.4), one could represent this game in extensive form: at the top of the game tree, Burger and Blackmun choose between *F* and *A*; whatever their choice, Nixon then chooses between "comply" (*C*) and "defy" (*D*).

Backward induction on this tree yields the same rational outcome as in the Figure 6.4 game. In this game, it is easy to see that "*D* if *F*, *C* if *A*" is a dominant strategy for Nixon: it yields payoffs as good as, and in at least one case better than, the payoffs yielded by any of his other three strategies, whatever the strategy choice of Burger and Blackmun. Given this unconditionally best strategy on the part of Nixon, it is reasonable to assume that Burger and Blackmun will anticipate Nixon's choice, assuming they (as well as Nixon) have complete information about the Figure 6.4 revised payoff matrix—or at least an intuitive understanding of the strategic situation as presented here. To maximize *their* payoff, Burger and Blackmun will choose the strategy that yields for them the highest payoff in the column associated with Nixon's dominant strategy. Because 3 is better than 1 for Burger and Blackmun in this column, one would therefore expect that they would choose their strategy *A*.

As already indicated, the Supreme Court did decide unanimously against Nixon. He was reportedly outraged by the Court's ruling, feeling himself "sold out" by his three appointees, Chief Justice Burger and Associate Justices Blackmun and Powell. Charles Colson claims that the president counted on all three justices. Others say he was certain of Burger and Blackmun. When he learned of the decision, Nixon used foul ("expletive-deleted") language to describe Burger. The president

Figure 6.4. Revised payoff matrix of White House tapes game

		Nixon			
		Comply (C) regardless	Defy (D) regardless	C if F, D if A	D if F, C if A
Burger and Blackmun	Decide for president (F)	(4,3)	(1,4)	(4,3)	(1,4)
	Decide against president (A)	(3,2)	(2,1)	(2,1)	(3,2)

Dominant strategy for Nixon

Key: (*x,y*) = (Burger and Blackmun, Nixon); 4 = best; 3 = next best; 2 = next worst; 1 = worst. Circled outcome is a Nash equilibrium.

could not believe that the Court's ruling had been unanimous. "Significantly, the President's greatest fury seems to have been directed not at the decision itself but at the three Justices who 'deserted' him" (Lukas 1976, 519).

In any event, the decision was unanimous, with no dissenting or concurring opinions. "It was the Court's seamless unity which made defiance so difficult" (Lukas 1976, 519). Eight hours after the decision was handed down, the president, through St. Clair, announced his compliance with the decision "in all respects."

In summary, the game-theoretic analysis seems to explain well, in terms of the foregoing reconstruction of the players' strategies and preferences for outcomes, why the players acted as they did. Yet not only is the outcome that occurred not the most desirable one from the viewpoint of either player, but both players also might have done better had the president been a little more reassuring.

Observe that the lower right (3,2) outcome is the unique Nash equilibrium in the Figure 6.4 matrix. Paradoxically, however, *both* players could have done better if they had chosen strategies associated with either of the two (4,3) outcomes in the Figure 6.4 matrix; as in Prisoners' Dilemma, therefore, (3,2) is a Pareto-inferior Nash equilibrium. Furthermore, observe that the (4,3) outcomes both involve the choice by Burger and Blackmun of deciding for the president, and the choice by Nixon of compliance. In theory, the president can induce this choice by selecting either comply (*C*) regardless or *C* if *F*, *D* if *A* in the Figure 6.4 matrix.

Unfortunately for the players, however, neither of the (4,3) outcomes is in equilibrium: Nixon in each case has an incentive to depart unilaterally from the strategies associated with them to try to bring about his best outcome, (1,4).[7] Not only are the (4,3) outcomes not in equilibrium, but Nixon's two strategies associated with these outcomes are also dominated by his (dominant) strategy, D if F, C if A.

For these reasons, therefore, it is hard to see how both players could have done better, even though the opportunity existed. Only if Burger and Blackmun had believed that their dissent would not trigger presidential defiance could they have voted their (presumed) convictions with equanimity. The public record shows that Burger and Blackmun never received any assurance that the president would comply if the Court split. On the contrary, Nixon and his spokesmen, as indicated earlier, continually held out the possibility of defying a Supreme Court decision that was not "definitive."

Thus, Burger and Blackmun had no choice—despite their disagreement with some arguments of the special prosecutor—but to decide against the president.[8] Thereby the Supreme Court decision was rendered unanimous and both players in the White House tapes game lost out, in a sense, on greater payoffs that—at least in principle—were attainable.

The public probably gained from this "noncooperative" solution, however. If one identifies the public with the special prosecutor in the White House tapes case, it seems likely that the special prosecutor, who set up the game that I have described, though he was not himself a player, would rank the outcome that actually occurred as the best of the four possible outcomes. This is certainly a reasonable inference from Jaworski's remarks immediately after the Court decision: "I feel right good over what happened. We can move ahead now. . . . I'm especially pleased it was a unanimous decision. It doesn't leave any doubt in anyone's mind."[9]

It seems worth pointing out that a variety of bizarre motives ("need to fail," "death wish") and personality traits ("self-destructive") have been attributed to Richard Nixon. The analysis here, however, suggests that his stance in the White House tapes case, which pushed his confrontation with the special prosecutor and then the Supreme Court beyond the point of no return, was not at all strange. Rather, Nixon was simply caught up in an intractable game that, perhaps with greater prescience, he could have avoided.

Political leaders of all different stripes have similar failings and lack of foresight. The consequences of these failings, I believe, can be well understood within the game-theoretic framework used in this and previous chapters. In Nixon's case, his reason for resigning in the end was commonplace and sensible: "I no longer have a strong enough political base [to complete the term of office]" (*New York Times* Staff, 1974, p. vii). This rationale is as good as his reason for obeying the Supreme Court's edict—that he could not do better by defiance. Thus, even a political leader as complex and enigmatic as Nixon seems at root a rational actor.

But if this is the case, why did he threaten the Court in the first place? The preferences that this threat in part gave rise to, depicted in the Figure 6.3 game, define Game 72 in Figure 5.6. In this game, Burger and Blackmun have a deterrent threat of deciding against the president unless he complies, and Nixon has a compellent threat of compliance, both of which induce (4,3) as the (common) threat outcome.

This result does not change in the 2 × 4 game of Figure 6.4, except for one critical difference: Burger and Blackmun cannot switch back to voting against the president once they vote in his favor, because the sequence of decisions (Court decides, Nixon responds) is fixed exogenously—the institutions dictate this order of choice. Because the Court cannot retract its decision, it has no real threat if Nixon chooses defiance.

On the other hand, Burger and Blackmun can make defiance unappealing, as they in fact did, by making the Court decision unanimous. But this is an action taken beforehand—not a threat of future reprisal—to induce compliance. In other words, it is not just a warning of worse things to come but a move, like the Nixon alert decision, that sends a stronger signal. Unlike the alert decision, though, it cannot be retracted.

Not being able to negotiate directly with Nixon, the Court had little alternative. Although the game was not to be repeated, the Court's reputation certainly did matter to Burger and Blackmun, as explained earlier. So they took what might be called preventive action, precisely because they had no recourse if Nixon defied after the Court rendered its verdict.

Nixon, as the second-moving player, did have recourse. However, this obviated his compellent threat; he could not credibly commit himself to compliance because the Court acted first and he had a free hand afterward. In fact, he undercut what credibility he did have with his implicit threat of defiance.

His decision to impugn the Court's authority seems intimately related to his desire to *prepare* the public for his defiance. Nixon seemed to have realized that if his rejection of the Court's decision came out of the blue, it might cause an uproar that would drive him from office.

Unfortunately for Nixon, though, he cultivated the ground too well. Burger and Blackmun were so shocked by the possibility that Nixon would defy the Court that they withdrew their apparently sincere support for his cause.

That they would act in this matter took Nixon by surprise, but was his threat irrational? Consider his alternative. If he had not issued his threat and, as a consequence, Burger and Blackmun had sided with him, I believe Nixon's defiance of the Court—without warning—would indeed have stunned the nation. Doubtless, Nixon would have been impeached and then convicted if he had not resigned. Moreover, a pardon by Gerald Ford, if Nixon were convicted by the Senate, would almost certainly have been out of the question. Everyone would have suffered through such an ordeal, not least Nixon himself.

In light of this alternative scenario, I think Nixon's veiled threat was not a foolish tactic. In the final phase of Watergate, Nixon was basically in a no-win situation, no matter how hard he maneuvered. That his threat backfired, therefore, does not mean that a better choice was available.

Of course, one might question whether Nixon acted rationally in getting himself into such straits by initiating the cover-up. Muzzio (1982) offers some surprising answers that again point to a shrewd and resourceful, if not always wise, president carefully plotting his moves.

6.5. Conclusions

In the Polish conflict of 1980–81 between Solidarity and the Communist Party, as I modeled it, there was a unique Nash and nonmyopic equilibrium that was favorable to the party. Yet Solidarity had the ability to threaten a worse outcome (for both players).

Solidarity's threat was in fact credible in the beginning, and the union temporarily gained some concessions from the party. But these were not to last, because the party, with Soviet support, could also use threat power to redress the imbalance and reinstitute the equilibrium, which it eventually did. By 1989, however, a calamitous economic situation forced the party to moderate its position by allowing Solidarity representation in the Polish parliament.

Threats are effective if they are backed up by the wherewithal to carry them out. But the threatened player must also recognize that the threatener will act—even to his or her own detriment—if the threat is ignored. Given both the power and the resolve to implement threats (should this prove necessary), threats can serve either to deter or to compel desired behavior, as the Polish conflict illustrated in the 1980–81 period.

The problem with threats, of course, is that the threatener as well as the threatenee will in general be hurt if the threatener is forced to carry them out, thereby making them sometimes appear quite incredible. This was not the case for Burger and Blackmun; they took all too seriously Nixon's implied threat of defying a less-than-unanimous Supreme Court. To stave off defiance, or at least make it as uninviting as possible, they sided with the rest of the Court in their opposition to the president.

The White House tapes game was not a Prisoners' Dilemma (only one player had a dominant strategy, whereas both do in Prisoners' Dilemma), but it had some of its earmarks. Although the tapes game had deleterious ramifications for the players, the country as a whole probably avoided a trap, even if its citizens were astonished and outraged by Watergate.

Nixon probably could not have chosen a better course of action, given his desperate situation toward the end of the fiasco. When he resigned and Gerald Ford took over, there was a feeling that a new chapter had been opened. Indeed, the new president sought to wipe the old slate clean by proclaiming in his inaugural statement that "our long national nightmare is over" (*New York Times* staff 1974, p. vii).

Both Poland and the Unites States suffered greatly, albeit in very different ways, from their domestic upheavals. In each case, the protagonists were skilled and clever in their use of threats, even if their aims were not always lofty. But the games they found themselves embroiled in made compromise difficult, though threats on occasion may stabilize cooperation, as seen in the case of the international crises in Chapter 4.

Whether threats facilitate or impede negotiated settlements depends very much on the game being played. What unfolded in the two domestic crises considered in this chapter is illuminated by both the theory of threats and the game theory presented earlier, showing how rational players may entrap themselves in less-than-desirable outcomes from which there may be no escape.

Notes

[1]This section is adapted from Brams and Hessel (1984) with permission.

[2]Walesa was opposed to the strike because he considered the Polish situation too precarious, both internally and externally. Defending his position, he said: "We must move step by step, without endangering anybody. . . . I am not saying that there will be no confrontation over some important issue . . . but now the society is tired and wants no confrontation" (*Solidarność*, April 10, 1981, p. 1).

[3]This and the next two sections are adapted from Brams and Muzzio (1977a, 1977b) with permission; additional background information can be found in these articles and in Muzzio (1982). For a general discussion of "social traps," see Cross and Guyer (1980).

[4]Data on case agreement can be found in the November issues of *Harvard Law Review* (1971–75). On the concurrence of Burger and Blackmun, see *New York Times* (July 1, 1974, p. 10) and Totenberg (1975).

[5]For a discussion of the importance of the majority-rule principle in the Court, see Norton (1923), Clarke (1923), Pillen (1924), and Warren (1924).

[6]It can be reasonably argued that the president preferred to comply with a unanimous decision (IV) than a "nondefinitive" ruling that he had been threatening to ignore (I), so (IV,I). The reversal of the ranking of the two compliance

outcomes leads to essentially the same results as I shall subsequently describe, except that the equilibrium becomes (3,3) rather than (3,2), and the paradox of rational choice discussed in Section 6.4 disappears.

[7]Interestingly, *no* outcomes in the Figure 6.3 matrix—not those associated with (4,3) or (3,2)—are in equilibrium, but this fact is not relevant to the present analysis because I have already established that this representation does not depict the game that was actually played.

[8]Their decision, it should be noted, gave them the benefit of influencing the contents of the majority opinion. Indeed, Burger wrote the opinion, but there is no evidence (after several rewritings) that it was "weakened" over what it would have been if he and Blackmun had dissented (Muzzio 1982, 148–49).

[9]*New York Times,* July 25, 1974, p. 22. H. R. Haldeman corroborated Jaworski's view, quoted in Section 6.3, about the consequences of a nonunanimous Court decision: "If the Supreme Court had handed down a [nonunanimous] majority decision, Nixon would have defied the Court and refused its order to turn over the tapes" (Haldeman with DiMona 1978, 310); see also Nixon (1978, 1020).

Chapter 7
Bargaining in Legislatures

7.1. Introduction

In this chapter I analyze legislative bargaining in two different settings. In each case, the bargaining involves more than two players, so the models I develop assume an n-person game.[1] In neither setting, however, do I assume that the players can make binding agreements, rendering the games noncooperative. That is, if the players reach an agreement, it is because they find it in their interest to do so.

The first situation involves vote trading in legislatures, wherein members may vote against their interests on roll calls that do not matter to them greatly in exchange for support from other members on more salient roll calls. Because vote trading provides a means, albeit limited, for legislators to register their intensities of preference across a set of issues, its supporters have argued that it better approximates a free market in which individual interests can better be satisfied. I contrast this view with that of an older and more skeptical school of thought that deplores vote trading—or logrolling, as it is popularly known—because of its presumed ill effects on the public good.

To try to clarify and resolve these different viewpoints, I develop a model of vote trading, demonstrating that all traders may end up in an n-person Prisoners' Dilemma under certain circumstances. Even if legislators recognize that they all may end up worse off by choosing their dominant strategies of trading, it is difficult for them to extricate themselves from this "paradox of vote trading." Moreover, the formation of coalitions, whose members attempt to realize positive benefits through vote trading and prevent other members from partaking of them, may be vulnerable to challenges by other coalitions, which may lead to indefinite cycling.

In short, it is hard to see how the paradox can be avoided, either by legislators who act singly or by those who form coalitions that attempt to restrict vote trading. Examples of such trades, and conditions under which they are most likely to occur, are discussed.

The second bargaining situation in legislatures that I analyze concerns how parties, after a parliamentary election that gives no single party a majority of seats, attempt to reach agreement on a governing coalition. The usual payoffs to a party for joining such a coalition are concessions on policy and the award of ministerial posts in the government, roughly in proportion to the number of its seats in the parliament.

Because the relatively unstructured bargaining that occurs after a parliamentary election is difficult to model, I narrow the focus to study the effects that a new voting system, called "coalition voting," might have in making parties more responsive to voters. This voting system gives voters, whose votes determine the order in which coalitions can attempt to form a government, direct control over what parties participate in a government. With this additional structure, one can model coalition voting's probable effects on bargaining among parties in parliamentary systems based on proportional representation.

Under coalition voting, voters have two different kinds of votes. The first kind is a "party vote," which voters can cast for as many parties as they like. However, each party approved of does not receive one vote; instead a party vote is divided evenly among all parties of which the voter approves, which determines the seat shares of the parties in parliament.

The second kind of vote is a "coalition vote," which counts for all majority coalitions that are acceptable because they include all parties that the voter designates Y ("yes") and no parties that the voter designates N ("no"). The majority coalition acceptable to the most voters becomes governing, provided that the parties it comprises agree.

I show that coalition voting encourages parties, before an election, to reconcile their differences and form coalitions that are likely to have broad appeal. Such party coalitions, insofar as they formulate joint policies expressing the collective interests of their members, facilitate voter choices, producing a convergence of voter and party/coalition interests.

Optimal strategies of voters and parties are investigated, with a measure of "bargaining strength" proposed to study what payoffs (e.g., in terms of ministerial posts) a party in a governing coalition might expect. Coalition voting's most likely empirical effects in faction-ridden multiparty systems, like those of Israel and Italy, are also considered. From a normative perspective, I argue that coalition voting is a relatively simple and practicable reform that, by encouraging the resolution of interparty disputes, would foster consensus formation and more coherent policies in party-list systems.

7.2. Judgments about Vote Trading

The conventional judgment on vote trading in legislatures is one of severe disapproval.[2] In the United States, at least, the usual idiom is "logrolling"; ever since its meaning was extended from the clearing of land and the building of houses to the description of legislative intrigue in the early nineteenth century, logrolling has always had pejorative connotations. The common sense of the language has been reinforced by the judgment of scholars. Schattschneider (1935, 293), in describing the writing of the Smoot-Hawley tariff of 1930, concluded: "To manage pressures [i.e., for vote trading] is to govern; to let pressures run wild is to abdicate." Furthermore, it seems likely that the widespread scholarly support for concentrated national leadership—as embodied, for example, in such writings as the report of the Committee on Political Parties of the American Political Science Association (1950), a report to which Schattschneider contributed substantially—was engendered in part at least by a desire to minimize vote trading.

Despite the long-standing unanimity of scholarly and popular judgment, however, it has been argued by a number of scholars in the last generation that vote trading is socially desirable because it allows the expression of degrees of intensity of preference. Buchanan and Tullock (1962, 145), for example, contend that the interests of a legislator (as well as voters) can be better met "if he accepts a decision contrary to his desire in an area where his preferences are weak in exchange for a decision in his favor in an area where his feelings are stronger"; hence, they say, "bargains among voters can, therefore, be mutually beneficial."

The authors do recognize that when bargains are concluded "in which the single voter does not participate, . . . he will have to bear part of the costs of action taken" (Buchanan and Tullock 1962, 145). But they nonetheless conclude that these external costs are on the average less than the benefits obtained so that, for the society as a whole, vote trading, or logrolling, is a desirable kind of activity.

In support of this argument, a small literature on the subject has developed. Tullock (1970) elaborated his earlier position. Coleman (1966) argued that logrolling is a device both to avoid the paradox of voting (to be described in Section 7.5) and to arrive at optimal allocations. A number of writers have pointed out, however, that vote trading does not eliminate the paradox (Mueller 1967; Wilson 1969). But these same writers and others have taken pains to argue that it does improve allocations in the direction of Pareto superiority (Wilson 1969; Haefele 1970; Mueller, Philpotts, and Vanck 1972).

There is thus an intellectual confrontation between an older, popular tradition and newer developments in social science. To try to reconcile this conflict, I shall define the relationship between salience and utility in Section 7.3, where the assumptions of a model of vote trading will be described. Then I shall offer an example that demonstrates how, through vote trades that are all individually rational (to be defined in Section 7.3) for pairs of members of a voting body, every member may end up worse off than before. This is the *paradox of vote trading*, which can be viewed, as I will demonstrate, as an *n*-person Prisoners' Dilemma that extends the earlier two-person version (Section 4.2) to more than two players. Then I shall assess the significance of the vote-trading paradox in light of some empirical examples before turning to the analysis of parliamentary coalitions under coalition voting.

7.3. Definitions and Assumptions about Vote Trading

Assume that each member of a hypothetical voting body can rank all roll calls in terms of their salience. By *salience* I mean the difference that it makes to a member to be in the majority (i.e., win) versus the minority (i.e., lose). More precisely, if $u_i(M)$ is the utility member i associates with being in the majority (M) on a particular roll call—which may not be positive if i votes insincerely, as I shall presently show—and $u_i(N)$ is the utility i associates with being in the minority (N), then define i's salience for that roll call as

$$s_i = u_i(M) - u_i(N).$$

For the two roll calls shown in Table 7.1, the second is more salient to i than the first (because $s_i = 4$ on Roll Call 2 and $s_i = 2$ on Roll Call 1), whereas the first is more salient to member j than the second (because $s_j = 3$ on Roll Call 1 and $s_j = 1$ on Roll Call 2).

Note that even though $s_i > s_j$ on Roll Call 2, and $s_j > s_i$ on Roll Call 1, no comparisons of salience *between* members is made. Such interpersonal comparisons of salience, and the utilities associated with salience, are ruled out in the absence of any universal standard (e.g., based on money, power, or prestige) that can be presumed for all members in their evaluations of social choices.[3]

In the subsequent analysis, I shall continue the development of the example in Table 7.1 to illustrate the definition of vote trading. First, however, I state the assumptions of the model:

1. A voting body of (initially) three members, $V = \{i,j,k\}$.
2. A set of (initially) six roll-call votes, $R = \{1,2,3,4,5,6\}$, on each of

Table 7.1. Utility of Positions and Salience of Roll Calls for Two Members

Members	Utility and Salience					
	Roll Call 1			Roll Call 2		
	$u(M)$	$u(N)$	s	$u(M)$	$u(N)$	s
i	1	−1	2	2	−2	4
j	1	−2	3	1	0	1

which a member has a preference for either one of two *positions* (for or against): if two of the three members agree on a roll call (by voting either for or against), this is the majority position (M), whereas the third member is in the minority (N).

3. There are no roll calls on which all three members agree. Winning majorities are thus assumed to be always *minimal winning*, which means that if either member of the two-member majority changes his or her position on a roll call, this changes the majority outcome on that roll call. Thus, the votes of the majority members on all roll calls are *critical*.

4. Each member of the voting body can rank all roll calls in terms of the importance or *salience* of the outcome. (As I shall show, the differential salience that members attach to the outcomes of different roll calls is the condition that makes votes trades possible.)

5. Each member possesses *complete information* about the positions and salience rankings of all other members and can *communicate* with them.

6. The *goal* of each member is, through vote trading, to maximize his or her utility across all roll calls by being in the majority on the roll calls whose outcomes are most salient.

Clearly, if members value the outcomes on roll calls differently (Assumption 4), then it follows from the goal assumption (Assumption 6) that a rational member will be willing to give up a preferred position on one roll call to secure a preferred position on another roll call whose outcome is more salient. The mechanism by which this is accomplished is a *vote trade*. The possibility of a vote trade depends on the presence of two conditions (a third condition will be specified shortly) for any pair of members i and j who vote on Roll Calls 1 and 2:

(a) i is in the majority on Roll Call 1 and the minority on Roll Call 2;

(b) j is in the majority on Roll Call 2 and the minority on Roll Call 1.

A trade occurs when i (majority position holder) gives his or her support to j (minority position holder) on Roll Call 1 in return for the support of j (majority position holder) on Roll Call 2 (on which i is in the minority).

It is precisely the asymmetry of the positions of the two members on the two roll calls that permits an exchange of support. By Assumption 3, such an exchange will alter the majority outcome on each roll call because the switcher (i on Roll Call 1, j on Roll Call 2) casts a critical vote when the majorities are minimal winning. Under this circumstance, the minority position for which a member (i on Roll Call 2, j on Roll Call 1) receives support becomes the majority position when this support is given.

Simple as conditions (a) and (b) are, they say quite a bit about the occurrence of logrolling in real legislatures. It is apparent that, for a trade to be possible, the traders must be on opposite sides on two roll calls. One trader must be in the initial majority on the first roll call and the initial minority on the second. The other trader must be in the initial minority on the first roll call and the initial majority on the second. If these conditions cannot be met, then trading is not possible.

One obvious place it cannot be met is in legislatures with just two disciplined parties. To say that a party is disciplined is to say that all its members are on the same side on any roll call. Hence, if the members of a party are a majority on one roll call, they are a majority on all roll calls. For the two conditions for vote trading to be met, some of the party members must sometimes be in the minority, but they cannot be by reason of their being disciplined.

Consequently, in a legislature with just two disciplined parties, logrolling is extremely rare. This is probably one reason why so many American writers from Woodrow Wilson onward have admired the British Parliament, especially when it has approached the two-party situation in which the two conditions for a vote trade cannot be satisfied. They should have also admired the state legislatures of New York and Pennsylvania, for example, which party bosses have often run with an iron hand, because logrolling is equally impossible in them. But it has never been fashionable to admire boss rule.

Of course, once vote trading is banished from the legislature, political compromise goes on someplace else politically antecedent to the legislature. Thus, in state legislatures and city councils with disciplined parties, the compromise takes place in the majority caucus or in the mind of the boss. In England, the Cabinet serves as one place of compromise, and very probably something like vote trading goes on there. Because the Cabinet situation is unstructured in comparison with the situation in the Parliament, however, it is probably hard to identify the trades and compromises that do occur.

A third condition is necessary to ensure that a vote trade is individually rational for each member in a pair:

(c) The minority position for which a member receives support on a roll call changes an outcome that is more salient than the outcome on which the member switches his or her vote.

In other words, a trade is individually rational for a pair of members when it not only changes the outcomes of the two roll calls on which they exchange votes but also assures each member of a majority position on the roll call whose outcome is more salient. As I shall show later, however, the trades of other pairs of members may upset these calculations in such a way that the trades that produce positive gains for each pair of trading members may lower the collective benefits for all members of the voting body. Before discussing the interdependence of vote trades, though, "sincere" and "insincere" voting must be distinguished.

7.4. Sincere and Insincere Voting

By *sincere voting* I mean that a member of a voting body votes directly according to his or her preferences. This is to be contrasted with *insincere voting,* which is defined as voting against one's interest—that is, for a less-preferred rather than a more-preferred position on a roll call—when there is an incentive to do so. Insincere voting includes "sophisticated voting," to be analyzed in Chapter 8; but it also includes voting in situations wherein voters can communicate with other voters and negotiate agreements, which is not assumed in sophisticated voting.

Surely one of the main reasons for insincere voting is logrolling. Whatever one thinks of the propriety of this kind of behavior, it may be rational with respect to the goal postulated in Section 7.3 (Assumption 6). Consider again the situation assumed earlier of two members, i and j, whose (sincere) positions on Roll Calls 1 and 2 are such that i is in the majority on Roll Call 1, denoted by $M(1)$, and j is in the majority on Roll Call 2, denoted by $M(2)$. Similarly, let $N(1)$ and $N(2)$ denote the minority positions on these roll calls, which I assume are the positions, respectively, of j and i.

Now assume, as was the case in Table 7.1, that Roll Call 2 is the roll call whose outcome is more salient to i, and Roll Call 1 is the roll call whose outcome is more salient to j. This situation is summarized in Table 7.2, with the utilities associated with the positions of each member, originally given in Table 7.1, also shown. ("Total utility" is simply the algebraic sum of the utilities of each member across the two roll calls.)

Table 7.2. Positions and Utilities before Trading

Members	High		Low		Total Utility
	Position	Utility	Position	Utility	
i	N(2)	−2	M(1)	1	−1
j	N(1)	−2	M(2)	1	−1

Given the goal of each member to be in the majority on its most salient roll calls (Assumption 6), *i* would prefer to be in the majority on Roll Call 2 and *j* on Roll Call 1. I shall now show that each member can realize this goal through a vote trade.

To effect such a trade, each member will have to vote insincerely on the roll call whose outcome is less salient. Label the insincere positions of the members on these roll calls as M_d to signify support of a majority with which one disagrees (*d*). Assuming that the outcomes N and M_d are valued as equally bad—that is, on any roll call $u(M_d) = u(N)$ for each member—the utilities of the new positions of members after the trade, originally given in Table 7.1, are shown in Table 7.3. The value of the trade can be seen by comparing the total utilities of the members before (Table 7.2) and after (Table 7.3) trading, which increase for both from −1 to +1. The advantages of vote trading are apparent—there is a clear gain for both members from the trade—and one can easily understand why the notion of logrolling has been so attractive to contemporary scholars.

Nevertheless, there are some serious limitations. One is that the possibilities of trading are quite restricted. By Assumption 3, a switch is pointless unless the switcher casts a critical vote with respect to his or her initial majority. As a consequence, there is a maximum limit on logrolling: since it takes two critical members to trade, there can at most be as many trades as half the number of issues. In a temporal world, moreover, only a finite number of issues can be juggled at once. In a session of a typical national legislature, for example, there are probably no more than, say, two thousand roll calls, which gives a theoretical maximum of one thousand trades.

But, of course, many issues are trivial so that no trade is worthwhile; many others come up for decision so quickly that the fairly elaborate arrangements of logrolling are not possible; for many others it may be difficult for a member to discover another one with whom Conditions (a), (b), and (c) can be satisfied; and, finally, because roll calls come up serially so that many future roll calls cannot be anticipated and so that past roll calls are irrevocably settled, only a small subset of roll calls is available for trading at any one moment. In fact, it would seem, the

Table 7.3. Positions and Utilities after Trading

| Members | Salience | | | | Total Utility |
| | High | | Low | | |
	Position	Utility	Position	Utility	
i	$M(2)$	2	$M_d(1)$	−1	1
j	$M(1)$	1	$M_d(2)$	0	1

practical maximum of trades is at most one-tenth of the theoretical maximum. In a typical legislature (with, say, one hundred members) in a typical session, therefore, it may well be that the average member can expect to be involved in at most one trade that changes the outcomes of the two roll calls on which the trade is made.

The utilities given in Tables 7.2 and 7.3 are purely illustrative, for individually rational vote trades as I have defined them will always be profitable for the participating members, given the equivalence between the N and M_d positions assumed earlier. This equivalence assumption is justified by the fact that in the case of both N and M_d, a member's sincere position differs from the prevailing one, expressed in one case by *public nonsupport* of the majority position (i.e., voting with the minority, N) and in the other by *public support* of a majority position with which one privately disagrees (M_d). Although one might regard the hypocrisy of the latter position as distasteful if not unconscionable, it would seem that whether one's disagreement is public or private, the results are the same: one's preferred position on a roll call is thwarted by the majority, even if it is a majority one publicly supports.

For this reason I consider these positions equivalent in terms of the utilities associated with each. Indeed, implicit in the goal assumption (Assumption 6) is that a member's majorities on roll calls whose outcomes are less salient are negotiable; in particular, this member will be willing to sacrifice preferred positions on these roll calls—and form majorities inimical to his or her interests—if he or she can prevail on roll calls whose outcomes are more salient. I assume that these more salient outcomes override any ethical qualms associated with insincere voting—that is, the utilities are true expressions of preferences.

So far so good for the vote-trading members in the previous example: they both come out better off after the trade. Their good fortune is not costless to other members, however, for the reversal of the majorities on the two roll calls must occur at somebody's expense—namely, the third member of the voting body.

To see this difficulty, consider the original (sincere) positions of *i* and *j* on the two roll calls given in Table 7.2. By Assumption 2, a third member

k must take the majority position on both roll calls in order that two members support the majority on each roll call and one member the minority. Thus, the (sincere) positions of a third member k on Roll Calls 1 and 2 will necessarily be $M(1)$ and $M(2)$.

Now recall that after the vote trade of members i and j, the old minority positions become the new majority positions because of the switch of i on Roll Call 1 and j on Roll Call 2 to positions with which they disagree (see Table 7.3). Because of the critical nature of members' votes on roll calls, these switches produce new majorities on the roll calls. These new majorities, which i and j now together constitute on Roll Calls 1 and 2, recast the previous majority positions of k on these roll calls into minority positions, $N(1)$ and $N(2)$.

Thus, the costs of the favorable trade between members i and j fall on the nonparticipant, k. This follows from the fact that the number of majority and minority positions must remain constant by Assumption 2 (in a three-members body, a 2:1 ratio of M's and N's must be preserved on all roll calls under simple majority rule), so all switches in positions produced by the vote-trading members on each roll call will perforce generate an equal number of involuntary outcome changes (from majority to minority) for the nontrading member. If that member k associates the same utilities with the majority and minority positions on the two roll calls as i (see Table 7.1), then the vote trade between members i and j drops k's total utility from $+3$ to -3, as shown in Table 7.4.

If the gains from a vote trade can be wiped out by "external costs" (defined in the next paragraph), the enthusiasm of logrolling's proponents may be misplaced. Indeed, it is quite possible to imagine a system in which everyone gains from individual trades—and so has a positive incentive to logroll—and yet everyone also loses if all such trades are carried out. This is the paradox of logrolling to whose illustration I shall turn in Section 7.5.

External costs are costs that one bears as a result of the actions of others. They are to be contrasted with internal costs, which result from one's own action. The noise that comes from a pneumatic drill is an internal cost with respect to the driller because it is part of what the driller must suffer to earn his or her pay. But to the neighbor at the construction site, the noise is an external cost; it must be borne not in order to get something else but merely because he or she is there.

Debate is never-ending about the existence of some external costs. (For example, does the noise of the drill really bother the neighbor, or does that person see a chance, by complaining of the noise—even though it is not bothersome—to blackmail the contractor?) But it seems impossible to doubt the existence of external costs in vote trading. Consider the position of some member who is not party to a trade: because the trade

Table 7.4. Positions and Utilities of Left-Out Member before and after Trading

Member k	Salience				Total Utility
	High		Low		
	Position	Utility	Position	Utility	
Before Trading	M(2)	2	M(1)	1	3
After Trading	N(2)	−2	N(1)	−1	−3

brings about a different winner on a roll call, the nontrader bears an external cost if he or she were originally in the majority; or the nontrader receives an external gain if he or she were in the original minority. In the example, k is entirely passive throughout the entire transaction, but two of k's positions are reversed from majority to minority.

External costs have mostly been ignored in the writings of those who extol the benefits of vote trading.[4] Yet they must by Assumption 3 on critical votes be present: because trading changes the outcomes, there must always be innocent bystanders who suffer. Although the size of their losses in particular cases will depend on the amounts of utility associated with their salience rankings, it is possible to show that in particular cases suffering is general and universal, which is the paradox of logrolling.

In summary, it would appear that the optimal joint strategy of a pair of vote-trading members *i* and *j* is to vote insincerely on the roll calls whose outcomes are less salient and sincerely on the roll calls whose outcomes are more salient. The trade puts both members on the side of the majority on both roll calls, one of which (the roll call whose outcome is more salient) each member agrees with, the other of which he or she disagrees with. The external cost which this trade imposes on *k* in the example is to change his or her previous majority positions on both roll calls into minority positions.

7.5. Initial Trades and the Paradox of Vote Trading

I now turn to a simple example to demonstrate that vote trades that are individually rational for pairs of members in a voting body may leave all members worse off after the trades. Assume that roll calls are voted on serially, so that future roll calls are not necessarily anticipated when current roll calls are considered. This assumption about the voting process, by the way, is quite different from the assumption made in the previously cited works of proponents of vote trading, where it is typically laid down that all roll calls are simultaneously before the legislature. In such a system, support can be traded back and forth in all possible ways, but in the present system support can be traded only with respect to the subset of roll calls currently before the legislature or anticipated to come before it.[5] The rationale for this more restrictive assumption is simply that it accords with a crucial feature of the real world.

In order for each of the three members (i, j, and k) of the postulated voting body to be able to trade with the two other members, the trading must occur over a minimum of six roll calls. This is so because there is a total of three different pairs of members in the three-member voting body—(i,j) (j,k), and (i,k). Because a trade by each pair involves two different roll calls, there must be at least six different roll calls if all three pairs are to engage in vote trading. In general, on any single round of trading there can at most be as many trades as half the number of roll calls, because on any trade support is exchanged between members on two different roll calls, which I assume cannot serve as the basis for more than one trade.

Given an *initial* set of trades among pairs of members, ignore for the moment the *subsequent* possible trades that these initial trades may set up. As I will show later, however, an indefinitely large number of possible trades may follow from the initial trades, so the number of roll calls on which members vote serves to limit only the number of initial trading possibilities. Moreover, a member may have a choice of more than one trading partner on two roll calls, but this and other possible complications of the simple example that I shall elaborate in this section will be reserved for the later discussion.

To illustrate the paradox of vote trading wherein each member is worse off after trading, consider a voting body whose members' positions on six roll calls, indexed by the numbers 1 through 6 in parentheses, are indicated in Table 7.5. For each member assume that the salience of the outcome of each roll call decreases from left to right in each row of the table. Thus, for i the outcome of Roll Call 1 is most salient, the outcome of Roll Call 6 least salient; on both roll calls, i's position is the majority position.

Vote trades can readily be identified for each pair of members in Table 7.5. Thus, i can trade with k on Roll Calls 3 and 6. That is, on i's least salient Roll Call, 6, i votes against his or her interest and gains thereby from k's switch on i's third most salient roll call, 3. Similarly, on k's next-to-least salient roll call, 3, k votes against his or her interest and gains thereby on his or her roll call of next-higher salience, 6. This trade is indicated in Table 7.5 by solid lines connecting the positions of members i and k; other trades between i and j and between j and k are indicated by dotted and dashed lines, respectively.

After the three trades indicated in Table 7.5 have been made, the

Table 7.5. Positions of Members before Initial Trades on Six Roll Calls

Member	High Salience → Low Salience						Trades	Switches	Key
	Majority and Minority Positions of Members before Trades								
i	$M(1)$	$M(2)$	$N(3)$	$N(4)$	$M(5)$	$M(6)$	with k	to $M_d(6)$	——
							with j	to $M_d(5)$	....
j	$M(3)$	$M(6)$	$N(5)$	$N(2)$	$M(1)$	$M(4)$	with i	to $M_d(4)$	....
							with k	to $M_d(1)$	------
k	$M(5)$	$M(4)$	$N(1)$	$N(6)$	$M(3)$	$M(2)$	with j	to $M_d(2)$	------
							with i	to $M_d(3)$	——

situation will be as shown in Table 7.6 (ignore for now the subsequent trades indicated in this table), where the two most salient M's for each member have been replaced by N's, the medium salient N's by M's, and the two least salient M's by M_d's (majority positions with which members disagree). As a result of the trades, the winning positions on all six roll calls are reversed.[6]

This is a dismal result for all three members. On the debit side, each member not only loses a majority position on his or her two most salient roll calls but also acquires a majority position, contrary to the member's interests, on his or her two least salient roll calls. For thus losing on the two most and the two least salient roll calls, on the credit side a member gains only on his or her two medium salient roll calls. Because members have greater utility for their two most salient roll calls than for their two medium salient roll calls, they lose overall by trading (their voting insincerely on their two least salient roll calls simply increases their loss from trading). Each member, then, is doubly hurt by trading.

Any set of utilities consistent with the salience rankings in the example can be used to illustrate this conclusion and gauge its magnitude. For example, assume for each member that the utility he or she associates with voting with the majority (M) on the roll call whose outcome is most salient is 6, on the next most salient is 5, and so on to the least salient, whose utility is 1. Assume further that the utility each member associates with voting with the minority (N) is 0 on all roll calls. Then the salience for each member,

$$s = u(M) - u(N),$$

will be $6 - 0$ on the the most salient roll call, $5 - 0$ on the next most salient, and so forth, which is consistent with the ordinal salience rankings.

Table 7.6. Positions of Members after Initial Trades on Six Roll Calls

Member	High Salience → Low Salience Majority and Minority Positions after Initial Trades						Trades	Switches	Key
i	$N(1)$	$N(2)$	$M(3)$	$M(4)$	$M_d(5)$	$M_d(6)$	with j with k	to $M(6)$ to $M(5)$	—— ....
j	$N(3)$	$N(6)$	$M(5)$	$M(2)$	$M_d(1)$	$M_d(4)$	with k with i	to $M(4)$ to $M(1)$	------- ——
k	$N(5)$	$N(4)$	$M(1)$	$M(6)$	$M_d(3)$	$M_d(2)$	with i with j	to $M(2)$ to $M(3)$	.... -------

Before trading, M's on each member's two most salient roll calls give him or her $6 + 5 = 11$ utiles, N's on each member's two next most salient roll calls $0 + 0$ utiles, and M's on each member's two least salient roll calls $2 + 1 = 3$ utiles, for a total utility of 14. After trading, assuming $U(M_d) = u(N) = 0$, N's on each members' two most salient roll calls give him or her $0 + 0 = 0$ utiles, M's on each member's two next-most-salient roll calls $4 + 3 = 7$ utiles, and M_d's on each members two least salient roll calls $0 + 0 = 0$ utiles, for a total utility of 7. Thus, for these particular utilities, which are consistent with the ordinal salience rankings assumed in this example, trading halves each member's total utility from 14 to 7. The paradox is confirmed: all members are absolutely worse off from trading—in this case, by a factor of two.

It might be thought that this result could be avoided by a different set of initial trades. But it is apparent in light of the situation as given in Table 7.5 that such trades are not possible. Member i, for example, wants to gain on Roll Calls 3 and 4 by getting someone to switch on these roll calls. But i cannot trade with j on Roll Call 3 because this would force j to switch on his or her most most salient roll call, which is in clear violation of condition (c) of individual rationality (Section 7.3). Therefore, i *must* trade with j on Roll Call 4, exactly as in Table 7.5. By a similar argument, each of the other two members in this table is constrained to exactly those trades indicated in it.

7.6. Subsequent Trades and the Instability of Vote Trading

The example in Table 7.5 shows that the paradox is inherent in the ordinal relationships and is not dependent on particular utility numbers, which I used simply to provide one illustration of salience and utility values in this example. Following the trades indicated in Table 7.5, however, the situation depicted in Table 7.6 is not in equilibrium. The positions generated by the initial set of trades are themselves unstable and generate the new set of trades shown in Table 7.6. Except that the majorities that the members trade are now ones with which they disagree, Conditions (a), (b), and (c), which ensure an individually rational vote trade, are all met for the trading pairs indicated in this table.

M_d's, however, can be traded like M's. In fact, there is an added incentive to switch an M_d on a roll call of lower salience than an M, because one switches from a majority with which one disagrees back to a majority with which one agrees. To illustrate, in the initial trading in the example, it was rational for i to support k on Roll Call 6 by switching from $M(6)$ (see Table 7.5) to $M_d(6)$ (see Table 7.6). But, as indicated in Table 7.6, after this initial trade it is now rational for i to switch back to $M(6)$ so that he or she can support j on Roll Call 6 in return for k's support on Roll Call 1.

What happens after members make these subsequent trades? It is easy to show that when members trade their M_d's back for M's, their positions after the subsequent trades will bring the trading back to where it started (i.e., the positions of members given in Table 7.5). This reversion of members after two rounds of trading back to their original positions, with nothing gained and nothing lost (except the costs of trading), is an immediate consequence of the two switches in position made by members' voting insincerely on the initial round but sincerely once again on the subsequent round. Because each member has only one sincere position on each roll call, the initially postulated sincere positions of members, and the sincere positions after the subsequent trades, must be the same.

Voting that involves first a switch to a position contrary to one's preference on a roll call and then a reverse switch back may seem more devious than sincere. But this is only the beginning. For after a reverse shift, when everybody assumes once again his or her original sincere position, there is no reason to believe that pairs of members will not plunge themselves once again into a new round of trades that are individually rational. Indeed, the inexorable logic of individual rationality dictates that if a member is willing to double-cross an old trading partner in order to improve his or her position through another trade, that member would be willing to triple-cross a new trading partner, and so on.

The consequence of all members' acting in this self-serving fashion is that trading continues indefinitely—in theory, at least, if not in practice. The lack of an equilibrium that could break this cycle at any point means that there is no guarantee that even the improved benefits to all, as before the initial or after the subsequent trades in the example, will halt the process. In practice, only when roll calls are actually voted on will the process of vote trading be terminated.

The instability of the positions of members after the initial trades is underscored by the fact that a member always has an incentive to switch his or her M_d positions back to their original M positions, even if the other members refuse to trade. For even without the cooperation of the other members, the switches themselves will increase each member's utility.

As an illustration in terms of the utilities given earlier, any single member in Table 7.6 would gain $1 - 0 = 1$ utile by switching from M_d to M on his or her least salient roll call, and $2 - 0 = 2$ utiles on his or her next least salient roll call, for a total utility gain of 3.[7] In fact, in *all* cases of vote trading, the generation of M_d's on the initial trades are by their nature positions that members would like to get rid of—and can, by reneging on vote-trading agreements. They are, therefore, unstable.

7.7. The Consequences of Refusing to Trade

In theory, it would seem, one possible way in which members might transcend the disturbing logic of individual rationality would be to make irrevocable trading agreements. Even if members have no ethical compunctions about reneging on pairwise agreements that turn out to be no longer individually rational to honor, it is possible that the penalties (e.g., reprisals by other members) for acting duplicitously may in the long run outweigh any benefits that accrue from trading. If this is the case, it would be rational for all members to honor trading agreements made on the initial round of trading.

To assume that the individual-rationality assumption is operative for only one round of trading, however, seems in some ways artificial. Although the blatant disregard of earlier agreements may seem duplicitous behavior that members could not get away with over the long haul, there is not much basis for believing this fact will bind them to their initial vote-trading agreements, especially when these agreements lead to a collective disaster for all, as the example illustrating the paradox demonstrated.[8] This is the worst possible situation when all members trade; with apparently nothing to lose, any behavior, however unscrupulous, would seem justified on the part of members who are trying to extricate themselves from this distressing situation.

As distressing as the everybody-worse-off situation is after the initial round of vote trading, members would do still worse by refusing to trade. For example, if in Table 7.5 i refused to trade with j and k, but j and k were willing to trade with each other, the positions of i on the six roll calls after this trade would be:

$$N(1) \quad N(2) \quad N(3) \quad N(4) \quad M(5) \quad M(6).$$

These positions are clearly inferior to the positions of i if he or she had traded with j and k (see Table 7.6),

$$N(1) \quad N(2) \quad M(3) \quad M(4) \quad M_d(5) \quad M_d(6),$$

for the majorities i agrees with on Roll Calls 3 and 4 are more salient than the majorities he or she would have been left with on Roll Calls 5 and 6 had i not traded. In terms of the utilities given earlier, i's total utility, summed across the six roll calls from most to least salient, would be

$$0 + 0 + 0 + 0 + 2 + 1 = 3$$

if i refused to trade, and

$$0 + 0 + 4 + 3 + 0 + 0 = 7$$

if i agreed to trade.

Similarly, it is possible to show that it would not be in the interest of either j or k to refuse to trade if the other two members did trade. Since it is individually rational for the other pair always to trade, there is no way to freeze the desirable status quo positions shown in Table 7.5. This means that despite the unfavorable consequences for all members set loose by the trades depicted in Table 7.5, it is irrational for any single member to refuse to trade.

Conceivably, the members might escape the paradox of Table 7.6 by all agreeing not to make the trades depicted in Table 7.5. For example, it might be said that if the members had foresight, they would refuse to make trades at all, lest the trades lead to the realization of the paradox. Self-restraint is not easy, however. Suppose each member makes no trade but anticipates a trade between the pair that does not include him or her. That is, this member behaves with self-restraint but—with a conservative appreciation of the harm others can do—anticipates the worst from them.

This situation is analogous to an n-person Prisoners' Dilemma, which is simply an extention to n players ($n > 2$) of the two-person Prisoners' Dilemma discussed in Section 4.2. If any member suspects that the others may not abide by their agreements not to trade, then this member's best strategy is to trade. Because it is also rational to trade when other members do not trade, trading is the dominant strategy for each member. Thus, with every member forced to trade in order to behave rationally, each perversely may come to a worse end than if he or she did not trade and always voted sincerely.

This problem is equivalent to the problem of collective action in the theory of collective (or public) goods, as Hardin (1971, 1982) and others have shown.[9] As applied to vote-trading situations, it means that every pair of members that can benefit from trading has no incentive to cooperate with other members whose positions they might adversely affect by trading. This makes it impossible for members of a voting body to reach a collective agreement not to trade unless there are sanctions (e.g., group norms) penalizing such actions.

7.8. The Consequences of Forming Coalitions

In Section 7.7 I showed that the refusal of i to trade, given that j and k trade with each other, leads to a more undesirable outcome for i than if he or she also traded. Just as i comes out worse off by refusing to trade, it follows from the assumption of individual rationality that j and k come out better off.

Exactly how much better off, with i out of the picture, is worth considering. In the case of j, for example, trading with k changes j's positions from those given in Table 7.5 to

$$M(3) \quad M(6) \quad N(5) \quad M(2) \quad M_d(1) \quad M(4)$$

after the pair exchanges support on Roll Calls 1 and 2. Had i not refused to trade with j and k, j's positions after the three trades by all pairs of members on Roll Calls 3 and 6, 4 and 5, and 1 and 2 would have been (see Table 7.6)

$$N(3) \quad N(6) \quad M(5) \quad M(2) \quad M_d(1) \quad M_d(4).$$

While j does pick up a majority that he or she agrees with on the third-most-salient roll call (i.e., 5) in exchange for voting insincerely on the least salient roll call (4), j forfeits majorities on his or her two most salient roll calls (3 and 6) when i "cooperates" (by trading) rather than refuses to trade. In terms of the utilities given earlier, j's total utility (summed across the six roll calls from most to least salient) is

$$6 + 5 + 0 + 3 + 0 + 1 = 15$$

when i refuses to trade, and

$$0 + 0 + 4 + 3 + 0 + 0 = 7$$

when i does trade with the other two members. This difference, of course, is mostly due to the external costs inflicted upon j by the vote trade between i and k, to which j is not a party.

The apparent lesson that follows from this example, which applies no matter which single member (i, j, or k) refuses to trade, is that two members can do better by agreeing to trade with each other but not the third member—that is, by forming a coalition whose members pledge to trade only with each other. Thereby they can obtain the benefits of trading and avoid the external costs of others' trades.

To be sure, this solution to the paradox simply denies that Conditions (a), (b), and (c) in Section 7.3, which define an individually rational trade, are operative for all members, but it is one way to cut the Gordian knot. It is comparable to cooperative solutions to Prisoners' Dilemma in which, with communication allowed and the suspects able to make binding agreements, they agree never to confess and thereby thwart the prosecutor. In the absence of enforceable agreements, however, there may be instabilities in such solutions simply because they are not individually rational. So it is here.

Refer again to Table 7.5, and suppose j and k coalesce on Roll Calls 1 and 2. Member i is excluded, but i may propose to coalesce with j instead on Roll Calls 4 and 5. Once this alternative is proposed, j prefers the coalition with i on Roll Calls 4 and 5 to the coalition with k on Roll Calls 1 and 2 simply because j gains more from an improvement on more salient Roll Call 5 than from an improvement on less salient Roll Call 2; also, j loses less from voting insincerely on least salient Roll Call 4 than from so voting on next-to-least salient Roll Call 1. (Put somewhat differently, in j's salience ranking in Table 7.5, the roll calls on which j trades with k are "embedded" in the roll calls on which j trades with i and hence are clearly inferior.) Thus, j prefers coalition $\{i,j\}$ to coalition $\{j,k\}$, and of course i—who is in the former but not the latter—also prefers $\{i,j\}$ to $\{j,k\}$. One can then write $\{i,j\}$ D $\{j,k\}$, where "D" means that the former coalition dominates the latter in that both members of the former prefer it to the latter.

By a similar argument it can be shown that $\{j,k\}$ D $\{i,k\}$ and $\{i,k\}$ D $\{i,j\}$. Putting these statements together, there is an *intransitive* preference ordering of all two-member (majority) coalitions—that is, each is preferred by some other coalition, resulting in the following cycle:

$$\{i,j\} \text{ D } \{j,k\} \text{ D } \{i,k\} \text{ D } \{i,j\}.$$

Thus, when vote trading is unrestricted, there may be no single coalition that is dominant, or preferred by its members to every other. In the present example, there is always one member of every two-member coalition who can be tempted by the offer of the third (left-out) member to defect and form a new coalition, from which both derive greater total utility. Hence, the system is unstable because the third (left-out) member has not only an incentive to break up an existing coalition but also always can do so by offering an alternative coalition that is preferred by one coalition member to the existing one.

It can be shown that vote trading, even in the absence of the paradox of vote trading, is a product of the same conditions that lead to the *paradox of voting*.[10] To illustrate the latter paradox, in Table 7.7 I have given the preferences of each member for the possible trades that might be made. Thus, i's highest preference is for the trade on Roll Calls 3 and 6 with k, because 3 is the most salient roll call on which i can improve his or her position and 6 is the least salient on which i can vote insincerely. Similarly, i's medium preference is for the trade on Roll Calls 4 and 5 with j; i's lowest preference is for the trade on Roll Calls 1 and 2 (between j and k) on which i is left out. If, now, the members vote on which trades they wish to occur, the outcome will be an intransitive social arrangement:

{3,6} is socially preferred to {4,5} by i and k,

{4,5} is socially preferred to {1,2} by i and j,

{1,2} is socially preferred to {3,6} by j and k,

so the arrangement is again a cycle,

$$\{3,6\} > \{4,5\} > \{1,2\} > \{3,6\},$$

where ">" indicates a majority preference (i.e., by two of the three members).

In sum, no trade is preferred to all other trades, so none could defeat all others in a series of pairwise contests. This is equivalent to the earlier demonstration that no coalition can defeat all others. Because there is no preferred set of trades on which to base a stable coalition, no stable coalition is possible. The paradox of vote trading cannot, therefore, be simply solved by waving it away with a coalition. Rather, it is inherent in the nature of the legislative process and, given certain configurations of preferences and external costs, cannot be avoided.

This lack of an equilibrium is significant, for it shatters any hope one might harbor that a dominant collective preference can be ensured through vote trading.[11] Such instability extends the previous conclusions in Section 7.6 about the cyclic nature of vote trading for individual members of a voting body to proper subsets of members, whose formation as coalitions that attempt to exclude vote trades with other members

Table 7.7. Preferences of Members for Trades

Member	Preferences for Trades		
	Highest	Medium	Lowest
i	(3,6)	(4,5)	(1,2)
j	(4,5)	(1,2)	(3,6)
k	(1,2)	(3,6)	(4,5)

offers no guarantee that trading cycles can be banished once and for all. There seems, therefore, to be a fundamental disequilibrium in vote trading that is driven by the assumption of individual rationality.

7.9. Empirical Examples of the Paradox of Vote Trading

The popular distrust of logrolling probably stems from an intuitive, incomplete, but nonetheless sure comprehension of the vote-trading paradox, or at least of the external costs on which it is based. To assess the validity of this popular distrust requires that one estimate the likelihood that the paradox arises in real legislatures. If it arises frequently, then surely the popular distrust has a reasonable basis. If it arises only rarely, however, then one probably ought to conclude that logrolling is a socially useful technique to approach collectively rational (i.e., Pareto-superior) states of the world. Even though there seems no systematic way to investigate real-world frequencies of the paradox, one can specify types of circumstances in which it is likely to occur and then estimate the likelihood of these circumstances.

The crucial element of the paradox is external costs, which of course depend on the specific trade. It is always the case, however, that more people gain than lose on each switch, for the gainers (including the critical member who switches) necessarily constitute a majority of members. Consequently, in a system of trades—and usually for each participant as well—more instances of gain occur than do instances of loss. But gains and losses are not necessarily equal in magnitude, so the paradox occurs when, in a system of trades, members generally lose more when they lose than they gain when they gain. The question then is: Under what real-world circumstances might these large losses be expected to occur?

Patently, if there is only one trade, the paradox is impossible because the gainers on this trade cannot suffer external costs on another, which does not exist. Therefore, if trades are occasional and isolated and not part of a system of interrelated bargains, losses are probably less than gains for many if not most members of the legislature. This kind of sporadic logrolling is often found in American legislatures, wherein party discipline is not usually very strong, but it is not the kind so earnestly recommended by the several scholars cited earlier in this chapter. Rather, the kind they applaud is that in which members engage in a constant round of bargaining in order to arrive at optimal outcomes over the whole set of issues in the legislative session. Unfortunately, it is exactly this kind of logrolling that probably increases the likelihood of the vote-trading paradox.

If one can separate out his reformist concerns, this is what Schatt-schneider (1935) seems to have perceived about the writing of the Smoot-Hawley tariff. Those members who joined the tariff combination for a price on some issue (usually a tariff on something manufactured in their districts) gained an advantage for their constituents. Such a large number joined, however, that protection was made indiscriminate—nearly every-body got something. Thereby international trade was discouraged and disrupted—to the disadvantage of everybody in the society. To the extent that the Smoot-Hawley tariff deepened and extended the Great Depres-sion in the 1930s, even the gainers probably suffered more than they gained.

One can see the same process at work in, for example, the river and harbor bills of the twentieth century when they ceased to have the charac-ter of vital internal improvements that they had had in the nineteenth century. A majority gains from the pork in such barrels, else the bill would not pass. But there are also losses, external costs. Once taxes are paid, the net gains of the gainers are probably quite small. And if the projects are for the most part economically useless (e.g., locks on a canal that only a few pleasure boats use), then the costs probably exceed the gainers' gains; if the projects are positively harmful (e.g., dikes on a river that would otherwise support wetlands and a higher water table), then their absolute losses almost certainly exceed the gainers' gains.

Still other possible cases come easily to mind. A long-term example is the system of income tax exemptions and deductions, which are distrib-uted so that they actually provide savings for only an unidentifiable few (in many cases, the wealthy). At the same time, they probably assess higher costs against nearly everybody, especially by distorting the market for certain goods and by discouraging certain kinds of investment. An-other and even longer-term example is the proliferation of military bases throughout the country, each providing a small economic benefit to its neighborhood but, by their inefficiency, considerably increasing in sum the military cost for everybody.

As these examples suggest, the bills and circumstances likely to occasion paradoxes are those that bring together an interrelated set of issues, many of which are of interest to only a few legislators. Tax bills, internal improvement bills, redistributions of income, to cite but a few cases, seem especially prone to providing the kind of situation in which the paradox can easily arise. As these kinds of bills occupy a good part of any legislature's time, it must be concluded that the paradox of vote trading is a real fact of political life. One suspects that, because of it, logrolling leads more often away from, rather than toward, Pareto-superior social allocations.

With a bow in the direction of reformers, both those who recommend and those who excoriate logrolling, it might be asked whether or not occurrences of the paradox can be prevented. The answer is, "probably not," short of highly unpalatable restrictions. Legislatures do occasionally adopt self-denying ordinances, like the so-called closed rule in the U.S. House of Representatives, a rule that prohibits amendments from the floor on which additional votes might be traded.[12]

Although this perhaps prevents the most gross and thoughtless types of logrolling, the anticipation of it probably forces the trading back off the floor into committee. Given all the rational pressures for trading, it is not really to be expected that a policy of self-denial will work. Stronger measures, like a system of responsible and disciplined parties, may well make trading impossible in the legislature, but they certainly cannot prevent it in the executive branch or in the party caucus.

It seems, then, that so long as one has the open kind of legislature in which any pair of members can trade, trading cannot be eradicated. Although its distributive effects may be beneficial to some or all members, the instances of logrolling in Congress discussed earlier suggest that this is frequently not the case. Speaking normatively, I conclude that the paradoxical consequences of logrolling are unpalatable and one probably ought to try—by such devices as closed rules and popular condemnation—to discourage the flagrant kinds of logrolling that generate paradoxes.

7.10. Choosing a Governing Coalition in a Multiparty System: Coalition Voting

Vote trading is not the only type of bargaining that occurs in legislatures. In multiparty systems (i.e., those with more than two parties) in which no single party gains a majority of seats after a parliamentary election, there is often furious bargaining among party leaders to try to put together a governing coalition.

Typically, the president of a country (or the king or queen in some cases) asks the leader of one of the major parties to try to form the government. If successful, this party leader usually becomes the prime minister. Success in this endeavor occurs when the party leader, by making concessions on policy and promising enough ministerial posts at the appropriate level to other parties, persuades them to agree to join his or her governing coalition. This leader has only a limited period of time to form the government (e.g., three weeks is the usual limit in Israel, three days in Greece) before someone else is given the opportunity. If the prospects look dim that anyone will be able to put together a coalition controlling a majority of seats, new elections might be called.

There is almost always intense bargaining among party leaders over the distribution of ministerial posts in a governing coalition. Although there is now a large empirical literature on the effects of a variety of factors (e.g., size of party, ideology, etc.) on who gets allocated what posts, rational-choice models about how the posts get distributed have, by and large, been found wanting (Browne and Dreijmanis 1982).

Instead of trying to construct a general model of coalition formation and bargaining in parliamentary democracies, I shall begin by describing a voting system called "coalition voting."[13] This system allows voters to express themselves directly on the question of *what* majority coalition will be governing, which they cannot do today. This lack of voter control has resulted in the making of some strange backroom deals, to the chagrin of many voters. Even voters who voted for the party of the prime minister often find themselves infuriated by the inclusion of parties in the governing coalition whose policies they oppose.

The idea of coalition voting was stimulated by the results of the Israeli parliamentary elections in November 1988. In this election, neither the Labor party on the left nor the Likud party on the right won a majority of seats; an agreement with different combinations of the religious parties could have given either major party the necessary seats to form a government. Consequently, both parties flirted with the religious parties, who won collectively 15 percent of the seats in the Knesset, over a period of several weeks in an effort to forge an alliance, but both failed in the end to reach an agreement. (Actually, there were several tentative agreements—even some that seemed binding—and bitter recriminations when these collapsed.)

After seven weeks of incessant bickering and tortuous negotiations, Labor and Likud decided to extend their tenuous relationship, which had been first established as the "national unity government" after the 1984 election (there were earlier national unity governments formed in 1967 and 1969). For the majority of (secular) Israelis, this outcome probably was preferable to an alliance of one of the major parties with the religious parties—and certainly to most American Jews, who were strongly opposed to the orthodox stand of these parties on the question of "who is a Jew." But still, as I shall argue later, this result was far from ideal.

A different result almost certainly would have occurred under *coalition voting* (CV), which is a voting procedure for electing a parliament, and choosing a governing coalition, under a party-list system of proportional representation (PR). Under CV, voters cast two different kinds of votes:

1. A *party vote*, divided equally among all parties the voter approves of, which determines the seat shares of the parties in parliament.

2. A *coalition vote* for all coalitions of parties that are *acceptable* because they include all parties that the voter designates Y ("yes") and no parties that the voter designates N ("no").

A majority coalition that has no superfluous parties, and is acceptable to the most voters according to the coalition vote, becomes governing, provided that the parties it comprises agree. I shall say more about the process of forming governing coalitions later.

To illustrate party and coalition votes, assume there is a set of five parties, $\{1,2,3,4,5\}$, and a voter casts a party vote for the subset $\{1,2\}$, giving each of the two parties in this subset $\frac{1}{2}$ a vote. In addition, assume that the voter designates Party 1 to be Y and Parties 4 and 5 to be N; by so doing, the voter indicates that coalitions $\{1\}$, $\{1,2\}$, $\{1,3\}$, and $\{1,2,3\}$ are acceptable.

If, say, only $\{1,2\}$ and $\{1,2,3\}$ have a majority of seats, then each of these two majority coalitions receives one coalition vote. But $\{1,2,3\}$ has a superfluous party (3), so it cannot become governing. Neither can nonmajority coalitions, $\{1\}$ and $\{1,3\}$, form a government, because they can be defeated by the complementary coalitions, $\{2,3,4,5\}$ and $\{2,4,5\}$, which do have a majority of seats.

I assume there to be no necessary relation between party and coalition votes. Thus, a voter might give the green party his or her entire party vote—in order to maximize its representation in parliament—but not want the greens to be in the governing coalition. By designating the green party to be N, and one or more mainstream parties to be Y, this voter can say that the greens should have voice (i.e., seats in parliament), but other parties should be in the government. It is likely, however, that the parties most voters will support with their party votes and their Y coalition votes will substantially overlap if not coincide.

Of the two votes under CV, the party vote is more in keeping with standard practice. As in most party-list systems, parties win seats in proportion to the number of votes they receive. This is the same under CV, except that the usual restriction on voting for exactly one party is lifted so that voters can vote for as many parties as they like.

This feature of CV mimics approval voting (AV), whereby voters can vote for as many candidates as they like in multicandidate elections without PR (Brams and Fishburn, 1978, 1983). But unlike AV, if a voter votes for more than one party, each party does not receive one vote—it depends on how many parties the voter voted for under CV, as I illustrated earlier.

Since AV was first proposed more than ten years ago, it has generated much interest as well as a good deal of controversy (see, e.g., the recent exchange between Saari and Van Newenhizen [1988], and Brams, Fishburn, and Merrill [1988]); I shall draw comparisons between it and CV later. I simply note here that AV and the party-vote aspect of CV resemble each other only in the physical act of voting: the voter indicates on a ballot all the alternatives (candidates under AV, parties under CV) of which he or she approves.

It is coalition votes that make CV radically different from AV. They allow the voter to use two different sieves, Y and N votes, to indicate that, for a coalition to be acceptable, some parties must always be included (Y) and some always excluded (N). All coalitions that survive this straining process receive a coalition vote, but only coalitions whose parties have a majority of seats can become governing.

By giving *voters* an ability to construct such majority coalitions, CV also encourages *parties* to coalesce, even before an election. Indeed, because coalition votes place a premium on precisely the majority coalitions that are most acceptable—as defined by the voters—they make it advantageous for parties to urge their supporters not only to cast their party votes for them alone but also to vote for and against certain other parties with their Y and N coalition votes. In this manner, the bane of multiparty systems under PR—disincentives to coalition formation—is attenuated.

Because CV gives voters two different kinds of votes, it is certainly more complex than AV. But this increase in complexity is balanced by an increase in the opportunity that CV affords voters to accomplish two goals:

- select with their party vote one or more parties that can best represent them in parliament;
- designate with their coaliton vote one or more majority coalitions to form the government.

Whereas parties will be motivated to solicit party votes exclusively for themselves, they will at the same time be motivated to strike compromises and reach policy agreements with other parties to try to build majority coalitions that voters will support with their coalition votes.

Insofar as they are successful, CV should mitigate the voters' choice problem. Indeed, precisely because voters can indicate acceptable coalitions directly on their ballots—and these help to determine the election outcome—CV forces the parties to pay greater heed to voters' individual as well as collective preferences. In particular, parties will have a strong incentive to iron out differences with potential coalition partners *before* the campaign in order to pose reasonable coalition-vote strategies to the voters during the campaign. That extant voting systems do not register electoral support for potential governing coalitions perhaps explains the paucity of models linking electoral competition and coalition formation in legislatures (Austen-Smith and Banks 1988; Laver 1989).

In Section 7.11 I shall define what is meant by a "majority" and a "minimal majority" coalition; the latter is assumed to be the only kind that can form a government. Next, "governing" coalitions, which are a subset of minimal majority coalitions, will be defined and illustrated. These definitions and assumptions will then serve as a springboard to discuss in Section 7.12 how the bargaining strength of parties might be determined under CV.

7.11. Majority, Minimal Majority, and Governing Coalitions

I begin by defining some concepts described in Section 7.10:

C: set of parties ($j = 1, \ldots, m$)

V: set of voters ($i = 1, \ldots, v$).

Party vote: Each voter i in V votes for a subset of parties P_i in C. Let $p_i = |P_i|$ be the number of parties in P_i. Each party j in P_i receives $1/p_i$ votes from i; the other parties receive no votes from i. Let v be the number of voters who do not abstain, and let v_j be the number of votes for party j. The proportion of seats won by party j is v_j/v. (Fractional seat assignments will be discussed later.)

Coalition vote: Each voter i in V votes for two disjoint subsets, Y_i and N_i, of C. The parties in Y_i are those that the voter indicates must be included in an acceptable governing coalition. The parties in N_i are those that the voter indicates must be excluded from an acceptable governing coalition. A coalition A in C is *acceptable* for voter i if and only if all Y_i are in A and no N_i are in A. Coalition A receives one vote from voter i if A is acceptable for i; otherwise, A receives no vote from voter i. Let $c(A)$ denote the number of coalition votes for coalition A.

A coalition A is said to be a *majority coalition* if it receives at least as many *party* votes as its complementary coalition $\overline{A} = C \backslash A$, the set of all parties that are in C and not in A. Equivalently, A is a majority coalition if the number of party votes it receives is at least half of the total:

$$v(A) = \sum_{j \in A} v_j \geq v/2.$$

Let M denote the *set* of all majority coalitions. Since there are m parties, there are 2^m coalitions, including the empty set $\emptyset$ and the grand coalition C. Moreover, because either a coalition or its complement will have a majority of party votes, the number of members of M will be at least 2^{m-1}; it will be greater if and only if there is some A such that $v(A) = v/2$, in which case there is a tie and both A and $\overline{A}$ are members of M.

Assume A is a member of M. Define A to be "minimal" if no other coalition that is a member of M is a proper subset of A. Let M^* denote the set of *minimal majority coalitions*. It will usually have far fewer members than M, but in all cases it has at least one member. Put another way, M^* eliminates from M all elements that are proper supersets of other elements in M—that is, majority coalitions that have superfluous members.

Presumably, if A is a member of M but does not need the votes of one or more of its parties to maintain its winning edge against $\overline{A}$, the superfluous members will not be adequately compensated and are likely to defect. Extra votes, however, may not be superfluous if there is uncertainty about who exactly is a loyal coalition member, so coalitions may form that are not minimal winning (Riker 1962). But having a bare majority of seats is not equivalent to being a minimal majority coalition, as the "national unity government" in Israel illustrates.

A is a *governing coalition* if A is a member of M^* and $c(A) \geq c(B)$ for all B that are members of M^*. Thus, a governing coalition is a minimal majority coalition that maximizes the coalition vote c over all minimal majority coalitions.

Let G denote the set of governing coalitions. Except for ties in c among members of M^*, G will have exactly one member.

The set of majority (M) and minimal majority (M^*) coalitions are based on party votes, whereas governing coalitions are chosen from M^* based on coalition votes. The congruence between these two different kinds of votes and general properties of CV are analyzed in Brams and Fishburn (1990). Here I simply note the twofold rationale for evenly dividing a voter's party vote among all parties of which he or she approves:

1. *Equality of voters.* Each voter counts equally in the apportionment of parliamentary seats. If there are 100,000 voters and 100 seats to be filled, for example, each voter accounts for 1/1000 seats, whether or not voters choose to concentrate their representation on one party or spread it across several.

2. *No-breakup incentive for parties.* Suppose that a voter's party vote is evenly divided among the parties voted for, but that a voter who votes for more parties casts more votes *in toto*. For example, if a voter votes for two parties, suppose that each party receives one vote (as under AV)

instead of half a vote. Then it might be profitable for a party to split, assuming its supporters continue to vote for both parts, to maximize its vote total and, therefore, its seats in parliament.

Allowing voters to distribute one vote unevenly across parties—or several votes, as under cumulative voting (presently used in a few local jurisdictions in the United States) and *panachage* (used in Luxembourg, Norway, Sweden, and Switzerland)—would obviously give voters more freedom to express themselves. But it would introduce complexities that would not only make voting impracticable in many systems but also alter the strategic incentives that I shall analyze in detail later.

7.12. Measuring Bargaining Strength under Coalition Voting

I begin by illustrating the concepts in Section 7.11 with a simple example. Assume $C = \{1,2,3\}$ and $v = 5$, so there are exactly three parties and five voters, which I indicate by the set $V = \{a,b,c,d,e\}$. Assume that each of the five voters divides his or her votes among one or two parties, as indicated in Table 7.8.

The vote totals for these parties, which determine how seats are apportioned to them in parliament, are also shown. Thus, Party 2, with 2 votes out of 5, receives 40 percent of the seats, whereas Parties 1 and 3, with 1.5 votes each, receive 30 percent of the seats each.

Note that not one of the three parties has a majority of party votes (i.e., more than 2.50), but every two-party coalition does:

$$\{1,2\}\text{---}3.5 \text{ votes}; \{2,3\}\text{---}3.5 \text{ votes}; \{1,3\}\text{---}3 \text{ votes}.$$

Because these coalitions as well as the grand coalition ($\{1,2,3\}$—5.00 votes) have more party votes than their complements, $M = \{12,13,23,123\}$, where the elements of M are the coalitions of parties indicated. Since $C = \{1,2,3\}$ is a superset of the other coalitions in $M, M^* = \{12,23,13\}$ does not include it. Finally, $G = \{12\}$ because 12 receives the most *coalition* votes:

$$c(12) = 3 \text{ (from voters } a, b, \text{ and } c);$$
$$c(23) = 2 \text{ (from voters } c \text{ and } d);$$
$$c(13) = 1 \text{ (from voter } e).$$

Although Coalitions 12 and 23 tie for the most party votes (3.5), the fact that 12 is supported by more voters *as a coalition* than 23 or 13 entitles it to be governing, or at least be given the first chance to form a government (more on this point shortly).

Table 7.8. Example of Coalition Voting

Voter	Party Votes			Coalition Votes	Coalitions Supported
	1	2	3		
a	½	½		$Y = \{1,2\}\ N = \{3\}$	12
b	1			$Y = \{1\}\quad N = \{3\}$	12
c		1		$Y = \{2\}$	12,23
d		½	½	$Y = \{2,3\}\ N = \{1\}$	23
e			1	$Y = \{1,3\}\ N = \{2\}$	13
Total	1.5	2.0	1.5		

In Section 7.10, I assumed an allocation rule that would assign fractional seats, giving each party exactly the proportion to which it was entitled on the basis of its party vote. Methods for assigning integer numbers of seats to parties, and apportioning legislative seats to districts in district-based legislatures, have been analyzed by Balinski and Young (1978, 1982). They recommend the Jefferson method for party-list systems, because it encourages smaller parties to coalesce into larger parties—by combining their votes, smaller parties will collectively obtain at least as many seats as they would obtain separately. Because CV already incorporates a strong incentive for ideologically proximate parties to coordinate their policies—if not merge (more on this question later)—I think the incentive of the Jefferson method may be unnecessary. A more "neutral" method, such as the Webster method, which Balinski and Young (1982) recommend for apportioning district-based legislatures, may work as well.

Although CV is meant to give a boost to the most approved majority coalitions, it is the parties themselves—or, more properly, their leaders—that must decide whether a governing coalition will actually form. In the earlier example, there is no guarantee that Parties 1 and 2 will be able to reach an agreement to form a new government.

If they do not, assume that the next-most acceptable coalition (23) is then given the opportunity to form a government. One might think that Party 2, which is a member of both Coalitions 12 and 23, could make extravagant demands on Party 1 (e.g., for ministerial posts), knowing that it would still have an opportunity with Party 3 to form a government if Coalition 12 failed to reach an agreement.

However, Coalition 13, which might comprise the left and right parties and be least acceptable to the voters, would still be a possibility should Coalition 23 fail to reach an agreement. Moreover, since Party 3 is the common member of Coalitions 23 and 13, it replaces Party 2 as the party in the advantageous position if Coalition 12 fails to form.

Although Coalition 13 enjoys little support from the voters, it might emerge as more than a theoretical possibility. In fact, a temporary coalition of the conservative New Democracy party and two Communist parties formed in Greece in 1989 in order to bring charges against members of the center (Socialists), so this phenomenon is not unprecedented.

How might one measure the bargaining strength of parties in a hierarchical ordering of coalitions, with the governing coalition at the top (12 in the earlier example, followed by 23 and then 13). Such a measure could be a useful indicator of the payoff a party might expect if it became a member of a governing coalition.

First observe that there will always be at least one common member of every pair of coalitions in M^* if the members do not tie in party votes. Thus in the example, Party 2 is the common member of 12 and 23, which are the first and second coalitions in M^* that would be asked to form a government, based on their coalition votes.

For illustrative purposes, assume that if two parties have the opportunity to form a governing coalition, there is a 50 percent chance that they will actually agree to do so. In the example, therefore, Party 2 has a probability of being in a government of

$$.5 + (.5)(.5) = .75,$$

where .5 is the probability of 12's succeeding initially, and (.5)(.5) is the probability of 12's failing initially and 23's succeeding next. By similar reasoning, Party 1 has a probability of being in a government of

$$.5 + (.5)(.5)(.5) = .625,$$

where the second term reflects 12's failing, 23's failing, and then 13's succeeding. Party 3 has a probability of being in a government of

$$(.5)(.5) + (.5)(.5)(.5) = .375,$$

where the first term reflects 12's failing and 23's succeeding, and the second term reflects 12's failing, 23's failing, and then 13's succeeding.

Of course, there may not be a government. The probability of this outcome, and the three other outcomes in which one of the two-party coalitions forms, are

12 forms: .5
23 forms: (.5)(.5) = .25
13 forms: (.5)(.5)(.5) = .125
No government forms: (.5)(.5)(.5) = .125,

which necessarily sum to 1 since they are mutually exclusive and exhaustive events.

Consider again the probabilities that each party is in the government. Normalizing these probabilities of .75, .625, and .375 for parties 2, 1, and 3, respectively, one can define the *bargaining strength* (*BS*) of each party to be

$$BS(2) = .43 \qquad BS(1) = .36 \qquad BS(3) = .21.$$

Plainly, Party 2's common presence in the first two coalitions to be asked to form a government helps it the most, with Party 1's common presence in the first and third coalitions hurting it somewhat. But Party 3 is hurt most, primarily because it suffers from the 50-percent chance that Coalition 12 will form a government at the start and consequently exclude it.

In fact, the 50–50 chance that Party 3 will be left out may be far too conservative. The fact that Coalition 12 is in G may make it an overwhelming favorite to form (say, above 90 percent). The "50 percent assumption" is arbitrary and was made simply to illustrate one way of calculating the differential advantage that parties higher in the coalition-vote hierarchy have in negotiating for ministerial posts, concessions on policy, and so on.

BS might also be used to approximate a division of spoils between coalition partners. If Coalition 12 forms, for example, the division between Parties 1 and 2 would be 5 to 6 according to *BS*, though the party votes of 1 and 2 (1.5 and 2, respectively, in the example) would surely also have to be taken into account. Of course, whether *BS* or other factors reflect the allocation of ministerial posts or other empirical indicators of party strength cannot be determined unless and until CV is actually used.

Complicating the determination of a party's bargaining strength, either as a member of G or as an heir apparent if G fails to form a government, is the size of the majority coalition. Insofar as the size principle is applicable (Riker 1962), having an overwhelming majority might be a coalition's Achilles heel. If, for example, 12 is such a coalition but 23 is minimum winning (making 13 somewhere in between), Party 2 might have good reason to sabotage a coalition with Party 1 in order to consummate an agreement with Party 3 at the next stage. Presumably, Party 3 would be less demanding of Party 2 than of Party 1 because not only is 23 not in G but it also has fewer supporters to pay off.

It is certainly possible for coalitions other than those that are governing to strike a deal in the end, despite the wishes of the voters. With a majority of seats, these coalitions could presumably assume the reins of power, even if most voters did not approve of them.

There are at least two ways of countering deal-making that blatantly defies voter approval. One is to permit only governing coalitions to try to form a government; if they fail, new elections would be held.

I prefer the less drastic procedure, suggested by the example, of giving governing coalitions priority in trying to form a government. Only if they fail would other coalition possibilities be entertained, in descending order of the size of the coalition vote of the different minimal majorities.

In the latter case, the parties to the negotiations would know what alternatives, if any, there were to fall back on if a deal fell through. Because the numbers approving of the various minimal majority coalitions would also be known, the repercussions from flouting voter desires would be glaringly evident.

The severe lack of approval of Coalition 13 in the earlier example would surely render it a dubious choice. But perhaps the fact that it has a majority of seats and theoretically could form a government, if Coalitions 12 and 23 do not form, would prevent Party 2 from exploiting its common presence in Coalitions 12 and 23 to force Parties 1 and 3 to "give away the store" in order to be selected as a coalition partner. If worst came to worst, Parties 1 and 3 would always have each other.

7.13. Possible Uses of Coalition Voting

CV seems an attractive procedure for coordinating if not matching voters' and parties' interests in a party-list system. Because the most compatible (i.e., acceptable) majority coalitions get priority in the formation of a government, both voters and parties are encouraged to weigh coalition possibilities. Even before the election, parties might negotiate alliances and offer joint policy positions, better enabling voters to know what a coalition stands for if it should form the next government. "Citizen electoral control," as Powell (1989) puts it, which varies considerably in democracies today, would be enhanced.

Under AV, by contrast, candidates do not form alliances but instead enjoy a premium in votes by taking positions that are acceptable to as many voters as possible—without, at the same time, appearing bland or pusillanimous, which might cost them votes. The fractional approval votes of CV give it some flavor of AV, but, just as significant, the coalition votes help to ensure that both voters and parties think beyond single best choices to coherent coalitions that can govern. This is not a factor in single-winner elections, to which AV is best suited.

But, as noted earlier, AV and CV are equivalent in allowing the voter to make multiple choices. To be sure, CV imposes greater burdens on voters than AV by asking them to cast two different kinds of votes that fulfill different purposes. Party-vote strategies that determine seat assignments would seem unproblematic for voters—most voters would probably vote for a single favorite party to maximize its seat representation. On the other hand, the choice of a coalition-vote strategy is not so straightforward, especially if there are more than three parties.

Consider again the case of Israel, mentioned briefly in Section 7.10. Israeli voters, anticipating that no single party would win a majority of seats in the 1988 election, would have been able directly to express themselves on what coalitions of parties they found they could best live with, if not like. With 27 parties running, and 15 that actually gained one or more seats in the Knesset, the opportunities for building coalitions would have been manifold.

As in the election itself, it appears likely that about two-thirds of the voters would have voted for Labor or Likud. A substantial number of these voters probably would have voted for both major parties, at least as compared to voting for one of the major parties and the religious parties. But more likely still, broad coalitions on the left and right probably would have arisen, reflecting the main secular dimensions of Israeli politics (Bara 1987). On the other hand, if the religious parties had significantly moderated their demands—anticipating that otherwise they would be left out of a governing coalition—then they might have made themselves acceptable to greater numbers of voters, probably on the right.

Whatever the alignments, CV almost certainly would have had a considerable impact on the campaign and election results. But what sentiment the coalitions that emerged would have reflected is difficult to say. What seems clear is that small and relatively extremist parties, while keeping their most fervent supporters and their seats proportionate to their numbers, would have hurt their chances of being in a governing coalition unless they broadened their appeal and allied themselves with other parties that could boost their chances.

The alliance of Labor and Likud that was finally consummated might not have been different under CV if the religious parties had persisted in their demands and the smaller parties on the left and right had not tried to ally themselves with the major parties. But surely the path to achieving this result would have been smoother.

This possible consequence of using CV is by no means slight, because the weeks of infighting among politicians, and large-scale demonstrations by citizens, not only wracked the society during the protracted negotiations but engendered deep cleavages that remain today. However, it is also possible that more compatible groupings of parties would have emerged, and a more ideologically coherent coalition would have won under CV.

Israel may be a special case—one observer has characterized its coalitions as "fragile" (Seliktar 1982)—but it is not alone in experiencing difficulties in establishing durable coalitions under a party-list system. Another example is Italy, which has had 49 governments since World War II, an average of more than one a year (Riding 1989).

Lijphart (1984) classifies Italy as a "consensus" democracy precisely because cleavages in the society have necessitated restraints on majority rule. To be sure, the frequent shifts in Italian governments probably have not had a great impact on the country's economy, national defense, or foreign policy, in part because the same people—mostly Christian Democrats—have governed for over 40 years, shuffling ministry portfolios among one another.

In fact, there have been only 18 persons since World War II to serve as prime minister. But, as Haberman reports, with 13 parties in parliament and a style of government that is more patronage-driven than policy-driven,

> many Italian political leaders sense that the national mood is changing, that people have grown tired of the old politicking and want governments that last longer than the average life of a flashlight battery. There is a desire for predictable, enforceable and sustainable policies, they say, and it has grown keener with the approaching economic integration of Europe in 1992. (Haberman 1989)

Indeed, CV probably could help to promote what Haberman later reports is "a widely shared desire: a restructuring of political forces to give Italian voters a choice between a few dominant parties or coalitions, offering clear programs and capable of taking turns at the helm (Haberman 1989). That bargaining among parties would be more productive and promote more coherent policies under CV must, of course, remain an hypothesis until CV is tried out. But, as I have attempted to show, bargaining is likely to be more responsive to voter interests.

7.14. Conclusions

The two models of bargaining in legislatures developed in this chapter illustrate problems that may arise in n-person games—in one case, over the trading of votes; in the other, over the formation of parliamentary coalitions. There does not seem to be any obvious solution to the vote-trading problem, but coalition voting offers a possible solution to unseemly governing coalitions that form and have little voter support.

I showed in the case of vote trading that external costs can wipe out the private gains of members on pairwise trades and leave everyone worse off after the trades. This so-called paradox of vote trading is rooted in an n-person Prisoners' Dilemma in which the noncooperative strategy of trading dominates the cooperative strategy of not trading for all members.

The three-member example I used to illustrate the analysis can be embedded in any legislature; and, of course, the three members can be three factions. Thus, for at least some configurations of preferences of legislators, there may be no equilibrium that is Pareto-superior.

Several examples of issues in which interests are relatively private, and for which support can therefore more readily be exchanged, were suggested as those most likely to engender vote trading and, under certain conditions, the paradox. Devices that limit vote trading on such issues, like the closed rule, have in some cases been institutionalized, which may discourage rampant trading and its most objectionable effects. These restrictions, however, usually do not prevent vote trading entirely but simply push it back to more private settings, where exchanges occur in a smaller market among fewer traders.

More generally, one may interpret vote trading as simply one way in which support develops around some issues and not others. Its effect is no different in principle from that which occurs when provisions are added to and subtracted from bills that gain some supporters and lose others. It is reasonable to assume, then, that vote trading—in one form or another—is pervasive in legislatures, and probably other bargaining settings as well, so the paradox is doubtless a general phenomenon.

The formation and break-up of coalition governments in parliamentary systems can be viewed in terms of the success or failure of political parties to reach agreement either on joint policy positions or the allocation of ministerial posts among coalition members. But even when parties reach agreement, their agreement may be at the expense of voters' interests.

CV diminishes the problem of politicians' ignoring voters' expression of interests. Indeed, it induces party leaders to try to reconcile their differences, insofar as possible, before an election and might even encourage mergers of parties. Because voters benefit from forcing coalitions to surface before, not after, an election, their task of choosing a coalition, as allowed under CV, is better informed.

Thus, CV seems well equipped to produce a convergence of voter and party/coalition interests, which Downs (1957) suggested, to the contrary, would be absent in multiparty systems. In fact, parties might find it in their interest to be as ambiguous as possible about compromises they would make to enter a coalition, thwarting voters who seek clarity in order to make more informed choices in the election. If vagueness is dispelled at all, it is usually after the election, when forced upon the parties by the necessity of forming a government.

The coalition-inducing and voter-responsive properties of CV should commend it to politicians in a party system like Israel's, which has been repeatedly torn by corrosive conflict that reflects in part the divided nature of that society, or Italy's, whose ephemeral governments seem ill-suited to making the tough choices required for the future. Similarly, in other countries (e.g., Belgium) that may be divided along ethnic, linguistic, racial, religious, or other lines—or simply have a tradition of factional conflict—CV would seem to offer hope for promoting greater reconciliation and compromise, not because it is in the public interest (however defined) but rather because it is in the parties' self-interest if they desire to participate in a governing coalition.

These advantages of CV, in my opinion, justify a somewhat complex seat-determination and coalition-selection process. The intricacies of the Hare system of single transferable vote (STV), which has been widely used in both public and private elections, are no less easy to understand—even by mathematicians (Brams 1982)—but these do not seem to burden the average voter.

In fact, because the voters under CV have only to indicate approval (with P and Y votes) and disapproval (with N votes) of parties—but do not have to rank them, as under STV—CV facilitates the task of voting, particularly if there is a large number of parties. In addition, the parties, fueled by their desire to be in a governing coalition, will, in all likelihood, present the voters with reasonable coalition strategies after bargaining among themselves, which should further ease the voters' burdens in deciding upon acceptable majority coalitions. All in all, I see no unusual practical difficulties in implementing CV in party-list systems.

Notes

[1] Applications of n-person game theory and related formal tools to real-life multiparty negotiations are relatively rare. Some notable exceptions include McDonald (1975), Raiffa (1982), and Sebenius (1984).

[2] This and the next eight sections of this chapter are adapted from Riker and Brams (1973) with permission.

[3] For a detailed discussion of this important, but often misunderstood, aspect of utility theory, see Luce and Raiffa (1957, chap. 2).

[4] An exception is Coleman (1966, 1121), who observes in passing that the inclusion of such costs requires a "much more extensive calculation," but he does not try to develop it. In a more recent article (Coleman 1969), Coleman provides an explicit calculation and concludes that vote trading will be generally profitable only under conditions of "absolutely free and frictionless political exchange" that preclude arbitrary decision rules (e.g., majority rule); see also Coleman (1973) for computer simulation models of vote trading.

[5]What comes before a legislature may very well be a product of vote trades in committees, where support is typically exchanged among members on the provisions of a single bill rather than on wholly different bills.

[6]Note that for each member, the M to N changes and N to M changes from Table 7.5 to Table 7.6 arise from other members' switches, not from a member's changing the positions which he or she supports; the latter changes occur only on roll calls on which a member's position changes from M to M_d.

[7]If all three members switched back from M_d's to M's on their two least salient roll calls in Table 7.6, they would thereby effect three pairwise vote trades, and the total utility gain to each member would be 7. This follows from the fact that the total utility of each member before trading—and after the subsequent trades, when there is a reversion to the original positions—is 14, but after the initial trades only 7, as I showed earlier. Hence, by reclaiming their initial positions before the initial vote trading, each member gains the difference of $14 - 7 = 7$.

[8]Even in the case where the rules or norms of a legislature absolutely proscribe the breaking of trading agreements, this would not prevent members from calculating the probable behavior of others, others' calculations about their own calculations, and so forth. This mental juggling of anticipated trades may well carry beyond the initial round of vote trading into subsequent rounds—at least in the course of their thinking, if not in the course of their actual trading—in a manner not unlike the calculations underlying the theory of moves. Even though members would not be able to cancel old trades, then, the irrevocable trades they do make will not necessarily be what I have called "initial trades." Trading cycles (and possible paradoxes), in other words, might be generated by some artful combination of mental constructions and physical trades—even when agreements are considered binding and trades cannot be undone.

[9]A *collective good* is one that, when supplied to some members of a collectivity, cannot be withheld from other members of that collectivity. Thus, a vote trade that changes the majorities on two rolls is a collective good (or bad, depending on one's preferences) to all other members of the voting body as well.

[10]Bernholz (1973, 1974); Miller (1975); and the exchange among Koehler (1975), Bernholz (1975), and Oppenheimer (1975). Furthermore, the paradox of vote trading is not dependent on the majority-rule assumption (Uslaner and Davis 1975).

[11]For the case in which the preferences of members for outcomes on roll calls can be expressed in terms of utilities, Park (1967) has shown that there is in general no equilibrium if there is a majority that can, through vote trading, improve the payoffs to all its members over those without vote trading. Furthermore, he has shown that if there is an equilibrium with vote trading, it must be exactly the same as the outcome without vote trading. But Coleman (1967) argues that Park's assumptions are unrealistcally restrictive.

[12]Baron and Ferejohn (1989) contrast the effects of closed and open rules in a noncooperative sequential model of the legislative process.

[13]Most of the remaining discussion of coalition voting is adapted from Brams and Fishburn (1990).

Chapter 8
Bargaining Power

8.1. Introduction

The measures of bargaining strength ($BS1$ and $BS2$) that I illustrated in section 7.12 were developed to assess the power of political parties in a parliamentary system using coalition voting. In this chapter I shall propose a measure of bargaining power that is not specific to any particular institutional arrangements but rather, in fact, quite general. After distinguishing it from another well-known measure of power, I shall use it to compare the power of representatives, senators, and the president in the U.S. federal system.

Although this measure seems to give more realistic results than other measures, it ignores information about the preferences that players might have in a particular situation. Such preferences help to define all the games previously analyzed. While ignoring this information enables one to model phenomena at a higher level of abstraction and obtain more general results, it has its costs.

One cost is that bargaining power, as used here, may not translate into actual power in a specific conflict once players know and take account of each others' preferences. For example, an "opposition" coalition may form to counter the ostensibly most powerful actor—based on its prerogatives, as given by the formal rules—if this actor poses a threat to the interests of the coalition members. Such a coalition may not only stymie this actor but, more surprising, may be able to achieve this result without communication or coordination among its members.

I explore this anomaly by defining and illustrating the "paradox of the chair's position." The paradox is germane not only to chairs of voting bodies but also to actors in less structured settings. As a case in point, I analyze the negotiating strategies of parties to the 1954 Geneva conference, which was convened to try to settle the conflict in Indochina at the time.

One of the players in this conflict (the "chair") had, seemingly, more power than the others because its preferred outcome would prevail in the event of no settlement. According to the logic of the paradox, this fact put this player in a vulnerable position: if the other players acted strategically, it would suffer its worst outcome. Recognizing this problem, though, the powerful player apparently deceived the others into thinking its preference ranking was different from what it was by making a false announcement. Thereby the chair was able to escape the paradox and induce its next-best outcome by "tacit deception," which did not reveal its misrepresentation.

Still, bargaining power based on institutional arrangements—independent of the preferences of the members of the institutions—is important, even if there are ways of subverting institutions. This is the kind of power that is frequently written into a contract or a constitution, as in the case of the U.S. federal system. But if these contracts or constitutions set the ground rules, actors may be able, by cleverness or cunning, to manipulate the rules to induce a superior outcome for themselves.

Their success in doing so may depend as much on luck as political skill, as Riker (1986) showed in a series of case studies. Whatever the mixture of ingredients, however, the success of political machinations is often short-lived. Indeed, a patchwork agreement may be a bargain with the devil, as the Indochina settlement reached in Geneva—which began to unravel shortly after the agreement was signed, culminating in the Vietnam War ten years later—demonstrated.

Before looking at the strategic uses of power, I shall first discuss the meaning of power in a specific context. Then I shall consider how it might be measured generally, comparing one measure of the president's power with data on presidential vetoes.

8.2. Power in the U.S. Federal System

The Founding Fathers had a good deal to say about the relative power of the House and Senate in the debate over the Constitution. Thus, while considering the two houses to be "co-equal" branches in *Federalist* No. 63 (*Federalist Papers*, p. 388), Madison averred in No. 58 that the House would have "no small advantage" over the Senate (p. 358). Similarly, in No. 66 Hamilton indicated that the House would be "generally a full match, if not an overmatch, for every other member of government" (p. 403); in particular, he predicted that the House's "mean influence . . . will be found to outweigh all the peculiar attributes of the Senate" (p. 404).

In Brams (1989) I used the Banzhaf (1965) index of voting power to assess the predictions of Hamilton and Madison. The model of voting power employed by Banzhaf identifies "critical" members of winning coalitions. A member is considered critical or essential when its sole defection from a coalition would change that coalition from a winning one to a losing one. In Banzhaf's model, the power of one member relative to another member is proportional to the number of coalitions in which each is critical.

Applying this model to the federal system comprising Congress and the president—whose relevant features will be described in detail later—produces the following Banzhaf power values:

President = .03803; Senator = .00329; Representative = .00146

Insofar as the power of the Senate may be thought of as the sum of the power of its 100 members, and that of the House as the sum of the power of its 435 members, the power of the Senate and House, respectively, are .32881 and .63316, giving the House nearly twice as much power as the Senate.

The superiority of the House over the Senate is corroborated by data indicating that the House, when it initiates either ordinary legislation or a veto override, more often gains the assent of the Senate than when the Senate initiates these actions and tries to gain the assent of the House (Brams 1989). But although the theoretical index and empirical data agree on the relative power of the two houses, the president's Banzhaf power of 3.8 percent seems way out of line with the actual legislative power that most presidents exercise.

True, the president's Banzhaf power is 11.6 times that of an individual senator, and 26.1 times that of an individual representative. But the president's structural coequality with the *entire* House and Senate in the passage of legislation, and his or her qualified veto—enabling the president to prevent the passage of a bill unless overridden by at least two-thirds majorities of both houses—would seem to put the president in a unique class as an individual. Indeed, one would expect that the president would be more powerful than either house, perhaps even as powerful as two-thirds of both houses. Yet what theory would imply this consequence, and how it could be corroborated empirically, are by no means clear.

Another well-known index of voting power, due to Shapley and Shubik (1954), gives the president a somewhat more reasonable 16.0 percent of all power in the tricameral federal system comprising the House, Senate, and president (wherein the president is considered a one-member house).[1] On the other hand, the Shapley-Shubik index is based on a rather implausible model of coalition formation—in which all orders of joining a coalition are considered equally likely (Brams 1975a; see also Dubey and Shapley 1979; Lucas 1983; and Straffin 1983)—which seems not at all descriptive of how alliances between the president and members of Congress form and agreements are reached, or how two-thirds majorities in Congress coalesce, on occasion, in order to override a presidential veto.

In the first part of this chapter, I shall propose the application of a voting power index, due to Johnston (1978), that is related to the Banzhaf index but makes a crucial modification in it that substantially boosts the power of the president.[2] Briefly, the Johnston index, unlike Banzhaf's, distinguishes between being critical in a winning coalition when one is uniquely so and when one shares this critical role with other actors, in which case one's power is proportionately reduced.

I do not propose the Johnston index, however, merely because it elevates the president to a preeminent position, seemingly more commensurate with his or her actual power in the federal system. Rather, I believe that the Johnston index captures, better than any other index, a feature of power that explains why most presidents have been so successful in shaping legislation and, even when opposed by majorities in both houses of Congress, preventing their vetoes from being overridden.

To begin the analysis, I shall propose criteria for measuring the *bargaining power* of an actor—that is, the power conferred on him or her by the rules for enacting bills or resolutions in either a single voting body or a set of interlocking institutions like the U.S. federal system (as specified in the Constitution). I shall not only show that the Johnston index satisfies these criteria but also argue, using a simple hypothetical example, that it gives more plausible numerical results than the Banzhaf index in certain situations.

Next I will illustrate the application of the Johnston index to the federal system in two cases: (1) when a bill has a fifty-fifty chance of passage by each house of Congress; and (2) when a bill, vetoed by the president, has a fifty-fifty chance of being overridden in each house by two-thirds majorities. In these cases, each actor's probability of being critical is maximized, rendering comparisons among the different actors—the president, senators, and representatives—most meaningful. These are situations in which the outcome is most up for grabs; each actor will presumably exert himself or herself to the maximum in such situations, providing an acid test for comparing relative bargaining power.

The president's bargaining power, as will be demonstrated, is different in these two cases. Consistent with the theoretical analysis, empirical data on the success of veto override attempts by Congress confirm the president's efficacy in preventing his or her veto from being overridden, though data that could be used to test the efficacy of the president in getting his or her legislation passed have not been analyzed. I will conclude the first part of this chapter with some comments on the application of the Johnston index to the measurement of presidential power.

8.3. What Should a Power Index Measure?

I assume, initially, that an actor is powerful to the extent that he or she

1. *alone* can decide outcomes; or
2. *alone* can prevent outcomes from being decided.

But there are few actors in the world who are dictators or hold veto power in the above senses, so it is appropriate to relax these criteria somewhat.

Thus, an actor might have a veto but not be the only actor with such a prerogative, as is true of the five permanent members of the U.N. Security Council. Their vetoes on the Council, as it turns out, give each 10.1 times as much power, according to the Banzhaf index (Brams 1975), as each of the ten nonpermanent members on the Council.

But this index probably understates the voting power of the permanent members. For whenever a permanent member can, by vetoing a resolution, prevent its passage, so can any of the 4 other permanent members. By comparison, whenever a nonpermanent member can, by changing its vote, prevent passage by the requisite majorty of 9 votes (out of 15 which must include the 5 permanent members), so can 3 other nonpermanent members, not to mention the 5 permanent members. In other words, a permanent member shares its power with fewer other members than a nonpermanent member, which presumably reflects the permanent member's greater power.

I will not calculate here precisely the effects of this sharing, because it would take me too far afield of the present case study of a president's bargaining power. With this example in mind, however, let me add an additional criterion for measuring bargaining power: an actor is powerful to the extent that he or she,

3. *with the fewest other actors,* can decide outcomes.

In other words, the powerful may share their decision-making capability, but they share it with as few other actors as possible.

So far, I have not defined bargaining power. Roughly speaking, I mean by such power having control over outcomes, with an actor's bargaining power increasing as fewer and fewer other actors exercise similar control.

More precisely, define a winning coalition to be *vulnerable* if, among its members, there is at least one whose defection would cause the coalition to lose. Call such a member *critical*. If only one player is critical, then this player is uniquely powerful in the coalition. Thus, a president in a coalition that includes himself or herself, 52 senators, and 219 representatives (in each house, one more than a simple majority) is uniquely powerful.[3] If, however, a coalition comprises exactly 51 senators, 218 representatives, and the president, then the president—and everybody else in the coalition—shares power with $51 + 218 = 269$ other players. In this coalition, because a total of 270 players are critical, I assume that each has only $\frac{1}{270}$ of the power.

To define bargaining power, consider the set, V, of all vulnerable coalitions. The *Banzhaf power* of player i is the number of vulnerable coalitions in which i is critical, divided by the total number of critical defections of all players, or i's *proportion of critical defections*. Mathematically expressed, for each vulnerable coalition $c \in V$, set

$$v_i(c) = \begin{cases} 1 & \text{if } i \text{ is critical in } c \\ 0 & \text{if } i \text{ is not critical in } c, \end{cases}$$

which counts the critical defections of i. Then the Banzhaf power of player i is defined to be

$$B(i) = \sum_{c \in V} v_i(c) / [\sum_{j=1}^{n} \sum_{c \in V} v_j(c)],$$

where $\sum_{c \in V}$ represents the summation over all vulnerable coalitions in V, and n is the number of members (players). Thus, $B(i)$ is a fraction in which the numerator is the number of instances in which player i is critical, and the denominator is the total number of instances in which all players are critical.

To develop a second measure of power, first count the number of players who are critical in each vulnerable coalition c. Call the inverse of this number the *fractional critical defection* of that coalition, or $f(c)$. [Thus, if there are two critical members of c, $f(c) = \frac{1}{2}$.] The *Johnston power* of player i is the sum of the fractional critical defections of all vulnerable coalitions in which i is critical, divided by the total number of fractional critical defections of all players, or i's *proportion of fractional critical defections*. Mathematically expressed, for each vulnerable coalition $c \in V$, set

$$f_i(c) = \begin{cases} f(c) & \text{if } i \text{ is critical in } c \\ 0 & \text{if } i \text{ is not critical in } c, \end{cases}$$

which counts the fractional critical defections of i. Then the Johnston power of player i is defined to be

$$J(i) = \sum_{c \varepsilon V} f_i(c) / [\sum_{j=1}^{n} \sum_{c \varepsilon V} f_j(c)].$$

Thus, $J(i)$ is a fraction in which the numerator is the sum of i's fractional critical defections, and the denominator is the sum of all players' fractional critical defections.

It is worth noting that, for each vulnerable coalition $c \varepsilon V$, the summation of $f_j(c)$ across all players j, which necessarily includes all players who are critical in c, is 1. By summing *this* summation across all $c \varepsilon V$—in effect, reversing the order of summation given in the denominator of the above fraction—it can be seen that the denominator must equal the total number of vulnerable coalitions.

This means that the Johnston power of player i may be thought of as *the probability that, given a vulnerable coalition* c *is selected at random, and then a critical member of* c *is chosen randomly,* i *is that critical member.* This interpretation also extends to *sets* of members. In the federal system, for example, S might be the entire Senate; then $J(S) = \sum_{i \varepsilon s} J(i)$ is the probability

that some senator is the critical member selected by the above random procedure.

Before deriving the formal power of players in the federal system, it is instructive to calculate the Johnston power of players in a simple weighted voting body to illustrate how it differs from the Banzhaf power. Consider the body [3; 2,1,1], which includes one 2-vote member and two 1-vote members, designated 2, 1_a, and 1_b. (Although the 1-vote members have the same weight, it is useful to distinguish them with subscripts in calculating their power, which is identical.) The *decision rule* is indicated by the first number inside the brackets and is a simple majority: 3 (out of 4) votes is the minimum number of votes necessary to make actions binding on all the members.

In this game, (2,1) is a vulnerable *arrangement,* or combination in which members of the same weight are indistinguishable. This arrangement subsumes two vulnerable *coalitions,* or subsets in which members of the same weight are distinguishable—one that includes one of the 1-vote members, $\{2,1_a\}$, the other that includes the other 1-vote member, $\{2,1_b\}$ (see Table 8.1). Similarly, (2,1,1) is a vulnerable arrangement, but it

Table 8.1. Banzhaf and Johnston Power in Weighted Voting Body [3; 2,1,1]

Vulnerable Arrangement	No. of Vulnerable Coalitions	Critical Defections (CDs)		Fractional CDs	
		2-Voter	1-Voter	2-Voter	1-Voter
(2,1)	2	2	1	½ × 2	½ × 1
(2,1,1)	1	1	0	1 × 1	0
Total	3	3	1	2	½
$B(i)$		⅗	⅕		
$J(i)$				⅔	⅙

subsumes only one vulnerable coalition, $\{2,1_a,1_b\}$, which happens to be the *grand coalition* (i.e., the coalition of all members).

The numbers of critical defections of the 2-vote member (3), and each of the two 1-vote members (1 each), in all vulnerable coalitions sum to 5; these possibilities are shown in Table 8.1. Thus, $B(2) = ⅗$ and $B(1) = ⅕$. The number of fractional critical defections of the 2-vote member (2), and the two 1-vote members (½ each), sum to 3, so $J(2) = ⅔$ and $J(1) = (½)/3 = ⅙$. Hence, the 2-vote member has *three* times as much formal power as either of the 1-vote members by the Banzhaf index, but *four* times as much by the Johnston index.

The reason, of course, that the 2-vote member does better according to the Johnston index is that it is uniquely powerful in the $\{2,1_a,1_b\}$ vulnerable coalition: it does not share its criticality with other members, so its power is not divided. By comparison, in the (2,1) arrangement, where 2 appears twice as often as 1_a or 1_b, the two members of each vulnerable coalition share equally in being critical, giving each a fractional critical defection of ½.

I previously offered a probabilistic interpretation of power according to the Johnston index. The Banzhaf power of player i may be interpreted as *the probability that a randomly chosen critical defection is cast by* i. Thus, in the weighted voting body [3; 2,1,1], five critical defections (3 for the 2-voter and 1 each for the two 1-voters, as shown in Table 8.1) are possible; given that these defections are equiprobable, the 2-vote member casts a randomly selected critical defection with probability ⅗.

Under the Johnston index, it is not critical defections that are equiprobable. Instead, first vulnerable coalitions are considered to be equiprobable; once a vulnerable coalition is randomly selected, its critical members are taken to be equally likely to defect. In the example, the 2-vote member doubly benefits from these equiprobability assumptions: first, that a vulnerable coalition will be chosen (2 is in all of them); second, that a critical member within each will be chosen (2 is the only critical member in one of them).

But is it reasonable to assume that $\{2,1_a,1_b\}$ is as likely to form as either $\{2,1_a\}$ or $\{2,1_b\}$? Although vulnerable, $\{2,1_a,1_b\}$ is not a minimal majority in the sense that *every* member's defection would cause it to be losing (Section 7.11). Likewise, it is not minimal winning, having only the bare minimum of votes (3 in this instance) necessary to be winning. To the degree that coalitions tend to be minimal winning, as Riker (1962) argues is the case in situations that approximate n-person, zero-sum games of complete and perfect information (the "size principle"), then the inclusion of $\{2,1_a,1_b\}$ in the definition of bargaining power would seem dubious.

Its inclusion seems especially problematic in the case of the Johnston index, because the 2-vote member derives a full 50 percent of its fractional critical defections from $\{2,1_a,1_b\}$, whereas in the case of the Banzhaf index it derives only 33 percent of its critical defections. Yet this "problem" with the Johnston index, I contend, is precisely its virtue when applied to the federal system, in which information is often incomplete and imperfect, in violation of assumptions on which the size principle is based. For instance, a minimal-winning coalition of exactly 51 senators, 218 representatives, and the president—in which 270 defections are critical—virtually never occurs.

Occasionally there is exactly a minimal majority in one house, making all its members critical along with the president, but on the vast majority of bills that the president signs, the president is the only critical member. (When the president vetoes a bill and the veto is overridden, the president is never critical, which is a case I shall consider later.) The Johnston index accords the president unique power when coalitions in the House and Senate are not minimal winning, whereas the Banzhaf index assumes that such a critical defection counts no more than when the president shares his or her disruptive power with exactly 218 representatives or 51 senators, or all 269 legislators.

Because greater-than-minimal-winning coalitions are the norm in both houses of Congress, and because the president is uniquely powerful in these (except when these coalitions are two-thirds majorities in veto override attempts), I believe that the bargaining power of the president should—consistent with Criteria 1 and 2 given earlier in this section—reflect this unique role. When the president is not uniquely powerful, the president's power should, consistent with Criterion 3, be reduced to the degree that this power is shared with other players.

There is another reason why players who are critical in coalitions that are not minimal winning can be thought to possess greater power.

In a minimal winning coalition, every player is critical, making each player indistinguishable on the basis of criticality. As players are added to such a coalition (the added members are necessarily noncritical), some of the players in the original minimal winning coalition cease to be critical as well.

As long as some player is critical, the expanding coalition is vulnerable. In such an expanding coalition, the longer a player remains critical, the more essential that player is to its winning; conversely, the more easily replaced a player is, the less likely it is that this player will be critical (in large yet vulnerable coalitions, in particular). Thus, the inclusion of vulnerable but not minimal winning coalitions in the definition of bargaining power is a way of measuring the "irreplaceability" of players, which I take to be a central feature of this kind of power.

In Section 8.4, I shall show how the Johnston power of the president, a senator, and a representative can be calculated. For reasons that will become evident, this calculation will be separated into two cases, one involving the passage of bills signed by the president, the other the overriding of bills vetoed by the president.

The bargaining power of the president in these two cases will then be considered in light of veto data on conflicts between the president and Congress. To assess how often the president prevails after casting a veto, data on vetoes, and successful and unsuccessful override attempts, are suggestive but hardly conclusive. In the case of the passage of legislation, I indicate data that might be examined to test the validity of the Johnston index, but no attempt to collect or analyze such data has been made here.

8.4 The Power of Approval and Disapproval

The president, Senate, and House are interconnected by constitutional decision rules that allow for the enactment of bills supported by at least a simple majority of senators, a simple majority of representatives, and the president; or at least two-thirds majorities in both the Senate and House without the support of the president (i.e., in order to override a veto). To be sure, this conceptualization ignores the fact that a majority of the Supreme Court can, in effect, veto a law by declaring it unconstitutional (see n. 1); it also ignores the countervailing power that Congress and the states have to amend the Constitution and thereby nullify Supreme Court rulings. Nevertheless, although other actors may affect the outcome, it seems useful to abstract those relationships among the actors having the most immediate impact on the enactment of bills into laws.

Before calculating the bargaining power of actors in the federal system,

I introduce notation that will be useful for counting vulnerable coalitions. The standard notation for the number of combinations that can be formed from m objects taken n at a time is

$$\binom{m}{n} = \frac{m!}{n!(m-n)!}.$$

The exclamation point (!) indicates a *factorial* and means that the number it follows is multiplied by every positive integer smaller than itself (e.g., $4! = 4 \times 3 \times 2 \times 1 = 24$).

To illustrate the meaning of combinations with a simple example, suppose that one wishes to calculate the number of ways of choosing a subset of three voters from a set of four, designated by the set $\{a,b,c,d\}$. Clearly, a subset containing three voters can be formed by excluding any one of the original four, yielding four different subsets of three voters: $\{a,b,c\}$; $\{a,b,d\}$; $\{a,c,d\}$; and $\{b,c,d\}$. In simple cases like this one, the number of subsets of a given size can thus be found by complete enumeration; in more complicated cases (like those to be developed shortly), a direct calculation is the only feasible one. In the illustrative example, the direct calculation confirms that the number of combinations of four objects taken three at a time is

$$\binom{4}{3} = \frac{4!}{3!1!} = \frac{(4 \times 3 \times 2 \times 1)}{(3 \times 2 \times 1)(1)} = 4.$$

Consider now the number of combinations in which the defection of the president, a senator, or a representative is critical, and the fractional critical defections—or simply f's—that these combinations contribute to each player's Johnston power.

1. *President.* One way for the president's defection from a vulnerable coalition to be critical is if it includes him or her, at least a simple majority of senators, and at least a simple but less than a two-thirds majority of representatives (i.e., between 218 and 289)—in order that the president can prevent the override of a veto in the House. This can occur in

$$\binom{1}{1}\left[\binom{100}{51} + \binom{100}{52} + \ldots + \binom{100}{100}\right]\left[\binom{435}{218} + \binom{435}{219} + \ldots + \binom{435}{289}\right]$$

ways. Let H be the number of supporters in the House and S be the number in the Senate. In each of the above arrangements, the f's of the president (p) are:

$f(p) = 1$, except when $S = 51$, $H > 218$, in which case $f(p) = \frac{1}{52}$;
or when $H = 218$, $S > 51$, in which case $f(p) = \frac{1}{219}$;
or when $S = 51$, $H = 218$, in which case $f(p) = \frac{1}{270}$.

A president's defection from a vulnerable coalition will also be critical when the coalition includes the president, at least a two-thirds majority of representatives (simple majorities were counted in the previous calculation), and at least a simple but less than a two-thirds majority of senators (i.e., between 51 and 66)—in order that the president can prevent the override of his veto in the Senate. This can occur in

$$\binom{1}{1}\left[\binom{435}{290} + \binom{435}{291} + \ldots + \binom{435}{435}\right]\left[\binom{100}{51} + \binom{100}{52} + \ldots + \binom{100}{66}\right]$$

ways. The f's of the president are

$f(p) = 1$, except when $S = 51$, $H > 289$, in which case $f(p) = \frac{1}{52}$.

2. *Senator.* For the defection of a senator (s) to be critical, a vulnerable coalition must include exactly 50 of the *other* 99 senators (so that the focal senator's defection would kill action by the Senate), the president, and at least a simple majority of the House, which can occur in the following number of ways:

$$\binom{99}{50}\binom{1}{1}\left[\binom{435}{218} + \binom{435}{219} + \ldots + \binom{435}{435}\right];$$

$f(s) = \frac{1}{52}$, except when $H = 218$, in which case $f(s) = \frac{1}{270}$;

or it must include exactly 66 of the *other* 99 senators (so that the focal senator's defection would kill action by the Senate in an override attempt), at least a two-thirds majority of the House, and exclude the president, which can occur in the following number of ways:

$$\binom{99}{66}\left[\binom{435}{290} + \binom{435}{291} + \ldots + \binom{435}{435}\right]\binom{1}{0};$$

$f(s) = \frac{1}{67}$, except when $H = 290$, in which case $f(s) = \frac{1}{357}$.

3. *Representative.* For the defection of a representative to be critical, a vulnerable coalition must include exactly 217 of the other 434 representatives (so that the focal representative's defection would kill action by

the House), the president, and at least a simple majority of the Senate, which can occur in the following number of ways:

$$\binom{434}{217}\binom{1}{1}\left[\binom{100}{51} + \binom{100}{52} + \dots + \binom{100}{100}\right];$$

$f(r) = \frac{1}{219}$, except when $S = 51$, in which case $f(r) = \frac{1}{270}$;

or it must include exactly 289 of the *other* 434 representatives (so that the focal representative's defection would kill action by the House in an override attempt), at least a two-thirds majority of the Senate, and exclude the president, which can occur in the following number of ways:

$$\binom{434}{289}\left[\binom{100}{67} + \binom{100}{68} + \dots + \binom{100}{100}\right]\binom{1}{0};$$

$f(r) = \frac{1}{290}$, except when $S = 67$, in which case $f(r) = \frac{1}{357}$.

In counting combinations in which a senator or representative is critical in an override attempt, I have implicitly assumed that the way he or she voted initially (i.e., in the non-override vote) does not change. Indeed, for the purposes of this calculation, there is only one vote: the power of a Senate or House member accrues from being critical in his or her house either when the president assents or when the president dissents (i.e., casts a veto)—but not both. For if a senator or representative could be critical in achieving both a simple majority on the first vote and a two-thirds majority on the override attempt, this would imply that at least $\frac{2}{3}$ − $\frac{1}{2}$ = $\frac{1}{6}$ of the members of his or her house changed their votes on the override vote.

Counting both votes toward a senator's or representative's bargaining power would imply that a president can simultaneously sign a bill (making a member of a simple majority in one house critical) and veto the bill (making a member of a two-thirds majority in one house critical), which is obviously nonsensical. In counting critical defections, therefore, I assume in effect that all players vote the same way on both the original bill and the override attempt (if it occurs); this is equivalent to assuming that only one vote is taken.

In fact, however, the combinatorial contribution that the Senate and House veto-override power makes to the Johnston (and Banzhaf) power of individual senators and representatives is negligible compared to the power that these players obtain from their non-override power. This is because, in order for the override to contribute to a senator's or representative's power, one house must have at least a two-thirds majority while the other house must have exactly a two-thirds majority. In relative terms, this can occur in very few ways compared to getting less lopsided majorities.

The veto override ability of both houses, therefore, contributes only a miniscule amount to the bargaining power (Johnston or Banzhaf) of their members; their powers would be virtually the same if the House and Senate could not override presidential vetoes by two-thirds majorities. Yet the veto power of the two houses *seems* significant—and, indeed, it can be shown to be so *if* separated from the members' ability to be critical in the passage of legislation (more on this later).

Based on the above calculations, the Johnston power values of the president, a senator, and a representative are:

$$J(p) = 0.770 \qquad J(s) = 0.00156 \qquad J(r) = 0.000169.$$

For the entire Senate (S) and the entire House (H),

$$J(S) = 0.156 \qquad J(H) = 0.0736.$$

Thus, a senator is 9.22 times as powerful as a representative, which translates into the Senate as an institution being 2.12 times as powerful as the House. But it is the president, with 77 percent of the power, who is the truly dominant figure in the federal system, according to the Johnston index.[4]

Before trying to assess the significance of these figures, it is useful to make a separate calculation that better captures the power of players in situations wherein Congress attempts to override a presidential veto. I make this calculation for two reasons: (1) Congress's ability to override a presidential veto has essentially no effect on the Johnston (or Banzhaf) power of players, as just computed; and (2) the situation in which a presidential veto might be overridden is qualitatively different from one in which no override attempt is made.

To be specific, the Banzhaf and Johnston indices presume a situation wherein each player is equally likely to support or oppose the issue in question. This feature, coupled with the large sizes of the Senate and House, causes both indices to depreciate to insignificance the effect of veto overrides because such overrides are so unlikely to occur under the equiprobability hypothesis. In fact, if the Constitution were amended to end veto overrides, the president's power, as measured by either index, would increase by less than one ten-billionth (10^{-10}).

Clearly, an override attempt is not only likely to be made, but also will most hang in balance, when the probability that a senator or representative will vote to override a veto is ⅔. In this situation of maximum uncertainty, each player will presumably strive to the utmost to affect the outcome, making this the acid test of bargaining power in veto override attempts.

One can modify the calculations to focus on the veto override process. This is most easily done by simply assuming that each senator and each representative has probability ⅔ of supporting the legislation, and, of course, probability ⅓ of opposing it. The previous calculations are then modified term by term, with each count of Senate or House support multiplied by appropriate probabilities. Thus, for example,

$$\binom{100}{51} \text{ becomes } \binom{100}{51}\left(\frac{2}{3}\right)^{51}\left(\frac{1}{3}\right)^{49};$$

$$\binom{99}{66} \text{ becomes } \binom{99}{66}\left(\frac{2}{3}\right)^{66}\left(\frac{1}{3}\right)^{33};$$

$$\binom{435}{218} \text{ becomes } \binom{435}{218}\left(\frac{2}{3}\right)^{218}\left(\frac{1}{3}\right)^{217}.$$

In effect, the combinatorial terms are weighted by the probabilities of getting the requisite numbers—on each side of the override vote—so as to make the president, a senator, or a representative critical. All other aspects of the calculations, including the counting of fractional critical defections, are unchanged.

The difference between the earlier "approval" (passage) and present "disapproval" (override) calculations is really one of degree, not kind. To see this, substitute the probability of ½ for both ⅔ and ⅓ in the disapproval calculations. Thereby every combinatorial term is multiplied by ½ raised to the same power (535), which can be factored out of the approval calculations. This means that the Johnston (and Banzhaf) indices, which measure the *relative* (passage) power of the different players, simply incorporate the implicit assumption of equal probabilities, which could be ignored earlier because they cancel out.

Both the passage and override calculations can be thought of as founded on *probabilities* that each player is critical. The Banzhaf index normalizes these probabilities so that they sum to one, giving equal weight to every critical defection. The Johnston index is based on a different normalization, giving greater weight to the defections of players who are critical with fewer other players. In addition, in the override calculation just described, wherein the most likely outcome is assumed to be a ⅔ − ⅓ split in favor of override in each house, the combinations themselves are, in effect, weighted by this assumed split, whereas in the passage case they are (equally weighted) by an assumed ½ − ½ split.

Does the president do better if the test of strength is on passage—when the probability that a member of either house will support him or her is ½—or on override attempts—when the probability that a member of either house will support him or her is ⅓? In each case, there are even odds in a house that the vote will go for or against the president, but the latter situation is definitely more favorable to the president, as the following Johnston power values for the override calculations show:

$$J(p) = 0.886 \quad J(s) = 0.000762 \quad J(r) = 0.0000856$$
$$J(S) = 0.0762 \quad J(H) = 0.0373$$

Compared with the passage values, the president jumps from 77 percent to 89 percent, and the power of the Senate and House as institutions are cut significantly (the Senate from 15.6 to 7.6 percent, the House from 7.3 to 3.7 percent). Intuitively, in the veto-override case, the power of senators and representatives is shared on average with ⅔ of their colleagues, depressing their power relative to the president's and that of the Senate and House as well.

In Section 8.5, I will consider the implications of these results, introducing some data on vetoes cast by presidents and sometimes overridden by Congresses. No systematic data on the passage of bills have been collected that might be used to compare with the earlier theoretical calculations, however, so at this stage the results are quite tentative.

8.5. Empirical Evidence of Presidential Power

The primary justification of the Johnston index rests on the fact that it gives proportionately more power to those actors who share their criticality in vulnerable coalitions with fewer other actors. Additionally the Banzhaf index, which counts all critical defections the same, gives the president less than 4 percent of all power in the federal system, which seems inordinately low.

The Johnston index gives the president 77 percent of all power in the passage calculations, but it is hard to think of how this figure might be validated by data. Because it is based on the assumption that a vulnerable coalition forms, one might examine all roll calls in which there is a minimal majority in at least one house versus larger majorities in the two houses (in which case only the president is critical if the majorities are not two-thirds or greater).

In the latter case, the president is all-powerful, given that the majorities are not two-thirds majorities or greater against the president. In the former cases, the president must share his or her power, so the relative frequencies of these two cases—presumably on important bills—might give some empirical estimate of the likelihood that each player is critical, which could then be compared with the Johnston values.

Minimal majorities might be too strict a standard on which to base the power of senators and representatives. Close votes that are not minimal on bills the president supports might indicate situations, before the vote is taken, in which the president may well fail to prevail. In these situations, given uncertainty about the final tally, the president's power might also be considered less than total. The president's record in getting such legislation enacted, especially that on which he or she takes a strong public stand, might be taken as an empirical measure of passage power.

A final reckoning of the president's power versus that of the Senate or House (and their members) seems elusive, however, because it is not measured simply by roll calls and the closeness of votes. A host of other factors comprise and help determine what is usually meant by presidential power, including the president's prestige, relations with the media, negotiation skills with Congress, and so on (Neustadt 1980). Nonetheless, close roll call votes, in which members of Congress may be critical, give one the opportunity to assess presidential power quantitatively and compare it with the kinds of formal calculations presented here.

The veto override calculation seems somewhat easier to relate to empirical data. Excluding "pocket vetoes" (42.5 percent of all presidential vetoes that have been cast)—whereby a president, by taking no action, prevents passage of a bill if Congress adjourns within ten days after the bill is sent to the president—which cannot be overridden, the forty presidents from George Washington (1789–97) to Ronald Reagan (1981–89) have cast a total of 1,419 vetoes. Only 103, or 7.3 percent, have been overridden by Congress in this almost two-hundred year span of time (Stanley and Niemi 1990, 256), suggesting that Congress's constitutional authority has not endowed it with great power to override presidential vetoes (Roberts 1986). This 93-percent success rating of the president, moreover, does not include cases in which the president's threat of a veto deterred Congress from even bringing up a bill for a vote.

But, one should remember, presidents will not be inclined to veto bills they expect to be overridden, except perhaps to make a political statement. And Congress will not be inclined to write bills that will be readily vetoed unless it seems possible for the veto to be overridden. These forces obviously affect the veto data, so one must be circumspect in treating them as an objective measure of presidential power.

When the president did veto legislation, one or both houses of Congress made the attempt to override only 256, or 18.3 percent, of the 1,398 nonpocket vetoes cast by presidents through 1984 (U.S. Senate 1978; U.S. Senate 1985). Of these, Congress was successful in overriding 40.6 percent. Although this is not a fantastic success rating in enacting legislation that the president opposed, it would appear that the bills on which an attempt was made to override a presidential veto were among the most important passed by Congress (Jackson 1967).

Overall, however, it seems fair to say that Congress's constitutional authority to override presidential vetoes has not dramatically augmented its control over legislation. In fact, almost half of all presidents (nineteen) never had a veto overturned, including John Kennedy (1961–63) and Lyndon Johnson (1963–69).

In short, presidents cast a large shadow, which suggests that their 89-percent Johnston power on override attempts may not be far off the mark. At a minimum, a president is probably the equal of the two-thirds majorities of Congress necessary to overturn a veto, giving him or her at least 67 percent of the power in the federal system. Perhaps with this reserve of strength in mind, Hamilton, in *Federalist* No. 73 (*Federalist Papers*, p. 445), strongly argued that the "qualified negative" (veto) was certainly preferable to an "absolute negative," in which the president would have all the (negative) power. But even with this limitation, Woodrow Wilson (1885, 52) characterized the president's veto power as "beyond all comparison, his most formidable prerogative," and this indeed appears to be the case (Spitzer 1988).

The formal calculations indicate that a president's power of both approval and disapproval exceeds 67 percent if power can be rooted in a player's criticality—diminished by others who also are critical—in vulnerable coalitions. Although I believe this notion of power is eminently reasonable, it still needs to be corroborated by more and better data.

Previous empirical data, which are consistent with the Banzhaf index (Brams 1989) but not the Johnston index, show the House to be more powerful than the Senate. Generally, the smaller an institution (including the presidency), the more likely its members are critical with fewer others, which explains this discrepancy between the Banzhaf and Johnston indices. But even if the Johnston index does not account for the relatively greater success of the House in conflicts with the Senate, it does show the president to be preeminent, which—while perhaps not exactly the intent of the Founding Fathers—seems by and large true today.

8.6. The Paradox of the Chair's Position

I suggested that the Johnston index is a reasonable measure for comparing the president's bargaining power with that of senators and representatives. This index, however, does not take into account the preferences that the president, senators, and representatives may have in a particular situation. Rather, it reflects an actor's criticality—with and without others—in all vulnerable coalitions.

When players choose strategies consistent with their preferences, the greater resources (e.g., votes or other institutional prerogatives) that an actor has may not translate into greater power in specific situations. Thus, an actor more critical by the Banzhaf or Johnston indices may not be able to obtain a better outcome than an actor who is less critical in certain circumstances.

For example, it would seem that the chair of a voting body would have more power than other members if it has a tie-breaking vote in addition to a regular vote. Yet, under circumstances to be spelled out shortly, a chair may actually be at a disadvantage relative to other members.

As an illustration, assume there is a set of three voters, $V = \{X,Y,Z\}$, and a set of three alternatives, $A = \{x,y,z\}$. Assume that voter X prefers x to y to z, indicated by xyz; voter Y's preference is yzx, and voter Z's is zxy.

These preferences give rise to a paradox of voting (discussed in Section 7.8) because the social ordering is intransitive: although a majority (voters X and Z) prefer x to y, and a majority (voters X and Y) prefer y to z, a majority (voters Y and Z) prefer z to x. Because the majorities that prefer each alternative over some other in a series of pairwise contests are in a cycle that returns to its starting point,

$$x > y > z > x, \text{ where ">" indicates "defeats,"}$$

there is none that can defeat all others; appropriately, they are referred to as *cyclical majorities*.

The fact that every alternative that receives majority support in one contest can be defeated by another alternative in another contest demonstrates the lack of a clearcut winner or social choice. But now assume that the voting procedure is the plurality procedure, whereby the alternative with the most votes wins, and that X has more votes than either of the other two voters but not enough to win if the other two voters both vote for another alternative.

Under a different interpretation, X may be considered to have the same number of votes as the other two voters but, in the event of a three-way tie, can act as the chair and break ties. In either event, it would appear that X has some kind of edge over the other two voters, Y and Z.

If voting is sincere, X will prevail because each voter will vote for the alternative he or she ranks first. By being able to make the decisive choice in the case of a three-way split, X can ensure the selection of x.

Curiously, however, X's apparent advantage in voting power over the other two voters disappears if voting is "sophisticated" (to be defined shortly). First, note that X has a dominant strategy of "vote for x," which is never worse, and sometimes better, whatever the other two voters do. Thus, if the other two voters vote for the same alternative, it wins, and

X cannot do better than vote sincerely for *x*. On the other hand, if the other two voters disagree, *X*'s tie-breaking vote (as well as regular vote) for *x* will be decisive in *x*'s selection. Hence, *X*'s sincere vote is at least as good as, and sometimes better than, voting for *y* or *z*, whatever the circumstances.

Given this choice on the part of *X*, *Y* and *Z* face the strategy choices shown in Figure 8.1. Their dominated strategies are crossed out, leaving *Y* two undominated strategies, "vote for *y*" and "vote for *z*," and *Z* one *undominated* strategy, "vote for *z*." In the case of *Y*, "vote for *x*," which always leads to *Y*'s worst outcome, is dominated by *Y*'s other two strategies. In the case of *Z*, "vote for *z*" is actually a dominant strategy, or a unique undominated strategy, because it is at least as good and sometimes better than *Z*'s other two strategies, whatever strategy *Y* adopts.

If voters have complete information about each other's preferences, then they can perceive the situation in terms of the top matrix in Figure 8.1 and eliminate the dominated strategies that are crossed out (first reduction). The elimination of these strategies gives the bottom matrix in Figure 8.1. Then *Y*, choosing between "vote for *y*" and "vote for *z*" in this matrix, would cross out "vote for *y*" (second reduction), now dominated because that choice would result in *x*'s winning due to the chair's tie-breaking vote; instead, *Y* would choose "vote for *z*," ensuring *z*'s election, which is *Z*'s best outcome but only the next-best outcome for *Y*.

In this manner *z*, which is not the first choice of a majority and could in fact be beaten by *y* in a pairwise contest, becomes the *sophisticated outcome*. In general, the successive elimination of dominated strategies by voters, insofar as this is possible, is called *sophisticated voting*, and the strategies that remain after all eliminations are made are called *sophisticated strategies*.[5]

The sophisticated outcome is a Nash equilibrium because, given *X*'s choice of "vote for *x*" and *Z*'s choice of "vote for *z*," *Y* cannot do better than choose "vote for *z*." But *Z* has no reason to depart from "vote for *z*," given *X*'s choice of "vote for *x*"; and because *X*'s choice is dominant, *X* has no incentive to deviate from "vote for *x*."

In game-theoretic terms, sophisticated voting produces a different and smaller game in which some formerly undominated strategies in the larger game become dominated in the smaller game. The removal of such strategies—sometimes in several successive stages—in effect enables sophisticated voters to determine what outcomes eventually *will* be chosen by eliminating those outcomes that definitely *will not* be chosen. Thereby voters attempt to foreclose the possibility that their worst outcomes will be chosen by the successive removal of dominated strategies, given the presumption that other voters will do likewise.

How does sophisticated voting affect the chair's presumed extra voting

Figure 8.1. Sophisticated voting outcome, given X chooses "vote for x"

First Reduction

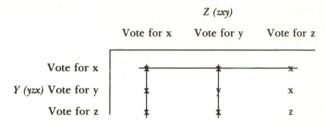

Second Reduction

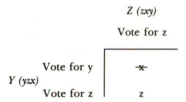

Note: The dominated strategies of each voter are crossed out in the first reduction, leaving two (undominated) strategies for Y and one (dominant) strategy for Z. Given these eliminations, Y would then eliminate "vote for y" in the second reduction, making "vote for z" the sophisticated strategies of both Y and Z, with z the sophisticated outcome.

power? Observe that the chair's tie-breaking vote is not only not helpful but positively harmful: it guarantees that X's worst outcome (z) will be chosen if voting is sophisticated! The illusory nature of the chair's extra voting power in such situations is called the *paradox of the chair's position.*

If this result seems anomalous, it is perhaps worth investigating how often the preferences of three voters will be such that the chair, despite possessing a tie-breaking vote, will not get its first choice if voting is sophisticated. In situations in which two or all three voters rank one alternative best, this alternative will obviously be chosen under both sincere and sophisticated voting. The situations that are of interest, therefore, are those in which all three voters have different first preferences, which I call *conflict situations.*

There are six ways in which each individual may order the set of three alternatives {x,y,z}: *xyz; xzy; yxz; yzx; zxy;* and *zyx.* Hence there are $6^3 = 216$ ways in which three individuals can express their preferences.

Now once the chair has chosen an ordering, of which there are six possibilities, there are four orderings that give the second voter a first choice different from the chair's, and two orderings that give the third voter a first choice different from both the chair's and the first voter's. Thus, there are $6 \times 4 \times 2 = 48$ distinct conflict situations.

For a social intransitivity to occur, preferences cannot be *value-restricted*: the first, second, and third choices of the three voters must all be different—that is, there must be a disparity in views at all levels.[6] In the three-voter, three-alternative example, once one voter has chosen a preference scale from among the six possibilities (e.g., *xyz*), a second voter has a choice between the only two preference scales (*yzx* and *zxy*) on which none of the alternatives is ranked in the same position as on the first voter's preference scale. Given the choice of the first two voters, the third voter is limited to just one preference scale (i.e., the one the second voter does not choose).

Consequently, given three alternatives, there are $6 \times 2 \times 1 = 12$ ways in which three individuals can choose preference scales that yield an intransitive social ordering. The probability, therefore, of a social intransitivity is $12/216 = 1/18 \approx .056$, assuming all preference scales are equiprobable, which can be generalized to more voters' voting on more alternatives (Brams 1976, 41–43; Brams 1985a, 65–66).

Besides the 12 paradox-of-voting situations, 24 of the remaining 36 conflict situations are vulnerable to the paradox of the chair's position, though not in as drastic a form as the paradox-of-voting situations that ensure the chair's worst choice under sophisticated voting.[7] In these circumstances, either the chair's second choice is chosen or the result is indeterminate (i.e., there is more than one sophisticated outcome). In none of these cases, however, can the chair's tie-breaking vote induce its first choice if voting is sophisticated.

Given this unfortunate state of affairs for a chair, it is reasonable to ask whether a chair (or the largest voting faction), with apparently greater voting power, has any recourse in such situations. Otherwise, the strategic calculations of sophisticated voting would appear inevitably to nullify the chair's edge over the other voters.

Consider the paradox-of-voting situation used to illustrate the paradox of the chair's position. The sophisticated outcome is z, which is supported by both Y and Z. Clearly, X has no voting strategy that will alter the sophisticated outcome, X's worst.

This result also holds in the other conflict situations in which the sophisticated outcome is either indeterminate or the second choice of the chair. Such a consequence would appear to be pretty dismaying for a chair: in 36 of the 48 cases in which the most-preferred outcomes of all three voters differ, sophisticated voting undermines the chair's apparent power advantage—specifically, its ability to obtain a most-preferred outcome, which it would obtain if voting were sincere. Moreover, there appears to be no voting strategy that can restore this power. Does any escape remain for a chair once sincerity in voting is lost?

8.7. The Chair's Counterstrategy of Deception

A chair is often in the unique position, after the other voters have already committed themselves, of being the last voter to have to make a strategy choice. Yet this position does not furnish a ready solution to the chair's problem if voting is truly sophisticated, for sophisticated voting implies that voters act both on their own preferences and on a knowledge of the preferences of the other voters. Therefore, the order of voting is immaterial: all voters can predict sophisticated choices beforehand and act accordingly. Even a chair's (unexpected) deviation from a sophisticated strategy cannot generally effect for it a more favorable outcome.

Assume for purposes of the subsequent analysis that the chair, by virtue of its position, can obtain information about the preferences of the other two voters, but the other two votes cannot obtain information about the chair's preference. Assume further that each of the two regular members is informed of the other's preference. If voting is to be sophisticated, the chair's preference must be made known to the regular members; however, the chair is not compelled to tell the truth. The question is: Can a chair, by announcing a preference different from its true preference, induce a more-preferred sophisticated outcome?

I explored the effects of a deceptive announcement in a different context in Section 4.4, where I hypothesized that Krushchev, terrified by the possibility of nuclear escalation in the Cuban missile crisis, induced the cooperative outcome in the Figure 4.3 version of this crisis by deceiving the United States. In the present case, recall that the chair, having the tie-breaking vote, will always have a dominant strategy if voting is sophisticated. Indeed, the other voters need only know (and believe) the chair's announced first choice, and not its complete preference scale, to determine what its sophisticated choice will be.

Define a *deception strategy* on the part of the chair to be any *announced* most-preferred outcome that differs from its *honestly* most-preferred outcome. Call the use of a deception strategy by the chair *tacit deception,* because the other members, not knowing the chair's true preference, are not able to determine whether its announcement is an honest representation of its most-preferred outcome. Tacit deception will be profitable for the chair if it induces a social choice that the chair prefers to the sophisticated outcome (based on the chair's honest representation of its preferences).

As an illustration, consider the paradox-of-voting situation discussed in Section 8.6. The chair (X), by announcing its first choice to be outcome y rather than x, can induce the (manipulated) sophisticated outcome y, which it would prefer to z. This can be seen from the reductions shown in Figure 8.2. Note that the first-reduction matrix gives the outcomes as Y and Z *perceive* them, after X's deceptive announcement of y as its first choice (it does not matter in what order x and z are ranked after y). Y's elimination of dominated strategies "vote for x" and "vote for z," and Z's elimination of dominated strategy "vote for y," give the second-reduction matrix shown in Figure 8.2, which cannot be reduced further because each of Z's two remaining strategies yield y. Thus, tacit deception, by changing the outcome from z to y, is profitable for X (as well as Y).

Assume now that X as chair actually chooses "vote for x" after announcing its (dishonest) preference for y. Then the (manipulated) sophisticated outcome will be x, the chair's first preference. In other words, the chair can induce its most-preferred outcome by announcing a bogus preference for y and, contrary to the announcement, voting honestly in the end. Because y, the tacit-deception outcome, is not a Nash equilibrium, X can benefit by voting for x, contrary to its announced preference for y.

Call this kind of deception, which involves not only announcing a deception strategy but taking *deceptive action* as well, *revealed deception*. This deception is revealed in the voting process and is clearly more profitable for X than tacit deception in a paradox-of-voting situation.

In general, a dishonest announcement by the chair may improve its position somewhat, as in the paradox-of-voting situation just illustrated, wherein a dishonest announcement ensures passage of the chair's next-best outcome. Such an announcement, however, followed by the chair's vote for its most-preferred outcome (thereby flouting this announcement) is still better: it ensures the chair's best outcome (x in the example) in the 36 conflict situations in which there is a paradox of the chair's position.

Of course, revealed deception becomes apparent after the vote—unless the vote is secret—and probably cannot be used very frequently. If it were, the chair's announcements would quickly become unbelievable and lose their inducement value.

The deception strategy game I have sketched for the chair can naturally be played by a regular member if he or she is privy to information that the chair and the other regular member are not. (The results of such special knowledge will not duplicate those for the chair, however, because the chair has an extra resource—the tie-breaking vote.) I shall not carry this analysis further, though, because my main purpose has been to demonstrate that there is a resolution (of sorts) to the paradox of the chair's position.[8] It requires, however, that the information available to some players in the game be restricted, which has the effect of endowing one player (the chair) with still greater resources.

Figure 8.2. Tacit deception outcome, given X chooses "vote for y"

First Reduction

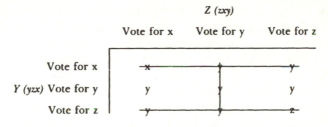

Z (*zxy*)

	Vote for x	Vote for y	Vote for z
Vote for x	x̶	y̶	y̶
Y (*yzx*) Vote for y	y	y	y
Vote for z	y̶	y̶	z̶

Second Reduction

Z (*zxy*)

	Vote for x	Vote for z
Y (*yzx*) Vote for y	y	y

Note: The dominated strategies of each voter are crossed out in the first reduction, leaving two (undominated) strategies for Z and one (dominant) strategy for Y. Given these eliminations, Z's two undominated strategies, both yielding y, remain undominated in the second reduction—so no strategies are in fact crossed out—making "vote for y" the sophisticated strategy of Y and both "vote for x" and "vote for z" the sophisticated strategies of Z. The (manipulated) sophisticated outcome is y, which is a product of tacit deception; if X actually voted for x after falsely announcing a first choice of y, the (manipulated) sophisticated outcome would be x, but X's deception would be revealed.

This, it must be admitted, is itself a rather deceptive way out of a problem that seems genuine. If voting is sophisticated, or if coalitions can form, the chair, despite the added weight of its position, will not necessarily enjoy greater control over outcomes than the other members. In fact, the reverse might be the case, as the paradox-of-voting situations illustrate.

Strangely enough, in these situations a chair can obtain its best outcome without deception if the voting system used is *approval voting*, whereby the voters can vote for as many alternatives as they like (briefly discussed in Section 7.10 as a prelude to the analysis of coalition voting). Under this system, each voter would choose between two undominated strategies: vote for his or her best, or two best, outcomes.[9] The sophisticated strategies of the three voters turn out to be {x,y}—vote for both x and y—for X (the chair), {y,z} for Y, and {x,z} for Z, which yields x when the chair breaks a three-way tie in favor of x. However, the chair may also do worse under approval voting than *plurality voting* (i.e., where voters are restricted to voting for only one alternative) if the preferences of the voters are different, so approval voting provides no panacea for a chair who suffers vis-à-vis the other voters because of the extra resources that it commands.

Two similar paradoxes may arise under either plurality or approval voting, whereby a chair does worse by (1) having both a regular and tie-breaking vote versus having only a tie-breaking vote (no-vote paradox); or (2) having a tie-breaking vote and participating versus not participating in the election at all (no-show paradox) (Brams, Felsenthal, and Maoz 1986; Brams, Felsenthal, and Maoz 1988). These consequences of sophisticated voting seem paradoxical because a chair in each case has ostensibly greater power (a tie-breaking vote in the no-show paradox, a regular vote in addition to the tie-breaking vote in the no-vote paradox) that it would do better without or not using. Moreover, because the encumbrances that the extra resources create cannot be foreclosed under either plurality or approval voting, the paradoxes are not a peculiarity of the voting system used.

All these paradoxes make clear that power defined as control over outcomes is not synonymous with power defined in terms of control over resources, at least those that a chair may possess.[10] The strategic situation facing voters intervenes and may cause them to reassess their strategies in light of the additional resources that a chair possesses. In so doing, they may be led to "gang up" against the chair—that is, to vote in such a way as to undermine the impact of the chair's extra resources, handing the chair a worse outcome than it would have achieved without them. These resources in effect become a burden to bear, not power to relish.

But as Farquharson (1969, 51) points out, Y and Z do not form a coalition against X in the sense of coordinating their strategies and agreeing to act together in a cooperative game, wherein binding agreements are possible. Rather, they behave as isolated individuals; at most they could be said to form an "implicit coalition." Such a coalition does not imply even communication between its members but simply agreement based on their common perceived strategic interests.

8.8.   The Geneva Conference Game

I know of no real-life instances in which the paradox of the chair's position manifested itself in a voting situation. On the other hand, Zagare (1979) has argued that the preferences of participants at the Geneva conference on Indochina in 1954 approximated those of the paradox of voting. While no participant could be legitimately assumed to possess either greater weight or a tie-breaking vote, the player who preferred the status quo had an advantage because this outcome would prevail if there were no settlement of the conflict. Not only did this fact seem to be well understood by the participants, but the preference of the advantaged player was somewhat of a mystery to the other players, enabling this player to make a false announcement and tacitly deceive the other players.

I shall retrace Zagare's argument, and present some of his evidence and that of others, in this section. An interesting question that his analysis raises is whether such negotiations—in which there is not only extensive communication among parties but also much bargaining that, in the end, leads to an agreement—is properly modeled by a noncooperative game of incomplete information that purports to explain strategizing in an anonymous voting situation. I believe the answer to this question is affirmative, but first let me recount the game.

In 1953 France was deeply engaged in a war with the Democratic Republic of Vietnam (the DRV or Vietminh) in Indochina. France received military aid from the United States and Great Britain, the Vietminh from the Soviet Union and China, but neither side's allies played active roles in the fighting. In the fall of 1953, with the war stalemated, pressure mounted on the French government of Joseph Laniel to negotiate a settlement with the Vietminh.

As dissatisfaction with the war grew and domestic support crumbled, the French left made it increasingly difficult for the Laniel government to pursue a military solution. Peace feelers from the Vietminh, and a more cooperative attitude on the part of the Soviet Union toward the West, intensified the forces on the French to negotiate.

As the prospects for a negotiated settlement apppeared to increase, three distinct collective and individual players became identifiable: the Western Alliance; the Sino-Soviet bloc; and the Vietminh. The Western Alliance was led by the United States and included France, Great Britain, and the quasi-independent State of Vietnam (SVN). The Chinese and the Soviets shared the same Communist ideology and had, at the time, similar strategic interests. Vietminh control over a large portion of Vietnam gave them autonomy as an independent player.

The military situation for the French had rapidly deteriorated in early 1954; their defeat at Dienbienphu the day before the Indochinese phase of the Geneva conference opened in May 1954 epitomized their waning influence. Likewise, the influence of the British was diminished by their lack of any significant military force in the region. Finally, the Western-supported SVN was not only internally weak but also totally dependent on American aid and so played a limited role in the Western Alliance. Thus, it was the preference of the United States that dominated the Alliance, though differences among its members on occasion produced rifts.

I shall describe shortly the preferences of the Alliance and the other players for the possible outcomes they foresaw as emerging from their talks in Geneva. But first consider what these outcomes were—at least before the French defeat at Dienbienphu—using the notation of Section 8.6:

x: the status quo, resulting in a continuation of the conflict, with the French probably replaced by the United States as the main protagonist;

y: a military solution, probably resulting in a permanent partition of Vietnam;

z: a military *and* political solution, probably resulting in DRV President Ho Chi Minh's victory in a general election.

If x were the outcome, not only would the war continue but its prosecution would almost surely require American intervention, which some U.S. leaders supported. Outcome y was proposed by the French but was probably most supported by the Sino-Soviet bloc, which wanted to limit discussion at the conference to military matters and to delay negotiating a political settlement, including the possibility of future elections, until after a cease-fire. Outcome z was proposed by DRV Prime Minister Pham Van Dong, who argued that military and political matters could not be separated and should therefore be discussed concurrently.

The consequences of outcome x were seen differently by two of the players. While U.S. intelligence reports predicted that "the over-all French Union position in Indochina [would] . . . deteriorate" by mid-1954, the United States nevertheless believed that increased American aid and a political program designed "to win sufficient native support" would enable the French to reverse their disadvantageous military position (*Pentagon Papers* 1971, 405). By contrast, the DRV was convinced that the French would succumb and, consequently, a continuation of the war would result in their hegemony over all of Vietnam, though undoubtedly at considerable cost.

As for outcome y, the French proposal was seen by all participants as tantamount to a permanent partition, because any temporary partition to enforce a cease-fire would likely become permanent. Outcome z was viewed by the participants to mean immediate French withdrawal from Vietnam, followed by a general election that "would be attended by almost certain loss of the Associated States to Communist control" (*Pentagon Papers* 1971, 449).

Among the three players, the following three coalitions of two each would be decisive:

1. the Western Alliance and the Sino-Soviet bloc;
2. the Sino-Soviet bloc and the Vietminh;
3. the Western Alliance and the Vietminh.

Coalition 1 could dictate any outcome because, although the Vietminh held de facto control in Indochina, they could continue to do so only with Soviet and Chinese aid or with Western acquiescence. Coalition 2 would be decisive because the Western Alliance could not prevent it from implementing outcome x or y; furthermore, it would be difficult for the West to subvert outcome z without suffering a serious propaganda loss. As Le Thi Tuyet (quoted in Zagare 1979, 402) pointed out, "Washington did not like the idea of a partition [but] it could not effectively prevent it." Finally, the members of Coalition 3 could, as the belligerents, obviously stop the war and effect any of the three outcomes.

Thus, the Geneva conference game had the earmarks of a simple-majority voting game in which any two players could, by their choice of an outcome, realize its choice. The problem, of course, was that the preferences of the players were diametrically opposed, as seen from the following rankings:

Western Alliance: xyz;

Sino-Soviet bloc: yzx;

Vietminh: zxy.

These are in fact the paradox-of-voting preferences of the example illustrated in Sections 8.6 and 8.7, which Zagare (1979) justifies in some detail. Because the rankings of the Western Alliance and the Vietminh are fairly evident, I will say little about them subsequently.

The least apparent ranking is the Sino-Soviet preference for y over z and x. For the Soviets, continuing the war (outcome x) raised the possibility of a nuclear confrontation with the United States, for which they were woefully unprepared; acceptance of z would also create problems for them in Soviet-bloc states that did not have free elections. Even though unfavorable to the Vietminh, y was therefore preferable to x or z.

For the Chinese, a united Vietnam (x), which would in all likelihood dominate Cambodia and Laos, would create a potential rival, whereas a partitioned Vietnam would pose no serious threat. Moreover, y would help to preserve harmony in the Communist bloc and was therefore better than z. By comparison, the Vietminh most feared partition (y), and it remains somewhat of a mystery why they accepted it (Burke and Greenstein 1989, 99). They were also unhappy with x because if the French were defeated, they viewed with trepidation the possibility of

American or Chinese intervention that would either result in their defeat or undermine their autonomy.

Because the preferences of the players in the Geneva conference game are cyclical, any agreement by one coalition to form—in support of a particular outcome—would not be stable, as shown in Section 7.8 for all the two-member coalitions in the paradox-of-vote-trading example. Moreover, there is no obvious "chair" in the Geneva conference game that, in the event of a three-way division over the three outcomes, could break a deadlock in favor of one. However, because a deadlock would presumably result in a continuation of the status quo (x), which the Western Alliance ranked first, the strategic situation can be conceptualized *as if* the Western Alliance were the chair.

If this is true and the three players make sophisticated choices, then the outcome is z, the worst outcome for the Western Alliance (Section 8.6). Apparently recognizing the possibility that Coalition 2, comprising the Sino-Soviet bloc and the Vietminh, would form in support of z, the Western Alliance, consistent with the deception analysis of Section 8.7, chose to dissemble. By so doing, it does not so much change the status quo as make it an orphan by withdrawing support from it.

Zagare (1979) documents how U.S. Secretary of State John Foster Dulles, commencing in March 1954, began to soften his position on opposing Communist aggression in Indochina. Leaving open the precise limits of American tolerance, he implied an American willingness to compromise. President Dwight D. Eisenhower went further a month later and hinted that the United States would be willing to negotiate a settlement at Geneva and reach a modus vivendi with the Communists. Finally, a week after Eisenhower's remarks in April, Dulles all but ruled out the use of American force in the region.

Altogether, the United States conveyed the strong impression that it favored a "temporary" partition. Zagare summarizes the press response:

> During the first week of May, several Saigon dailies and the New York *Herald Tribune* reported that the American government was willing to accept the partition of Indochina under satsifactory conditions. On May 6, the New York *Times* stated that the United States had decided to seek a "protracted armistice" at Geneva. (Zagare 1979, 405)

Despite public appearances, however, Dulles privately told the British that he desired to continue the conflict and even contemplated American intervention after a certain point, not unlike the Inchon landings in Korea. Information on American conditions for intervention in Vietnam, including a possible air strike, was also conveyed to the French; its publication precipitated a two-week deadlock in the Geneva talks.

With the fall of the Laniel government in June, the various parties (including the United States) evinced a new willingness to iron out their differences quickly. An agreement calling for a cease-fire and the separation of French and Vietminh forces was signed in July.

As foreseen by some, the all-Vietnamese elections, scheduled in 1956, were never held, and Vietnam remained divided. Less than ten years later, of course, the United States found itself once again enmeshed in the conflict. But this time, having made a major commitment of American forces, there would be no easy escape.

To return to 1954, the evidence is by no means incontrovertible that the United States, by deceiving the Soviets and Chinese into thinking that its first choice was *y*, was thereby able to induce this as the (manipulated) sophisticated outcome. Also plausible as an explanation for this result is that the United States knew that a compromise acceptable to at least one other player could not be built around *x*; it therefore settled for *y* as its fall-back position, which was the first choice of the Sino-Soviet bloc.

What the second interpretation fails to explain is the glaring discrepancy between the U.S. public position—indicating a willingness to compromise by accepting the partition of Vietnam—and the apparent private desire of some U.S. leaders, including Admiral Arthur W. Radford, chairman of the Joint Chiefs of Staff, and Vice President Richard M. Nixon (Burke and Greenstein 1989, 10, 65), to win militarily if the status quo continued. Indeed, this "obvious contrast between the public and private comments of the Eisenhower Administration officials and organs" was noted in the *Pentagon Papers* (1971, vol. 1, p. 177). Thus, the U.S. acceptance of its fallback position was more deceptive than honest.

Dulles, in particular, did not simply retreat from his hard-line position. Before the French defeat at Dienbienphu, he had pressed for American military intervention, which Eisenhower vetoed in large part because of a lack of support from Congressional leaders and allies (Burke and Greenstein 1989, 74–89). Dulles presumably would have been willing to scuttle the agreement at Geneva, and reveal his deception, if the chances for the defeat of the Vietminh had improved and Eisenhower had supported intervention.

Dulles in fact believed that, after defeating the French, the Vietminh were militarily exhausted; the Western Alliance might still triumph if the conflict continued. Yet an alliance between the Vietminh and the Soviets and Chinese could make this task extremely difficult. In the end, then, it was better to prevaricate, first by being deliberately ambiguous about U.S. aims and policy, effectively making the game one of incomplete information—not only for the other players but for the British and French as well (Randall 1969, 91).

That uncertainty made more plausible a gradual shift toward support

258 / Bargaining Power

of y, which in effect became the new status quo. Thus, on June 8 Dulles said that "the United States has no intention of dealing with the Indochina situation unilaterally"; shortly thereafter, the Americans and British agreed in effect to a partition of Vietnam that they hoped would prevent a total Communist takeover. In the end, the gradual but unmistakable movement by the West toward y—even if brought about through tacit deception—made an agreement possible with the Chinese and Soviets, who in turn pressured the Vietminh to go along.

It was a bitter pill for the Vietminh to swallow. But by 1965, the Vietcong guerrillas in South Vietnam, whom the Vietminh supported, constituted a serious military threat to South Vietnam. President Lyndon Johnson reluctantly approved large-scale military intervention by the United States to try to preserve the solution achieved in Geneva, but now this status quo proved vulnerable.[11]

The Vietnam War ended for America in 1973 with the signing of peace accords in Paris. (The peace talks in Paris had begun in 1968 and were not untainted by deceptive pronouncements, as Zagare [1977] demonstrates.) In 1975, after withdrawal of American forces from Vietnam, the Vietminh overran South Vietnam and saw their dream of a united Vietnam finally realized—more than twenty years after the Geneva talks and, of course, at a terrible cost.

8.9. Conclusions

Power is probably the most suggestive concept in the vocabulary of political scientists. It is also one of the most intractable concepts, bristling with apparently contradictory meanings and implications. To explore some of these, I began by defining bargaining power as the ability of actors to control outcomes.

This ability was operationalized in terms of two different measures, each based on the criticalness of actors in coalitions. I argued that the Johnston index provides a more accurate portrayal of the power of the president in the federal system than does the Banzhaf or Shapley-Shubik indices. By distinguishing situations in which an actor is uniquely critical from those in which he or she shares this ability with other actors, the Johnston index makes the president more than the equal of the two-thirds majorities in both houses of Congress needed to override a presidential veto.

The veto data I briefly assayed tend to support the preeminence of the president in the federal constellation. From the Founding Fathers to Woodrow Wilson to contemporary commentators, there has been much speculation but very little formal analysis of the sway of the president over other actors in the system. The Johnston index, in my opinion, provides a reasonable benchmark of the president's constitutionally based power of approval and disapproval.

The Johnston and other indices, while applicable to voting bodies and other rule-governed systems like the federal system, ignore the preferences of actors. Instead, they focus exclusively on what the rules of the game—constitutional or other—imply about an actor's ability to disrupt a winning coalition. But an actor's bargaining power depends not just on his or her criticalness in all possible coalitions that might form but also on what is desired in a particular situation, and coalitions that might form to implement those desires.

Thus, preferences may upset the commonsensical notion that the greater the proportion of resources (such as votes) that an actor has, the greater is his or her power. A chair in a voting body, which can cast a tie-breaking vote in addition to a regular vote, may be at a disadvantage vis-à-vis the regular members once the strategic calculations of voters, based on their preferences, are factored into the equation.

I showed possible ways that a chair may circumvent the paradox of the chair's position through tacit or revealed deception. Lacking an example of this paradox in a real-life voting body, I indicated how its logic may apply to the strategic choices of players in, and the outcome of, the 1954 Geneva negotiations on the Indochinese conflict. More specifically, the United States appeared to have deceived the other players about its preference in order to induce a better outcome than it would have realized otherwise.

To be sure, these negotiations were not simply a voting game in which players behaved entirely individualistically. The negotiations extended over several months; many proposals and much information was exchanged, which surely contributed to the sophistication of the players. Thus, it seems no accident that the sophisticated voting model, with possible deception by one of its players, fits well the apparent facts. Specifically, the United States, by hiding its (true) preferences and conveying through various channels a false preference ordering, constructed a settlement quite favorable to itself.

But this resolution of the conflict was only temporary, signifying that an agreement built on deception is unlikely to possess long-run stability. Indeed, a tacit deceiver, as was the United States, may have an incentive, by revealing his or her deception, to try to effect an even better outcome. Although the United States did not abrogate the Geneva accord calling for a cease-fire, it ignored the accord on future elections.

In addition, the United States supported anti-Communist insurgents in the region several years before the Vietnam War. By the same token, North Vietnam and Communist movements with which it was allied received support from the Soviet Union and China. Evidently, the parties to the Geneva agreement never foresaw it as providing a permanent solution but rather one that would be driven by other forces.

Although the United States escaped the paradox of the chair's position in 1954, its escape smacked more of evasion. A more permanent solution, as subsequent events proved, required force to implement, which is another way of saying that the "game" over the longer term was not a cooperative one. A settlement, to be binding, could not be simply agreed to but instead had to be enforced.

If settlements built on a foundation of deception are fragile, what does it mean to have bargaining power? The paradox of the chair's position in fact reflects more the absence of such power than its presence, because the chair's tie-breaking vote—or, equivalently, extra voting weight—is for naught. Indeed, this prerogative has a rueful effect in some situations: it ensures that the chair's last choice will be chosen under sophisticated voting.

Potential chairs, beware! One may maximize one's influence, or effect on the outcome, by relinquishing the chair, not seeking it out. Although the chair can improve its position through a policy of either tacit or revealed deception, the use of such a strategy depends on having information about the preferences of other members that they do not have about the chair's—and even then the "solution" may not be stable, as the later undercutting of the Geneva accords illustrates. On the other hand, changing the voting system may work to the chair's advantage, as I indicated in the case of approval voting, but such a switch offers no guarantee, for the paradox of the chair's position seems quite independent of the voting system used.

The ramifications of this paradox extend to other political arenas. In international relations, countries that steer clear of alliance involvements—as Austria and Switzerland have done in Western Europe—or pledge themselves not to develop nuclear weapons—as most countries in the world today have done by signing the Nuclear Nonproliferation Treaty—would seem examples in which shunning certain prerogatives or resources may redound to the advantage of the shunner. In fact, when a policy of apparent self-denial fosters superior outcomes for those doing the denying, it might better be characterized as a policy of self-enhancement. Under what strategic conditions the less powerful (in resources) become the more powerful (in securing better outcomes for themselves) is an intriguing question on which little research has been done.

That there is a linkage, however tenuous, between resources and control over outcomes is underscored by the analysis of bargaining power based on the Johnston index. The president *is* powerful by being able to influence the choice of an outcome in many situations. At the same time, the president is not always successful; his or her preferences may set in motion forces that counter them, as occurs when there is a paradox of the chair's position. In defining power, therefore, "control over outcomes" should, at some level, reflect control that tends to satisfy one's preferences or advance one's goals. If bargaining does not do this, then it will presumably be eschewed.

Notes

[1]Although a majority of the Supreme Court is able to declare legislation unconstitutional, thereby exercising a veto of a sort, the Court will not be considered an actor in the present analysis. Chamberlin (1989) has extended the Banzhaf calculations in Brams (1989) to the Court—showing it to be intermediate in power between the president and the House and Senate—but the qualitatively different role it plays in the federal system makes power comparisons with the other players questionable.

[2]This analysis is adapted from Brams, Affuso, and Kilgour (1989) with permission.

[3]In fact, because the vice-president is able to break a 50-50 tie, 50 senators, not 51, may constitute a simple majority—but only if the president, through the vice-president, favors this coalition of 50. The other coalition of 50 is not sufficient to win—in fact, the tie-breaking vote of the vice-president will cause it to lose—so a simple majority for it will be 51 senators.

To avoid such considerations in measuring power, wherein the position of a president on a bill matters, I exclude the vice-president as a player from the subsequent analysis. This exclusion has virtually no effect on the later conclusions, though it should be borne in mind that the vice-president has the same defection possibilities as a senator when there is a 50-50 tie.

On the other hand, when the vote is 51-49, the vice-president is not critical, but a senator may be. Specifically, a senator's defection from the coalition of 51 will be critical if the vice-president is on the side of the original coalition of 49 (which becomes a coalition of 50 with the defection), but not critical if the vice-president is on the other side.

In sum, the vice president and each senator are always critical in a 50-50 tie, but the vice president is never critical when the vote is 51-49. By comparison, a senator may or may not be critical in the 51-49 situation (depending on which side he or she—and the vice president—are on), which probably makes the vice president roughly equivalent to a senator in terms of voting power. But because the vice president is really only a surrogate for the president in the role of president of the Senate, it is the president's power that is enhanced, albeit only slightly, over the figures to be given later.

[4]If the president, Senate, and House are considered simply three players, each as an institution has equal power if one ignores the president's veto power and Congress's veto override power. By contrast, the Banzhaf and Johnston indices assume that the power of the Senate and that of the House reside in the ability of their individual members to change their votes. In my opinion, this is a more

sensible perspective than treating these bodies as if they were single-minded blocs.

[5]Farquharson (1969) was the first to define and analyze sophisticated voting, which has been developed further in, among other places, Brams (1975) and Moulin (1983, 1986). The first discussion of the successive elimination of dominated strategies can be found in Luce and Raiffa (1957, 99–100) for repeated games.

[6]Sen (1966); for other characterizations of partial agreement that ensure a transitive social ordering, see Sen (1970, 169–71).

[7]For a breakdown, see Brams (1976, 168–75), which is based on Brams and Zagare (1977).

[8]For a more systematic analysis of deception voting strategies, see Brams and Zagare (1977, 1981).

[9]For a simple demonstration in the three-candidate case, see Brams (1978); more generally, see Brams and Fishburn (1983).

[10]Nagel (1975) argues that power is the causation of outcomes by preferences, linking preferences and outcomes in what he calls a descriptive (or empirical) model but not a formal (or deductive) model. The point of introducing preferences is to show the limitations of the "averaging" calculations underlying the power indices, which can be extremely useful in delineating, for example, how much the constitutional decision rules favor the president vis-à-vis a senator or representative. However, they do not show how preferences, say, on a particular bill may affect the outcome if voters are sophisticated. Such cases are discussed in, among other places, Brams (1976, 1985a) and Riker (1986).

[11]A game-theoretic model of escalation, based on a dollar auction in which the two highest bidders pay, is described in O'Neill (1986) and Leininger (1989), and is highly suggestive of how players may get themselves entrapped in a situation like Vietnam; see also Shubik (1971).

Chapter 9
Epilogue

In this book I have analyzed numerous negotiation games by developing different game-theoretic models of bargaining and arbitration, deriving theoretical consequences of the models, and using these models to interpret real-world cases. Chapter by chapter, some of the major themes are the following:

1. *Negotiation games have an ancient history.* The confrontation between Cain and God in the Bible illustrates that even when one player is in an obviously superior bargaining position, serious give-and-take may still occur. Rahab's harboring of the Israelite spies has the appearance of a straightforward exchange of favors, but it was conditioned on threats that helped to ensure that neither player would renege on the agreement. As arbitrator, Solomon first elicited the preferences of the two disputing women through deception before pronouncing judgment.

2. *There are procedures that induce honesty in bargaining.* The procedures that induce players to be honest include one in which a third party pays two bargainers a certain bonus if they reach an agreement; in principle the bonus may be recovered by taxing the players. Another honesty-inducing procedure imposes a penalty on the players that may result in the cancellation or diminution of a feasible settlement. An appraiser may prevent collusion under the bonus procedure and facilitate a settlement under the bonus and penalty procedures, as Jimmy Carter did at Camp David in 1978. Without rewards from the outside or a built-in risk of failure, however, there is no procedure that can eliminate posturing and exaggeration.

3. *Arbitration need not be by fiat but may cede different kinds of choices to the disputants.* Although arbitration, unlike bargaining, always leads to a settlement, different ways of arriving at the settlement may lead to different outcomes. Certain variations on final-offer arbitration (FOA) seem to hold promise, including procedures that promote convergence to the position of the arbitrator, possibly in stages, or to a middle position that is not necessarily the choice of the arbitrator. FOA, unalloyed, has

attractive features, too—principally its ability to induce two sides to reach their own agreement, lest they risk the possibility that a relatively extreme offer of the other side may be selected by the arbitrator. FOA has been used successfully to settle different kinds of disputes, including salary disputes in major league baseball. Less structured mediation/ arbitration/bargaining—illustrated by Henry Kissinger's shuttle diplomacy in the Middle East from 1973 to 1975—has, while difficult and protracted, also proven successful.

4. *Although crises exacerbate the problems of reaching agreements, the pressures of time may expedite back-and-forth exchanges and lead to settlements.* This is especially true when it is the superpowers who are embroiled in a crisis, because there is no third party that can readily step in and impose a settlement. The two empirical cases studied—the 1962 Cuban missile crisis and the 1973 U.S. alert decision during the Yom Kippur War—illustrate how moves and countermoves can be analyzed according to the theory of moves. In each crisis, the players appear to have made nonmyopic calculations and exercised power so as to ameliorate the crises.

5. *Two different kinds of threats—compellent and deterrent—may be effective in bargaining.* While intended to deter untoward actions of an adversary, threats, if carried out, are costly to the threatener as well as the threatened party. Their rationality derives from bolstering a player's reputation in repeated play of a game, in which the costs of a carried-out threat may be more than offset by the threat's increased deterrence value in later play. Although it is not always rational for a stronger player to carry out threats against a weaker player in a game with a definite termination point, the sequential-primary game illustrates why a weaker player, because of uncertainty, may capitulate.

6. *Compellent and deterrent threats were effective in one crisis, but in another a threat had unintended effects.* The Polish crisis of 1980–81 indicates how Solidarity's deterrent threat, and then the party's compellent threat, were invoked to implement different outcomes. When the economic situation deteriorated in Poland in the late 1980s, the game changed, allowing Solidarity to reassert itself. On the other hand, Richard Nixon's implicit threat against the Supreme Court in the Watergate scandal backfired, though his short-term calculations and actions in the White House tapes case were rational. However, Nixon probably did not fully appreciate his threat's long-term effects, but rational threats do not presume omniscience on the part of the players who make them.

7. *The distribution of public goods (or bads) and the stability of coalition governments are affected by vote trading and election rules.* Vote-trading probably occurs in most legislatures, but how individually rational trades can redound to the detriment of all has been somewhat of a puzzle, especially because a free market in votes would seem generally beneficial; the puzzle is explained in terms of an n-person Prisoners' Dilemma. The instability that plagues some multiparty parliamentary democracies, based on proportional representation, could be alleviated by an election

reform called coalition voting, which encourages bargaining and the formation of alliances among parties before an election. It would seem especially helpful in countries like Israel and Italy, each of which has more than a dozen parties in its parliament and has suffered from chronically unstable governments.

8. *The bargaining power of players is a function of both their preferences and the constitutional structures under which they act.* The bargaining strength of parties under coalition voting, illustrated in Chapter 7, is extended to the study of bargaining power in the U.S. federal system, comprising the president, members of the Senate, and members of the House of Representatives. Based on a new measure of voting power called the Johnston index, the president is shown to be the most powerful actor by far, despite Congress's power to override a presidential veto. But this kind of power, based on constitutional prerogatives alone, ignores player preferences. These preferences may stimulate the formation of an implicit coalition against the most powerful player in a game—or the status quo—illustrated by the 1954 Geneva talks on the future of Vietnam, wherein deception by one player apparently affected the outcome.

The game-theoretic models enhance one's strategic understanding of both the opportunities and limitations of negotiation. Whereas opportunities for resolving conflicts at all levels abound, many are lost because players are not forthcoming, norms and procedures do not exist or are manipulated, threats are made that undermine trust, and so on.

Rather than viewing these problems as pathologies, they are more properly seen as the strategic responses of rational actors in the negotiation games they play. Thus, for example, deception may not only be optimal against an opponent but may also prevent a conflict from exploding, to the distress of all players. Although one might decry the use of deception, it is hard to tell a player to shun it if it enhances his or her bargaining position or stabilizes a delicate situation that might otherwise unravel.

Because negotiations are intrinsically strategic, game theory provides powerful tools for their study. The tools I have used are varied, ranging from the noncooperative theory of incomplete-information games to the theory of moves to the cooperative theory dependent on decision rules.

Besides elucidating strategic behavior in real-life bargaining and arbitration situations, I have used the theory to derive consequences of rules and procedures that may help negotiators to narrow their differences and find common ground, for party leaders to build stable coalitions, and for heads-of-state to think ahead in crises and seek long-term solutions. While the study of negotiation games does not always offer crisp answers and instant advice, it provides a deductive logic for understanding the conditions that facilitate or impede negotiation.

Glossary

This glossary contains definitions of game-theoretic and related terms used in this book. Major topics that are discussed at length in the book (e.g., different bargaining and arbitration procedures; different measures of bargaining strength and bargaining power) are not included. Most terms are defined in relatively nontechnical language; more extended and rigorous definitions of some concepts (e.g., moving, staying, and threat power) can be found in the text.

Approval voting. Approval voting is a voting procedure in which voters can vote for as many alternatives as they like (i.e., approve of) in an election with more than two alternatives; the alternative with the most votes wins.

Backward induction. Backward induction is a reasoning process in which players, working backward from the bottom to the top of a game tree, anticipate each other's rational choices.

Bargaining problem. The bargaining problem is how to get players to reach a settlement that is in their mutual interest when it is in each player's individual interest to make exaggerated demands.

Cardinal utility. See *Utility.*

Coalition. A coalition is a subset of players that forms to achieve some end mutually beneficial to its members.

Coalition voting. Coalition voting is a voting procedure in which voters can cast two different kinds of votes in parliamentary elections based on proportional representation; their votes determine both the seat shares of parties and the coalition that becomes the governing one.

Common knowledge. Players in a game have common knowledge when they share certain information, know that they share it, know that they know that they share it, and so on ad infinitum.

Compellent threat. In repeated play of a sequential two-person game, a threatener's compellent threat is a threat to stay at a particular strategy to induce the threatened player to choose its (as well as the threatener's) best outcome associated with that strategy.

Complete information. A game is one of complete information if each player knows the rules of play and the preferences or payoffs of every player for all possible outcomes.

Conflict game. A conflict game is a game in which there is not a mutually best outcome; a no-conflict game is one in which there is such an outcome.

Conflict situation. In a three-member voting body, a conflict situation occurs when all three members have different first preferences.

Constant-sum (zero-sum) game. A constant-sum (zero-sum) game is a game in which the payoffs to the players at every outcome sum to some constant (zero); if the game has two players, what one player gains the other player loses.

Contingency. A contingency is the set of strategy choices made by players other than the one in question.

Cooperative game. A cooperative game, in which players can make a binding and enforceable agreement, concerns how the surplus generated by the agreement might be reasonably divided among the players.

Critical defection. A critical defection is a defection that transforms a vulnerable winning coalition into a losing coalition.

Cyclical majorities. Cyclical majorities occur when majorities of voters prefer alternative x to y, y to z, and z to x, indicating the lack of a transitive ordering; such majorities exist when there is a paradox of voting.

Deception strategy. In a game of incomplete information, a deception strategy is a player's false announcement of a preference to induce the other players to choose strategies favorable to the deceiver.

Decision rule. A decision rule specifies the subsets of actors (e.g., a simple majority in a voting body) that can take collective action that is binding on all the actors.

Distribution-free strategy. A distribution-free strategy is a strategy whose dominance in a game of incomplete information does not depend on knowledge of another player's "type."

Dominant strategy. A dominant strategy is a strategy that leads to outcomes at least as good as those of any other strategy in all possible contingencies, and a better outcome in at least one contingency. A strictly dominant strategy is a dominant strategy that leads to a better outcome in every contingency.

Dominated strategy. A dominated strategy is a strategy that leads to outcomes no better than those of any other strategy in all possible contingencies, and a strictly worse outcome in at least one contingency.

Effective power. Power is effective when possessing it induces a better outcome for a player in a game than when an opponent possesses it.

Equilibrium. See *Nash equilibrium; Nonmyopic equilibrium; Sequential equilibrium.*

Expected payoff. An expected payoff is the sum of the payoffs a player receives from each outcome, multiplied by its probability of occurrence, for all possible outcomes that may arise.

Ex-post efficiency. A bargaining procedure is ex-post efficient if, whenever the bargainers' reservation prices overlap, an agreement is implemented.

Extensive form. A game in extensive form is represented by a game tree, wherein players make sequential choices.

External costs. External costs are the costs that one bears as a result of the actions of others; they are sometimes referred to as a public bad.

Final outcome. In a sequential game, a final outcome is the outcome induced by rational moves and countermoves (if any) from the initial outcome, according to the theory of moves.

Forward induction. In an extensive-form game, forward induction involves using prior choices to signal future choices.

Fractional critical defection. A fractional critical defection is a critical defection diminished by the number of other coalition members who are critical.

Game. A game is the totality of rules of play that describe a strategic situation.

Game of partial conflict. A game of partial conflict is a variable-sum game in which the players' preferences are not diametrically opposed.

Game theory. Game theory is a mathematical theory of rational strategy selection used to analyze optimal choices in interdependent decision situations; the outcome depends on the choices of two or more actors or players, and each player has preferences for all possible outcomes.

Game of total conflict. A game of total conflict is a constant-sum game in which the best outcome for one player is worst for the other, the next- best outcome for one player is next-worst for the other, and so on.

Game tree. A game tree is a symbolic tree, based on the rules of play of a game, in which the vertices or nodes of the tree represent choice points or moves, and the branches represent alternative courses of action that can be selected by the players.

Governing coalition. Under coalition voting, a governing coalition is a minimal majority coalition with the greatest coalition vote.

Grand coalition. A grand coalition is the coalition of all the players in a game.

Incentive compatibility. A bargaining procedure is incentive compatible when the optimal response of one player to the other player's truthfulness is also to be truthful.

Incomplete information. Information is incomplete when one player does not know the preferences of another player or knows only the probability distribution that describes the player's type (or of some third party whose choices affect the outcome of a game).

Individual rationality. A bargaining procedure is (a priori) individually rational if a player never suffers a loss by being truthful; it is (interim) individually rational if a player may lose in any single trial but does not suffer an expected loss (over a sufficiently long series of trials) .

Initial outcome. In a sequential game, an initial outcome is the outcome that rational players choose when they make their initial strategy choices according to the theory of moves.

Just agreement. A just agreement is an agreement to which rational players would voluntarily subscribe.

Majority coalition. A majority coalition is a coalition with a sufficient number of members to make its decisions binding, as specified by some decision rule.

Maximin strategy. A maximin strategy is a strategy that maximizes the minimum payoff that a player can receive.

Minimal majority coalition. A minimal majority coalition is a majority coalition that contains no superfluous members.

Minimal winning coalition. A minimal winning coalition is a winning coalition that is smallest in size.

Minimax strategy. A minimax strategy is a strategy that minimizes the maximum payoff that an opponent can receive.

Mixed strategy. A mixed strategy is a strategy that involves a random selection from two or more pure strategies, according to a particular probability distribution.

Move. In a game in extensive form, a move is a choice point or node of the game tree, where one from a given set of alternative courses of action is selected by a player; in a two-person sequential game in normal form, it is a player's switch from one strategy to another in the matrix.

Moving power. In a two-person sequential game, moving power is the ability to continue moving when the other player must eventually stop.

Nash equilibrium. A Nash equilibrium is an outcome from which no player would have an incentive to depart unilaterally because the departure would immediately lead to a worse, or at least not a better, outcome.

Node. A node is a point or vertex in a game tree at which a player (or chance) makes a choice.

Noncooperative game. A noncooperative game is a game in which the players cannot make binding or enforceable agreements.

Nonmyopic calculation. In a two-person sequential game, nonmyopic calculation assumes players fully anticipate how each will respond to the other both in selecting their strategies initially and making subsequent moves and countermoves.

Nonmyopic equilibrium. In a two-person sequential game, a nonmyopic equilibrium is an outcome from which neither player, anticipating all possible rational moves and countermoves from the initial outcome, would have an incentive to depart unilaterally because the departure would eventually lead to a worse, or at least not better, outcome.

Normal (strategic) form. A game is represented in normal (strategic) form when it is described by an outcome or payoff matrix in which the players choose their strategies independently. The possible outcomes of the game correspond to the cells of the matrix.

Ordinal game. An ordinal game is a game in which each player can rank the outcomes but not necessarily assign payoffs or utilities to them.

Outcome (payoff) matrix. An outcome (payoff) matrix is a rectangular array, or matrix, whose entries indicate the outcomes or payoffs to each player resulting from each of their possible strategy choices.

Paradox of the chair's position. The paradox of the chair's position occurs when being chair (with a tie-breaking vote) hurts rather than helps the chair if voting is sophisticated.

Paradox of vote trading. A paradox of vote trading occurs when all voters benefit from making individually rational vote trades but, because of external costs incurrred from the trades of others, are worse off after trading.

Paradox of voting. A paradox of voting occurs when no alternative can defeat all others in a series of pairwise contests if voting is sincere.

Pareto-inferior (superior) outcome. An outcome is Pareto-inferior if there exists another outcome that is better for some players and not worse for any other player. If there is no other outcome with this property, then the outcome in question is Pareto-superior.

Payoff. A payoff is a measure of the value that a player attaches to an outcome in a game; usually payoffs are taken to be cardinal utilities.

Perfect information. A game is one of perfect information if each player, at each stage of play, knows the strategy choices of every other player up to that point.

Player. See *Rational player.*

Plurality voting. Plurality voting is a voting procedure in which voters can vote for only one alternative, and the alternative with the most votes wins.

Preference. Preference is a player's ranking of outcomes from best to worst.

Public good (bad). A public good (bad) is a good that, when supplied to some members of the public, cannot be withheld from other members; it may benefit (public good) or not benefit (public bad) the members.

Pure strategy. A pure strategy is a single specific strategy.

Random variable. A random variable is an uncertain quantity that can be described by a probability distribution.

Rational choice. A rational choice is a choice that leads to a preferred outcome, based on a player's goals.

Rational outcome. See *Nash equilibrium; Nonmyopic equilibrium.*

Rational player. A rational player is a player who makes rational choices, in light of the presumed rational choices of other players in a game.

Rational termination. Rational termination is a constraint, assumed in the definition of staying power, that prohibits the player without such power from moving from the initial outcome if it leads to cycling back to this outcome in a sequential game.

Reservation price. A reservation price is the price (or other terms for a settlement) at which a bargainer would be indifferent between reaching or not reaching an agreement.

Revealed deception. In a game of incomplete information, revealed deception involves falsely announcing one strategy to be dominant but subsequently choosing another strategy, thereby revealing the deception.

Revelation principle. The revelation principle says that, for any bargaining procedure, there exists an equivalent procedure that makes truthful revelation a Nash equilibrium.

Rules of play. The rules of play of a game describe the choices of the players at each stage of play, and how the outcome depends on these choices.

Saddlepoint. In two-person constant-sum games, a saddlepoint is an outcome that the minimizing player can guarantee will not be greater than the value, and the maximizing player can guarantee will not be less than the value, by choosing their minimax/maximin pure strategies.

Salience. Salience is the difference in utility that it makes for a player to be in the majority (i.e., win) versus the minority (i.e., lose) on a roll-call vote if voting is sincere.

Security level. The security level of a player is the best outcome or payoff that the player can ensure, whatever strategies the other players choose.

Sequential equilibrium. A sequential equilibrium is a Nash equilibrium that is rational with respect to the beliefs of the players in a game of incomplete information.

Sequential game. A sequential game is one in which players can move and countermove, in accordance with the theory of moves, after their initial strategy choices.

Sincere voting. Sincere voting is voting directly in accordance with one's preferences.

Size principle. The size principle says that only minimal winning coalitions will form in certain kinds of games.

Sophisticated voting. Sophisticated voting is voting that involves the successive elimination of dominated strategies, given that other voters act likewise.

Superior outcome. A superior outcome is an outcome preferred by all players to every other outcome in a no-conflict game.

Staying power. In a two-person sequential game, staying power is the ability of a player to hold off making a strategy choice until the other player has made one.

Strategy. A strategy is a complete plan that specfies the exact course of action a player will follow whatever contingency arises.

Supergame. A supergame is a game that comprises infinite repeated play of a nonsequential game.

Symmetric game. A symmetric game is one that is strategically the same for all players. In a two-person, normal-form symmetric game with ordinal payoffs, the players' ranks of the outcomes along the main diagonal are the same, whereas their ranks of the off-diagonal outcomes are mirror images of each other.

Tacit deception. In a game of incomplete information, tacit deception involves a player's falsely announcing one strategy to be dominant and subsequently choosing this strategy, thereby not revealing the deception.

Theory of moves. The theory of moves describes optimal strategic calculations in normal-form games in which the players can move and countermove from an initial outcome in sequential play.

Threat power. In a two-person sequential game that is repeated, threat power is the ability of a player to threaten a mutually disadvantageous outcome in the single play of a game to deter untoward actions in the future play of this or other games.

Transitivity. Preferences are transitive if, whenever x is preferred to y and y is preferred to z, x is preferred to z; if this is not the case, preferences are intransitive, leading to cyclical majorities and a paradox of voting.

Trap. A trap is a game in which the players' apparently rational strategies result in a Pareto-inferior outcome, whereby they are all worse off than had they chosen other strategies.

Undominated strategy. An undominated strategy is a strategy that is not dominated by any other strategy.

Utility. Utility is the numerical value, indicating degree of preference, that a player attaches to an outcome.

Value. In two-person constant-sum games, the value is the amount that the players can ensure for themselves by choosing minimax/maximin strategies.

Value-restrictedness. The preferences of three actors for three alternatives are value-restricted if the first, second, and third choices of the actors are all different.

Variable-sum game. A variable-sum game is a game in which the sum of the payoffs to the players at different outcomes is not constant but variable, so the players may gain or lose simultaneously at different outcomes.

Vote trade. A vote trade is an exchange between two voters in which each gives support to the other in return for receiving support on a more salient roll call.

Vulnerable coalition. A vulnerable coalition is a winning coalition from which the defection of at least one member would cause it to be losing.

Wise arbitration. Wise arbitration involves the setup of a game by an arbitrator to distinguish truthful from untruthful disputants, based on the disputants' choices in the game.

Zero-sum game. See *Constant-sum (zero-sum) game.*

Bibliography

Abel, Elie. 1966. *The Missile Crisis*. Philadelphia: Lippincott.

Achen, Christopher H., and Duncan Snidal. 1989. "Rational Deterrence Theory and Comparative Case Studies." *World Politics* 41, no. 2 (January): 143–69.

Allan, Pierre. 1982. *Crisis Bargaining and the Arms Race: A Theoretical Model*. Cambridge, MA: Ballinger.

Allison, Graham T. 1971. *Essence of Decision: Explaining the Cuban Missile Crisis*. Boston: Little, Brown.

American Political Science Association. 1950. *Toward a Responsible Party System*. New York: Rinehart.

Ascherson, Neal. 1982. *The Polish August: The Self-Limiting Revolution*. New York: Viking.

Ashenfelter, Orley, and David E. Bloom. 1984. "Models of Arbitrator Behavior: Theory and Evidence." *American Economic Review* 74, no. 1 (March): 111–24.

Aumann, Robert J. 1988. "Preliminary Notes on Irrationality in Game Theory." Department of Mathematics, Hebrew University, Jerusalem, Israel, preprint.

Aumann, Robert J., and Mordecai Kurz. 1977. "Power and Taxes." *Econometrica* 45, no. 5 (July): 522–39.

Austen-Smith, David, and Jeffrey Banks. 1988. "Elections, Coalitions, and Legislative Outcomes." *American Political Science Review* 82, no. 2 (June): 406–22.

Avenhaus, Rudolf, Steven J. Brams, John Fichtner, and D. Marc Kilgour. 1989. "The Probability of Nuclear War." *Journal of Peace Research* 26, no. 1 (February): 91–99.

Axelrod, Robert. 1984. *The Evolution of Cooperation*. New York: Basic.

Axelrod, Robert, and Douglas Dion. 1988. "The Further Evolution of Cooperation." *Science* 242 (9 December): 1385–90.

Baldwin, David A. 1989. *Paradoxes of Power*. New York: Basil Blackwell.

Balinski, M. L., and H. P. Young. 1978. "Stability, Coalitions and Schisms in Proportional Representation Sytems." *American Political Science Review* 72, no. 3 (September): 848–58.

Balinski, Michel L., and H. Peyton Young. 1982. *Fair Representation: Meeting the Ideal of One Man, One Vote*. New Haven, CT: Yale University Press.

273

Banzhaf, John F., III. 1965. "Weighted Voting Doesn't Work: A Mathematical Analysis." *Rutgers Law Review* 19, no. 2 (Winter): 317–43.

Bara, Judith (1987). "Israel 1949–1981." In Budge, Robertson, and Hearl (1987), 111–33.

Baron, David P., and John A. Ferejohn. 1989. "Bargaining in Legislatures." *American Political Science Review* 53, no. 4 (December): 1181–1206.

Barston, R.P. 1988. *Modern Diplomacy*. London: Longman.

Bartels, Larry M. 1988. *Presidential Primaries and the Dynamics of Public Choice*. Princeton, NJ: Princeton University Press.

Bazerman, Max H., and Henry S. Farber. 1985. "Arbitrator Decision Making: When Are Final Offers Important?" *Industrial and Labor Relations* 39, no. 1 (October): 76–89.

Bernholtz, Peter. 1973. "Logrolling, Arrow Paradox, and Cyclical Majorities." *Public Choice* 15 (Summer): 87–95.

———. 1974. "Logrolling, Arrow-Paradox and Decision Rules—A Generalization." *Kyklos* 77 (Fasc. 1): 41–62.

———. 1975. "Logrolling and the Paradox of Voting: Are They Really Logically Equivalent?" *American Political Science Review* 69, no.3 (September): 961–62.

Bialer, Seweryn. 1981. "Poland and the Soviet Imperium." *Foreign Affairs* 59, no. 3 (Fall): 522–39.

Binmore, Ken. 1990. *Essays on the Foundations of Game Theory*. Oxford, UK: Basil Blackwell.

Binmore, Ken, and Partha Dasgupta, eds. 1987. *The Economics of Bargaining*. Oxford, UK: Basil Blackwell.

Blechman, Barry M., and Douglas M. Hart. 1982. "The Political Utility of Nuclear Weapons: The 1973 Middle East Crisis." *International Security* 7, no. 1 (Summer): 132–56.

Blechman, Barry M., and Stephen S. Kaplan. 1978. *Force without War: U.S. Armed Forces as a Political Instrument*. Washington, DC: Brookings.

Blight, James G., and David A. Welch. 1989. *On the Brink: Americans and Soviets Reexamine the Cuban Missile Crisis*. New York: Hill and Wang.

Bok, Sissela. 1978. *Lying: Moral Choice in Public and Private Life*. New York: Pantheon.

Brams, Steven J. 1975a. *Game Theory and Politics*. New York: Free Press.

———. 1975b. "Newcomb's Problem and Prisoners' Dilemma." *Journal of Conflict Resolution* 19, no. 4 (December): 596–612.

———. 1976. *Paradoxes in Politics: An Introduction to the Nonobvious in Political Science*. New York: Free Press.

———. 1977. "Deception in 2 × 2 Games." *Journal of Peace Science* 2 (Spring): 171–203.

———. 1978. *The Presidential Election Game*. New Haven, CT: Yale University Press.

———. 1980. *Biblical Games: A Strategic Analysis of Stories in the Old Testament*. Cambridge, MA: MIT Press.

———. 1982. "Omniscience and Omnipotence: How They May Help—or Hurt—in a Game." *Inquiry* 25, no. 2 (June): 217–31.

———. 1983. *Superior Beings: If They Exist, How Would We Know? Game-Theoretic Implications of Omniscience, Omnipotence, Immortality, and Incomprehensibility.* New York: Springer-Verlag.

————. 1985a. *Rational Politics: Decisions, Games, and Strategy.* Washington, DC: CQ Press. Reprinted by Academic Press (1989).

————. 1985b. *Superpower Games: Applying Game Theory to Superpower Conflict.* New Haven, CT: Yale University Press.

————. 1986. "New, Improved Final-Offer Arbitration." *New York Times,* August 9, p. 22.

————. 1989. "Are the Two Houses of Congress Really Co-Equal?" In Bernard Grofman and Donald Wittman eds., *The Federalist Papers and the New Institutionalism.* New York: Agathon, pp. 125–14l.

————. 1990. "Practical Bargaining Procedures and Their Game-Theoretic Foundations." *Information and Decision Technologies,* forthcoming.

Brams, Steven J., Paul J. Affuso, and D. Marc Kilgour. 1989. "Presidential Power: A Game-Theoretic Analysis." In Paul Brace, Christine B. Harrington, and Gary King, eds., *The Presidency in American Politics.* New York: New York University Press, pp. 55–74.

Brams, Steven J., Dan S. Felsenthal, and Zeev Maoz 1986. "New Chairman Paradoxes." In Andreas Diekmann and Peter Mitter, eds., *Paradoxical Effects of Social Behavior: Essays in Honor of Anatol Rapoport.* Heidelberg, FRG: Physica-Verlag, pp. 243–56.

————. 1988. "Chairman Paradoxes under Approval Voting." In Gerald Eberlein and Hal Berghel eds., *Theory and Decision: Essays in Honor of Werner Leinfellner.* Dordrecht, Holland: D. Reidel pp. 223–33.

Brams, Steven J., and Peter C. Fishburn. 1978. "Approval Voting." *American Political Science Review* 72, no. 3 (September): 831–47.

————. 1983. *Approval Voting.* Cambridge, MA: Birkhäuser Boston.

————. 1990. "Coalition Voting." Preprint.

Brams, Steven J., Peter C. Fishburn, and Samuel Merrill, III. 1988. "The Responsiveness of Approval Voting: Comments on Saari and Van Newenhizen" and "Rejoinder." *Public Choice* 59 (November): 121–31, 149.

Brams, Steven J., and José E. Garriga-Picó. 1975. "Bandwagons in Coalition Formation: The 2/3's Rule." *American Behavioral Scientist* 18, no. 4 (March/April): 472–96. Reprinted in Hinckley (1976), pp. 34–58.

Brams, Steven J., and Marek P. Hessel. 1982. "Absorbing Outcomes in 2 × 2 Games." *Behavioral Science* 27, no. 4 (October): 393–401.

————. 1983. "Staying Power in 2 × 2 Games." *Theory and Decision* 15, no. 3 (September): 279–302.

————. 1984. "Threat Power in Sequential Games." *International Studies Quarterly* 28, no. 1 (March): 15–36.

Brams, Steven J., and D. Marc Kilgour. 1988. *Game Theory and National Security.* New York: Basil Blackwell.

————. 1989. "Bargaining Procedures That Induce Honesty." Preprint.

Brams, Steven J., D. Marc Kilgour, and Shlomo Weber. 1989. "Sequential Arbitration Procedures." Preprint.

Brams, Steven J., D. Marc Kilgour, and Samuel Merrill, III. 1990. "Arbitration Procedures." Preprint. To appear in Young (1991).

Brams, Steven J., and Samuel Merrill, III. 1983. "Equilibrium Strategies for Final-Offer Arbitration: There Is No Median Convergence." *Management Science* 29, no. 8 (August): 927–41.

———. 1986. "Binding Versus Final-Offer Arbitration: A Combination Is Best." *Management Science* 32, no. 10 (October): 1346–55.

———. 1989. "Final-Offer Arbitration with a Bonus." Preprint.

Brams, Steven J., and Douglas Muzzio. 1977a. "Game Theory and the White House Tapes Case." *Trial* 13, no. 5 (May): 48–53.

———. 1977b. "Unanimity in the Supreme Court: A Game-Theoretic Explanation of the Decision in the White House Tapes Case." *Public Choice* 32 (Winter): 67–83.

Brams, Steven J., and Donald Wittman. 1981. "Nonmyopic Equilibria in 2 × 2 Games." *Conflict Management and Peace Science* 6, no. 1 (Fall): 39–62.

Brams, Steven J., and Frank C. Zagare. 1977. "Deception in Simple Voting Games." *Social Science Research* 6 (September): 257–72.

———. 1981. "Double Deception: Two against One in Three-Person Games." *Theory and Decision* 13 (March): 81–90.

Browne, Eric C., and John Dreijmanis, eds. 1982. *Government Coalitions in Western Democracies*. New York: Longman.

Brune, Lester H. 1985. *The Missile Crisis of October 1962: A Review of Issues and References*. Claremont, CA: Regina.

Buchanan, James M., and Gordon Tullock. 1962. *The Calculus of Consent*. Ann Arbor, MI: University of Michigan Press.

Budge, Ian, David Robertson, and Derek Hearl, eds. 1987. *Ideology, Strategy and Party Choice: Spatial Analyses of Post-War Election Programmes in 19 Democracies*. Cambridge, UK: Cambridge University Press.

Burke, John P., and Fred I. Greenstein. 1989. *How Presidents Test Reality: Decisions on Vietnam, 1954 and 1965*. New York: Russell Sage Foundation.

Carrington, Tim. 1988. "Pentagon Halts Multiple Submissions of 'Best and Final Offers' by Contractors." *Wall Street Journal*, July 26, p. 62.

Chamberlin, John R. 1989. "Assessing the Power of the Supreme Court." In Bernard Grofman and Donald Wittman, eds., *The Federalist Papers and the New Institutionalism*. New York: Agathon, pp. 142–49.

Chass, Murray. 1988. "Arbitration: In Settlements, Size Counts." *New York Times*, February 21, p. S7.

———. 1990. "Players Big Winners as Arbitration Ends." *New York Times*, February 22, p. B14.

Chatterjee, Kalyan. 1981. "Comparison of Arbitration Procedures: Models with Complete and Incomplete Information." *IEEE Transactions: Systems, Man, Cybernetics*, SMC-11 (February): 101–9.

———. 1985. "Disagreement in Bargaining: Models with Incomplete Information." In

Alvin E. Roth, ed., *Game Theoretic Models of Bargaining*. New York: Cambridge University Press, pp. 9–26.

Chatterjee, Kalyan, John W. Pratt, and Richard J. Zeckhauser. 1978. "Paying the Expected Externality for a Price Quote Achieves Bargaining Efficiency." *Economic Letters* 1: 311–13.

Chatterjee, Kalyan, and William Samuelson. 1983. "Bargaining under Incomplete Information." *Operations Research* 31, no. 5 (September–October): 835–51.

Chayes, Abram. 1974. *The Cuban Missile Crisis: International Crises and the Role of Law*. New York: Oxford University Press.

Cioffi-Revilla, Claudio. 1983. "A Probability Model of Credibility." *Journal of Conflict Resolution* 27, no. 1 (March): 73–108.

Clarke, Edward H. 1971. "Multipart Pricing of Public Goods." *Public Choice* 11 (Fall): 19–33.

Clarke, John H. 1923. "Judicial Power to Declare Legislation Unconstitutional." *American Bar Association Journal* 9, no. 11 (November): 689–92.

Coleman, James S. 1966. "The Possibility of a Social Welfare Function." *American Economic Review* 56, no. 5 (December): 1105–22.

———. 1967. "The Possibility of a Social Welfare Function: Reply." *American Economic Review* 57, no. 5 (December): 1311–17.

———. 1969. "Beyond Pareto Optimality." In Sidney Morgenbesser, Patrick Suppes, and Morton White, eds., *Philosophy, Science, and Method: Essays in Honor of Ernest Nagel*. New York: St. Martin's, pp. 419–39.

———. 1973. *The Mathematics of Collective Action*. Chicago: Aldine.

Crawford, Vincent P. 1982. "A Comment on Farber's Analysis of Final- Offer Arbitration." *Journal of Conflict Resolution* 26, no. 1 (March): 157–60.

Cronin, Barry. 1989. "The Umpire Strikes Back." *Northwestern Perspective* 2, no. 3 (Spring): 2–7.

Cross, John G., and Melvin J. Guyer. 1980. *Social Traps*. Ann Arbor, MI: University of Michigan Press.

Daniel, Donald C., and Katherine L. Herbig, eds. 1982. *Strategic Military Deception*. New York: Pergamon.

d'Aspremont, Claude, and Louis-André Gérard-Varet. 1979. "Incentives and Incomplete Information." *Journal of Public Economics* 11, no. 1: 25–45.

Dayan, Moshe. 1981. *Breakthrough: A Personal Account of the Egypt-Israel Peace Negotiations*. New York: Knopf.

Detzer, David. 1979. *The Brink: Story of the Cuban Missile Crisis*. New York: Crowell.

Dinerstein, Herbert. 1976. *The Making of the Cuban Missile Crisis, October 1962*. Baltimore, MD: Johns Hopkins University Press.

Divine, Robert A., ed. 1971. *The Cuban Missile Crisis*. Chicago: Quadrangle.

Downs, Anthony. 1957. *An Economic Theory of Democracy*. New York: Harper and Row.

Dubey, Pradeep, and Lloyd S. Shapley. 1979. "Mathematical Properties of the Banzhaf Power Index." *Mathematics of Operations Research* 4, no. 1 (February): 99–131.

Elster, Jon. 1989a. *The Cement of Society: A Study of Social Order.* Cambridge, UK: Cambridge University Press.

———. 1989b. *Solomonic Judgements: Studies in the Limitations of Rationality.* Cambridge, UK: Cambridge University Press.

Evans, Roland, and Robert Novak. 1974. "Mr. Nixon's Supreme Court Strategy." *Washington Post,* June 12, p. A29.

Farber, Henry S. 1980. "An Analysis of Final-Offer Arbitration." *Journal of Conflict Resolution* 24 (December): 683–705.

———. 1981. "Splitting-the-Difference in Interest Arbitration." *Industrial and Labor Relations Review* 35, no. 1 (October):70–77.

Farber, Henry S., and Max H. Bazerman. 1986. "The General Basis of Arbitrator Behavior: An Empirical Analysis of Conventional and Final-Offer Arbitration." *Econometrica* 54, no. 4 (November):1503–28.

Farquharson, Robin. 1969. *Theory of Voting.* New Haven, CT: Yale University Press.

The Federalist Papers (Alexander Hamilton, James Madison, and John Jay). (1787–88), 1961. Edited by Clinton Rossiter. New York: New American Library.

Fischer, Roger. 1981. "Playing the Wrong Game?" In Jeffrey Z. Rubin, ed., *Dynamics of Third Party Intervention: Kissinger in the Middle East.* New York: Praeger, pp. 95–121.

Fraser, Niall M., and Keith W. Hipel. 1982–83. "Dynamic Modeling of the Cuban Missile Crisis." *Conflict Management and Peace Science* 6, no. 2 (Spring): 1–18.

Freeman, Richard B. 1986. "Unionism Comes to the Public Sector." *Journal of Economic Literature* 24, no. 1: 41–86.

Friedman, James W. 1986. *Game Theory with Applications to Economics.* New York: Oxford University Press.

Garthoff, Raymond L. 1989. *Reflections on the Cuban Missile Crisis,* rev. ed. Washington, DC: Brookings.

George, Alexander L., et al. 1983. *Managing U.S.-Soviet Rivalry: Problems of Crisis Prevention.* Boulder, CO: Westview.

George, Alexander L., and Richard Smoke. 1974. *Deterrence in American Foreign Policy: Theory and Practice.* New York: Columbia University Press.

Gibbons, Robert. 1988. "Learning in Equilibrium Models of Arbitration." *American Economic Review* 78, no. 5 (December): 896–912.

Glassman, Jon D. 1975. *Arms for the Arabs: The Soviet Union and War in the Middle East.* Baltimore, MD: Johns Hopkins University Press.

Glazer, Jacob, and Ching-to Albert Ma. 1989. "Efficient Allocation of a 'Prize'—King Solomon's Dilemma." *Games and Economic Behavior* 1, no. 3 (September): 222–233.

Graves, Robert, and Raphael Patai. 1963. *Hebrew Myths: The Book of Genesis.* New York: McGraw-Hill.

Green, Jerry R., and Jean-Jacques Laffont. 1979. *Incentives in Public Decision Making.* Amsterdam: North-Holland.

Grofman, Bernard, and Donald Wittman, eds. 1989. *The Federalist Papers and the New Institutionalism.* New York: Agathon.

Groves, Theodore. 1973. "Incentives in Teams." *Econometrica* 41, no. 4 (July):617–31.

Groves, Theodore, and John O. Ledyard. 1987. "Incentive Compatibility Since 1972." In Theodore Groves, Roy Radner, and Stanely Reiter, eds., *Information, Incentives, and Economic Mechanisms: Essays in Honor of Leonid Hurwicz*. Minneapolis, MN: University of Minnesota Press, pp. 48–111.

Groves, Theodore, and Martin Loeb. 1975. "Incentives and Public Inputs." *Journal of Public Economics* 4, no. 3 (August): 211–26.

———. 1979. "Incentives in a Divisionalized Firm." *Management Science* 25, no. 3 (March): 221–30.

Haberman, Clyde. 1989. "End May Be Near for Italy's Leader." *New York Times*, March 5, p. 9.

Haefele, Edwin T. 1970. "Coalitions, Minority Representation, and Vote-Trading Probabilities." *Public Choice* 8 (Spring): 75–90.

Hagerty, Kathleen M., and William P. Rogerson. 1987. "Robust Trading Mechanisms." *Journal of Economic Theory* 42, no. 1 (June): 94–107.

Haldeman, H. R., with Joseph DiMona. 1978. *The Ends of Power*. New York: Times Books.

Halloran, Richard. 1988. "Honesty Called 'Impossible' in Pentagon Bidding System." *New York Times*, July 28, p. A20.

Hardin, Russell. 1971. "Collective Action as an Agreeable *n*-Prisoners' Dilemma." *Behavioral Science* 16, no. 5 (September): 472–81.

———. 1982. *Collective Action*. Baltimore, MD: Johns Hopkins University Press.

Hinckley, Barbara J., ed. 1976. *Coalitions and Time: Cross-Disciplinary Studies*. Beverly Hills, CA: Sage.

Ho, Y. C., and B. Tolwinski. 1982. "Credibility and Rationality of Players' Strategies in Multilevel Games." *Proceedings of the 21st Conference on Decision and Control* (December 8–10).

Holsti, Ole R., Richard A. Brody, and Robert C. North. 1964. "Measuring Affect and Action in International Reaction Models: Empirical Materials from the 1962 Cuban Missile Crisis." *Journal of Peace Research* 1:170–89.

Hopmann, P. Terrence, and Daniel Druckman. 1981. "Henry Kissinger as Strategist and Tactician in the Middle East Negotiations." In Jeffrey Z. Rubin, ed., *Dynamics of Third-Party Intervention: Kissinger in the Middle East*. New York: Praeger, pp. 122–35.

Howard, Nigel. 1971. *Paradoxes of Rationality: Theory of Metagames and Political Behavior*. Cambridge, MA: MIT Press.

Intriligator, Michael D., and Dagobert L. Brito. 1984. "Can Arms Races Lead to the Outbreak of War?" *Journal of Conflict Resolution* 28, no. 1 (March): 63–84.

———. 1986. "Mayer's Alternative to the I-B Model." *Journal of Conflict Resolution* 30, no. 1 (March): 29–31.

Jackson, Carlton. 1967. *Presidential Vetoes: 1792–1945*. Athens, GA: University of Georgia Press.

Jaworski, Leon. 1976. *The Right and the Power: The Prosecution of Watergate*. Pleasantville, NY: Reader's Digest Press.

Johnston, R. J. 1978. "On the Measurement of Power: Some Reactions to Laver." *Environment and Planning A* 10, no. 8: 907–14.

Kennedy, Robert F. (1969). *Thirteen Days: A Memoir of the Cuban Missile Crisis.* New York: Norton.

Kilgour, D. Marc. 1984. "Equilibria for Far-sighted Players." *Theory and Decision* 16, no. 2 (March): 135–57.

———. 1985. "Anticipation and Stability in Two-Person Non-Cooperative Games." In Urs Luterbacher and Michael D. Ward, eds., *Dynamic Models of Internatonal Conflict.* Boulder, CO: Lynne Rienner, pp. 26–51.

Kochan, Thomas A. 1981. "Step-by-Step in the Middle East from the Perspective of the Labor Mediation Process." In Jeffrey Z. Rubin, ed., *Dynamics of Third Party Intervention; Kissinger in the Middle East.* New York: Praeger, pp. 122–135.

Koehler, David H. 1975. "Vote Trading and the Voting Paradox: A Proof of Logical Equivalence," and "Rejoinder." *American Political Science Review* 69, no. 3 (September): 954–60, 967–69.

Kreps, David M. 1990. *A Course in Microeconomic Theory.* Princeton, NJ: Princeton University Press.

Kreps, David M., and Robert Wilson. 1982a. "Reputation and Imperfect Information." *Journal of Economic Theory* 27, no. 2 (August): 253–79.

———. 1982b. "Sequential Equilibria." *Econometrica* 50, no. 4 (July): 863–94.

Lambert, J. P. 1988. "Voting Games, Power Indices, and Presidential Elections." *UMAP Journal* 9, no. 3 (Fall): 213–267.

Laver, Michael. 1989. "Party Competition and Party System Change: The Interaction of Coalition Bargaining and Electoral Competition." *Journal of Theoretical Politics* 1, no. 3 (July): 301–24.

Ledyard, John O. 1978. "Incentive Compatibility and Incomplete Information." *Journal of Economic Theory* 18, no. 1 (June): 171–89.

———. 1979. "Dominant Strategy Mechanisms and Incomplete Information." In Jean-Jacques Laffont, ed., *Aggregation and Revelation of Preferences.* Amsterdam: North-Holland, pp. 309–20.

Leininger, Wolfgang. 1989. "Escalation and Cooperation in Conflict Situations: The Dollar Auction Revisited." *Journal of Conflict Resolution* 33, no. 2 (June): 231–54.

Leininger, W., P. B. Linhart, and R. Radner. 1989. "The Sealed-Bid Mechanism for Bargaining with Incomplete Information." *Journal of Economic Theory* 48, no. 1 (June): 63–106.

Lijphart, Arend. 1984. *Democracies: Patterns of Majoritarian and Consensus Government in Twenty-One Countries.* New Haven CT: Yale University Press.

Lucas, William F. 1983. "Measuring Power in Weighted Voting Systems." In Steven J. Brams, William F. Lucas, and Philip D. Straffin, Jr., eds., *Modules in Applied Mathematics: Political and Related Models,* vol. 2. New York: Springer-Verlag, pp. 183–238.

Luce, R. Duncan, and Howard Raiffa. 1957. *Games and Decisions: Introduction and Critical Survey.* New York: Wiley.

Lukas, J. Anthony. 1976. *Nightmare: The Underside of the Nixon Years.* New York: Viking.

McCall, Brian P. 1990. "Interest Arbitration and the Incentive to Bargain: A Principal-Agent Aproach." *Journal of Conflict Resolution* 34, no. 1 (March): 151–67.

McDonald, John. 1975. *The Game of Business.* New York: Doubleday.

Majeski, Stephen J. 1984. "Arms Races as Iterated Prisoners' Dilemmas." *Mathematical Social Sciences* 7, no. 3 (June): 253–66.

Maoz, Zeev. 1983. "Resolve, Capabilities, and the Outcomes of Interstate Disputes." *Journal of Conflict Resolution* 27, no. 2 (June): 195–229.

Mayer, Thomas F. 1986. "Arms Races and War Initiation: Some Alternatives to the Intriligator-Brito Model. *Journal of Conflict Resolution* 30, no. 1 (March): 3–28.

Milgrom, Paul, and John Roberts. 1982. "Predation, Reputation, and Entry Deterrence." *Journal of Economic Theory* 27, no. 2 (April): 280–312.

Miller, Nicholas R. 1975. "Logrolling and the Arrow Paradox: A Note." *Public Choice* 21 (Spring): 107–110.

Moulin, Hervé. 1981. "Deterrence and Cooperation: A Classification of Two-Person Games." *European Economic Review* 15, no. 2 (April): 179–93.

———. 1983. *The Strategy of Social Choice.* Amsterdam: North Holland.

———. 1986. *Game Theory for the Social Sciences,* 2d ed. New York: New York University Press.

Mueller, Dennis C. 1967. "The Possibility of a Social Welfare Function: Comment." *American Economic Review* 57, no. 5 (December): 1304–11.

Mueller, Dennis C., Geoffrey C. Philpotts, and Jaroslav Vanck. 1972. "The Social Gains from Exchanging Votes." *Public Choice* 13 (Fall): 55–79.

Muzzio, Douglas. 1982. *Watergate Games: Strategies, Choices, Outcomes.* New York: New York University Press.

Myerson, Roger B. 1979. "Incentive Compatibility and the Bargaining Problem." *Econometrica* 47, no. 1 (January): 61–73.

Myerson, Roger B., and Mark A. Satterthwaite. 1983. "Efficient Mechanisms for Bilateral Trading." *Journal of Economic Theory* 29, no. 2 (April): 265–81.

Nagel, Jack H. 1975. *The Descriptive Analysis of Power.* New Haven, CT: Yale University Press.

Nash, John. 1951. "Non-Cooperative Games." *Annals of Mathematics* 54: 286–95.

Neale, Margaret A., and Max H. Bazerman. 1987. "Progressive Approximation Final-Offer Arbitration: Matching the Goals of a Conflict Domain. *International Journal of Management* 4, no. 1 (March): 30–37.

Neustadt, Richard E. 1980. *Presidential Power: The Politics of Leadership from FDR to Carter.* New York: Wiley.

New York Times Staff. (1974). *The End of a Presidency.* New York: Bantam.

Nixon, Richard M. 1978. *RN: The Memoirs of Richard Nixon.* New York: Grosset and Dunlap.

Norton, Thomas J. 1923. "The Supreme Court's Five to Four Decisions." *American Bar Association Journal* 9, no. 7 (July): 417–420.

O'Neill, Barry. 1986. "International Escalation and the Dollar Auction." *Journal of Conflict Resolution* 30, no. 1 (March): 33–50.

Oppenheimer, Joe. 1975. "Some Political Implications of 'Vote Trading and the Voting Paradox: A Proof of Logical Equivalence': A Comment." *American Political Science Review* 69, no. 3 (September): 963–66.

Osborne, Martin J., and Ariel Rubinstein. 1990. *Bargaining and Markets.* San Diego, CA: Academic.

Pachter, Henry M. 1963. *Collision Course: The Cuban Missile Crisis and Coexistence.* New York: Praeger.

Park, R. E. 1967. "The Possibility of a Social Welfare Function: Comment." *American Economic Review* 57, no. 5 (December): 1301–5.

The Pentagon Papers: The Defense Department History of United States Decisiomaking on Vietnam 1971. Senator Gravel Edition, 4 vols. Boston: Beacon.

Pillen, Herbert. 1924. *Majority Rule in the Supreme Court.* Washington, DC: Georgetown University.

Pomper, Gerald et al. 1989. *The Election of 1988: Reports and Interpretations.* Chatham, NJ: Chatham House.

Powell, G. Bingham, Jr. 1989. "Constitutional Design and Citizen Electoral Control." *Journal of Theoretical Politics* 1, no. 2 (April): 107–30.

The Prophets. 1978. Philadelphia: Jewish Publication Society.

Pruitt, Dean G. 1981. "Kissinger as a Traditional Mediator with Power." In Jeffrey Z. Rubin, ed., *Dynamics of Third Party Intervention: Kissinger in the Middle East.* New York: Praeger, pp. 136–47.

Quandt, William B. 1977. *Decade of Decisions: American Policy Toward the Arab-Israeli Conflict, 1967–1976.* Berkeley, CA: University of California Press.

———. 1986. *Camp David: Peacemaking and Politics.* Washington, DC: Brookings.

Radner, Roy. 1986. "The Internal Economy of Large Firms." *Economics Journal* 96 (Supplement): 1–22.

Raiffa, Howard. 1982. *The Art and Science of Negotiation.* Cambridge, MA: Harvard University Press.

Randle, Robert F. 1969. *Geneva 1954: The Settlement of the Indochinese War.* Princeton, NJ: Princeton University Press.

Rapoport, Anatol, and Melvin Guyer. 1966. "A Taxonomy of 2 × 2 Games." *General Systems: Yearbook of the Society for General Systems Research* 11: 203–14.

Rasmusen, Eric. 1989. *Games and Information: An Introduction to Game Theory.* Oxford, UK: Basil Blackwell.

Rehmus, Charles M. 1979. "Interest Arbitration." In Public Employment Relations Services, ed., *Portrait of a Process: Collective Negotiations in Public Employment.* Ft. Washington, PA: Labor Relations Press, pp. 209–33.

Riding, Alan. 1989. "Italy Has New Government with Andreotti at Head." *New York Times,* July 23, p. 17.

Riker, William H. 1962. *The Theory of Political Coalitions.* New Haven, CT: Yale University Press.

———. 1986. *The Art of Political Manipulation.* New Haven, CT: Yale University Press.

Riker, William H., and Steven J. Brams. 1973. "The Paradox of Vote Trading." *American Political Science Review* 67, no. 4 (December): 1235–47.

Roberts, Steven V. 1986. "Key to Strategy: The Pocket Veto." *New York Times*, September 18, p. B10.

Roth, Alvin E., ed. 1985. *Game-Theoretic Models of Bargaining*. Cambridge, UK: Cambridge University Press.

Rubin, Jeffrey Z., ed. 1981. *Dynamics of Third Party Intervention: Kissinger in the Middle East*. New York: Praeger.

Rubinstein, Ariel. 1982. "Perfect Equilibrium in a Bargaining Model." *Econometrica* 50, no. 1 (July): 97–109.

Saari, Donald G., and Jill Van Newenhizen. 1988. "Is Approval Voting an 'Unmitigated Evil'? A Response to Brams, Fishburn, and Merrill." *Public Choice* 59, no. 2 (November): 133–47.

Samuelson, William F. 1989. "Final-Offer Arbitration under Incomplete Information." School of Management, Boston University, preprint.

Sarna, Nahum M. 1970. *Understanding Genesis: The Heritage of Biblical Israel*. New York: Schocken.

Satterthwaite, Mark A., and Steven R. Williams. 1989. "Bilateral Trade with the Sealed Bid Double Auction: Existence and Efficiency." *Journal of Economic Theory* 48, no. 1 (June): 107–33.

Schattschneider, E. E. 1935. *Politics, Pressures and the Tariff*. New York: Prentice-Hall.

Schelling, Thomas C. 1966. *Arms and Influence*. New Haven, CT: Yale University Press.

Scigliano, Robert. 1971. *The Supreme Court and the Presidency*. New York: Free Press.

Sebenius, James K. 1984. *Negotiating the Law of the Sea*. Cambridge, MA: Harvard University Press.

Seliktar, Ofira. 1982. "Israel: Fragile Coalitions in a New Nation." In Eric C. Browne and John Dreijmanis, eds., *Government Coalitions in Democracies*. New York: Longman, pp. 283–314.

Selten, Reinhard. 1975. "Reexamination of the Perfectness Concept for Equilibrium Points in Extensive Games." *International Journal of Game Theory* 4, no. 1: 25–55.

———. 1978. "The Chain-Store Paradox." *Theory and Decision* 9, no. 2 (April): 127–59.

Sen, Amartya K. 1966. "A Possibility Theorem on Majority Decisions." *Econometrica* 34, no. 2 (April): 491–99.

Sen, Amartya K., 1970. *Collective Choice and Social Welfare*. San Francisco: Holden–Day.

Shapley, L. S., and Martin Shubik. 1954. "A Method of Evaluating the Distribution of Power in a Committee System." *American Political Science Review* 48, no. 3 (September): 787–92.

Sheehan, Edward R. F. 1981. "How Kissinger Did It: Step by Step in the Middle East." In Jeffrey Z. Rubin, ed., *Dynamics of Third Party Intervention: Kissinger in the Middle East*. New York: Praeger, pp. 44–91.

Shubik, Martin. 1971. "The Dollar Auction Game: A Paradox in Noncooperative Behavior and Escalation." *Journal of Conflict Resolution* 15, no. 1 (March): 109–11.

————. 1982. *Game Theory in the Social Sciences: Concepts and Solutions.* Cambridge, MA: MIT Press.

————. 1984. *A Game-Theoretic Approach to Political Economy.* Cambridge, MA: MIT Press.

Snyder, Glenn H., and Paul Diesing. 1977. *Conflict among Nations: Bargaining, Decision Making, and Systems Structure in International Crises.* Princeton, NJ: Princeton University Press.

Sorensen, Theodore C. 1965. *Kennedy.* New York: Harper and Row.

Spitzer, Robert J. 1988. *The Presidential Veto: Touchstone of the American Presidency.* Albany, NY: State University of New York Press.

Stanley, Harold W., and Richard D. Niemi, eds. 1990. *Vital Statistics on American Politics.* Washington, DC: CQ Press.

Stephenson, D. Grier, Jr. 1975. "'The Mild Magistracy of the Law': U.S. v. Richard Nixon." *Intellect* 103, no. 2363 (February): 288–92.

Stern, James L., Charles M. Rehmus, J. Joseph Loewenberg, Hirshel Kasper, and Barbara D. Dennis. 1975. *Final-Offer Arbitration: The Effects on Public Safety Employee Bargaining.* Lexington, MA: D. C. Heath.

Stevens, Carl M. 1966. "Is Compulsory Arbitration Compatible with Bargaining?" *Industrial Relations* 5, no. 2 (February): 38–52.

Straffin, Philip D., Jr. 1983. "Power Indices in Politics." In Steven J. Brams, William F. Lucas, Philip D. Straffin, Jr., eds., *Modules in Applied Mathematics: Political and Related Models.* New York: Springer-Verlag, pp. 256–321.

Straus, Donald B. 1981. "Kissinger and the Management of Complexity: An Attempt that Failed." In Jeffrey Z. Rubin, ed., *Dynamics of Third Party Intervention: Kissinger in the Middle East.* New York: Praeger, pp. 253–270.

Szafar, Tadeusz. 1981. "Brinkmanship in Poland." *Problems of Communism* 30, no. 3 (May/June): 75–81.

Taylor, Michael. 1987. *The Possibility of Cooperation.* Cambridge, UK: Cambridge University Press.

The Torah: The Five Books of Moses. 1967. Philadelphia: Jewish Publication Society, 2d ed.

Tirole, Jean. 1988. *The Theory of Industrial Organization.* Cambridge, MA: MIT Press.

Totenberg, Nina. 1975. "Behind the Marble, Beneath the Robes." *New York Times Magazine,* March 16, pp. 15ff.

Touval, Saadia. 1982. *The Peace Brokers: Mediators in the Arab-Israeli Conflict, 1948–1979.* Princeton, NJ: Princeton University Press.

Trockel, Walter. 1986. "The Chain-Store Paradox Revisited." *Theory and Decision* 21, no. 2 (September): 163–79.

Tullock, Gordon. 1970. "A Simple Algebraic Logrolling Model." *American Economic Review* 60, no. 3 (June): 419–26.

U.S. Senate. 1978. *Presidential Vetoes, 1789–1976.* Washington, DC: U.S. Government Printing Office.

————. 1985. *Presidential Vetoes, 1977–1984.* Washington, DC: U.S. Government Printing Office.

Uslaner, Eric M., and J. Ronnie Davis. 1975. "The Paradox of Vote Trading: Effects of Decision Rules and Voting Strategies on Externalities." *American Political Science Review* 69, no. 3 (September): 929–42.

Vickrey, William. 1961. "Counterspeculation, Auctions, and Competitive Sealed Tenders." *Journal of Finance* 16, no. 1 (March): 8–37.

von Neumann, John, and Oskar Morgenstern. 1953. *Theory of Games and Economic Behavior*, 3d ed. Princeton, NJ: Princeton University Press.

Wagner, R. Harrison. 1982. "Deterrence and Bargaining." *Journal of Conflict Resolution* 36, no. 2 (June): 329–58.

Warren, Charles. 1924. *The Supreme Court in United States History*, vol. 1. Boston: Little, Brown.

Watt, Richard M. 1982. "Polish Possibilities." *New York Times Book Review*, April 25, pp. 11, 19.

Weintal, Edward, and Charles Bartlett. 1967. *Facing the Brink: An Intimate Study of Crisis Diplomacy*. New York: Scribner.

Wiesel, Elie. 1977. *Messengers of God: Biblical Portraits and Legends*. New York: Pocket.

Williams, Steven R. 1987. "Efficient Performance in Two Agent Bargaining." *Journal of Economic Theory* 41, no. 1 (February): 154–72.

Wilson, Robert. 1969. "An Axiomatic Model of Logrolling." *American Economic Review* 59, no. 3 (June): 331–41.

———. 1985. "Reputations in Games and Markets." In Alvin E. Roth, ed., *Game-Theoretic Models of Bargaining*. New York: Cambridge University Press, pp. 27–62.

———. 1989. "Deterrence in Oligopolistic Competition." In James L. Stern, Robert Axelrod, Robert Jervis, and Roy Radner, eds., *Perspectives on Deterrence*. New York: Oxford University Press, pp. 157–90.

Wilson, Woodrow. 1885. *Congressional Government: A Study in American Politics*. Boston: Houghton Mifflin.

Wittman, Donald. 1986. "Final-Offer Arbitration." *Management Science* 32, no. 12 (December): 1551–61.

Wohlstetter, Albert. 1959. "The Delicate Balance of Terror." *Foreign Affairs* 37, no. 2 (January): 209–34.

Woodward, Bob, and Carl Bernstein. 1976. *The Final Days*. New York: Simon and Schuster.

Young, Peyton, ed. 1991. *Negotiation Analysis*, forthcoming.

Zagare, Frank C. 1977. "A Game-Theoretic Analysis of the Vietnam Negotiations: Preferences and Strategies 1968–73." *Journal of Conflict Resolution* 21, no. 4 (December): 663–84.

———. 1979. "The Geneva Conference of 1954: A Case of Tacit Deception." *International Studies Quarterly* 23, no. 3 (September): 390–411.

———. 1981. "Nonmyopic Equilibria and the Middle East Crisis of 1967." *Conflict Management and Peace Science* 5, no. 2 (Spring): 139–62.

———. 1983. "A Game-Theoretic Evaluation of the Cease-Fire Alert Decision of 1973." *Journal of Peace Research* 20, no. 1 (April): 73–86.

———. 1984. "Limited-Move Equilibria in 2 × 2 Games." *Theory and Decision* 16, no. 1 (January): 1–19.

———. 1985. "Toward a Reformulation of the Theory of Mutual Deterrence." *International Studies Quarterly* 29, no. 2 (June): 155–69.

———. 1987. *The Dynamics of Deterrence*. Chicago: University of Chicago Press.

Zartman, I. William. 1981. "Explaining Disengagement." In Jeffrey Z. Rubin, ed., *Dynamics of Third Party Intervention: Kissinger in the Middle East*. New York: Praeger, pp. 148–67.

Index

Abel, 1, 3–9, 25–26
Abel, Elie, 136n, 273
Abraham, 2
Absorbing outcome, 132
Achen, Christopher H., 135, 273
Adam, 3–4
Affuso, Paul J., xviii, 261n, 275
Afghanistan, 165
Agreement
  binding or enforceable, xiv, 120, 151,
    157, 189, 207, 252, 260
  feasible, 30–31, 34, 36–39, 45, 49–51,
    53, 58
Ahasuerus, King, 2
Allan, Pierre, 165n, 273
Alert decision crisis (1973), 101, 116–19,
    122, 127–35, 185, 264
Algorithm, 148, 166n
Allies, 164, 254–60
Allison, Graham T., 108, 136n, 273
Alternative dispute resolution (ADR), xiii
Altruism, 57
American Political Science Association,
    191
Appeasement, 164
Appraiser, definition of, 31, 45
Approval voting; see Voting, approval
Arabs, 93–94; see also Middle East
Arbitration
  in Bible, 1–2, 17, 25–26, 64, 263
  definition of, xiv, 64–65
  interest versus grievance or rights, 65,
    70
  relationship to bargaining, 32–33, 53–
    54, 56–57, 64–65, 68–69, 71, 92, 98,
    100n
Arbitration procedures, xv–xvi, 64–100,
    263–64
  bias under, 65–66
  bidding competition under, 71

Bonus FOA, 76, 79–82, 84–86, 88, 93,
    97–99, 100n
Combined, 67, 81–86, 88, 97–99, 100n,
    263
Conventional, 65–70, 74–75, 78, 80–83,
    85, 88, 91, 96, 98–99
convergence under, xv, 57, 64–100, 263
empirical analysis of, 67, 69–71, 96, 263
exaggeration or posturing under, 65,
    68–71, 81, 264
experimentation with, 90, 99
feedback under, 86, 96
Final-Offer (FOA), xiv, 66–100, 263–64
implementation of, 75, 84, 97
internal bonus under, 75–79, 81–82
learning under, 93, 96
normative analysis of, 69–70, 91–93
practicality of, 96, 98–99, 264
sequential, xv–xvi, 38, 59, 67–71, 86–
    89, 98–99, 263–64
Two-Stage and Multistage, 67–71, 86–
    93, 95–96, 98–99, 263–64
Arbitrator, independence of, 65, 69, 84,
    95
Ascherson, Neal, 172–73
Ashenfelter, Orley, 77–78, 84, 273
Assad, Hafez, 94–95
Atomic bomb, 74; see also Nuclear war
Aumann, Robert J., 34, 141, 273
Austen-Smith, David, 215, 273
Austria, 260
Avenhaus, Rudolf, 107, 136n, 273
Axelrod, 166n–67n, 273, 285

Backward induction, 8–9, 23, 114–16,
    120, 122–29, 140, 158–64, 182, 266
Baldwin, David A., 165n–66n, 273
Balinski, Michel L., 218, 273
Bandwagon, 154
Banks, Jeffrey, 215, 273

Banzhaf, John F., III, 228, 274; *see also* Power indices, Banzhaf
Bara, Judith, 222, 274
Bargaining
  in Bible, 1–17, 25–26, 165n, 263
  definition of, xiv, 33
  honesty in, xiii, xv, 29–63, 65, 100n, 263, 265
  relationship to arbitration, 32–33, 53–54, 56–57, 64–65, 68–69, 71, 92, 98, 100n
  sequential, 106, 110, 116
Bargaining power, xvi, 230–32, 235–36, 239, 244, 258–60, 265; *see also* Bargaining strength; Power indices
Bargaining problem, xiii, 29–30, 266
Bargaining procedures, xv, 29–63, 263
  bias under, 55, 61
  Bonus, 31, 39–52, 58, 60, 66, 100n, 263
  Bonus Appraisal, 31, 45–48, 51–52, 59–60, 62n, 66, 100n, 263
  budget balancing, 50, 52, 55
  Chatterjee-Samuelson, 34–41, 50
  exaggeration or posturing under, xiii, 35–37, 61, 100n, 263, 265
  Expansive Appraisal, 32–33, 53–57, 60–61, 64, 66, 100n, 263
  heuristic value of, 33
  implementation of, 31–33, 36, 39, 48–51, 58
  Penalty, 31–32, 48–51, 55–56, 58–61, 62n–63n, 66, 100n, 263
  Penalty Appraisal, 32, 47, 51–56, 58, 60, 62n, 64, 66, 100n, 263
  posted-price, 52, 63n
  practicality of, 33, 61
  sequential, 38–40, 62n
  subsidies under, 30, 41, 47, 50, 53
  tax assessment under, 31, 33, 43–45, 48, 50, 60, 66, 263
  vulnerability to collusion under, 31, 41–45, 47–48, 57, 60
Bargaining strength (BS), xvi, 190, 217–21, 227, 265
Baron, David P., 226n, 274
Barston, R. P., 70, 274
Bartels, Larry M., 154, 274
Bartlett, Charles, 136n, 285
Baseball, major league, 68, 71, 74–75, 78–79, 88–92, 97, 99, 264
Bazerman, Max H., 65, 68–69, 84, 89–90, 274, 278, 281
Begin, Menachem, xv, 58–59, 101
Belgium, 225
Berghel, Hal 275
Bernholz, Peter, 226n, 274
Bernstein, Carl, 180, 285

Betrayal, 12–13, 15, 25, 27n; *see also* Double-cross
Bialer, Seweryn, 170, 274
Bible, xv–xvi, 1–28, 30, 102, 263
  barter in, 11–12, 14–15
  deception in, 23–26, 28n, 263
  jealousy in, 3–4, 7–9
  murder in, 4–8, 25–26, 27n
  prostitution in, 10, 18, 25–26
  rationality in, 7, 26, 27n
  sin in, 4, 6
  supernatural in, 1
  see also Arbitration, in Bible; Bargaining, in Bible
Binmore, Ken, 62n, 163, 274
Blackmail, 198
Blackmun, Harry, 176–87
Blechman, Barry M., 137n, 274
Blight, James G., 136n, 274
Bloom, David E., 78, 84, 273
Bluff, 144
Bok, Sissela, 28n, 274
Bonuses; *see* Arbitration procedures, Bonus FOA and internal bonuses under; Bargaining procedures, Bonus and Bonus Appraisal
Boss rule, 194
Brace, Paul, 275
Brams, Steven J., 3, 27n–28n, 37, 62n, 74, 77–78, 81, 84, 86, 89, 92, 99n, 112–13, 121, 132–33, 135, 136n, 138–39, 160, 165n–67n, 187n, 213–14, 216, 225, 226n, 228–29, 231, 244, 248, 252, 261n–262n, 273–76, 280, 282, 284
Breakdown outcome/strategy, 144–47, 173–74
Brezhnev, Leonid, 116, 130, 137n
Brinkmanship, 115–116, 147, 166n, 172
British Parliament/Cabinet, 194
Brito, Dagobert L., 136n, 279
Brody, Richard A., 116, 279
Browne, Eric C., 212, 276, 283
Brune, Lester H., 136n, 276
Buchanan, James M., 191, 276
Budge, Ian, 274
Burch, Dean, 178
Burger, Warren, 176–87
Burke, John P. 255, 257, 276
Business, xiii, xvi, 160, 167n
Buzhard, Fred, 180

Cain, 1, 3–9, 19, 25–26, 27n, 165n, 263
Calculus, 72, 76, 80
Cambodia, 255
Camp David agreement (1978), xv, 33, 57–61, 62n, 101, 263

Canaan, 9
Caribbean, 104, 112
Carrington, Tim, 71, 276
Carter, Jimmy, xv, 57–60, 263
Catholicism, 155
Cease-fire game; *see* Alert decision crisis (1973)
Central Intelligence Agency, 105
Certiorari before judgment, 176, 179
Chain-store paradox, 162
Chamberlin, John R., 261n, 276
Chass, Murray, 71, 74, 79, 276
Chatterjee, Kalyan, 34–35, 37–38, 40, 99n, 276–77
Chayes, Abram, 136n, 277
Chicken, 102–7, 109, 120–29, 140–42, 145, 147, 152–54, 160, 163–64, 166n
China, People's Republic of, 253–57, 259
Christian Democratic party (Italy), 223
Cioffi-Revilla, Claudio, 165n, 277
Civil War, U.S., 178
Clarke, Edward H., 40, 277
Clarke, John H., 187n, 277
Closed rule, 211, 224, 226n
Coalition
    governing, 190, 212, 215–22, 268
    grand, 216–17, 234, 268
    implicit, 252, 265
    majority, 190, 213–18, 225, 268
    minimal majority, 215–18, 235, 243, 268
    minimal winning, 216, 220, 235–36, 268
    vulnerable, 232–39, 242, 244, 264
Coalitions, xvi, 30, 206–9, 211–26, 251–52, 254–61, 264–66
Coalition voting, xvi, 190, 211–27, 251, 265–66
    bargaining among parties under, 190, 211, 214–15, 217–25, 265
    bargaining strength (BS) under, xvi, 190, 217–21, 227
    coalition vote under, 190, 213–22, 225
    incentives to coalition formation under, 190, 214–15, 218, 221–25, 265
    party vote under, 190, 213–18, 221–22, 225
Coleman, James S., 191
Collective good; *see* Public good (bad)
Collision course, 105–6, 142, 163
Collusion
    under Bonus Procedure, 31, 41–44, 47–48, 60
    instability of, 42–43
Colson, Charles, 176, 182
Combinations, number of, 237
Command and control, 139

Commitment, 154, 164, 177
Common knowledge, xvi, 33–34, 37, 44–45, 52, 69, 71, 76, 266; *see also* Information
Communication
    in Cuban missile crisis, 110–11, 164
    lack of under sophisticated voting, 227, 252
    problems of, xiii, 120
    in sequential-primary game, 160
    in vote trading, 193, 195
Conflict, violent, 170–71
Conflict situation, 247–48, 250, 267
Congress, U.S., xvi, 211, 230, 235–36, 243, 256–58, 265
Constitution, U.S. 228, 230, 236, 240, 243–44, 262n, 265
Constitutional crisis, 178–79
Contingency, 14, 267
Court of Appeals, U.S., 176–77
Cover-up, 77, 175–76, 186
Cox, Archibald, 177
Crawford, Vincent P., 99n, 277
Credibility, 127, 130, 165n, 181, 185–86; *see also* Threats, credible
Crises
    alternative views of, 102, 104, 130, 135
    initiation of, 173
    see also Alert decision crisis (1973); Cuban missile crisis (1962); Polish crisis (1980–81); Watergate crisis (1973–74)
Critical defection, 228–30, 232–44, 258–59, 261n, 267–68
Critical distance, 84
Critical vote, 193–95, 198–99, 209
Cronin, Barry, 74, 277
Cross, John G., 187n, 277
Cuban missile crisis (1962), xvi, 101, 104–16, 122, 124, 131–33, 135, 154, 160, 164, 166n, 168, 174, 182, 249, 264
Cyclical majorities, 245, 267; *see also* Intransitivity; Paradox of voting; Preferences, cyclical

Daniel, David C., 136n, 277
Dasgupta, Partha, 62n, 274
d'Aspremont, Claude, 44, 62n, 277
David, 18
Davis, J. Ronnie, 226n, 284
Dayan, Moshe, 57, 94, 277
Dean, John ,176
Deception, xiii, xvi, xviii
    under bargaining procedures, 45, 61
    in Bible, 23–26, 28n, 263
    in Geneva conference (1954), 256–60, 265
    revealed, 250–51, 259–60, 270

strategy, 110–13, 135, 249, 253, 260, 267
tacit, 228, 249–51, 258–60, 270
in voting games, 228, 249–53, 256, 259, 262n
see also Collusion; Information, incomplete
Decision rule, 233, 236, 262n, 265, 267
Deduction, xvii, 265
"Definitive decision" (of Supreme Court), xvi, 168, 177–78, 184
"Delicate balance of terror," 116, 164
Dennis, Barbara D., 284
Détente, 132, 134
Deterrence, 74, 107, 113, 134, 136n, 139, 141–54, 159–64, 165n–66n, 171–75, 264
nuclear, 127, 164
Detzer, David, 136n, 277
Diekmann, Andreas, 275
Dienbeinphu, 253–54, 257
Diesing, Paul, 136n, 283
DiMona, Joseph, 188n, 279
Dinerstein, Herbert, 136n, 277
Dion, Douglas, 166n, 273
"Dirty tricks" (in Watergate crisis [1973–74]), 175
Discount factor, 49
Dishonor, 12, 108–9
Divine, Robert A., 111, 136n, 277
Dong, Pham Van, 254
Double-cross, 12, 15, 26, 104, 120, 203; see also Betrayal
Downs, Anthony, 224, 277
Dreijmanis, John, 212, 276, 283
Druckman, Daniel, 94–95, 279
Dubey, Pradeep, 229, 277
Dulles, John Foster, 256–58

Eberlein, Gerald, 275
Economics, xiii, 29, 31
Eden, 3
Efficiency; see Ex-post efficiency
Egypt, 33, 57–59, 68, 93–95, 101, 116–18, 130, 137n
Eisenhower, Dwight D., 256–57
Elections
ambiguous statements in, 224
negative advertising in, 156
in Vietnam, 254–55, 257, 259
see also Coalition voting; Presidential primaries; Voting
Elster, Jon, 28n, 62n, 277
England, 194, 253, 256–58
Entrepreneurs, 57
Equilibrium
Bayesian Nash, 35

collusion, 42–43, 48
Nash, definition of, 34, 269
nonmyopic, 101–2, 120–30, 132, 135, 136n–37n, 138–39, 141–43, 149–54, 163, 171–73, 186, 269
sequential, 161–64, 270
subgame perfect, 28n, 137n
Erlichman, John 176
Esau, 2
Escalation, 165, 173, 249, 262n
Esther, 2
Ethics; see Morality; Normative analysis; Trade-offs
Evans, Roland, 178, 278
Eve, 3–4
Executive privilege, 176
Expected payoff, definition of, 267; see also Expected profit, definition of; Expected utility, definition of
Expected profit, definition of, 36
Expected utility, definition of, 16
Ex-post efficiency, 30, 32, 41, 47, 50, 52, 55, 267
External costs, 65, 191, 198–99, 207–10, 223, 267

Factorial, 237
Fair division, xiv, xvi, 220
Fairness, 65, 69, 78, 84–85, 87–88, 91, 98, 172
Faith, 1, 14, 16, 98
Fall-back position, 257
Farber, Henry S., 68, 84, 99n, 274, 278
Farquharson, Robin, 252, 262n, 278
Favorite sons, 154–63
Felsenthal, Dan S. 252, 275
Ferejohn, John A., 226n, 274
Fichtner, John, 136n, 273
Firefighters, union of, 56, 65
Fischer, Roger, 93, 278
Fishburn, Peter C., xviii, 213–14, 216, 226n, 262n, 275
Ford, Gerald, 186–87
Founding Fathers, 228, 244, 258
France, 253–57
Franklin, Benjamin, 127
Fraser, Niall M., 136n, 278
Freeman, Richard B., 71, 75, 278
Friedman, James W., 62n, 162–63, 167n, 278

Games
characteristic function of, xvii
of conflict, 149, 163, 267
constant-sum (zero-sum), 39, 51, 60, 68, 72, 76, 100n, 146, 235, 267
cooperative, xiv, xvi, 157, 252, 260, 267

definition of, xiv, 1, 11, 268
different formal representations of, xv
in extensive form, 7, 11, 163, 182, 267, 269
final outcome of, 122, 268
initial outcome of, 121, 268
interpersonal relationship in, 167n
lack of foresight in, 184, 205
matrix, 11–12, 20, 137n
no-conflict, 148, 267
noncooperative, xiv, 32–34, 62n, 184, 189, 253, 265, 269
in normal (strategic) form, 20, 115, 137n, 138, 269
n-person, xv–xvi, 155, 189, 223–25, 235
ordinal, 27n, 102, 112, 127, 129, 132–33, 148, 163, 166n, 168, 269
of partial conflict, 103, 268
repeated, xvi, 43, 137n, 138–54, 158, 163, 165n–67n, 185, 262n, 264
rules of play of, 121, 227, 265, 268, 270
sequential, definition of, 121–22, 270
sequential-primary, xvi, 140–41, 154–67, 264
signaling in, xiv, 27n, 160, 165n, 185
symmetric/asymmetric, 103, 152, 271
theory of, xiv–xv, xvii–xviii, 1–2, 29, 101–2, 129–30, 135, 168, 184, 187, 246, 265, 268
of total conflict, 103, 146, 268
two-person, xv, 29, 68, 72, 140, 163, 165n
value of, 72
variable-sum, 51, 60, 103, 271
see also Information; Strategy
Game tree, 7–8, 11, 21–22, 113–116, 268
Garriga-Picó, José E., 166n, 275
Garthoff, Raymond L., 107, 278
Gaza, 59
Geneva conference (1954), xvi, 227–28, 252–60
George, Alexander L., 137n, 278
Gérard-Varet, Louis-André, 44, 62n, 277
Gibbons, Robert, 99n, 278
Glassman, Jon D., 130, 132, 278
Glazer, Jacob, 27n, 278
Goals, 19, 25, 105, 140, 165n, 193, 195–97
God, 1–13, 17, 25–26, 27n, 64, 165n, 263
guilt of, 6–7, 25
immortality of, 165n
mercy of, 5–7
power of, 6–7
Golan Heights, 94
Goldberg, Stephen B., 74
Gomorrah, 2
Good will, xiii, 57

Graves, Robert, 27n, 278
Great Depression, 210
Greece, 212, 219
Green, Jerry R., 62n, 278
Greenstein, Fred I., 255, 257, 276
Grofman, Bernard, 275–76
Groves, Theodore, 40, 44, 62n, 278–79
Guyer, Melvin, 149, 166n, 187n, 277, 282

Haberman, Clyde, 223, 279
Haefele, Edwin T., 191, 279
Hagerty, Kathleen M., 52, 279
Haldeman, H. R., 176, 188n, 279
Halloran, Richard, 71, 279
Haman, 2
Hamilton, Alexander, 228, 244, 278
Hardin, Russell, 206, 279
Harrington, Christine B., 275
Hart, Douglas M., 137n, 274
Hartley, David, 127
Hearl, Derek, 274
Herbig, Katherine L., 136n, 277
Hessel, Marek P., xviii, 113, 132–33, 138, 166n, 187n, 275
Hinckley, Barbara J., 275, 279
Hipel, Keith W., 136n, 278
Ho, Y. C., 165n, 279
Holsti, Ole R., 116, 279
"Honesty among thieves," 42; see also Collusion
Hopmann, P. Terrence, 94–95, 279
Hot line, 115, 134
House of Representatives, U.S., xvi, 178, 211, 228–30, 235, 244, 261n, 265
Howard, Nigel, 111, 279
Humphrey, Hubert, 166n

Ideology, 170, 222, 253
Impeachment, 178–80, 186
Incentive-compatibility, 30–31, 41, 268
Inchon landings, 256
Indeterminacy, 28n, 248
Indochina, 228, 252–56
Information
complete, 9, 62n, 157, 162, 182, 193, 235, 246, 266
imperfect, 235
incomplete, 32–34, 38, 46, 69, 110, 135, 136n, 160–62, 235, 249–50, 253, 257, 265, 268
perfect, 27n, 157, 159, 163, 235, 270
private, 39, 48, 99n
see also Common knowledge; Intelligence; Uncertainty
Intelligence, 134, 254
International relations, xv, 30, 59, 135, 164, 165n–66n, 260

International trade, 210
Intransitivity, 207–9, 271; *see also* Cyclical majorities; Paradox of voting; Preferences, cyclical
Intriligator, Michael D, 136n, 279
Irrationality, xiv, 4, 25, 59, 131, 137n, 141, 147, 185–86, 205; *see also* Rationality
Isaac, 2
Israel, 33, 57–58, 93–95, 116–18, 130–31, 134, 190, 212, 222, 225, 265
Israelites (in Bible), 1–2, 9–11, 13, 15, 25, 263
Italy, 190, 223, 225, 265

Jackson, Carlton, 244, 279
Jacob, 2
Jaworski, Leon, 175–77, 179, 184, 188n, 279
Jay, John, 278
Jefferson apportionment method, 218
Jericho, 1, 9–11, 13, 15
Jerusalem, 58
Jervis, Robert, 285
Jews, 212; *see also* Israelites (in Bible)
Job, 2
Johnson, Lyndon B., 134, 244, 258
Johnston, R. J., 230, 279; *see also* Power indices, Johnston
Jonah, 2
Jordan, 118
Joseph, 2
Joshua, 9, 11–13, 15–17, 27n
Just agreement, 14–15, 18, 25–26, 268

Kaplan, Stephen S., 137n, 274
Kasper, Hirshel, 284
Kefauver, Estes, 166n
Kennedy, John F., 106, 108, 110–11, 115, 155, 244
Kennedy, Robert F., 109, 136n, 279
Kilgour, D. Marc, xviii, 62n, 86, 89, 92, 99n, 136n–37n, 160, 165n–66n, 261n, 273, 275, 280
King, Gary, 275
Kissinger, Henry, xv–xvi, 30, 59, 68, 71, 93–96, 98, 101, 130, 134, 264
Knesset, 212, 222
Kochan, Thomas A., 93, 95, 280
Koehler, David H., 226n, 280
Korea, 256
Kreps, David M., 62n, 160–61, 280
Krushchev, Nikita, 106, 108, 110–11, 249
Kuron, Jacek, 171–72
Kurz, Mordecai, 141, 273

Laban, 2
Labor-management disputes, 30, 71, 75, 77–79, 97, 101
Labor party (Israel), 212, 222
Laffont, Jean-Jacques, 62n, 278, 280
Lambert, J. P., 229, 280
Laniel, Joseph, 253, 257
Laos, 255
Laver, Michael, 215, 280
Law, xiii, xvi, 25–26, 65
Leah, 2
Ledyard, John, 44, 62n, 278, 280
Legislatures; *see* Coalition voting; Vote trading
Leininger, Wolfgang, 37, 262n, 280
Lijphart, Arend, 223, 280
Likud party (Israel), 212, 222
Linhart, P. B., 37, 280
Litigation, xiii
Loeb, Martin, 44, 279
Loewenberg, J. Joseph, 284
Logrolling; *see* Vote trading
Loyalty, 12, 216
Lucas, William F., 229, 280, 284
Luce, R. Duncan, 225n, 262n, 280
Lukas, J. Anthony, 176, 178–79, 183, 280
Luterbacher, Urs, 280

Ma, Ching-to Albert, 27n, 278
McCall, Brian P., 99n, 280
McDonald, John, 225n, 280
McGovern, George, 175
Madison, James, 228, 278
Majeski, Stephen J., 166n, 280
Majority rule, 223, 225n–26n
Majority-rule principle, 179–81
Management science, 29
Maoz, Zeev, 165n, 252, 275, 281
Marbury v. Madison (1803), 181
Marshall, John, 181
Martial law, 174
Masada, 95
Mathematics, xv, xvii, 29, 62, 225, 232
Mayer, Thomas F., 136n, 281
"Med-arb," 93, 96, 98, 264
Mediation, xvi, 30, 71, 93–96, 98, 264
Merrill, Samuel, III, xviii, 74, 77–78, 81, 84, 92, 99n, 215, 275–76
Middle East, xv, 30, 57, 68, 93, 117, 130, 134, 264
Milgrom, Paul, 160, 281
Miller, Nicholas R., 226n, 281
Minh, Ho Chi, 254
"Minnesota Twins," 177
Misperceptions, xiii, 117; *see also* Perceptions
Mitchell, John, 176

Mitter, Peter, 275
Model
  definition of, xv
  formulation of, xvii–xviii
  testing of, xvii
Morality, 4–5, 7–9, 25–26, 27n, 195, 197,
  204; see also Normative analysis;
  Trade-offs
Morgenbesser, Sidney, 277
Morgenstern, Oskar, 73, 101, 284
Moscow, 115
Moses, 2, 9, 19
Moulin, Hervé, 62n, 138, 165n, 262n, 281
Mount Sinai, 2
Move (in game tree), 8, 269; see also The-
  ory of moves
Mueller, Dennis C., 191, 281
Multiparty systems, xvi; see also Coalition
  voting
Muzzio, Douglas, xviii, 136n–37n, 186,
  187n,–88n, 276, 281
Myerson, Roger B., 30, 37–38, 40–41, 44,
  50, 281

Nagel, Jack H., 262n, 281
Nash, John, 34, 281
National party convention, 154–55
National security, 160
National unity government (Israel), 212
Neale, Margaret A., 65, 69, 89–90, 281
Negotiation
  courses on, xiii
  definition of, xiv
  modeling of, xiii–xv, xvii–xviii
  relevance of game theory to, xv, xvii, 2,
  265
  role of theory in, xiii–xiv, 265
Neustadt, Richard E., 243, 281
Newcomb's problem, 27n
New Democracy party (Greece), 219
New Jersey, 78, 97
New York, 194
Niemi, Richard D., 243, 284
Nineveh, 2
Nixon, Richard M., xvi, 101, 116–17, 119,
  129–30, 132, 134–35, 137n, 168–69,
  175–88, 257, 264, 281
Nonmyopic calculation, 121, 264, 269; see
  also Equilibrium, nonmyopic
Normative analysis, xviii, 69–70, 91–93,
  190, 209–11, 214–15, 218, 221–25,
  264–65; see also Morality; Trade-offs
North, Robert C., 116, 279
Norton, Thomas J., 187n, 281
Novak, Robert, 178, 278
Nuclear Nonproliferation Treaty, 260

Nuclear war, 104, 106–8, 111, 115, 130,
  147, 164, 166n, 255
  probability of, 107, 115, 136n
  see also Threats, nuclear

Omniscience, 26n–27n, 32, 53, 59, 61, 264
O'Neill, Barry, 262n, 281
Oppenheimer, Joe, 226n, 281
Osborne, Martin J., 62n, 281
Outcome (payoff) matrix, definition of,
  11–12, 269

Pachter, Henry M., 136n, 282
Palestinian problem, 58
Panachage, 217
Paradox of chair's position, 227–28, 244–
  52, 259–61, 269
  in Geneva conference, 255–60
Paradox of vote trading; see Vote trading,
  paradox of
Paradox of voting, 208–9, 226n, 245, 248,
  250–52, 255–56, 269; see also
  Cyclical majorities; Intransitvity; Prefer-
  ences, cyclical
Pardon, presidential, 186
Pareto-inferiority, 103, 144–47, 152, 183,
  269
Pareto-superiority, 104, 143–44, 146–48,
  151–52, 209, 211, 224
Paris, 258
Park, R. E., 226n, 282
Parliament, selection of government in,
  190, 210–25
Patai, Raphael, 27n, 278
Payoff, 12, 39, 270; see also Expected pay-
  off, definition of; Preference; Utility
Pearl Harbor, 109
Pennsylvania, 194
Perceptions, 19, 117, 119, 130, 135, 137n,
  138–39, 169, 210, 246, 250; see also
  Crises, alternative views of; Mispercep-
  tions; Preferences, alternative repre-
  sentations of
Philpots, Geoffrey C., 191
Pillen, Herbert, 187n, 282
Player
  definition of, 11, 30, 270
  determination of in game, 9, 169, 176–
  77, 184
  stronger and quicker, 126, 128
  types of, 41, 161–62
Police, union of, 56, 65, 78
Polish crisis (1980–81), xvi, 154, 168–75,
  186–87, 264
  balance of power in, 169, 172–74, 186
Polish economy, 173–74, 186, 264
Polish parliament, 174, 186

Political parties, xvi, 154, 194, 210, 225, 227
Political science, xiii, xvi, 29, 135
Pomper, Gerald, 167n, 282
Pork-barrel legislation, 210–11
Powell, G. Bingham, Jr., 221, 282
Powell, Lewis, Jr., 178–79, 182
Power
    dependence on preferences, 227, 245–246, 252, 259, 261, 262n
    effectiveness of, 113, 133, 139–40, 143, 151–54, 163, 174–75, 186, 264, 267
    inefficacy of extra resources on, 227–28, 246–52, 259–60
    moving, 112–13, 132–33, 135, 140, 152, 163, 174–75, 269
    overlap of different kinds of, 153–54, 166n
    of parties in a parliament, xvi, 190, 217–21, 227
    staying, 112, 132, 133, 135, 140, 152–53, 163, 174–75, 271
    in U.S. federal system, 227–44, 258–59, 262n, 265
    threat, 112–13, 132–33, 135, 139–54, 160, 163, 165, 168, 172–75, 186, 271
    see also Bargaining power; Bargaining strength (BS); Power indices
Power indices, 262n
    Banzhaf, 228–35, 239–41, 245, 258, 261n
    empirical corroboration of, 229–31, 236, 242–44, 258
    Johnston, 230, 232–45, 258–60, 265
    Shapley-Shubik, 229, 258
Pratt, John W., 40, 277
Preemption, 126
Preference, 7, 270
    alternative representations of, 23, 27n, 102, 135, 187n–88n
    intensities of, 189
    transitive/intransitive, 207–9, 271
Preferences
    cyclical, 109, 133, 256
    deterioration of, 111
    strict, definition of, 27n
President, U.S., xvi, 175, 229–32, 235–44, 258–60, 261n–62n, 265
Presidential power; see Power indices; Power, in U.S. federal system
Presidential primaries, 154–55, 166n–67n
Preventive action (in Watergate crisis [1973–74]), 185
Prisoners' Dilemma, 27n, 102–4, 119–22, 127–29, 133–34, 136n, 142–43, 151–52, 158, 163, 166n–67n, 174–75, 183, 186–87, 192, 205, 207
    n-person, 189, 192, 205–7, 224, 264

Probability
    of being critical, 230, 233–34, 241
    of being in governing coalition, 219–20
Probability distribution, 33, 268
    continuous, 38, 43, 74, 82
    discrete, 37–38, 42–43, 74
    symmetric or unimodal, 74, 82–84, 88, 92, 97–98
Probit analysis, 78
Proportional representation, xvi, 190, 213, 264
Pruitt, Dean G., 95, 282
Psychology, xiii, 29
Public good (bad), 57, 62n, 189–90, 206, 226n, 264, 270
Public interest, 225
Public policy, 169

Quandt, William B., 59, 94, 282

Rabin, Yitzhak, 95
Rachel, 2
Radford, Arthur W., 257
Radner, Roy, 37, 62n, 278, 280, 282, 285
Rahab, 1, 9–17, 25–26, 27n, 263
Raiffa, Howard, 58, 77, 225n, 262n, 280, 282
Rakowski, Mieczyslaw, 171
Randall, Robert F., 257, 282
Random variable, 33, 41, 52, 56, 270
Rapaport, Anatol, 149, 166n, 282
Rashomon, 135
Rasmusen, Eric, 62n, 163, 282
Rational choice
    definition of, 9, 270
    lack of, 113, 184–87, 212
    one-sided versus two-sided, 124–25, 127
Rationality
    in bargaining, 32, 34, 44, 265
    in Bible, 7, 26, 27n
    of conflict, xiii–xiv
    individual, 32, 268
    interim individual, 44, 268
    a priori individual, 44
    of vote trading, 195, 197, 199, 202–9
    see also Irrationality
Rational outcome, definition of, 23
Rational player, definition of, 22
Rational termination, 133, 270
Reagan, Ronald, 243
Realpolitik, 132, 134
Rebekah, 2
Reciprocity, 43
Rehmus, Charles M., 67, 282, 284
Rehnquist, William, 176
Reiter, Stanley, 278
Reputation, 10, 165n, 185; see also Threats, and reputation

Reservation prices, definition of, 29, 270
Resolve, 112, 134, 165n, 186; *see also* Toughness
Retaliation, 139, 146, 164, 185, 204
Retribution, 6, 13, 164
Revelation principle, 40–41
Revenge, 4, 6, 9, 13, 15, 25
Riding, Alan, 223, 282
Riker, William H., xviii, 216, 220, 225n, 228, 235, 262n, 282
Risk, 164, 180, 264
Risk-aversity, 77, 81
Roberts, John, 160, 281
Roberts, Steven V., 243, 282
Robertson, David, 274
Rogerson, William P., 52, 279
Rossiter, Clinton, 278
Roth, Alvin E., 62n, 282, 285
Rubin, Jeffrey Z., 93–94, 278–80, 282–84
Rubinstein, Ariel, 62n, 281, 283

Saari, Donald G. 214, 283
Sadat, Anwar, xv, 58–59, 101, 117, 130
Saddlepoint, 73, 83, 270
St. Clair, James, 175–77, 183
Salience, 192–93, 195–203, 205–8, 226n, 270
Samuelson, William F., 34–35, 99n, 277, 283
Sanctions, 45, 57, 95, 206
Sarna, Nahum M., 26n, 283
Satan, 2
Satterthwaite, Mark A., 30, 37–38, 41, 44, 50, 281, 283
"Saturday Night Massacre" (in Watergate crisis [1973–74]), 117
Saudi Arabia, 93
Saul, 18
Schattschneider, E. E., 191, 210, 283
Schelling, Thomas C., 141, 146, 283
Scigliano, Robert, 178, 283
Sebenius, James K., 225n, 283
Security level, 112, 270
Seliktar, Ofira, 223, 283
Selten, Reinhard, 137n, 160, 162, 167n, 283
Sen, Amartya K., 262n, 283
Senate, U.S., xvi, 179, 186, 228–30, 233, 235, 244, 261n, 265, 284
Separation of powers, 178
Shapley, L. S., 229, 277, 283
Sheehan, Edward R. F., 94–96, 283
Show of force, 164
Shubik, Martin, 62n, 229, 262n, 283
Shuttle diplomacy, xv, 68, 71, 93, 98, 101, 264
Sinai, 57
Sirica, John, 176

Size principle, 220, 235, 270
Smoke, Richard, 137n, 278
Smoot-Hawley tariff, 191, 210
Snidal, Duncan, 135, 273
Snyder, Glenn H., 136n, 283
Socialism, 171
Socialist party (Greece), 219
Sociology, xiii
Sodom, 2
Solidarity, 168–74, 186–87, 264
Solomon, 1, 17–26, 27n, 110, 182, 263
Sorensen, Theodore, 115–16, 284
Soviet Union, 93, 101, 104–19, 129–34, 136n–37n, 165, 169, 172, 186, 253–57, 259
Sphere of influence, 112
Spitzer, Robert J., 244, 284
Spoiler, 154
Spoils, 220
Stability; *see* Equilibrium
Standing to sue, 176, 181
Stanley, Harold W., 243, 284
Stephenson, D. Grier, Jr., 178, 284
Stern, James L., 66, 74, 284–85
Stevens, Carl M., 66, 284
Stevenson, Adlai, 166n
Stopping rule, 122–23, 135
Straffin, Philip D., Jr., 136n, 229, 280, 284
Strategy
    "carrot-and-stick," 148, 165
    definition of, 11, 137n, 271
    distribution-free, 33, 41, 48, 267
    dominant, definition of, 14, 22, 42, 136n, 267
    dominated, definition of, 119, 267
    "junk," 147–48, 105
    maximin, 72, 268
    minimax, 73, 269
    mixed, 74, 269
    pure, 74, 136n, 270
    undominated, 246–47, 251, 271
Straus, Donald B., 93, 284
Suez Canal, 94
Supergame, 139, 271
Superior outcome, 14, 271
Suppes, Patrick, 277
Supreme Court, U.S., xvi, 168–69, 175–88, 236, 261n, 264
Switzerland, 260
Syria, 68, 93–95, 116–18
Szafar, Tadeusz, 173, 284

Taylor, Michael, 166n, 284
Ten Commandments, 25
Theory of moves, xvi, 101–2, 120–37, 166n, 226n, 264–65, 271
Third parties; *see* Appraiser, definition of;

Arbitration, definition of; Arbitration procedures; Arbitrator, independence of; Bargaining procedures, Bonus and Bonus Appraisal; Mediation
Threat behavior, 141
Threat outcome/strategy, 143–54, 163, 173–75, 185
Threats, xiv, 26, 42–43, 58, 68, 83, 95, 104, 130, 137n, 138–87, 227, 243, 255, 263–64
  compellent, 140, 146–53, 165, 168, 171, 173, 185–86, 264, 266
  costs of, 140, 154, 156, 165, 168, 264
  credible, 138–40, 144–46, 160, 162–64, 165n, 185–86
  deterrent, 140, 146–53, 165, 168, 171–73, 175, 185–86, 264
  empty, 144–45
  implementation of, 145, 147–49, 151–52, 170, 173–75, 186
  nuclear, 138–39, 147, 166n
  perverse effect of in Watergate crisis (1973–74), 175, 178, 183–87, 264
  in Polish crisis (1980–81), xvi, 154, 168–75, 186–87, 264
  rational, 144, 185–87, 264
  real, 144, 185
  and reputation, xvi, 127, 137n, 138–67, 185, 264
  veiled, 169, 186, 264
  vulnerability of outcomes to, 142–43, 163, 165, 168
  see also Power, threat
Timing, problem of, 137n, 154, 185
Tirole, Jean, 62n, 284
Tolwinski, B., 165n, 279
Totenberg, Nina, 176, 187n, 284
Toughness, 140, 161–62; see also Resolve
Toughness dilemma, 29
Touval, Saadia, 95, 284
Trade-offs, 30, 60–61, 68–70, 93
Transitivity, 208, 271
Trap, 169, 175, 181–87, 271
Treaty interpretation, 68, 70–71, 93, 97
Trockel, Walter, 167n, 284
Trust, xiv, 12, 16–17, 26, 27n, 42, 110, 151, 265
Truth, revelation of, 23–26, 30–63, 111, 249
Tucker, A.W., 119
Tullock, Gordon, 191, 276, 284
Turkey, 106, 111
Tuyet, Le Thi, 255

Uncertainty, 17, 31, 33, 52, 97, 160–62, 164, 241, 243, 257, 264; see also Information, incomplete

Unitary actor, 136n
United Nations Security Council, 117, 231
United States, 33, 57–58, 93, 95, 104–19, 129–34, 136n–37n, 154, 165, 187, 249, 253–62
United States v. Mitchell et al. (1974), 176
United States v. Nixon (1974), 178
Unraveling, 228, 265
Uslaner, Eric M., 226n, 284
Utility
  cardinal, 16, 102, 156, 166n, 266, 271
  expected, 12, 16
  interpersonal comparison of, 192
  and vote trading, 192–93, 195–99, 201–2, 204–7, 226n

Value-restrictedness, 248, 271
Vanck, Jaroslav, 191
Van Newenhizen, Jill, 214, 283
Vetoes, presidential, xvi, 229–31, 235–44, 258, 261n, 265
  empirical data on, 243–44, 258
  pocket, 243
Vickrey, William, 40, 284
Vietcong, 258
Vietminh, 253, 255–58
Vietnam, xvi, 165, 253–60, 262n, 265
Vietnam War, 228, 258–59
von Neumann, John, 73, 101, 284
Vote trade, 193–95, 272
Vote trading, 189–211, 223–26, 256, 264
  coalitions in, 189–90, 192, 206–9
  examples of, 190, 209–11, 224
  instability of, 202, 264
  judgments about, 191–92
  outside of legislatures, 194, 211, 224, 226n
  paradox of, xvi, 189–90, 192, 198–211, 223–24, 226n, 264, 269
  and party discipline, 194, 210-ll
  rationality of, 195, 197, 199, 202–7
  relationship to free market, 189, 264
Voting
  approval, 213–14, 216, 221, 51–52, 260, 266
  cumulative, 217
  Hare system of single transferable vote (STV), 223
  insincere, 192, 195–96, 199, 201, 203, 207–8
  plurality, 245, 252, 270
  sincere, 195, 197–99, 203, 245–47, 249, 270
  sophisticated, xvi, 195, 245–52, 256, 259–60, 262n, 270
  see also Coalition voting
Voting power; see Power indices
Vulnerablity of outcomes, 15, 104, 189,

228, 248, 258; *see also* Bargaining, procedures, vulnerability to collusion under; Coalition, vulnerable; Threats, vulnerability of outcomes to

Wagner, R. Harrison, 166n, 285
Walesa, Lech, 171–72, 174, 187n
War; *see* Nuclear war; Vietnam War; World War II
Ward, Michael D., 280
Warren, Charles, 187n, 285
Warren, Gerald, 177
Washington, D.C., 115, 175, 255
Washington, George, 243
Watergate crisis (1973–74), xvi, 117, 137n, 154, 168, 175–88, 264
Watt, Richard M., 174, 285
Weber, Shlomo, xviii, 86, 89, 92, 276
Webster apportionment method, 218
Weintal, Edward,136n, 285
Welsh, David A., 136n, 274
West Bank, 59
Western Alliance, 253–60
White House tapes case; *see* Watergate crisis (1973–74)

White, Morton, 277
Wiesel, Elie, 27n, 285
Williams, Steven R., 30, 283, 285
Wilson, Robert, 160–61, 165n, 191, 280, 285
Wilson, Woodrow, 194, 244, 258, 285
Winning, 66–67, 75–79, 100n, 154, 186, 232, 236, 261n
    minimal, 193–94, 216, 220, 235–36
Wise arbitration, 18, 23–24, 26, 27n, 272
Wittman, Donald, xviii, 71, 77, 99n, 121, 137n, 139, 275–76, 285
Wohlstetter, Albert, 136n, 285
Woodward, Bob, 180, 285
World War II, 59, 107, 137n, 164, 223

Yom Kippur War, xvi, 30, 68, 101, 104, 116–19, 264
Young, H. Peyton, 99n, 218, 273, 276, 285

Zagare, Frank C., xviii, 28n, 117, 118n, 130–32, 134, 136n–37n, 166n, 252–53, 255–56, 258, 262n, 276, 285
Zartman, I. William, 29, 94–95, 285
Zeckhauser, Richard J., 40, 276